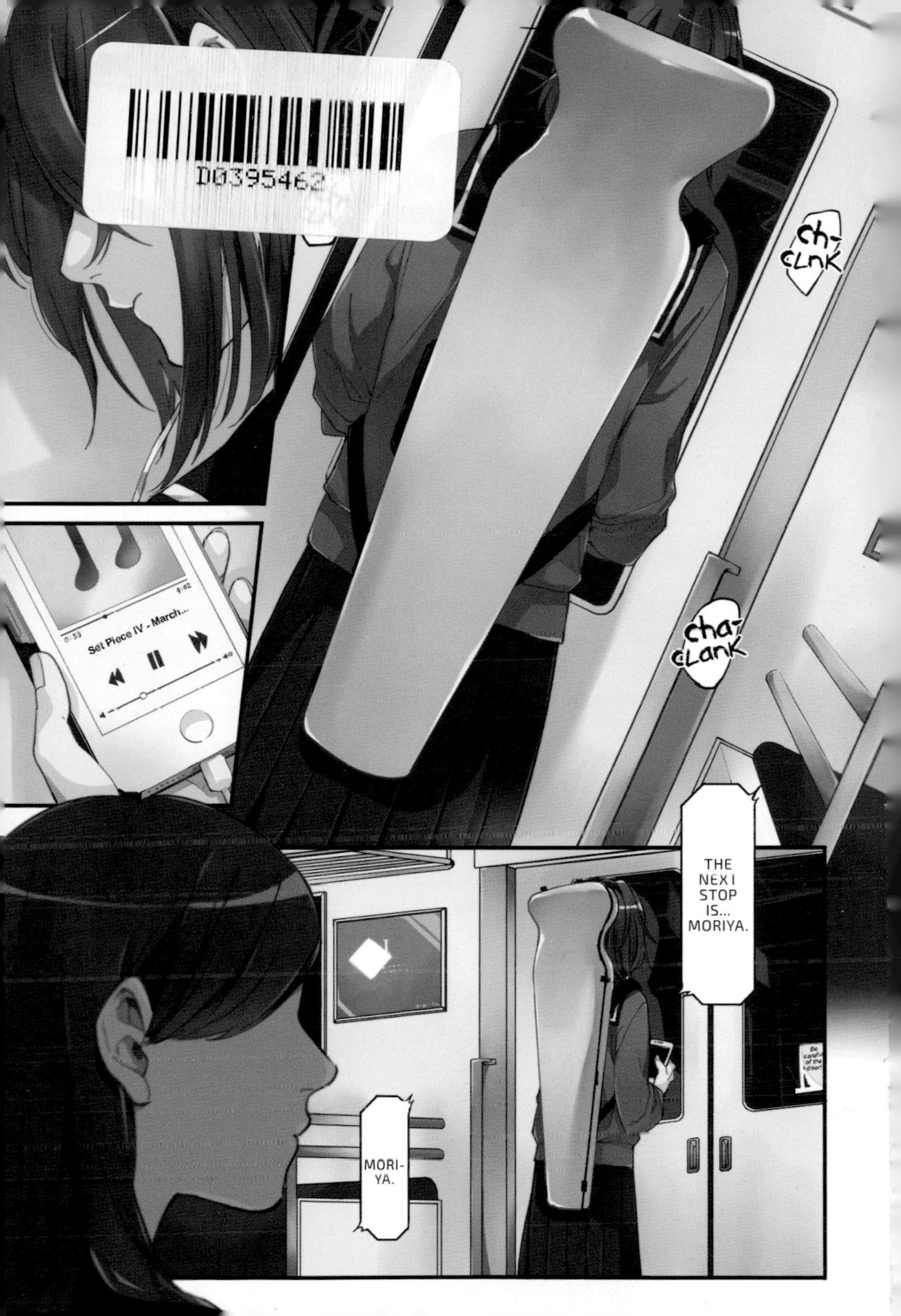
CH-CLNK
CHA-CLANK
0:53
4:02
Set Piece IV - March...
THE NEXT STOP IS... MORIYA.
MORI-YA.

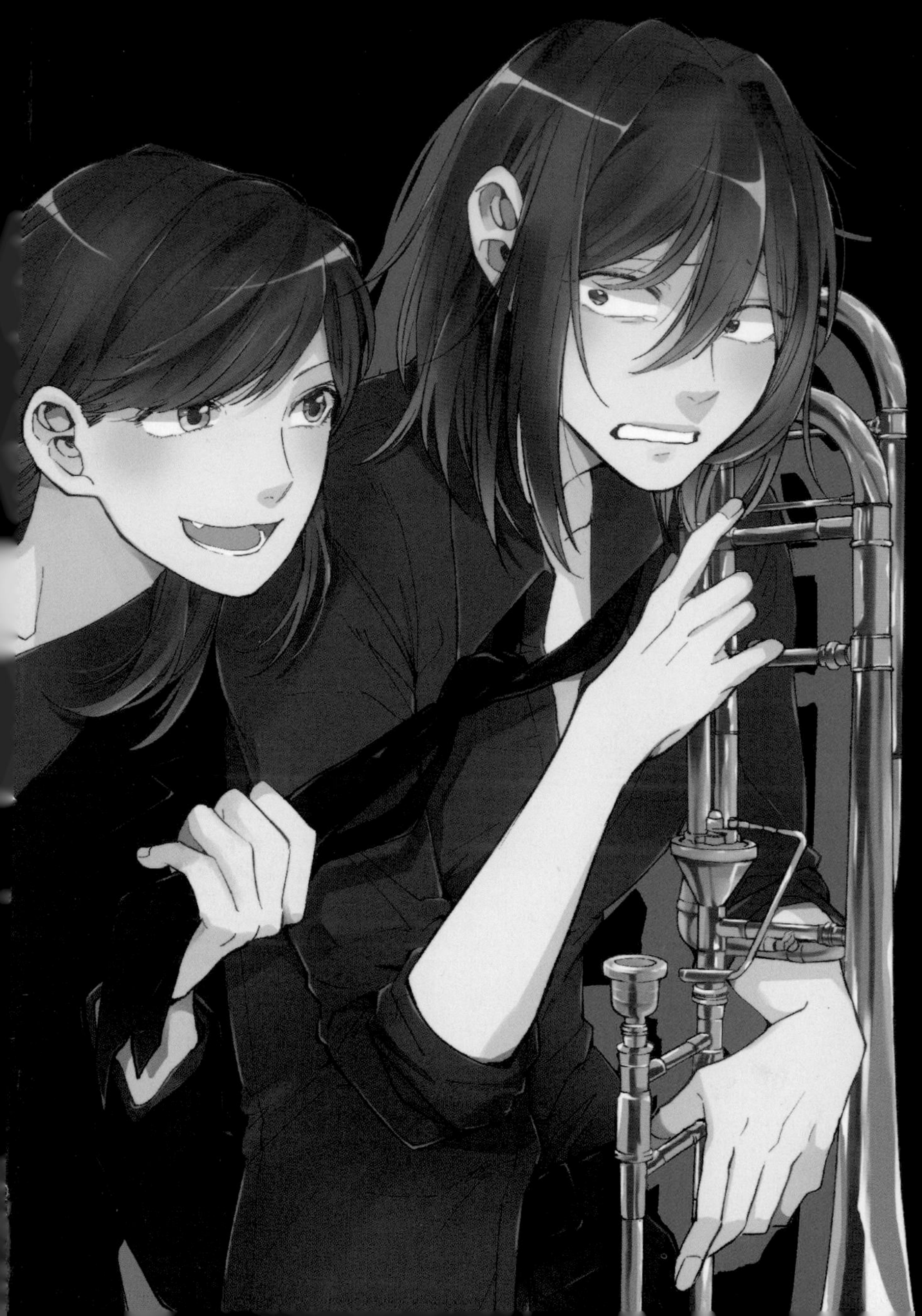

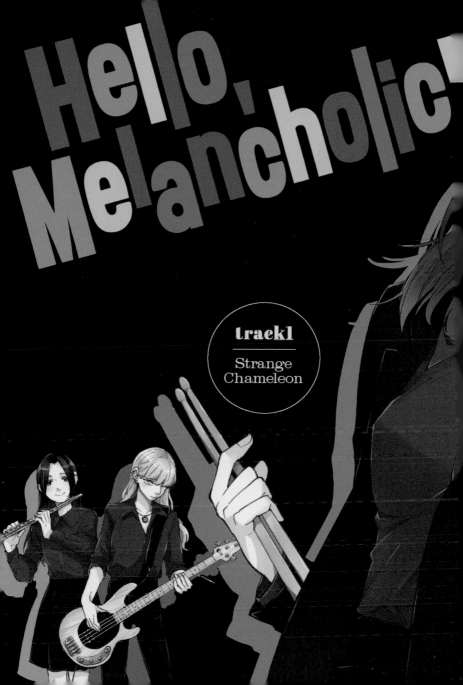

Hello, Melancholic!

track1

Strange
Chameleon

Hello, Melancholic!

story & art by
Yayoi Ohsawa

CONTENTS

track1
Stange Chameleon [001]

track2
Timing [067]

track3
Wandering Freak [101]

track4
Pierrot [135]

bonus track
[160]

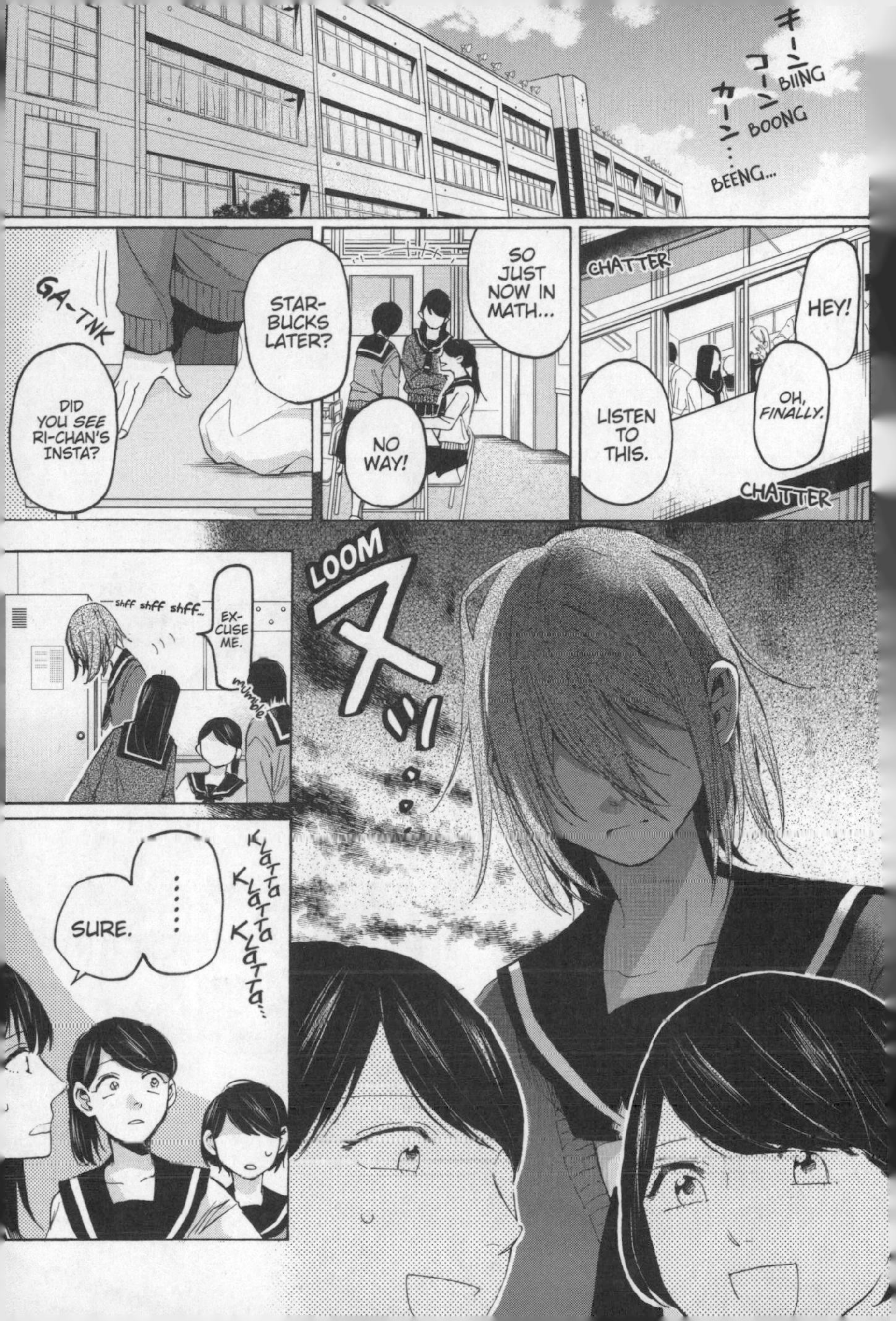
キーン
BIING
コーン
BOONG
カーン…
BEENG...
CHATTER
HEY!
OH, FINALLY.
LISTEN TO THIS.
CHATTER
SO JUST NOW IN MATH...
STAR-BUCKS LATER?
NO WAY!
GA-TNK
DID YOU SEE RI-CHAN'S INSTA?
LOOM
shff shff shff...
EX-CUSE ME.
mumble
......
SURE.
Klatta Klatta Klatta Klatta...

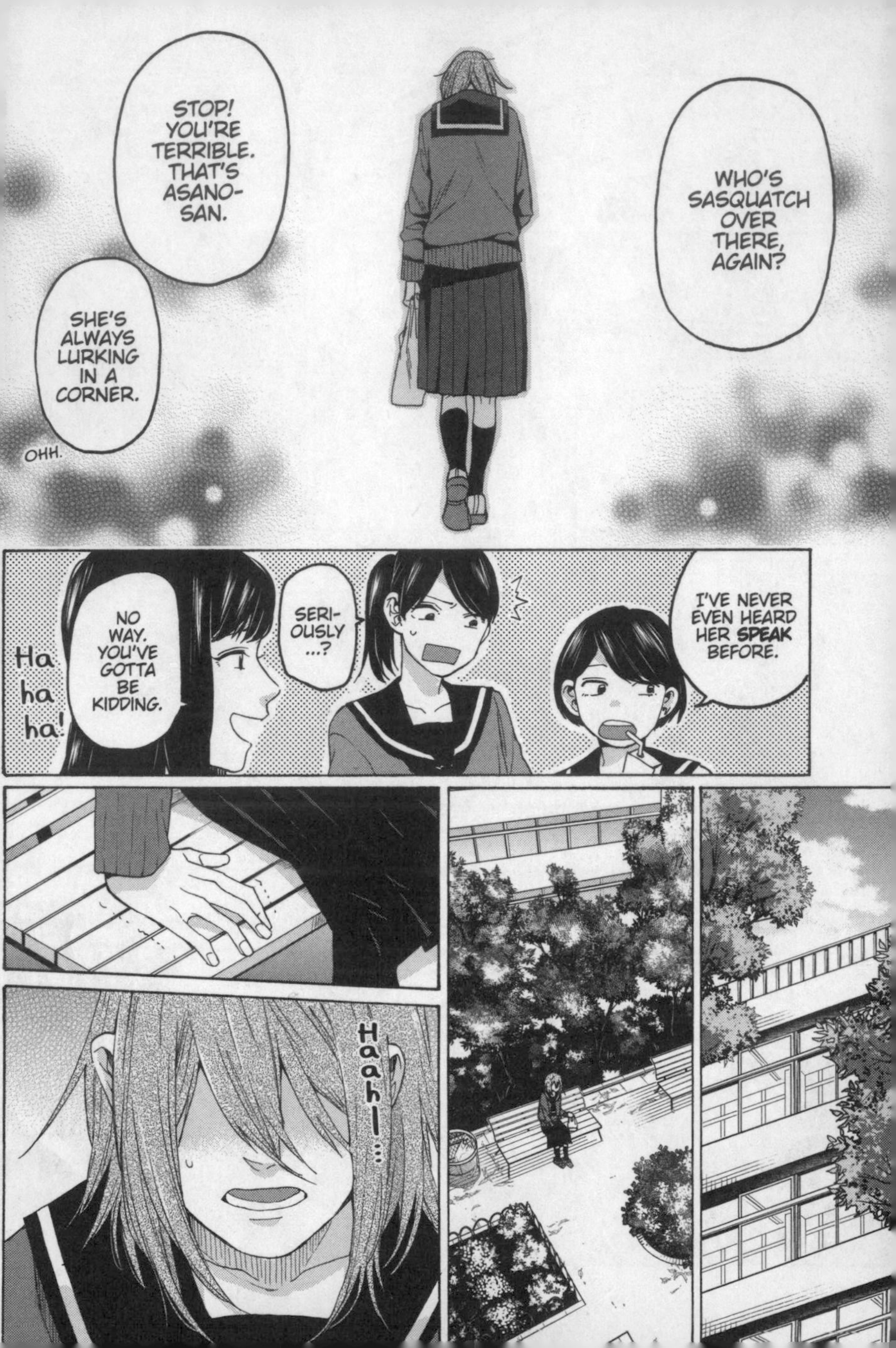
WHO'S SASQUATCH OVER THERE, AGAIN?
STOP! YOU'RE TERRIBLE. THAT'S ASANO-SAN.
SHE'S ALWAYS LURKING IN A CORNER.
OHH.
I'VE NEVER EVEN HEARD HER **SPEAK** BEFORE.
SERIOUSLY ...?
NO WAY. YOU'VE GOTTA BE KIDDING.
Ha ha ha!
Haah!...

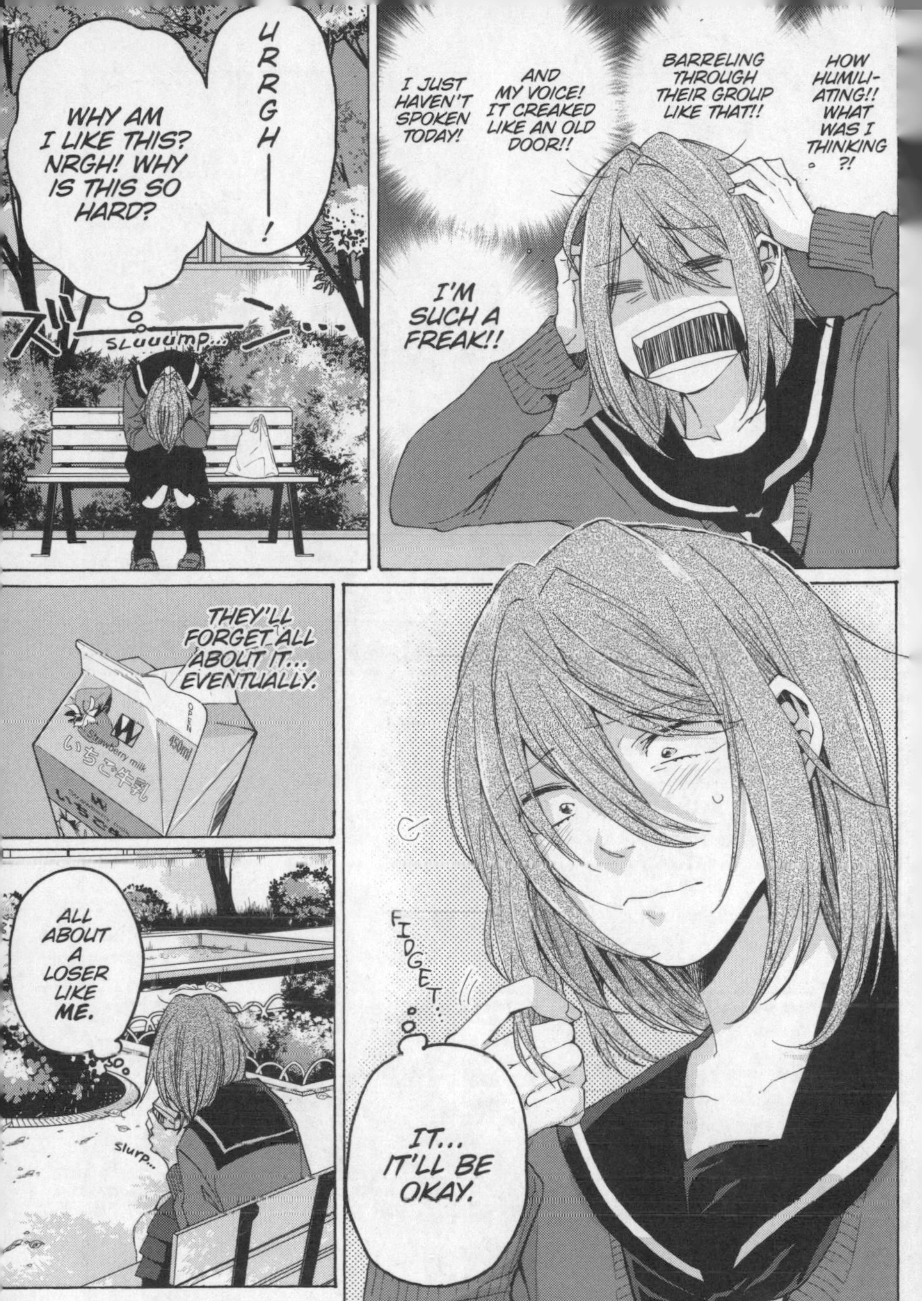
HOW HUMILIATING!! WHAT WAS I THINKING?!
BARRELING THROUGH THEIR GROUP LIKE THAT!!
AND MY VOICE! IT CREAKED LIKE AN OLD DOOR!!
I JUST HAVEN'T SPOKEN TODAY!
I'M SUCH A FREAK!!
URRGH—!
WHY AM I LIKE THIS? NRGH! WHY IS THIS SO HARD?
SLuuump...
FIDGET...
IT... IT'LL BE OKAY.
THEY'LL FORGET ALL ABOUT IT... EVENTUALLY.
Strawberry milk
いちご牛乳
450ml
OPEN
ALL ABOUT A LOSER LIKE ME.
slurp...

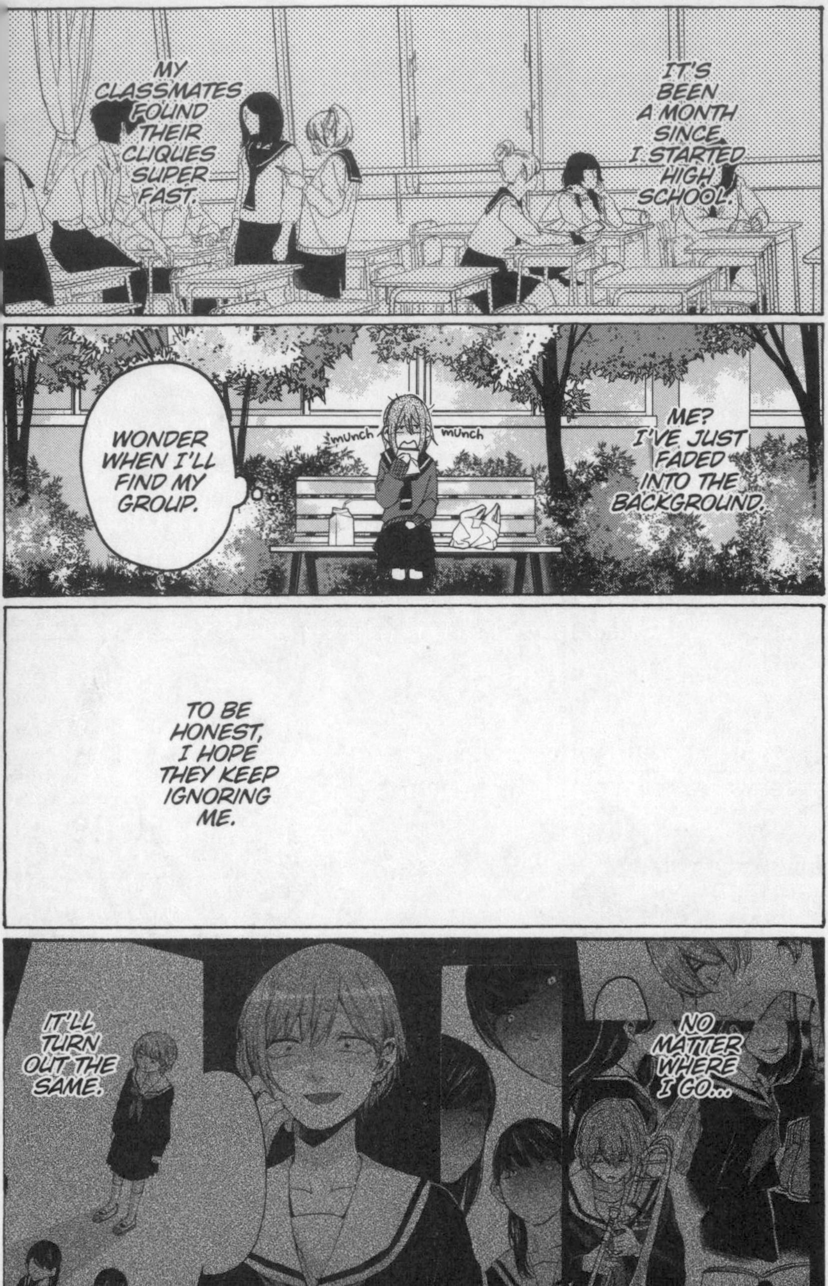
IT'S BEEN A MONTH SINCE I STARTED HIGH SCHOOL.
MY CLASSMATES FOUND THEIR CLIQUES SUPER FAST.
ME? I'VE JUST FADED INTO THE BACKGROUND.
munch
munch
WONDER WHEN I'LL FIND MY GROUP.
TO BE HONEST, I HOPE THEY KEEP IGNORING ME.
NO MATTER WHERE I GO...
IT'LL TURN OUT THE SAME.

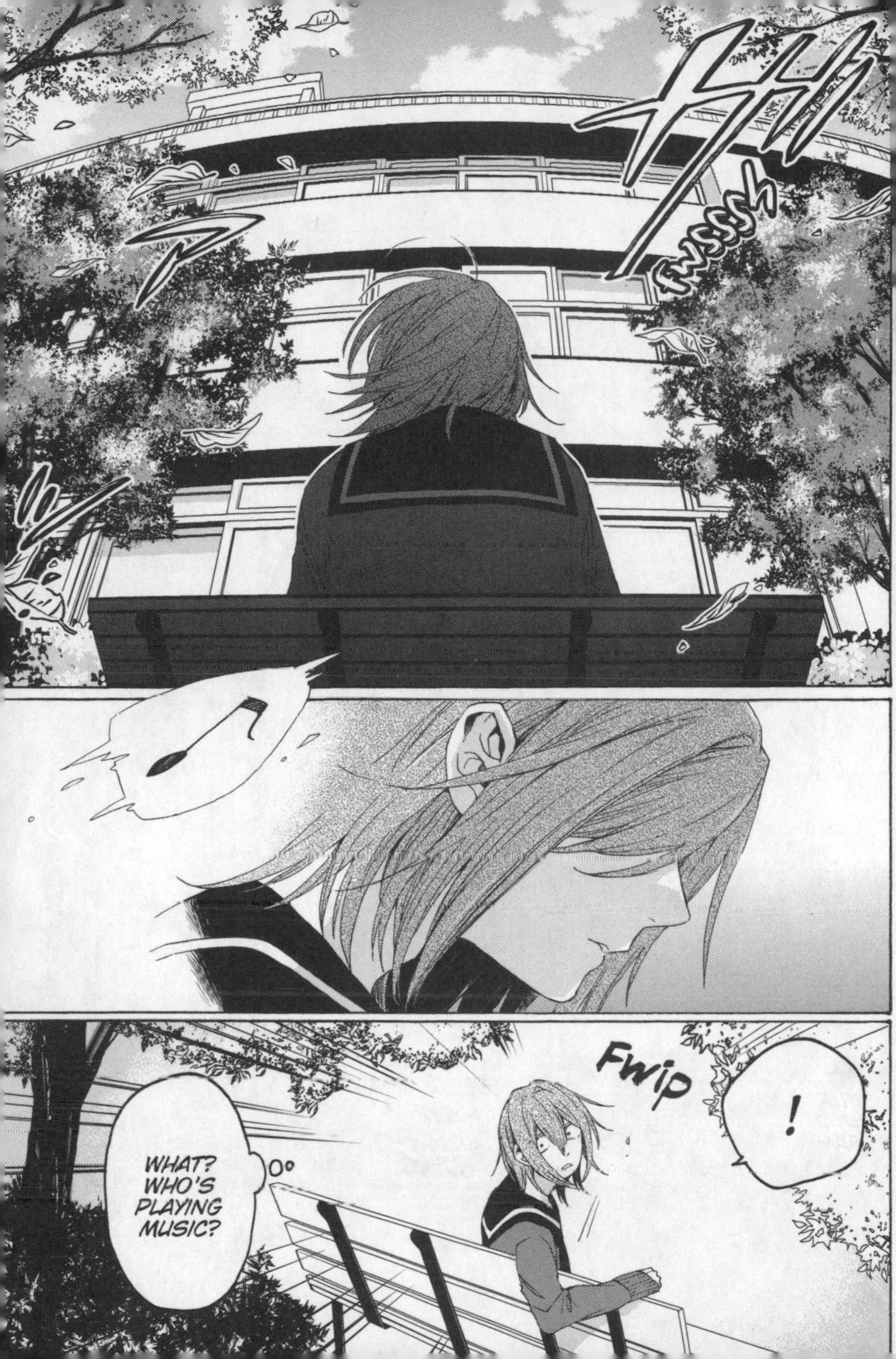
FWSSSH
Fwip
!
WHAT? WHO'S PLAYING MUSIC?

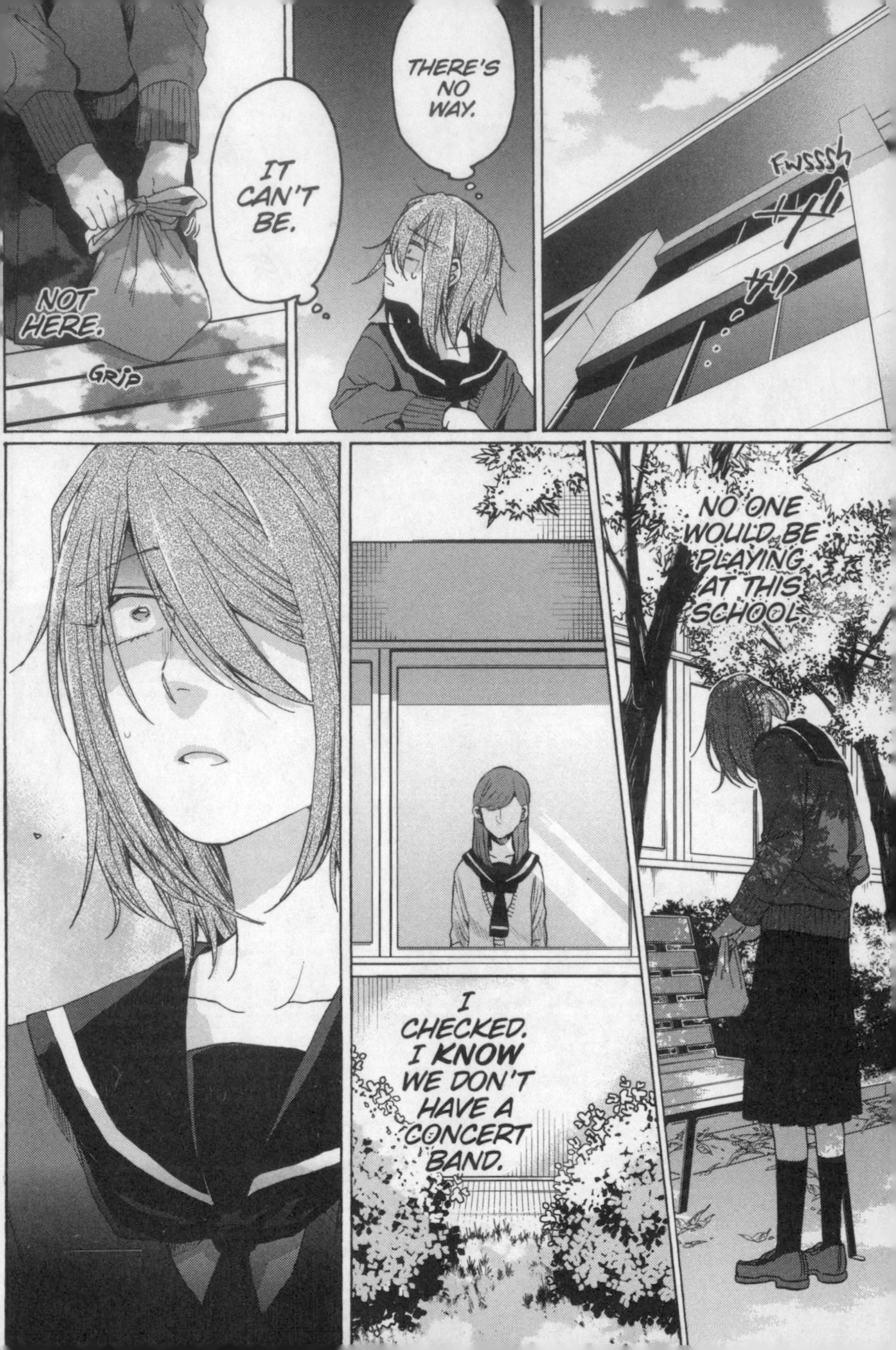
Fwsssh
THERE'S NO WAY.
IT CAN'T BE.
NOT HERE.
Grip
NO ONE WOULD BE PLAYING AT THIS SCHOOL.
I CHECKED. I KNOW WE DON'T HAVE A CONCERT BAND.

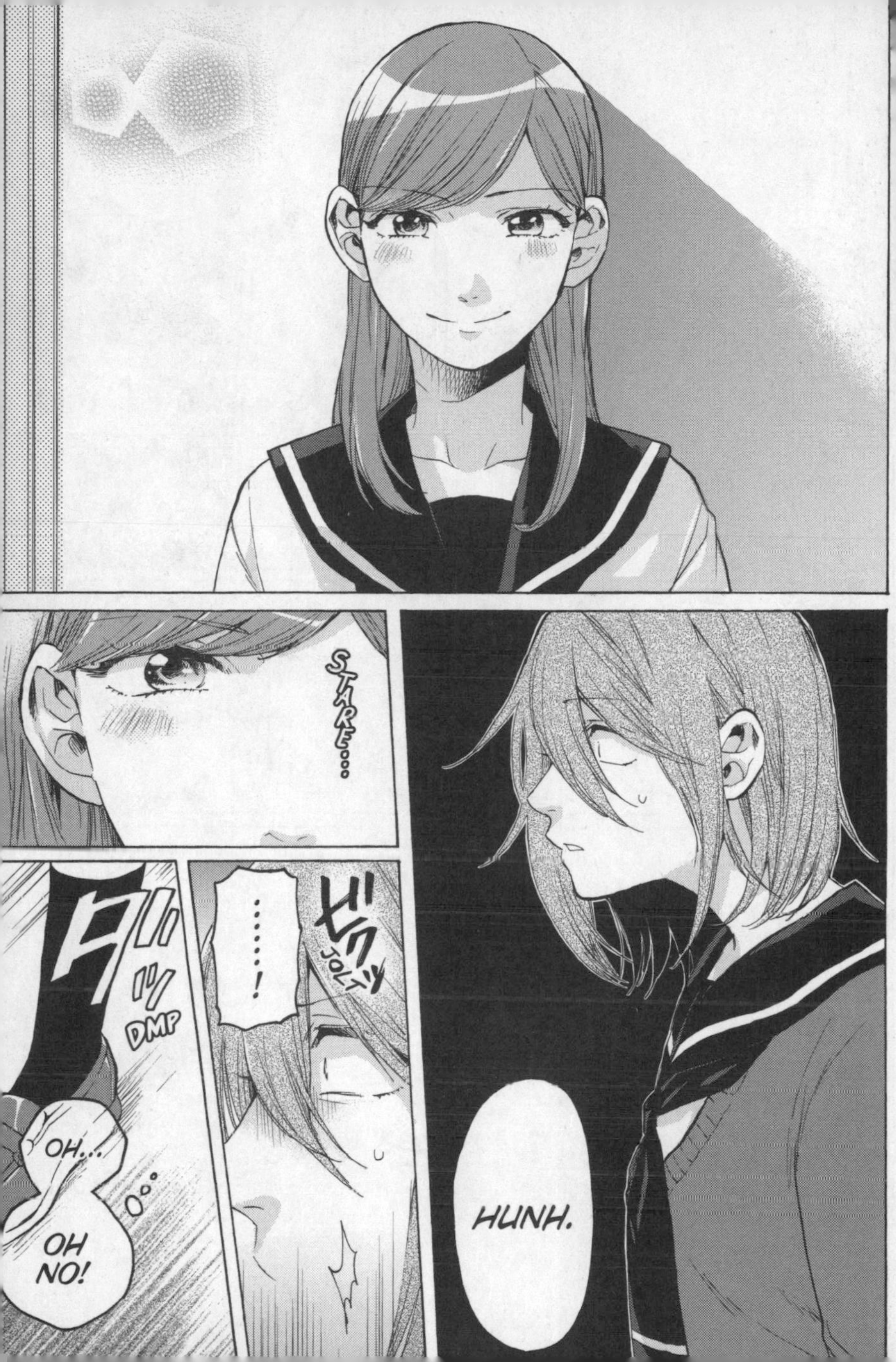
HUNH.
STARE...
......!
JOLT
DMP
OH...
OH NO!

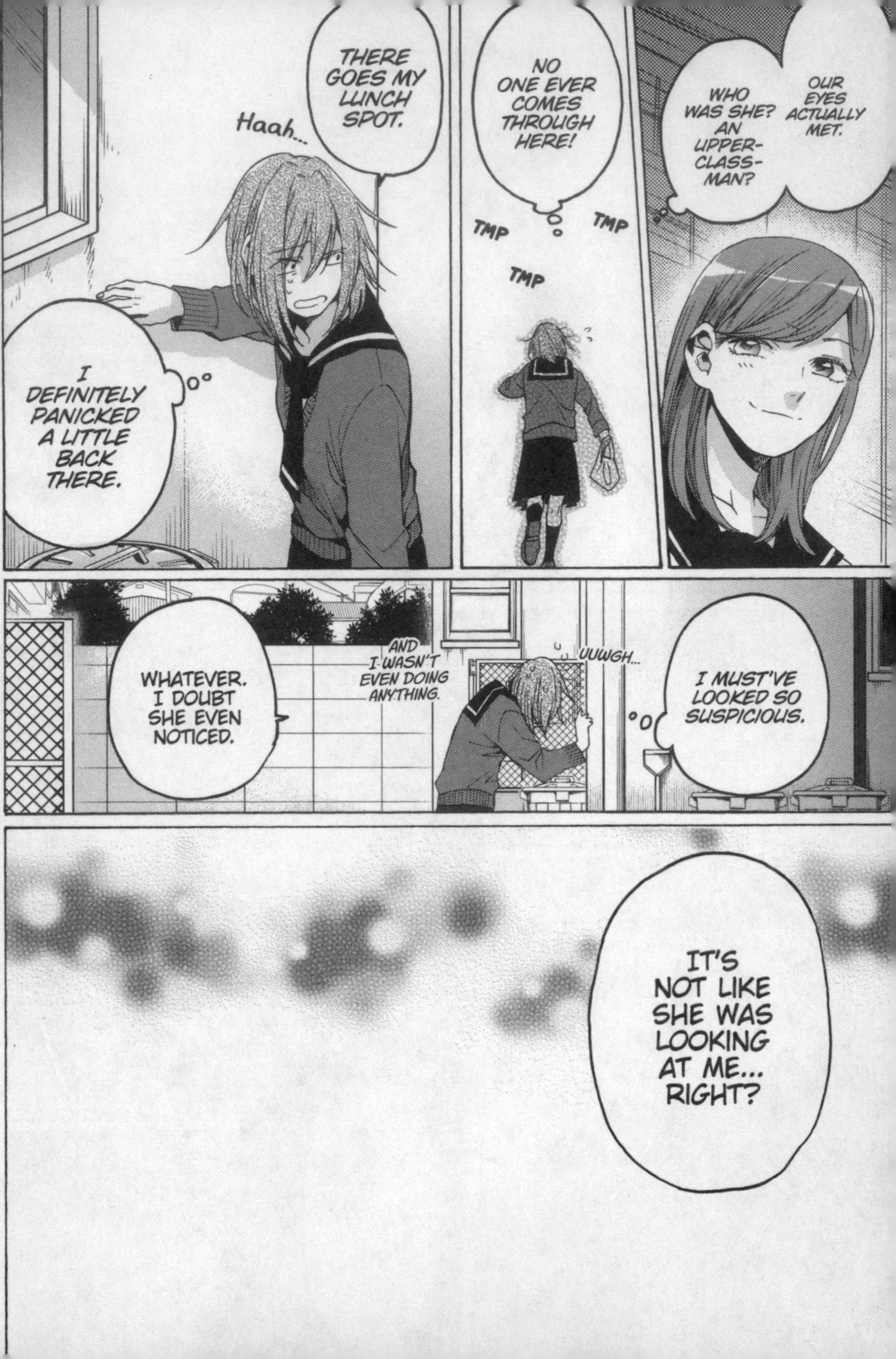
OUR EYES ACTUALLY MET.
WHO WAS SHE? AN UPPER-CLASSMAN?
NO ONE EVER COMES THROUGH HERE!
TMP
TMP
TMP
THERE GOES MY LUNCH SPOT.
Haah...
I DEFINITELY PANICKED A LITTLE BACK THERE.
I MUST'VE LOOKED SO SUSPICIOUS.
UUWGH...
AND I WASN'T EVEN DOING ANYTHING.
WHATEVER. I DOUBT SHE EVEN NOTICED.
IT'S NOT LIKE SHE WAS LOOKING AT ME... RIGHT?

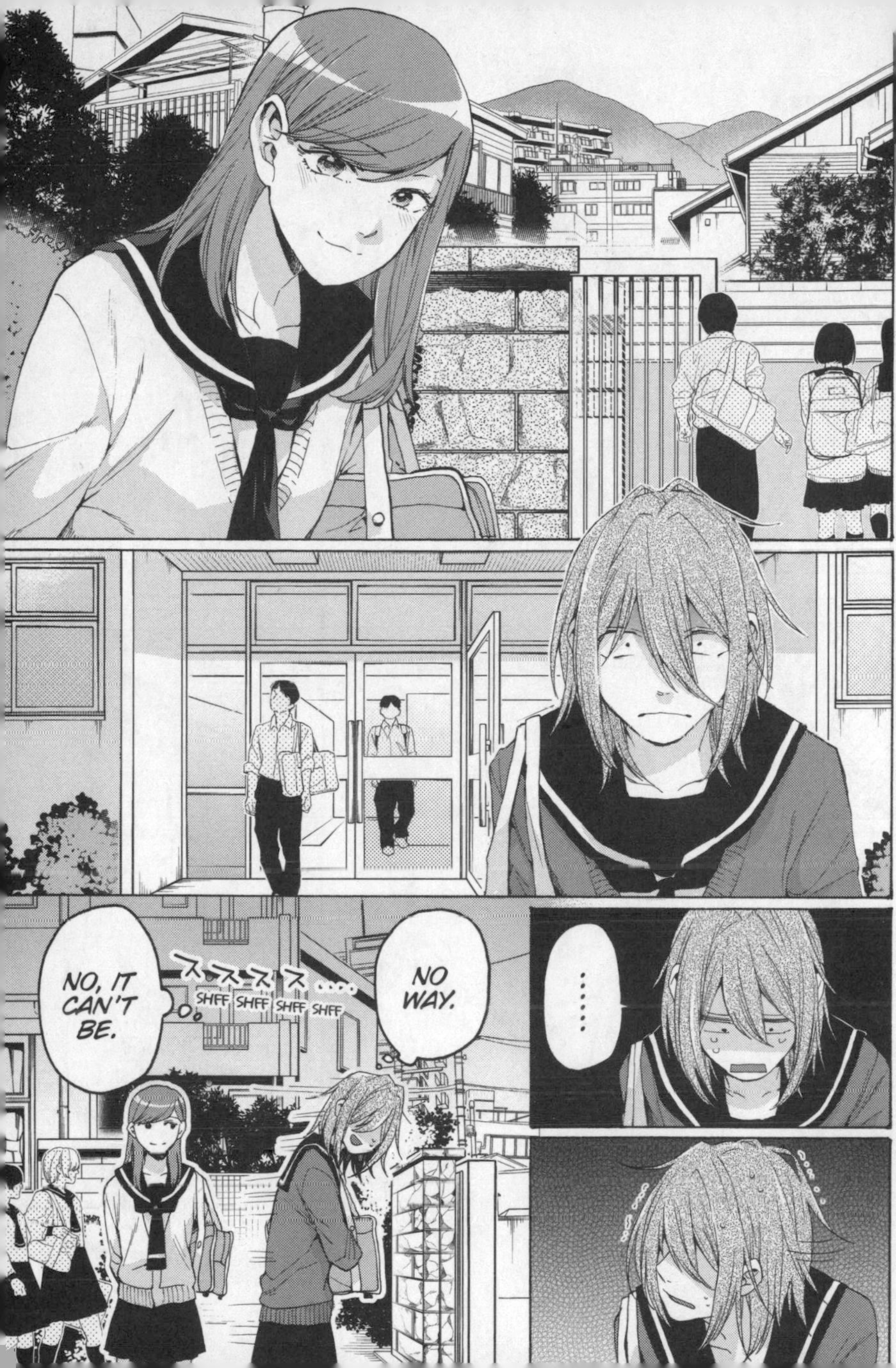
......
NO WAY.
ススススス....
SHFF SHFF SHFF SHFF
NO, IT CAN'T BE.

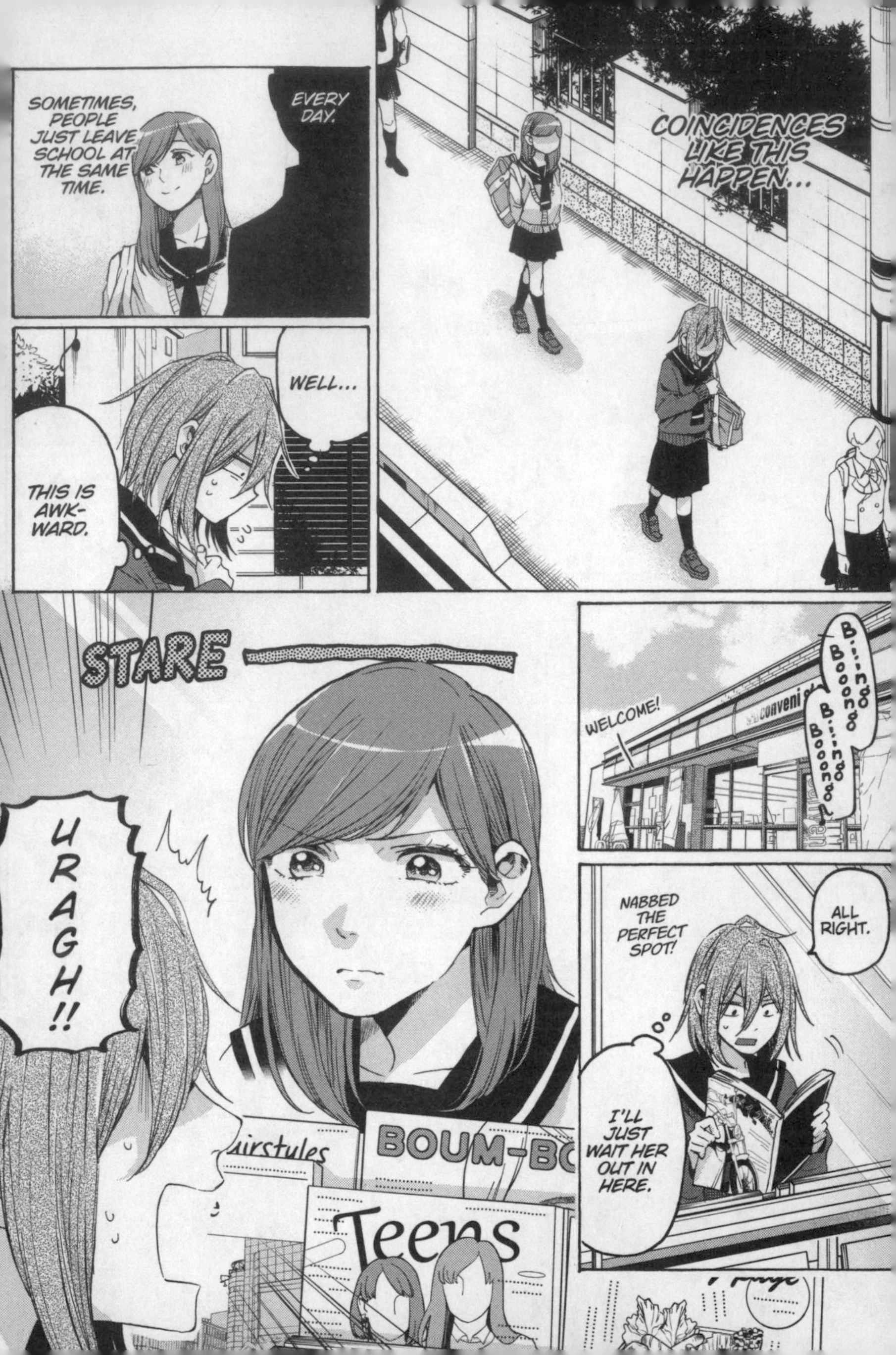
COINCIDENCES LIKE THIS HAPPEN...
EVERY DAY.
SOMETIMES, PEOPLE JUST LEAVE SCHOOL AT THE SAME TIME.
WELL...
THIS IS AWK-WARD.
B...ing Booong
B...ing Booong
WELCOME!
ALL RIGHT.
NABBED THE PERFECT SPOT!
I'LL JUST WAIT HER OUT IN HERE.
STARE
URAGH!!
Teens

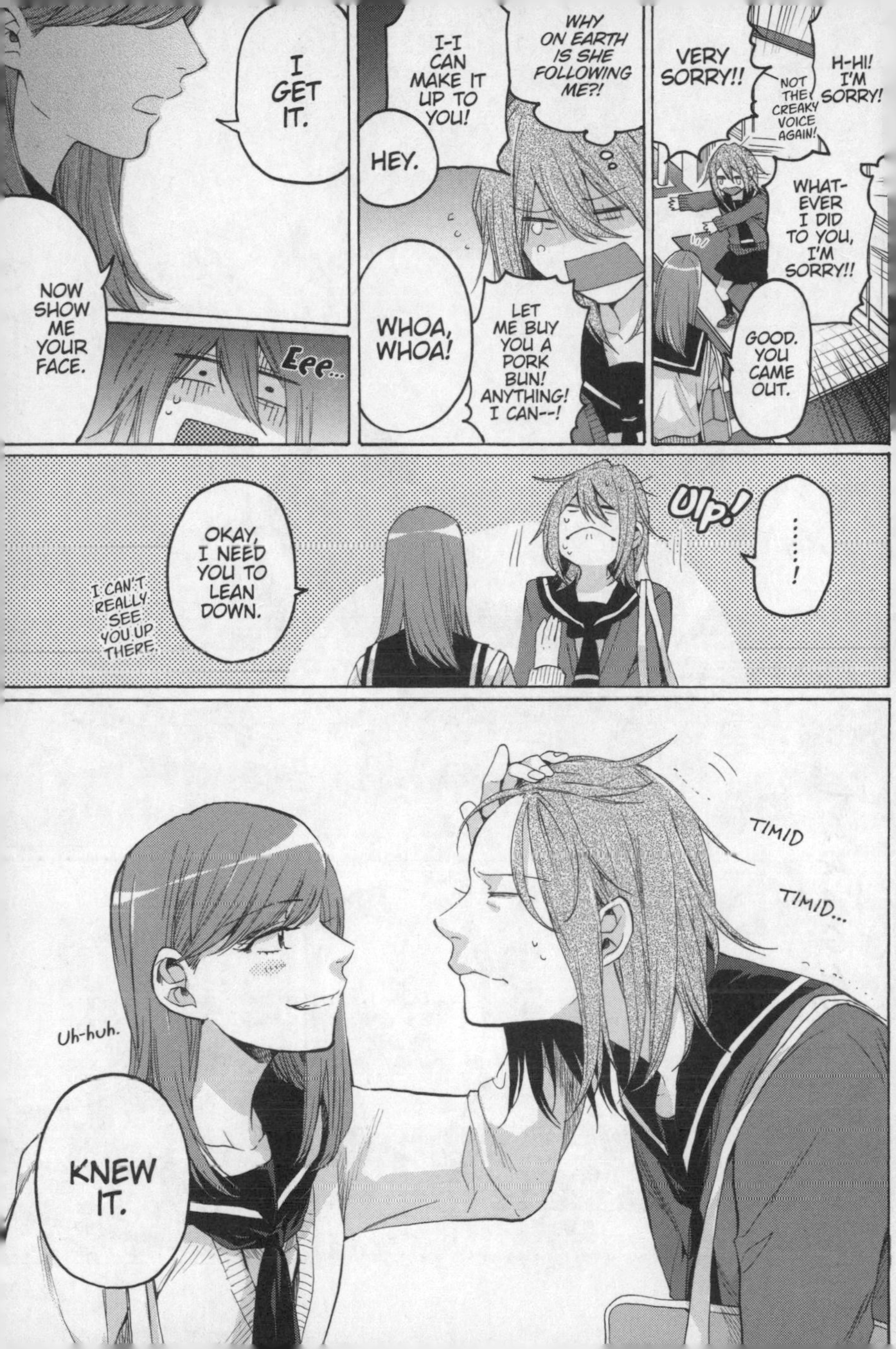
H-HI! I'M SORRY!
VERY SORRY!!
NOT THE CREAKY VOICE AGAIN!
WHAT-EVER I DID TO YOU, I'M SORRY!!
GOOD. YOU CAME OUT.
WHY ON EARTH IS SHE FOLLOWING ME?!
I-I CAN MAKE IT UP TO YOU!
HEY.
LET ME BUY YOU A PORK BUN! ANYTHING! I CAN--!
WHOA, WHOA!
I GET IT.
NOW SHOW ME YOUR FACE.
Eee...
......!
Ulp!
OKAY, I NEED YOU TO LEAN DOWN.
I CAN'T REALLY SEE YOU UP THERE.
TIMID
TIMID...
Uh-huh.
KNEW IT.

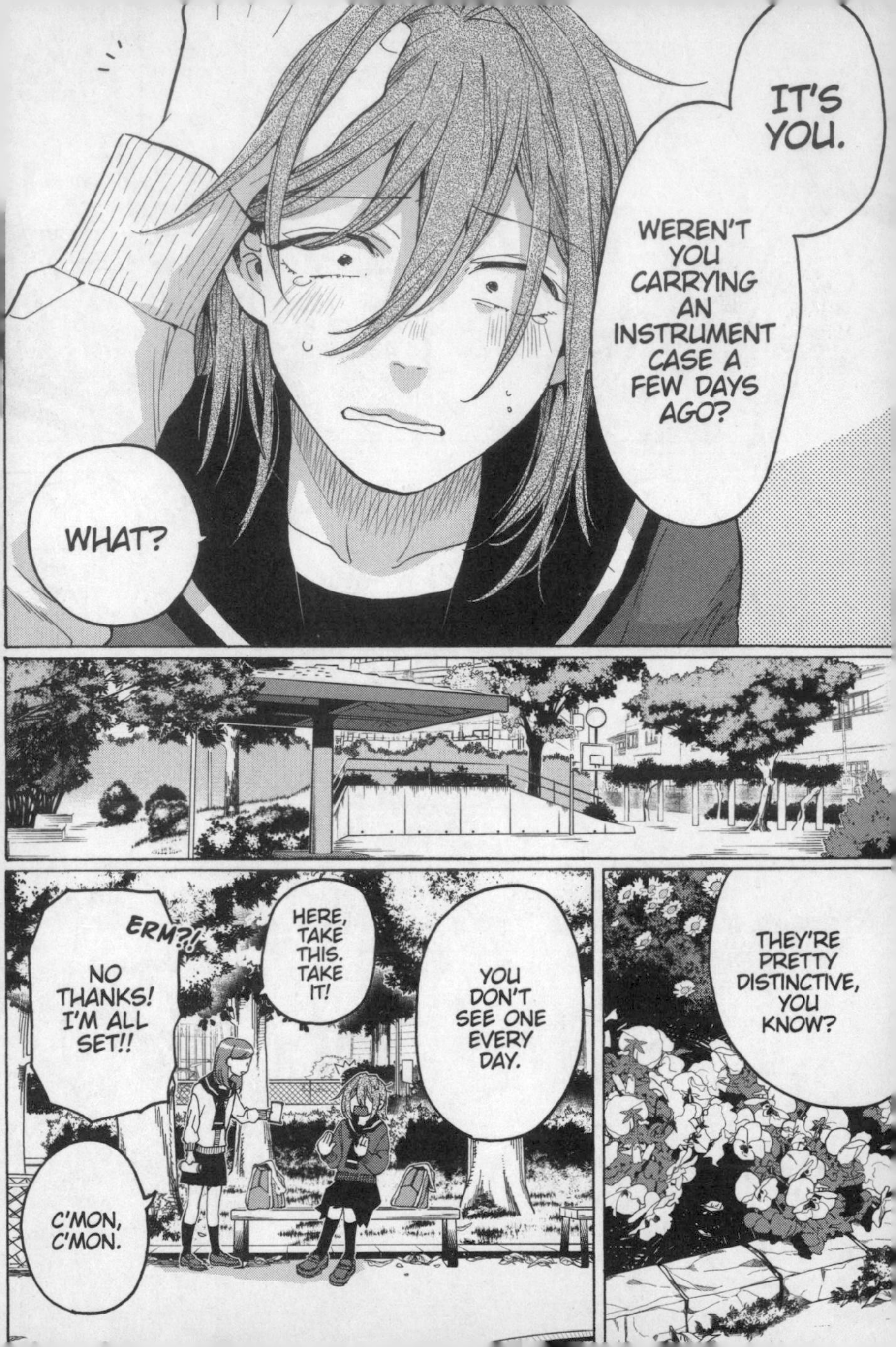
IT'S YOU.
WEREN'T YOU CARRYING AN INSTRUMENT CASE A FEW DAYS AGO?
WHAT?
THEY'RE PRETTY DISTINCTIVE, YOU KNOW?
YOU DON'T SEE ONE EVERY DAY.
HERE, TAKE THIS. TAKE IT!
ERM?!
NO THANKS! I'M ALL SET!!
C'MON, C'MON.

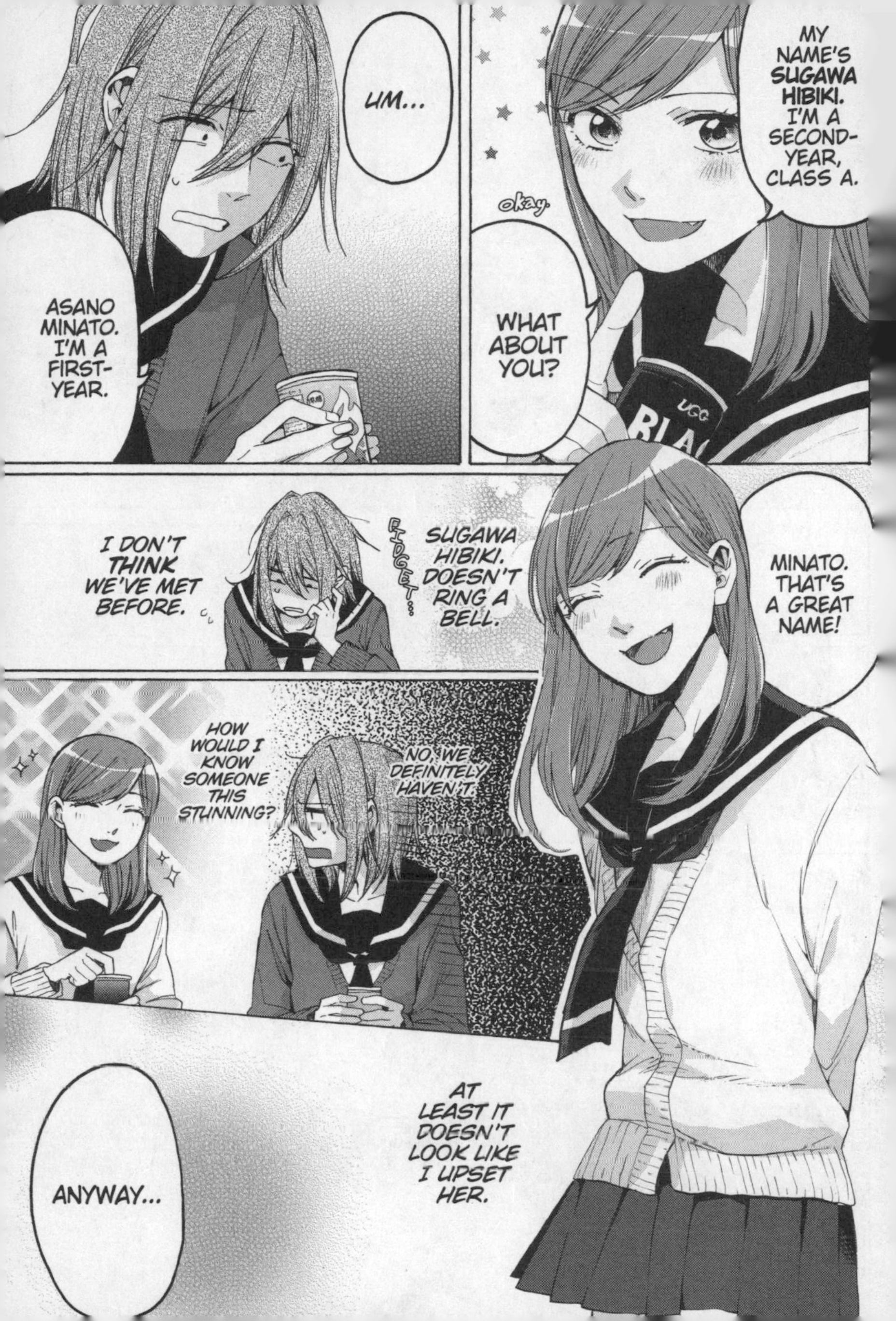
MY NAME'S SUGAWA HIBIKI. I'M A SECOND-YEAR, CLASS A.
okay.
WHAT ABOUT YOU?
UM...
ASANO MINATO. I'M A FIRST-YEAR.
MINATO. THAT'S A GREAT NAME!
SUGAWA HIBIKI. DOESN'T RING A BELL.
FIDGET...
I DON'T THINK WE'VE MET BEFORE.
NO, WE DEFINITELY HAVEN'T.
HOW WOULD I KNOW SOMEONE THIS STUNNING?
AT LEAST IT DOESN'T LOOK LIKE I UPSET HER.
ANYWAY...

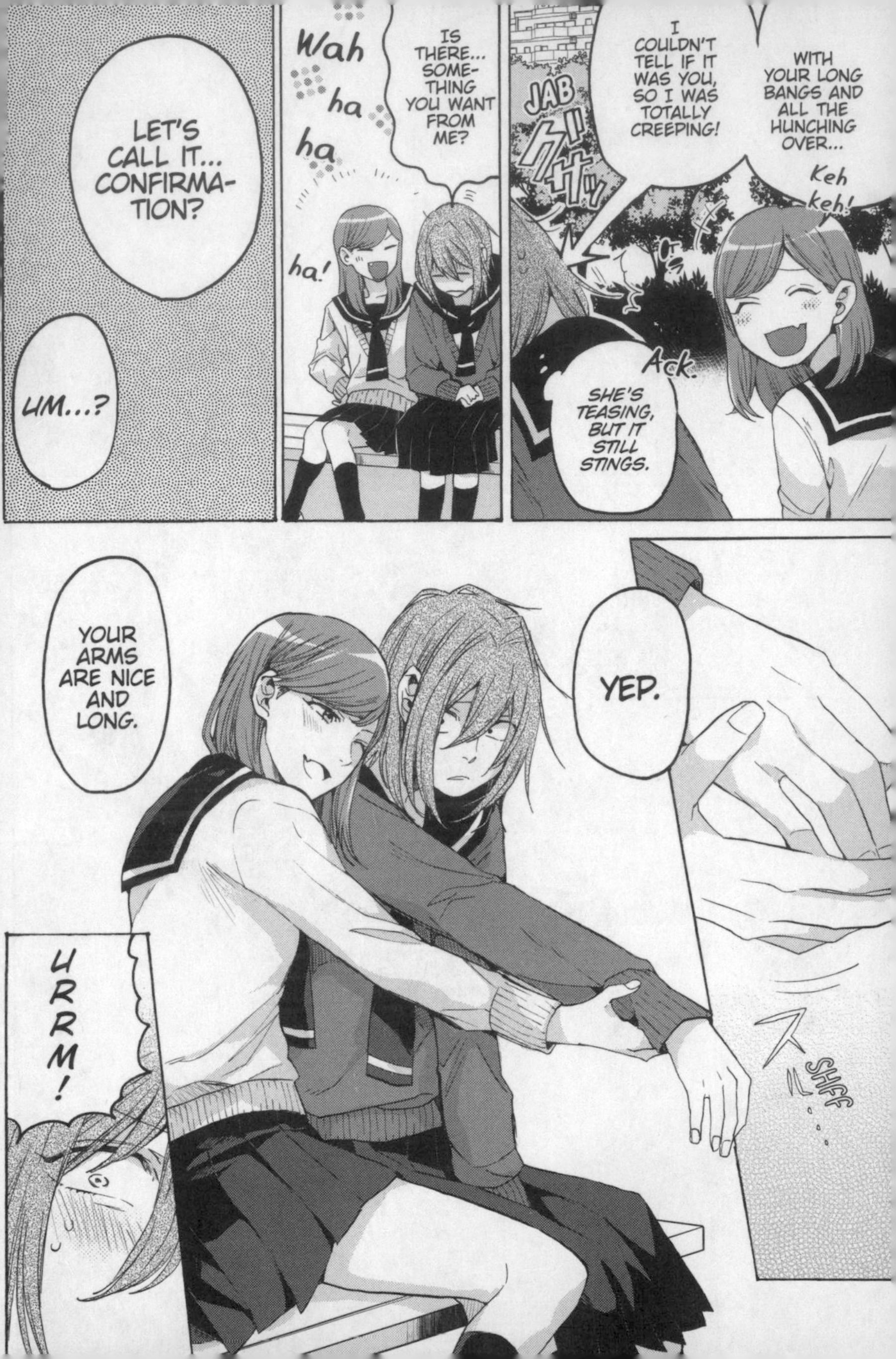
WITH YOUR LONG BANGS AND ALL THE HUNCHING OVER...
I COULDN'T TELL IF IT WAS YOU, SO I WAS TOTALLY CREEPING!
Keh keh!
JAB
Ack.
SHE'S TEASING, BUT IT STILL STINGS.
IS THERE... SOMETHING YOU WANT FROM ME?
Wah ha ha ha!
LET'S CALL IT... CONFIRMATION?
UM...?
YEP.
SHFF
YOUR ARMS ARE NICE AND LONG.
URRM!

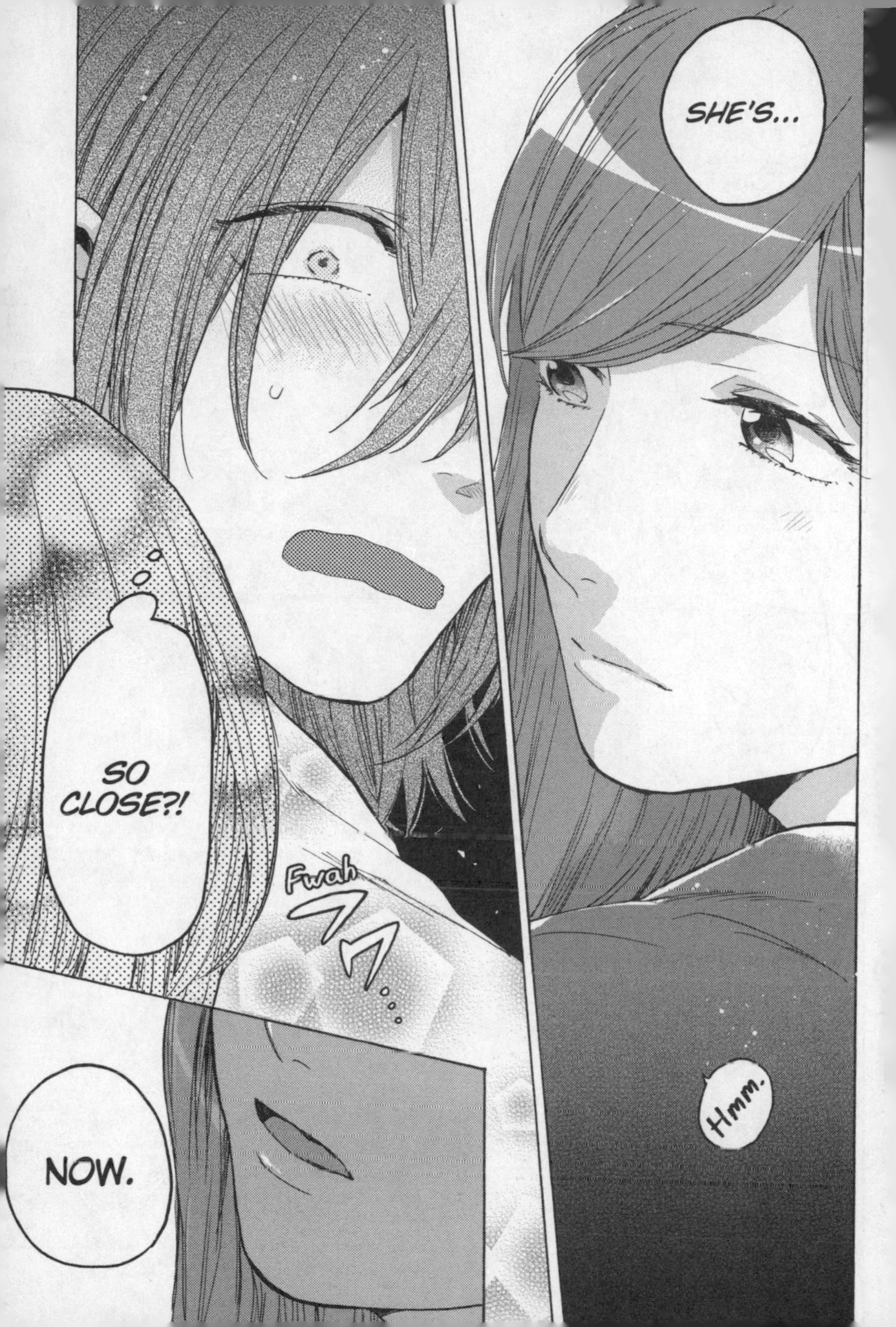
SHE'S...
Hmm.
SO CLOSE?!
Fwah
NOW.

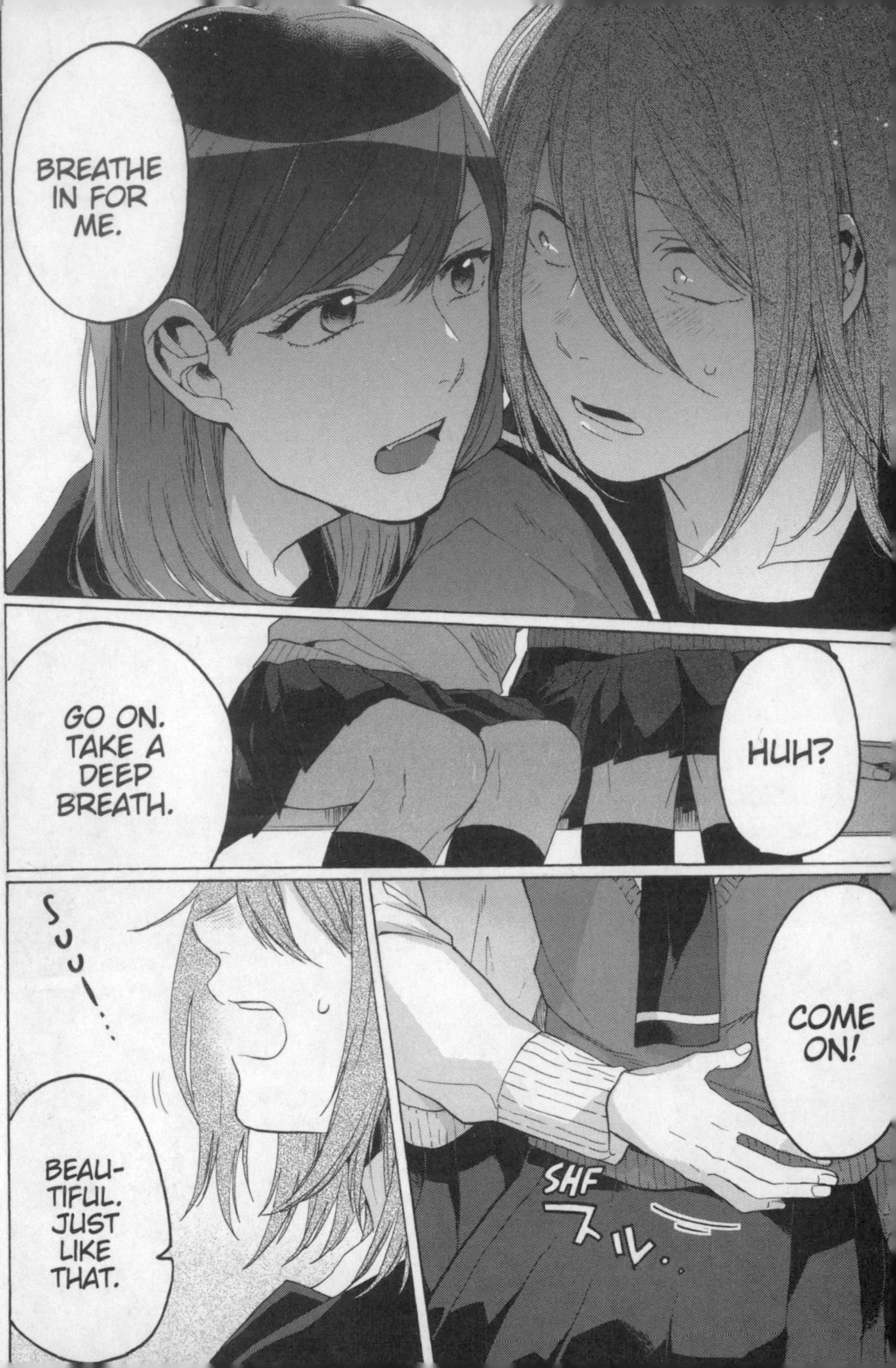
BREATHE IN FOR ME.
HUH?
GO ON. TAKE A DEEP BREATH.
COME ON!
SHF
スル..
SUUU...
BEAU-TIFUL. JUST LIKE THAT.

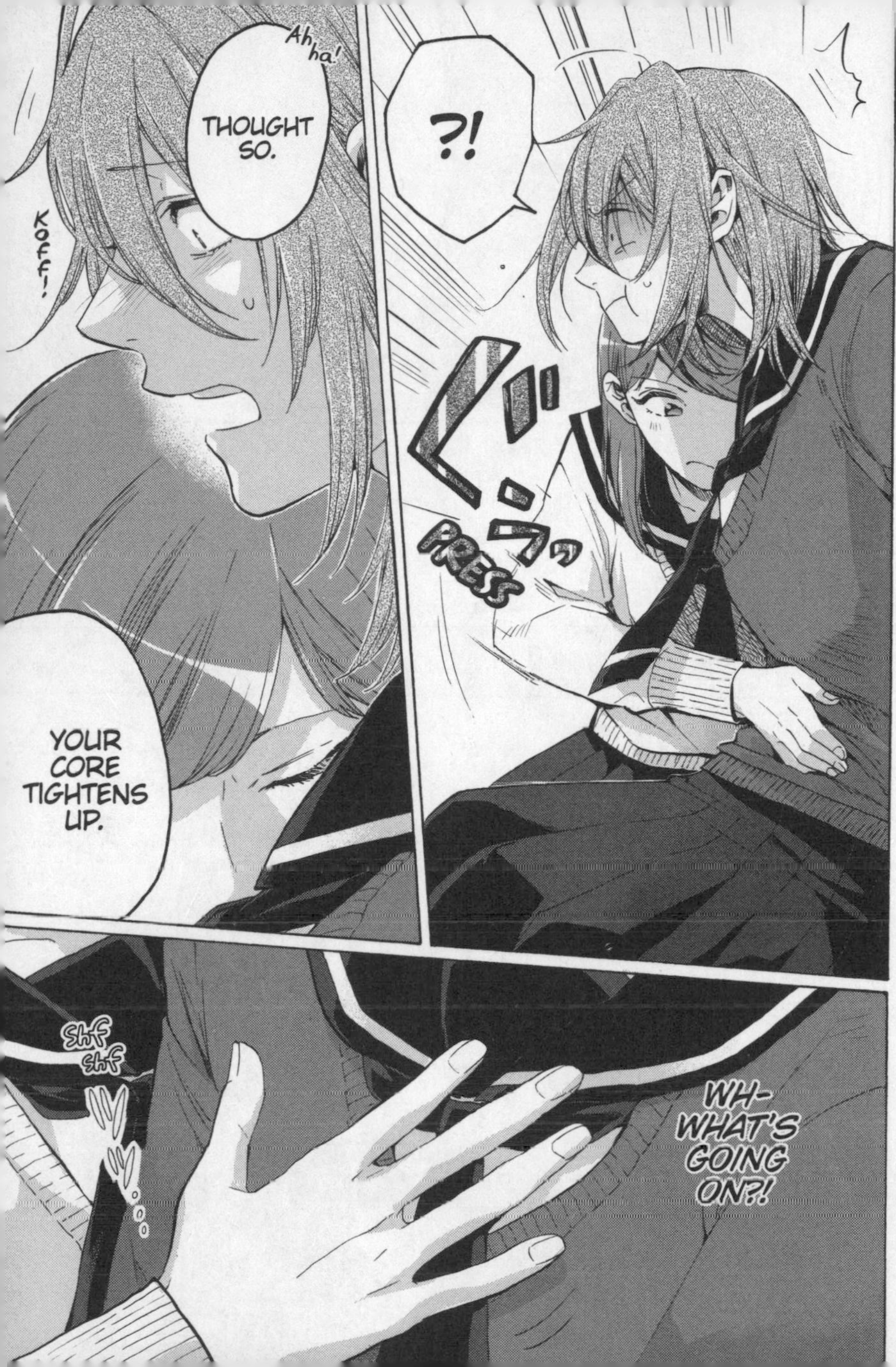
?!
PRESS
Ah ha!
THOUGHT SO.
Koff!
YOUR CORE TIGHTENS UP.
WH- WHAT'S GOING ON?!
Shf shf

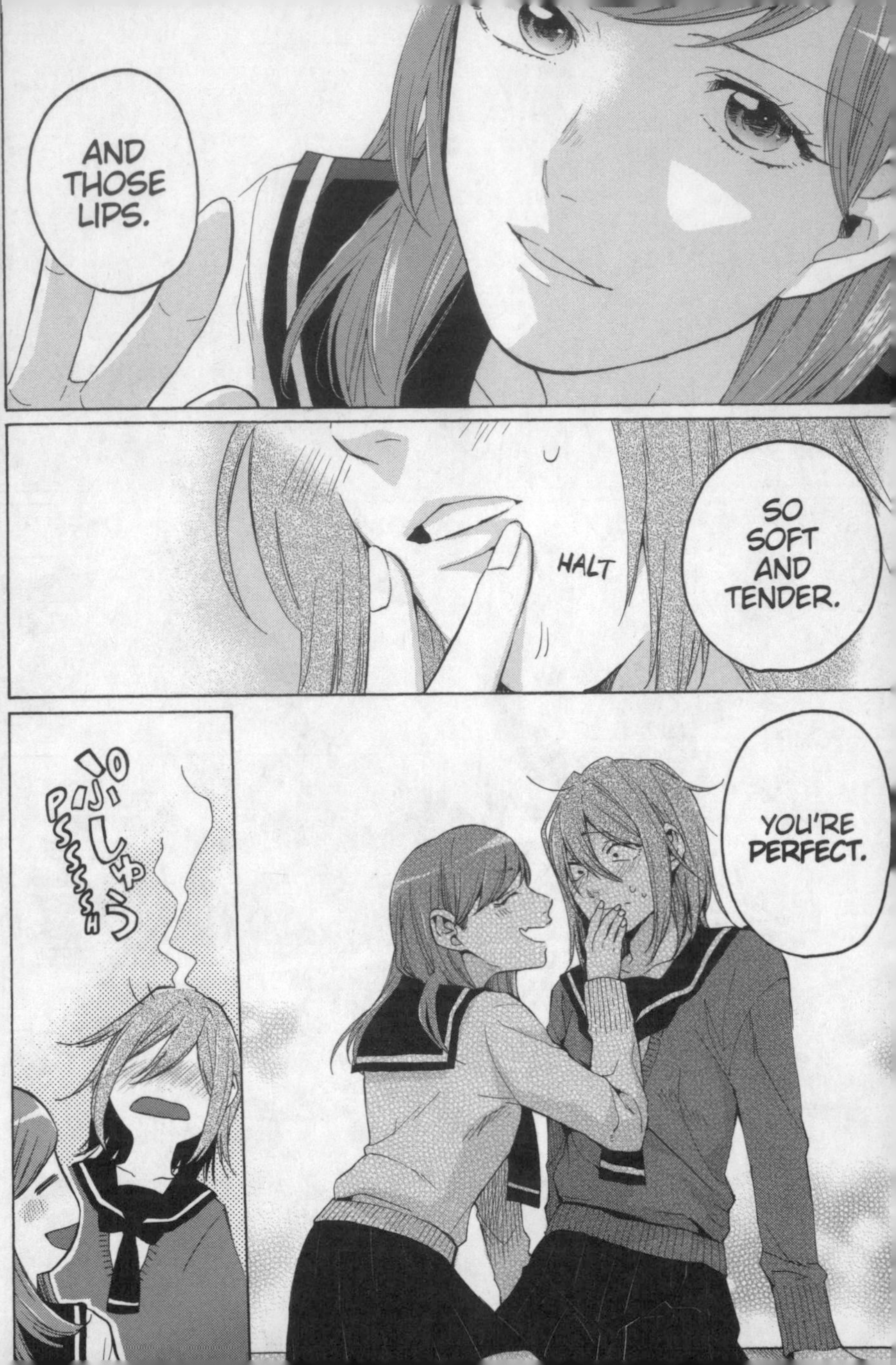
AND THOSE LIPS.
SO SOFT AND TENDER.
HALT
YOU'RE PERFECT.
PSSSSSH

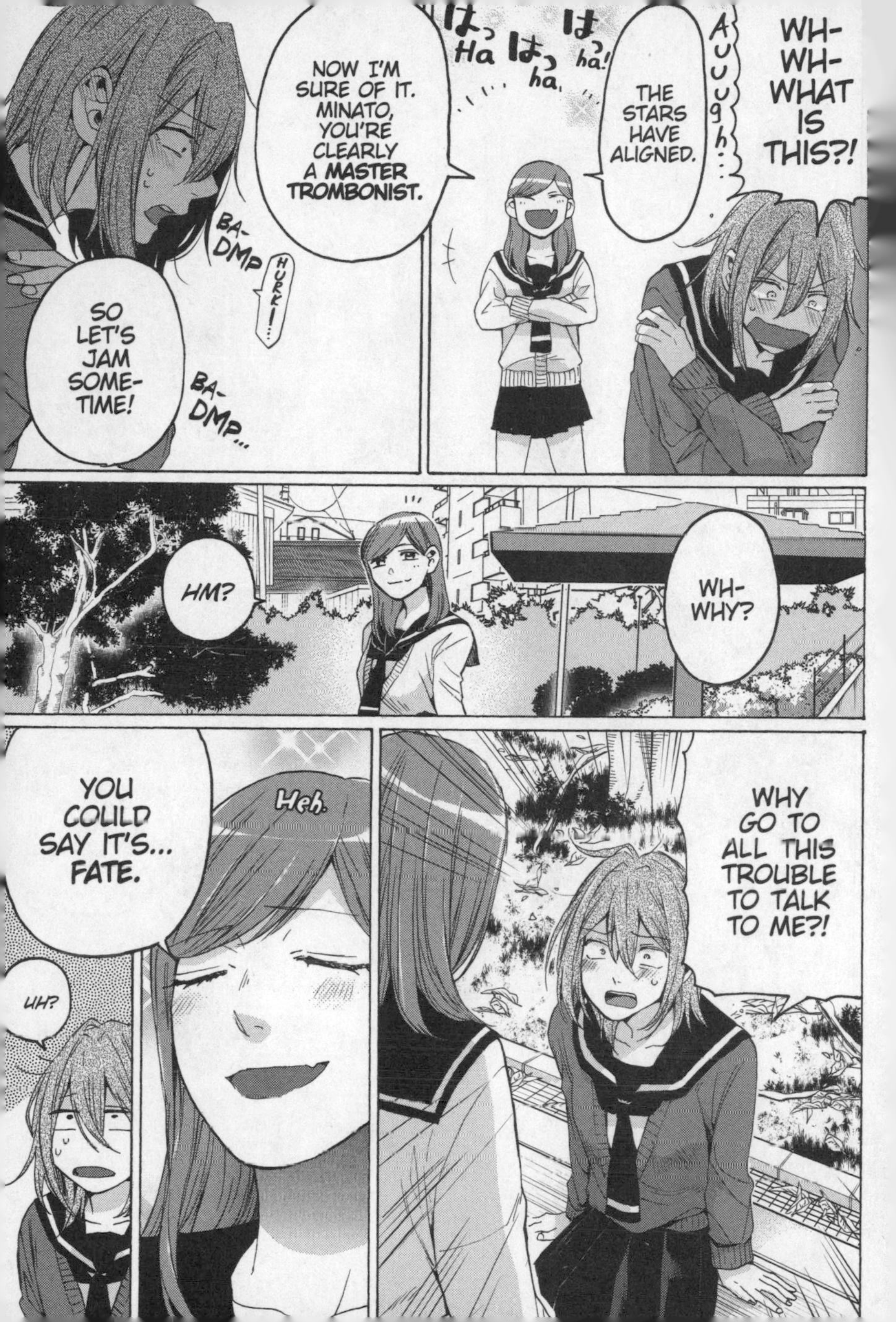
WH-WH-WHAT IS THIS?!
AUUUGH...
はっ は はっ
Ha ha! ha.
THE STARS HAVE ALIGNED.
NOW I'M SURE OF IT. MINATO, YOU'RE CLEARLY A **MASTER TROMBONIST.**
BA-DMP
HURK!...
SO LET'S JAM SOME-TIME!
BA-DMP...
WH-WHY?
HM?
WHY GO TO ALL THIS TROUBLE TO TALK TO ME?!
Heh.
YOU COULD SAY IT'S... FATE.
UH?

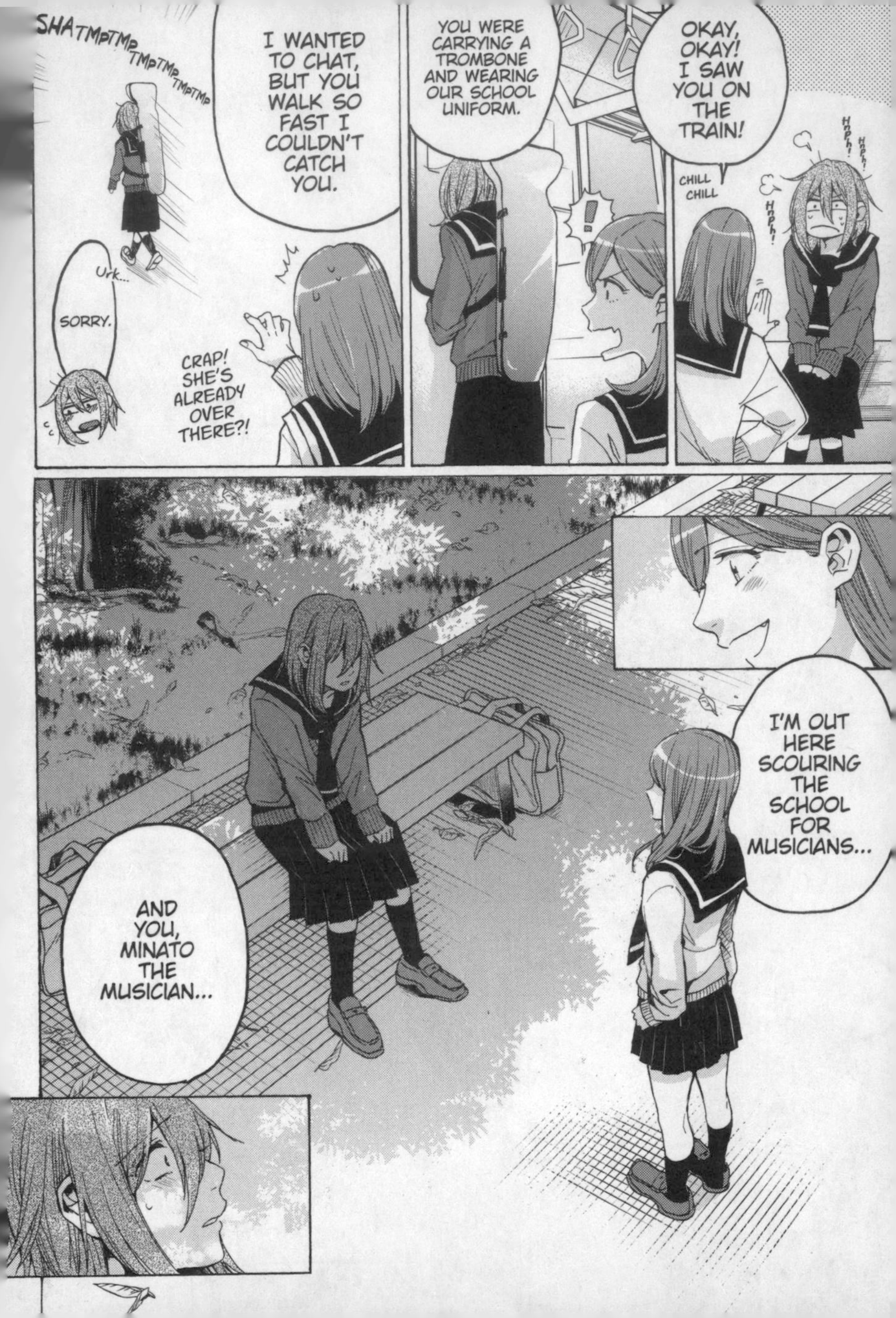
OKAY, OKAY! I SAW YOU ON THE TRAIN!
CHILL CHILL
Hnph! Hnph!
Hnph!
YOU WERE CARRYING A TROMBONE AND WEARING OUR SCHOOL UNIFORM.
!
I WANTED TO CHAT, BUT YOU WALK SO FAST I COULDN'T CATCH YOU.
SHA TMPTMP TMPTMP TMPTMP
CRAP! SHE'S ALREADY OVER THERE?!
Urk...
SORRY.
I'M OUT HERE SCOURING THE SCHOOL FOR MUSICIANS...
AND YOU, MINATO THE MUSICIAN...

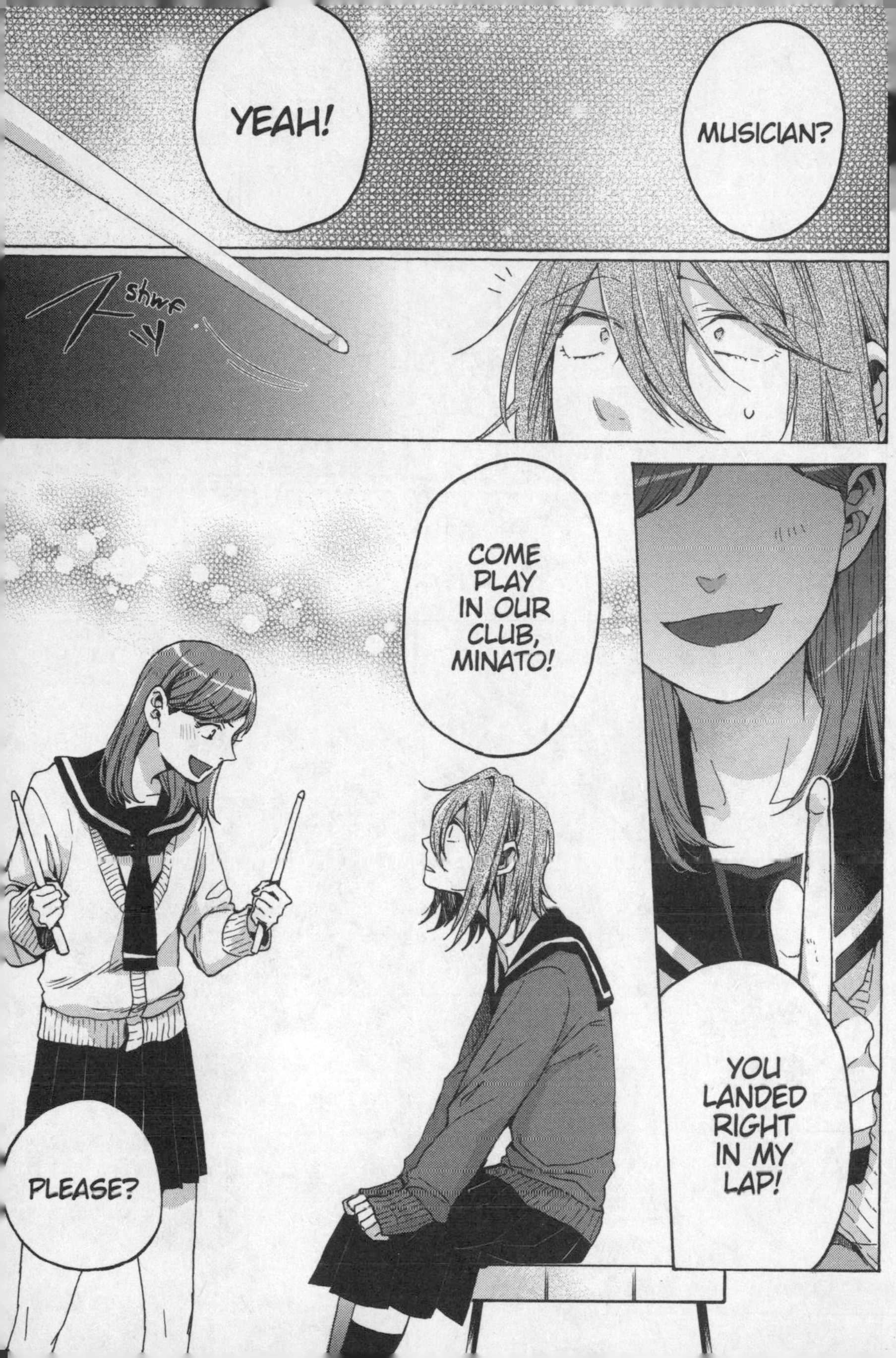
MUSICIAN?
YEAH!
shwf
YOU LANDED RIGHT IN MY LAP!
COME PLAY IN OUR CLUB, MINATO!
PLEASE?

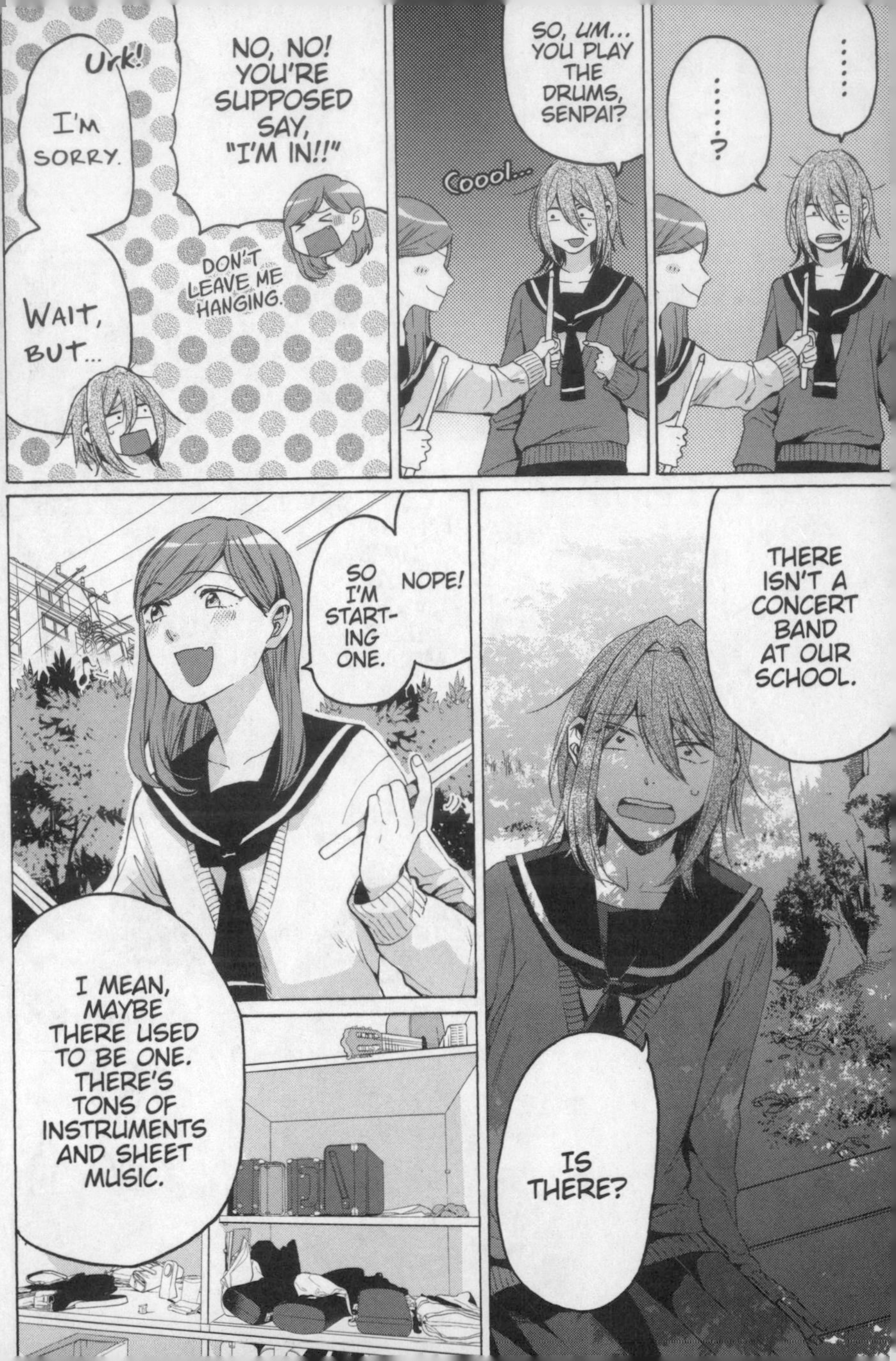
......
......?
SO, UM... YOU PLAY THE DRUMS, SENPAI?
Coool...
NO, NO! YOU'RE SUPPOSED SAY, "I'M IN!!"
DON'T LEAVE ME HANGING.
Urk!
I'M SORRY.
WAIT, BUT...
THERE ISN'T A CONCERT BAND AT OUR SCHOOL.
IS THERE?
NOPE!
SO I'M STARTING ONE.
I MEAN, MAYBE THERE USED TO BE ONE. THERE'S TONS OF INSTRUMENTS AND SHEET MUSIC.

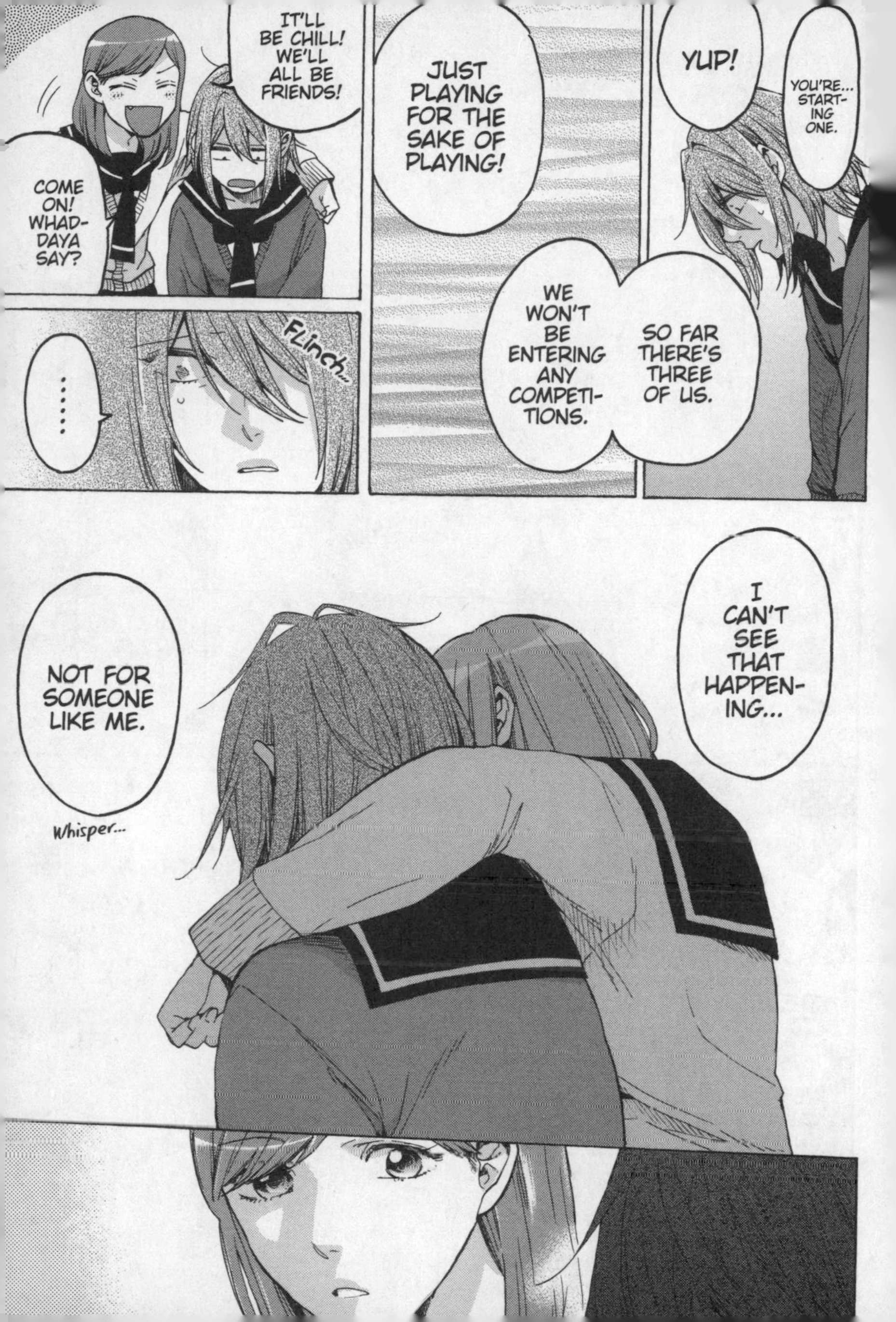

YOU'RE... START-ING ONE.
YUP!
JUST PLAYING FOR THE SAKE OF PLAYING!
SO FAR THERE'S THREE OF US.
WE WON'T BE ENTERING ANY COMPETI-TIONS.
IT'LL BE CHILL! WE'LL ALL BE FRIENDS!
COME ON! WHAD-DAYA SAY?
FLinch...
......
I CAN'T SEE THAT HAPPEN-ING...
NOT FOR SOMEONE LIKE ME.
Whisper...

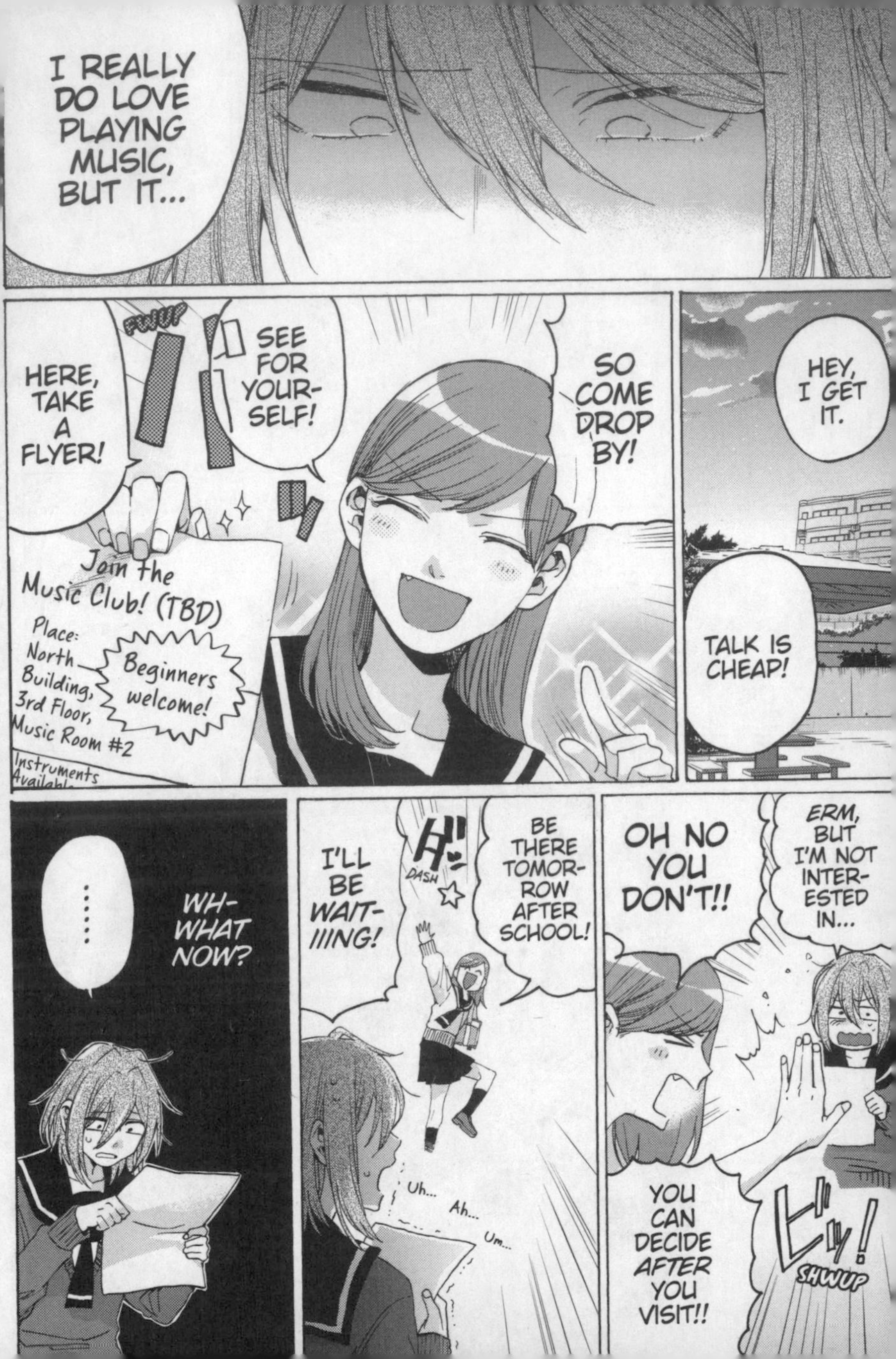
I REALLY DO LOVE PLAYING MUSIC, BUT IT...
HEY, I GET IT.
TALK IS CHEAP!
SO COME DROP BY!
SEE FOR YOURSELF!
FWUP
HERE, TAKE A FLYER!
Join the Music Club! (TBD)
Place: North Building, 3rd Floor, Music Room #2
Beginners welcome!
Instruments
ERM, BUT I'M NOT INTERESTED IN...
OH NO YOU DON'T!!
SHWUP
YOU CAN DECIDE AFTER YOU VISIT!!
BE THERE TOMORROW AFTER SCHOOL!
DASH
I'LL BE WAITIIING!
Uh...
Ah...
Um...
WH-WHAT NOW?
......

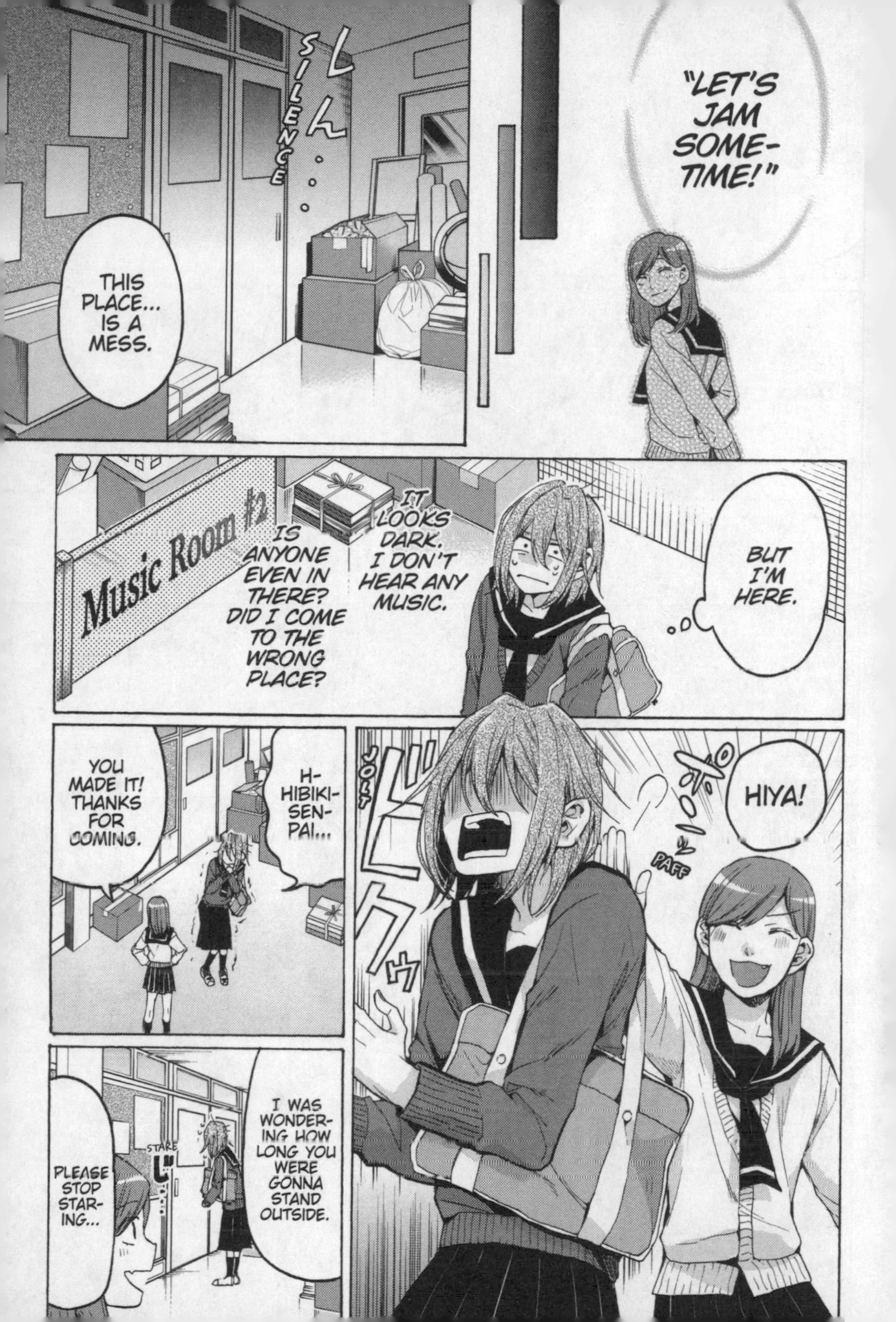
"LET'S JAM SOME-TIME!"
SILENCE
THIS PLACE... IS A MESS.
BUT I'M HERE.
IT LOOKS DARK. I DON'T HEAR ANY MUSIC.
IS ANYONE EVEN IN THERE? DID I COME TO THE WRONG PLACE?
Music Room #2
HIYA!
PAFF
JOLT
H-HIBIKI-SENPAI...
YOU MADE IT! THANKS FOR COMING.
I WAS WONDERING HOW LONG YOU WERE GONNA STAND OUTSIDE.
STARE
PLEASE STOP STARING...

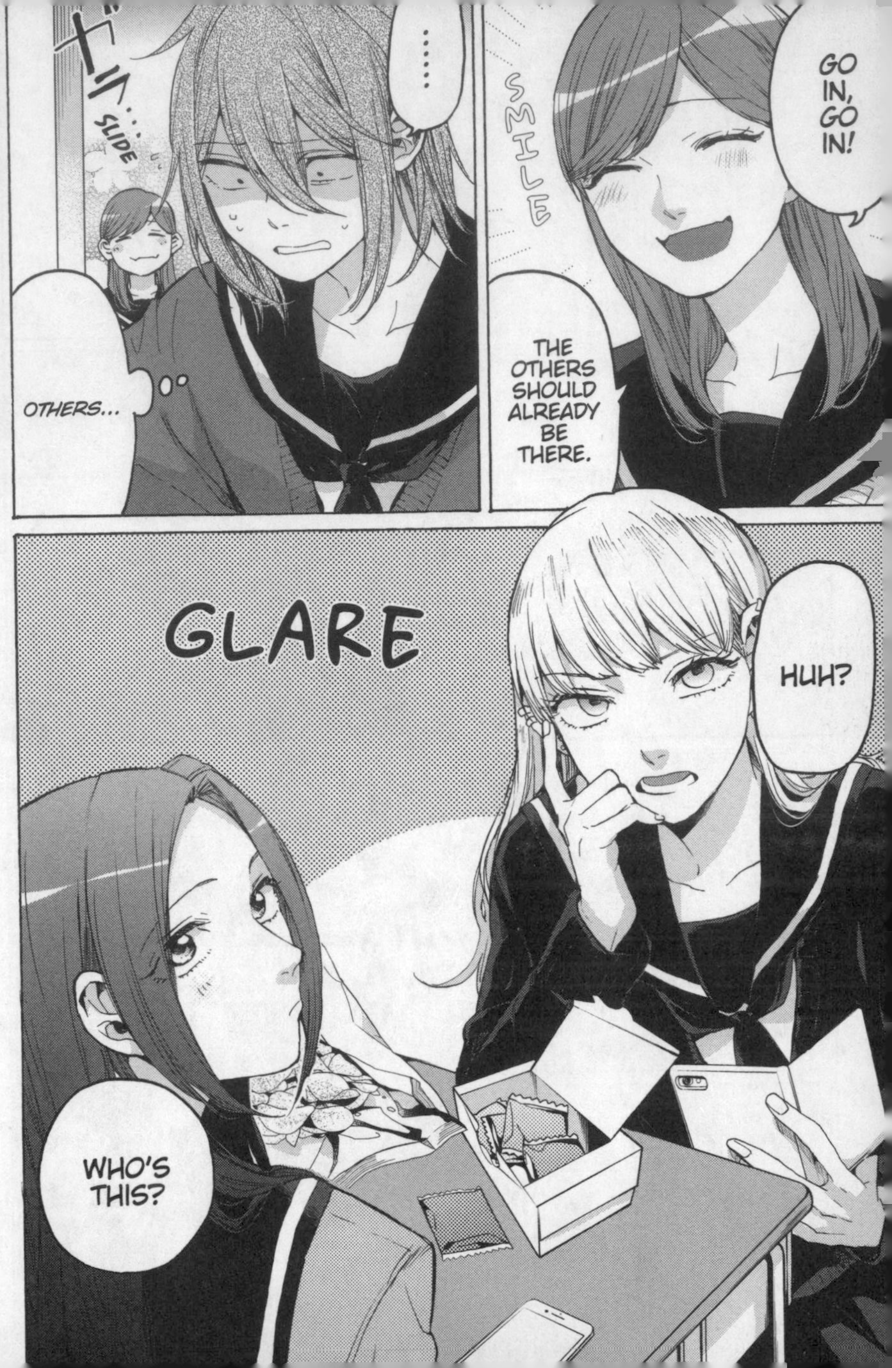
GO IN, GO IN!
SMILE
THE OTHERS SHOULD ALREADY BE THERE.
......
SLIDE
OTHERS...
GLARE
HUH?
WHO'S THIS?

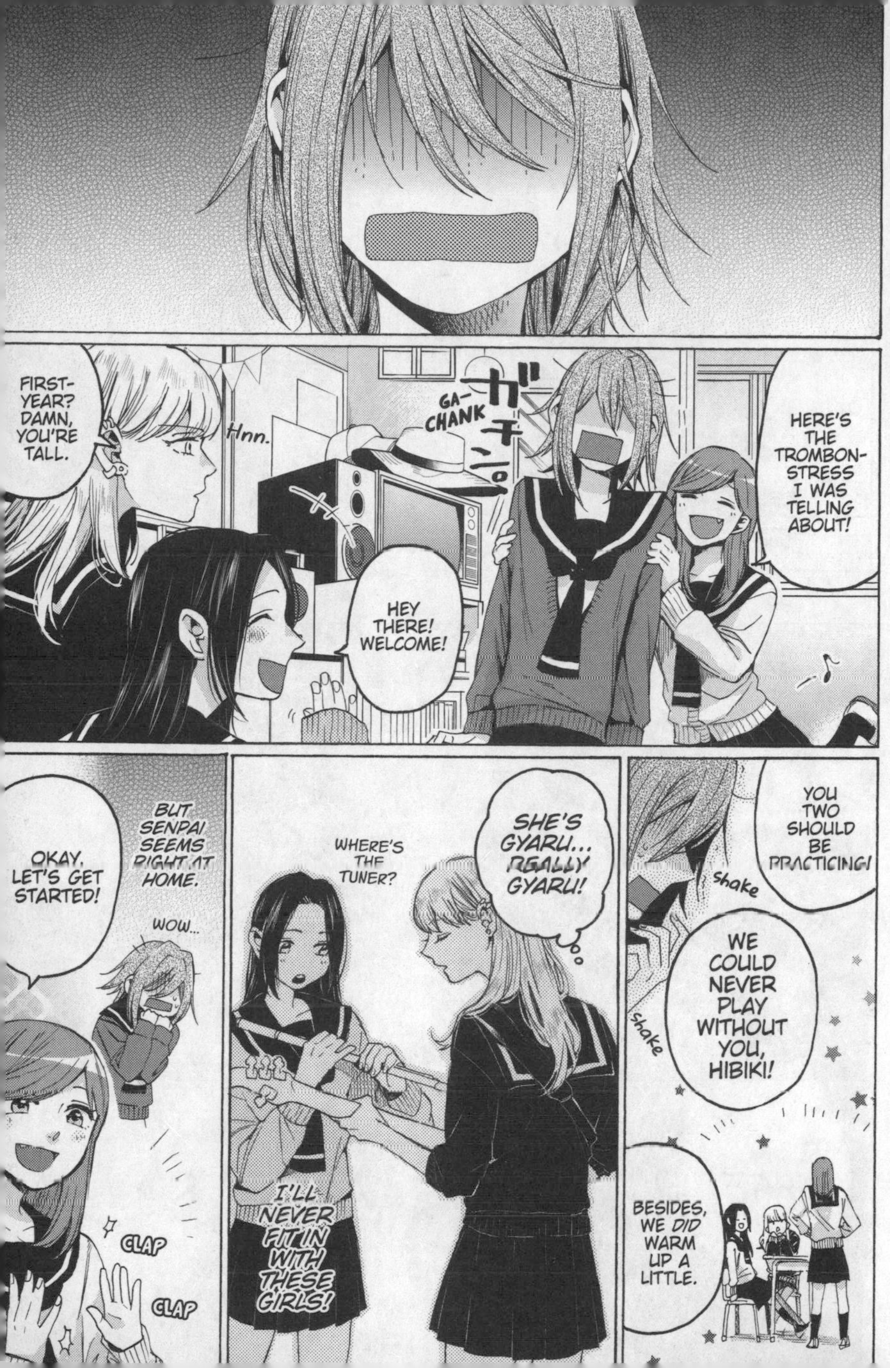
HERE'S THE TROMBONSTRESS I WAS TELLING ABOUT!
GA-CHANK
HEY THERE! WELCOME!
Hnn.
FIRST-YEAR? DAMN, YOU'RE TALL.
YOU TWO SHOULD BE PRACTICING!
Shake
WE COULD NEVER PLAY WITHOUT YOU, HIBIKI!
Shake
BESIDES, WE DID WARM UP A LITTLE.
SHE'S GYARU... REALLY GYARU!
WHERE'S THE TUNER?
I'LL NEVER FIT IN WITH THESE GIRLS!
BUT SENPAI SEEMS RIGHT AT HOME.
OKAY, LET'S GET STARTED!
WOW...
CLAP
CLAP

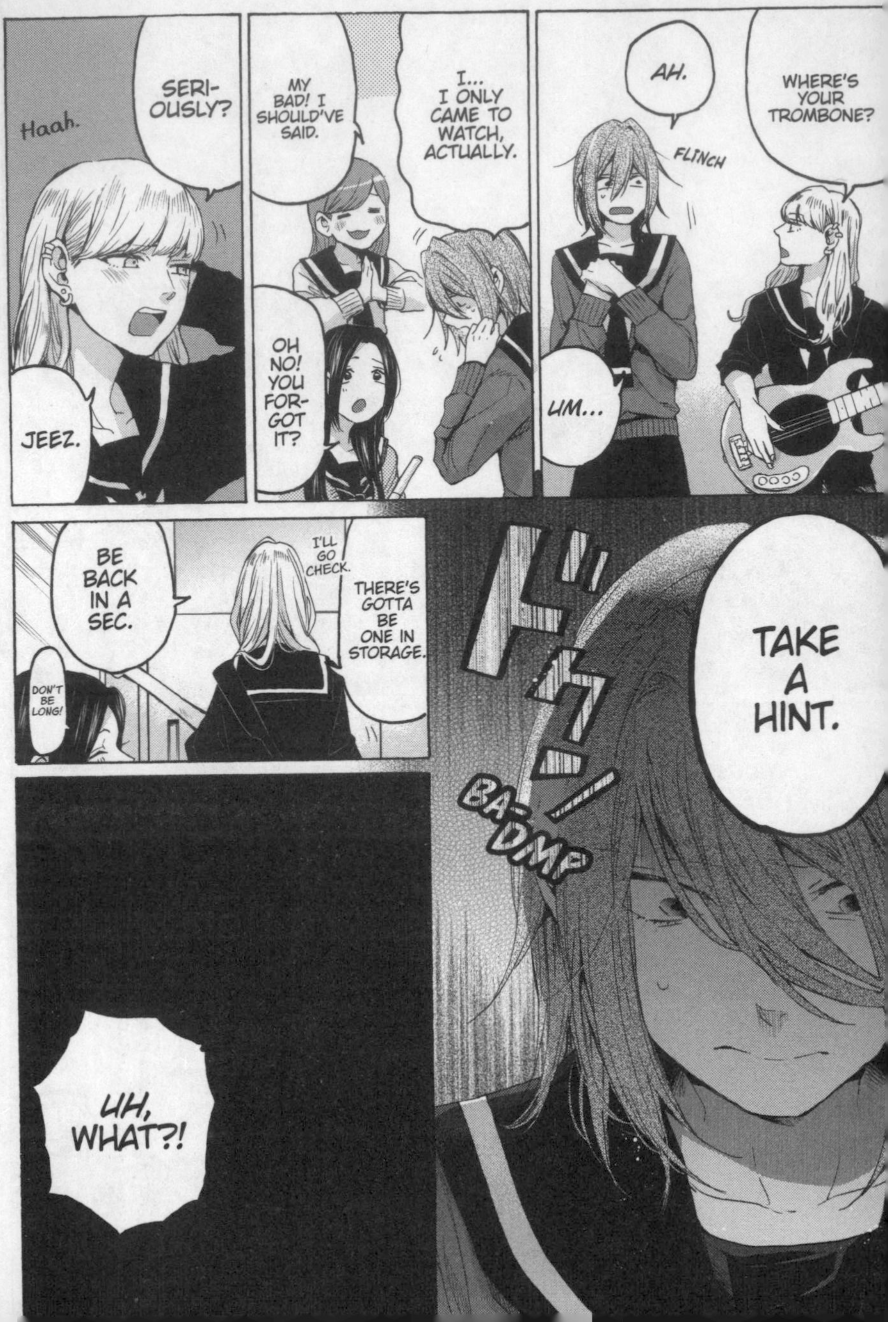
WHERE'S YOUR TROMBONE?
AH.
FLINCH
UM...
I... I ONLY CAME TO WATCH, ACTUALLY.
MY BAD! I SHOULD'VE SAID.
OH NO! YOU FOR-GOT IT?
SERI-OUSLY?
Haah.
JEEZ.
TAKE A HINT.
BA-DUMP
I'LL GO CHECK.
THERE'S GOTTA BE ONE IN STORAGE.
BE BACK IN A SEC.
DON'T BE LONG!
UH, WHAT?!

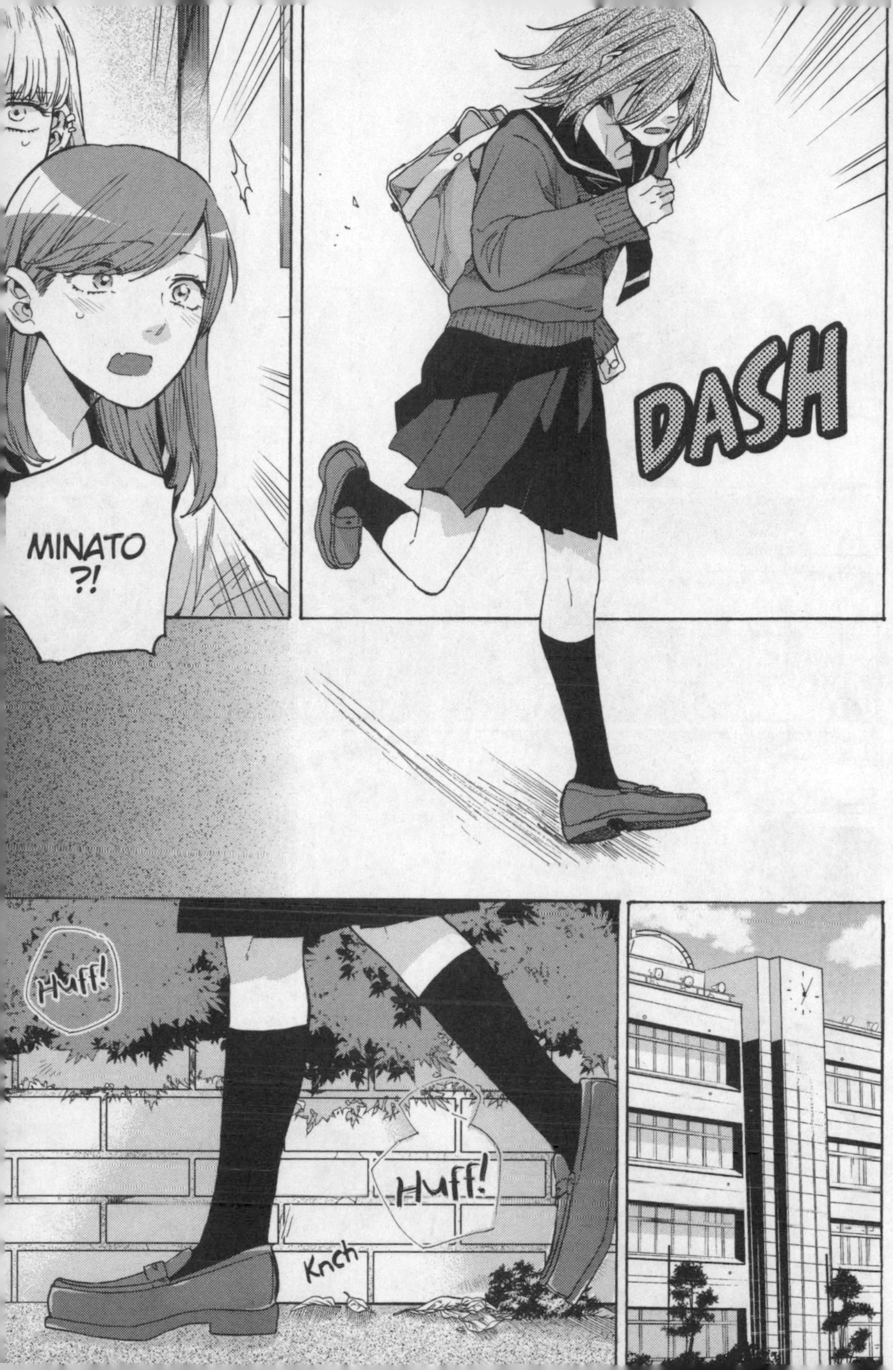
DASH
MINATO ?!
Huff!
Huff!
Knch

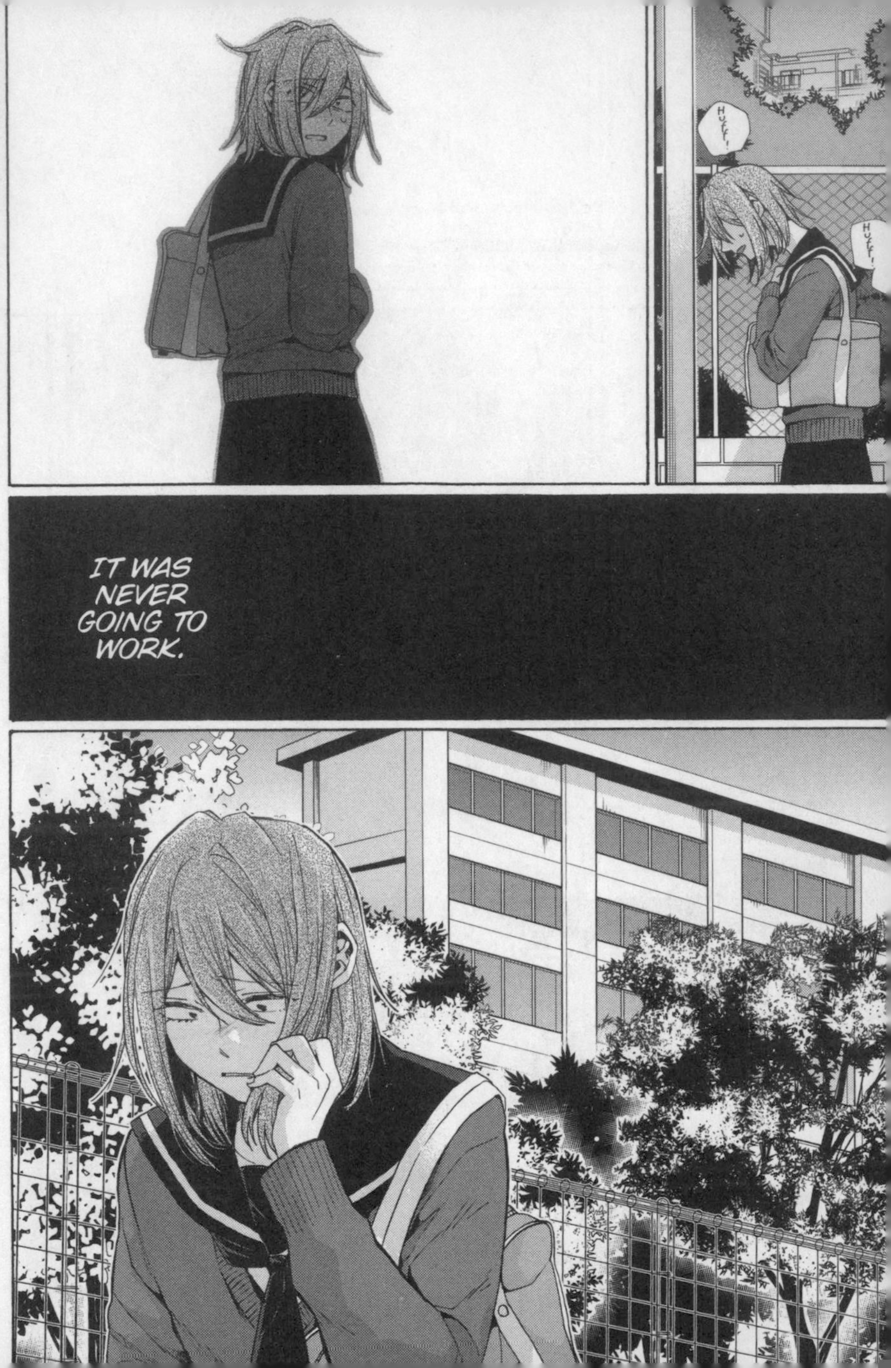
Huff!
Huff!
IT WAS NEVER GOING TO WORK.

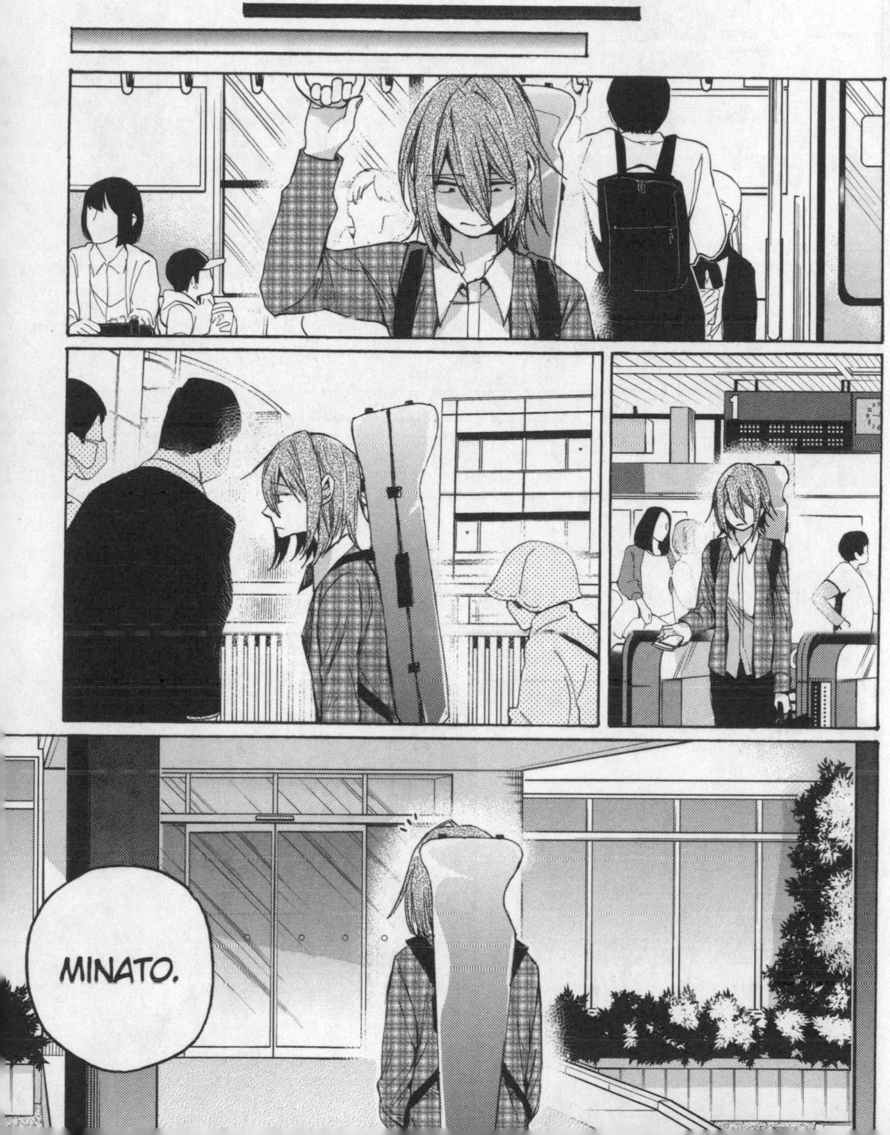
MINATO.

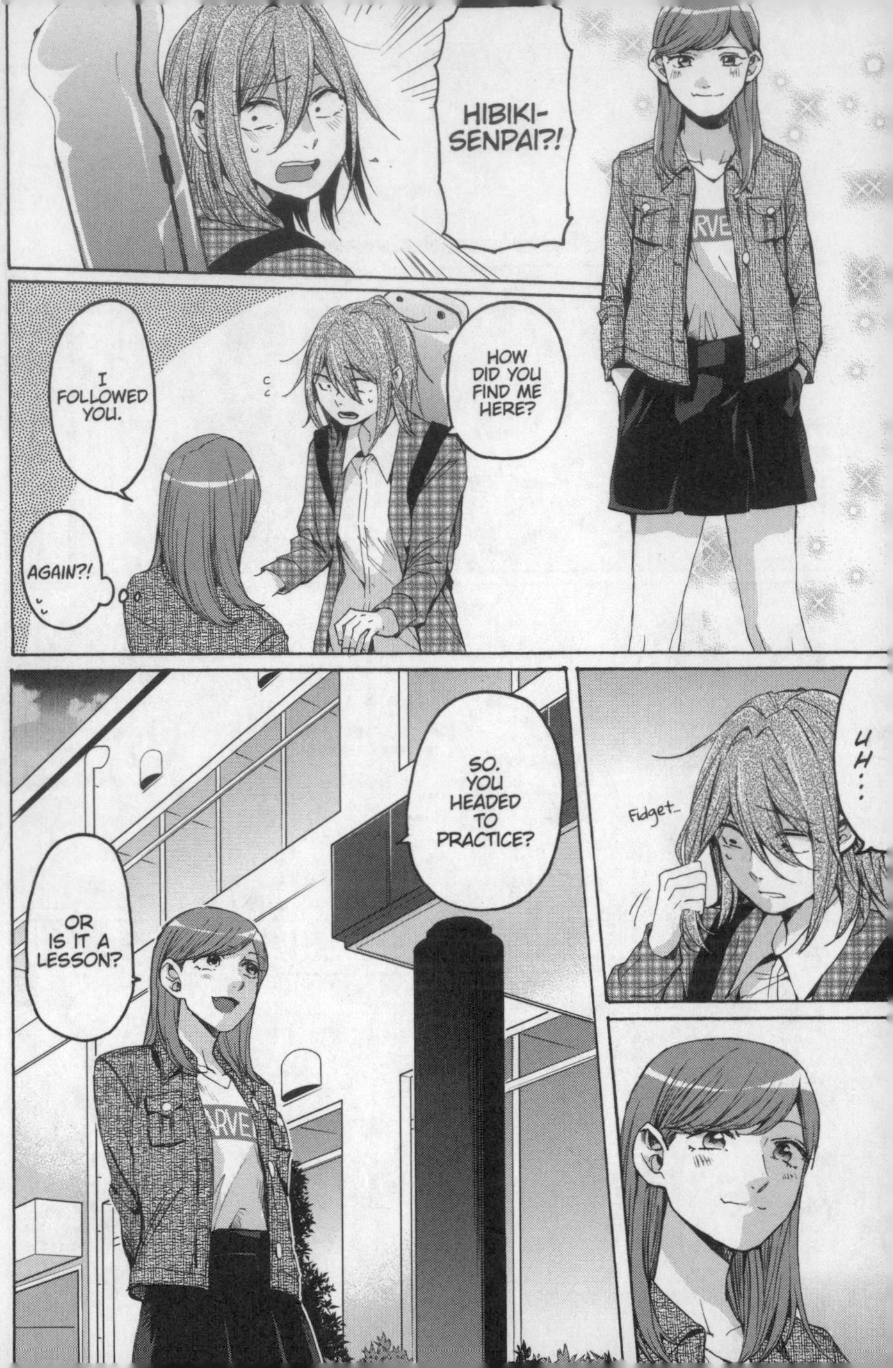
HIBIKI-SENPAI?!
HOW DID YOU FIND ME HERE?
I FOLLOWED YOU.
AGAIN?!
UH...
Fidget...
SO. YOU HEADED TO PRACTICE?
OR IS IT A LESSON?

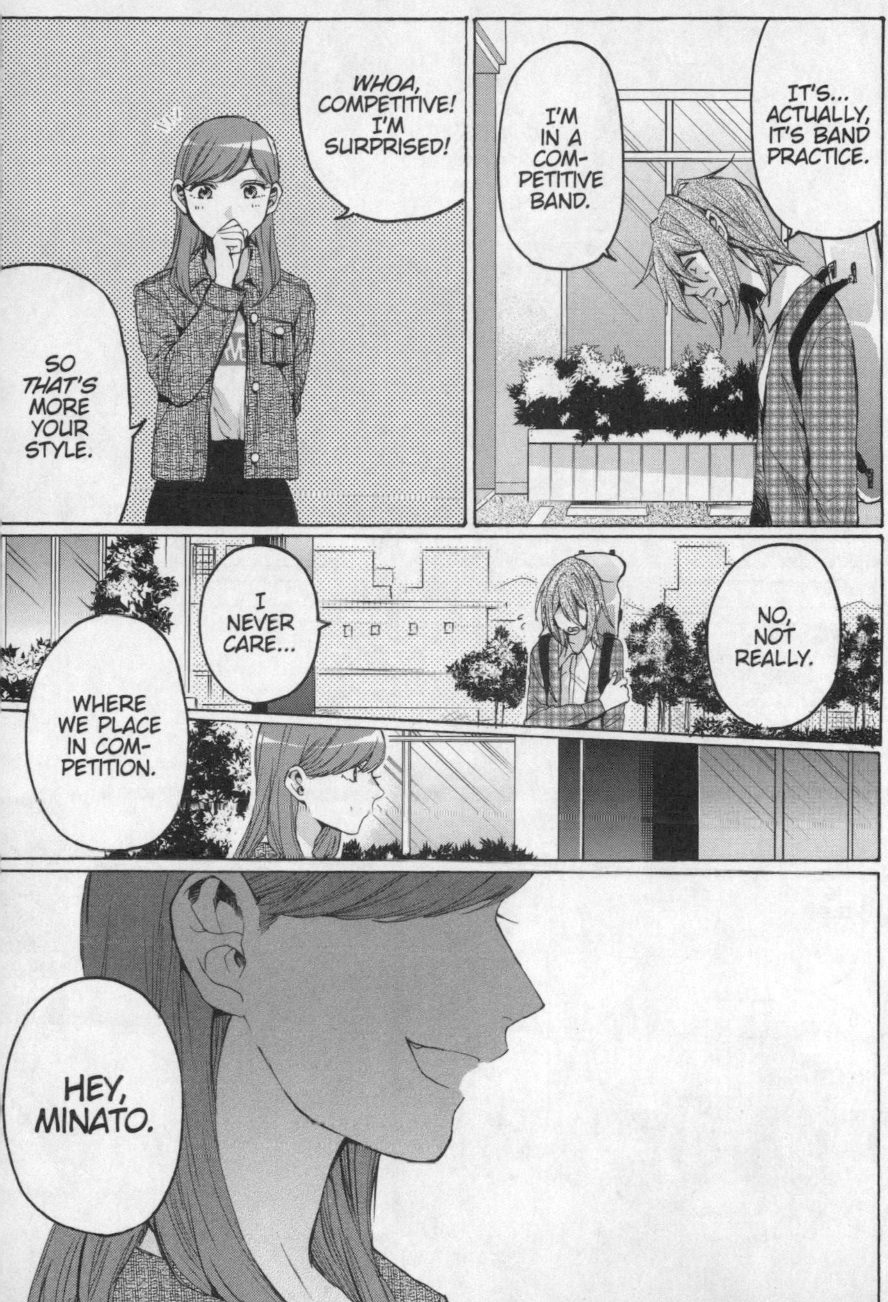
IT'S... ACTUALLY, IT'S BAND PRACTICE.
I'M IN A COM-PETITIVE BAND.
WHOA, COMPETITIVE! I'M SURPRISED!
SO THAT'S MORE YOUR STYLE.
NO, NOT REALLY.
I NEVER CARE...
WHERE WE PLACE IN COM-PETITION.
HEY, MINATO.

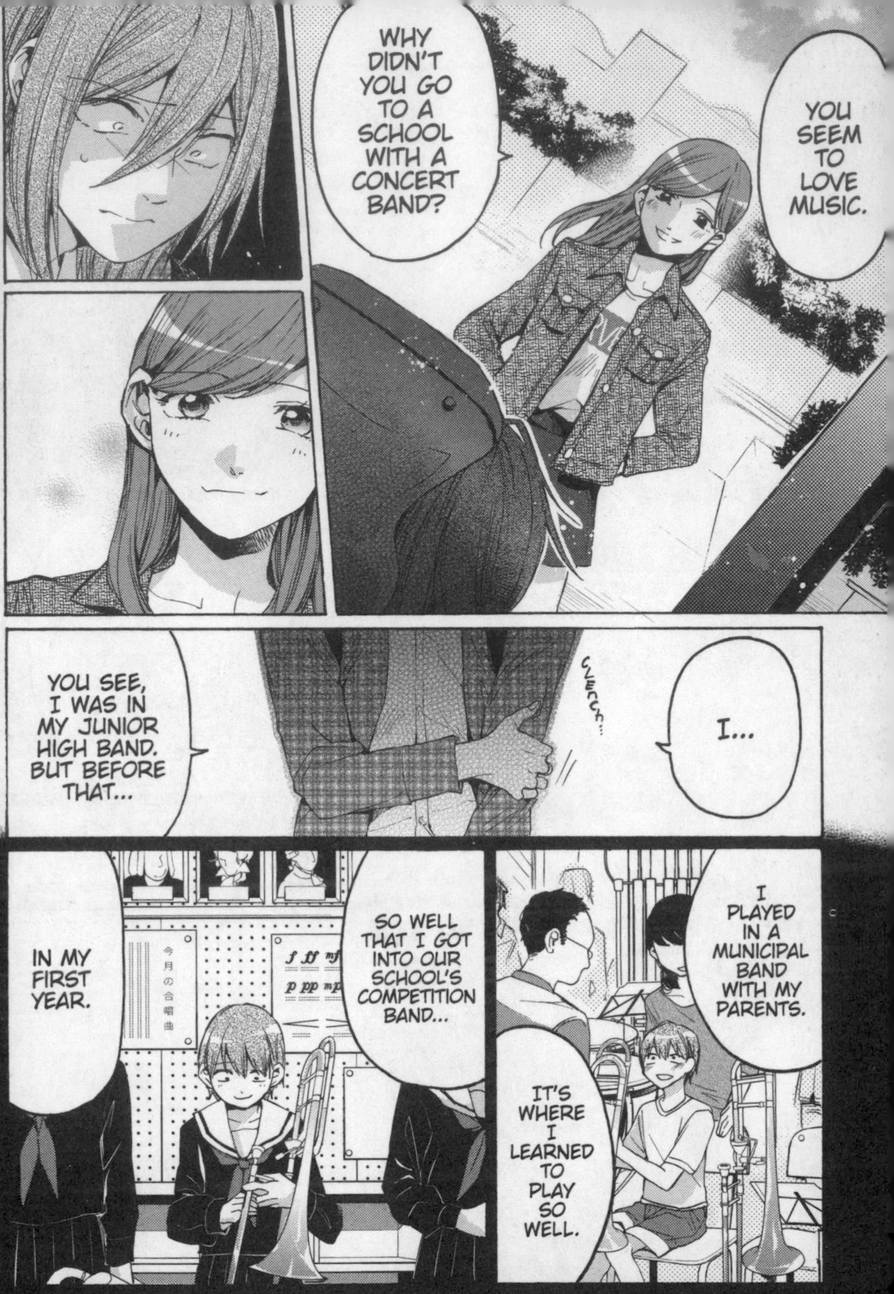
YOU SEEM TO LOVE MUSIC.
WHY DIDN'T YOU GO TO A SCHOOL WITH A CONCERT BAND?
I...
CLENCH..
YOU SEE, I WAS IN MY JUNIOR HIGH BAND. BUT BEFORE THAT...
I PLAYED IN A MUNICIPAL BAND WITH MY PARENTS.
IT'S WHERE I LEARNED TO PLAY SO WELL.
SO WELL THAT I GOT INTO OUR SCHOOL'S COMPETITION BAND...
IN MY FIRST YEAR.
今月の合唱曲

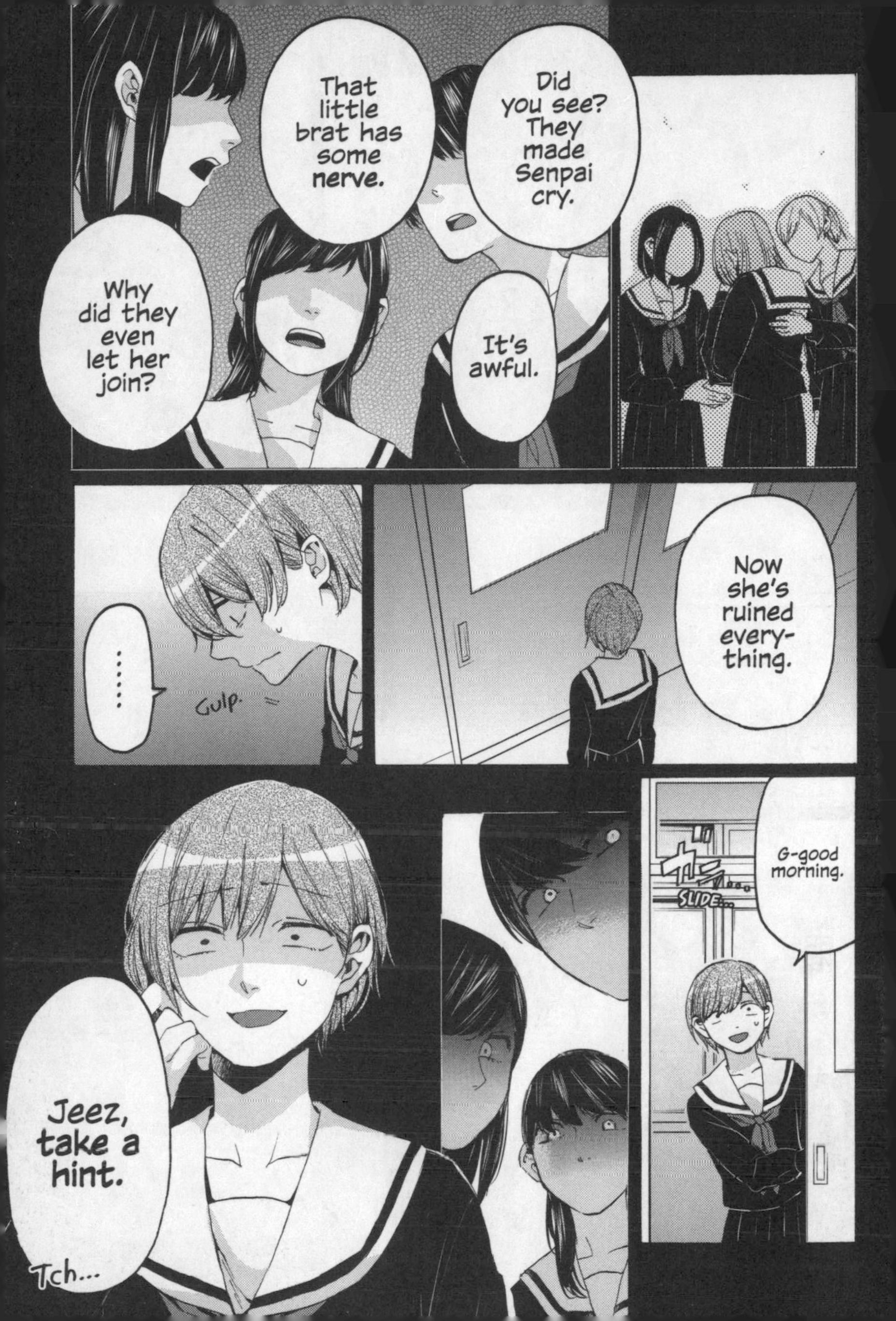
Did you see? They made Senpai cry.
That little brat has some nerve.
It's awful.
Why did they even let her join?
Now she's ruined everything.
......
Gulp.
SLIDE...
G-good morning.
Jeez, take a hint.
Tch...

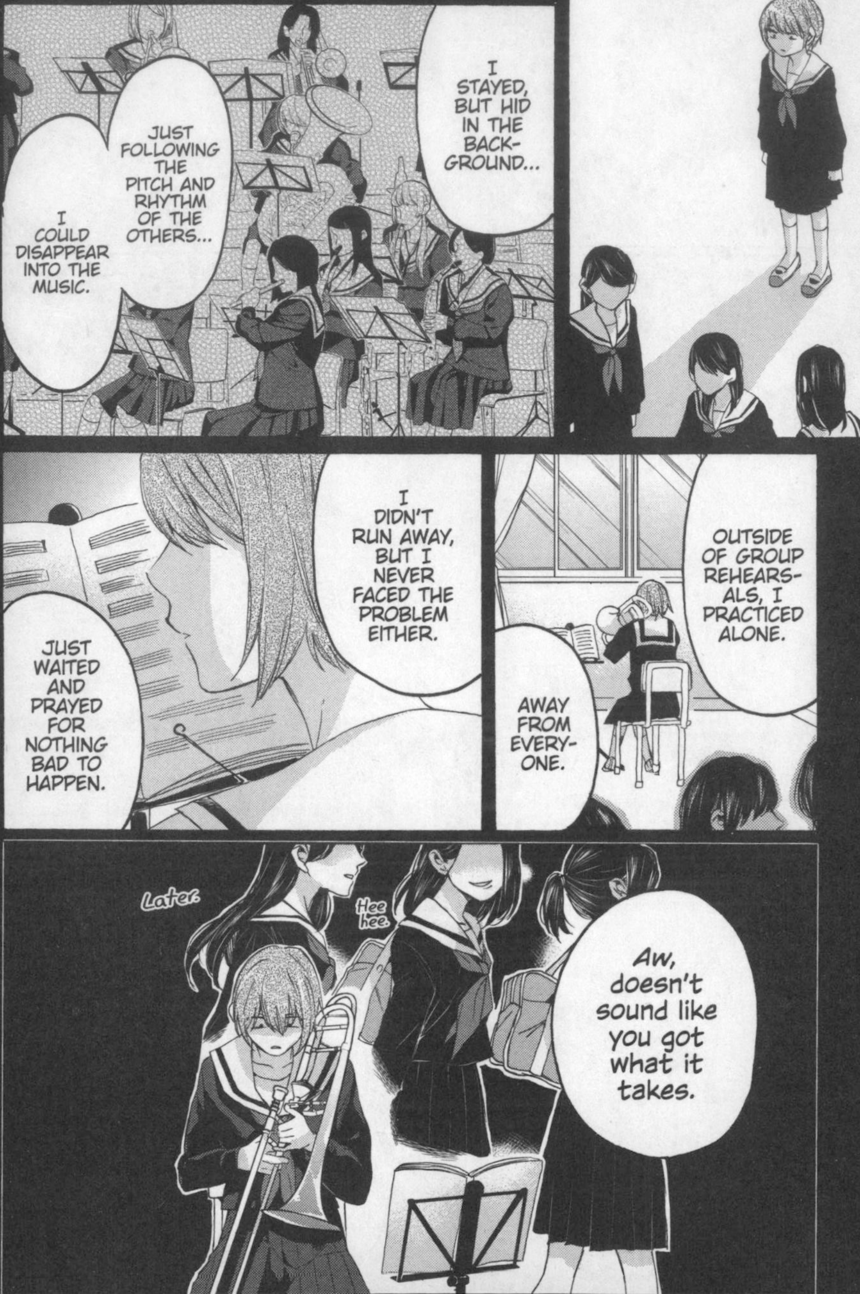
I STAYED, BUT HID IN THE BACKGROUND...
JUST FOLLOWING THE PITCH AND RHYTHM OF THE OTHERS...
I COULD DISAPPEAR INTO THE MUSIC.
OUTSIDE OF GROUP REHEARSALS, I PRACTICED ALONE.
AWAY FROM EVERYONE.
I DIDN'T RUN AWAY, BUT I NEVER FACED THE PROBLEM EITHER.
JUST WAITED AND PRAYED FOR NOTHING BAD TO HAPPEN.
Later.
Hee hee.
Aw, doesn't sound like you got what it takes.

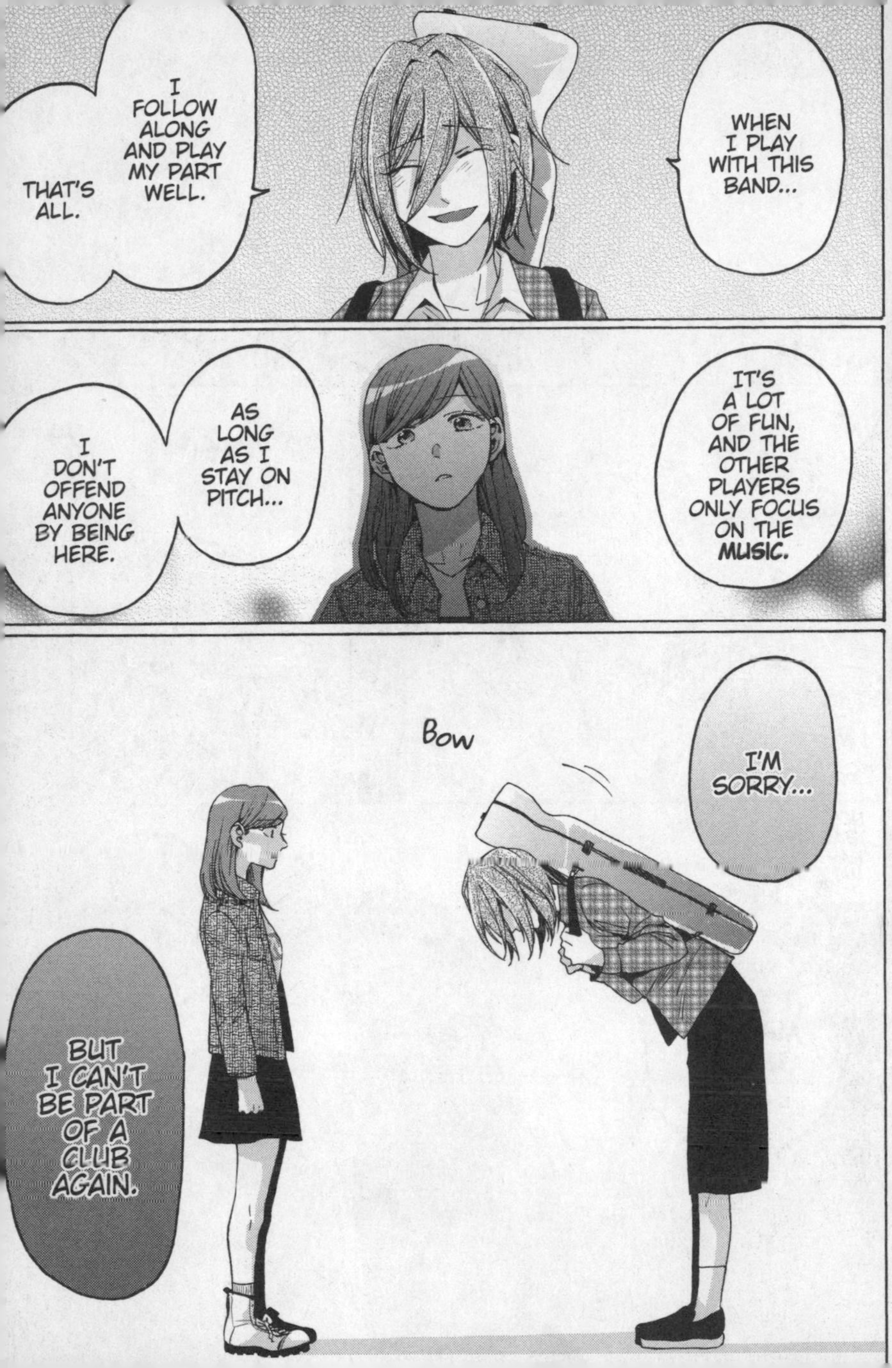
WHEN I PLAY WITH THIS BAND...
I FOLLOW ALONG AND PLAY MY PART WELL.
THAT'S ALL.
IT'S A LOT OF FUN, AND THE OTHER PLAYERS ONLY FOCUS ON THE MUSIC.
AS LONG AS I STAY ON PITCH...
I DON'T OFFEND ANYONE BY BEING HERE.
I'M SORRY...
Bow
BUT I CAN'T BE PART OF A CLUB AGAIN.

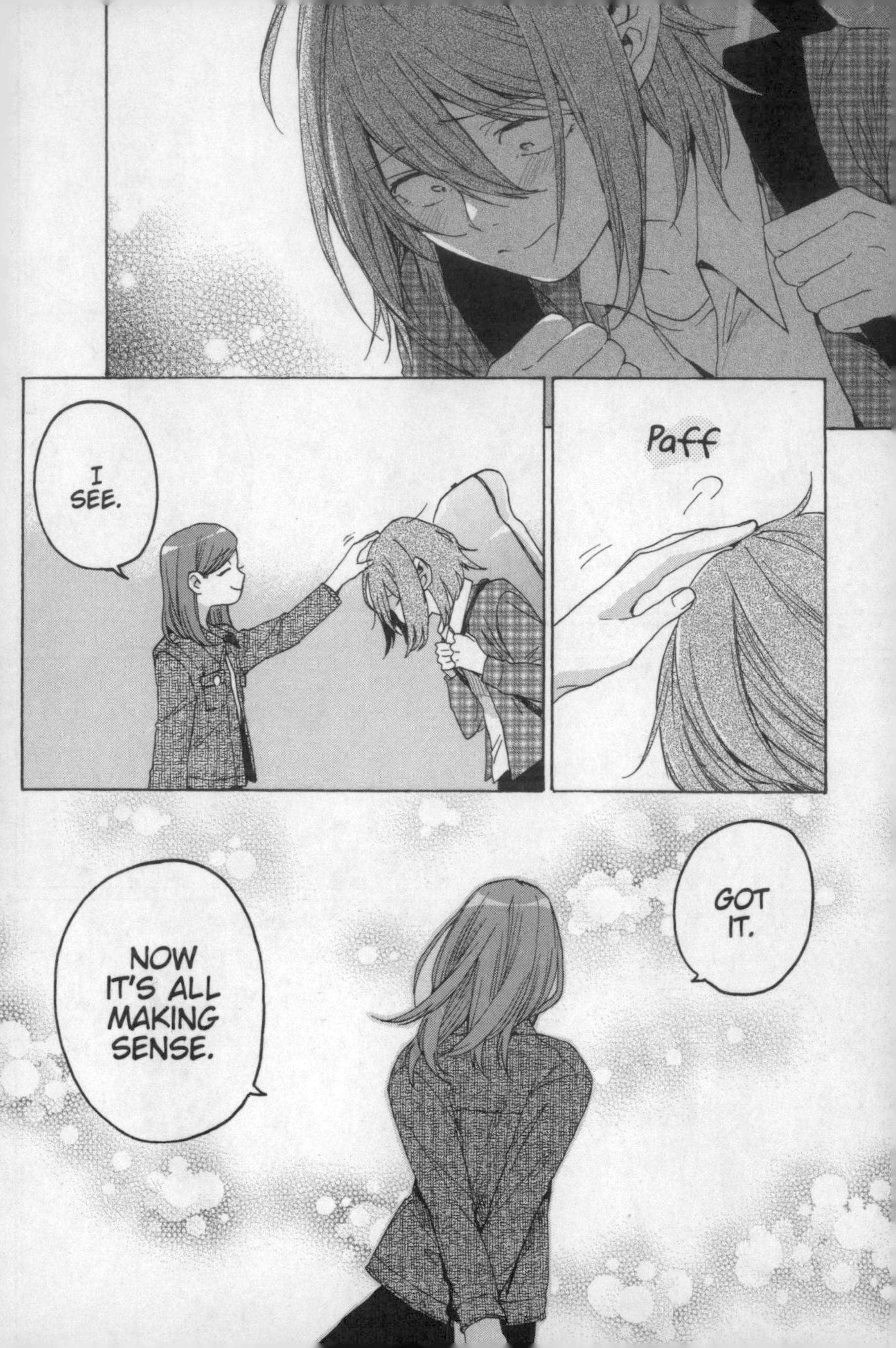
Paff
I SEE.
GOT IT.
NOW IT'S ALL MAKING SENSE.

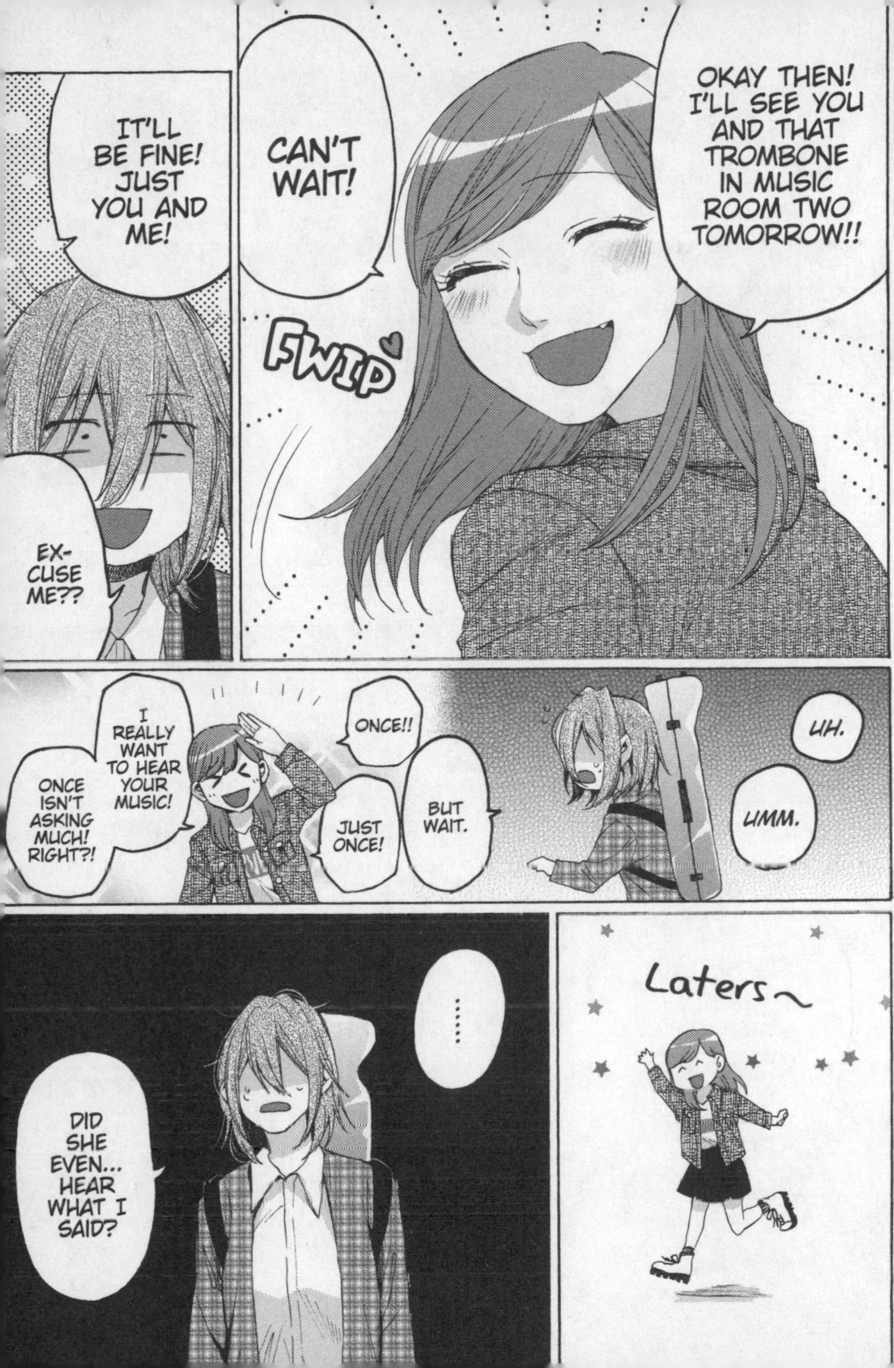
OKAY THEN! I'LL SEE YOU AND THAT TROMBONE IN MUSIC ROOM TWO TOMORROW!!
CAN'T WAIT!
FWIP
IT'LL BE FINE! JUST YOU AND ME!
EX-CUSE ME??
UH.
UMM.
ONCE!!
BUT WAIT.
I REALLY WANT TO HEAR YOUR MUSIC!
JUST ONCE!
ONCE ISN'T ASKING MUCH! RIGHT?!
Laters~
......
DID SHE EVEN... HEAR WHAT I SAID?

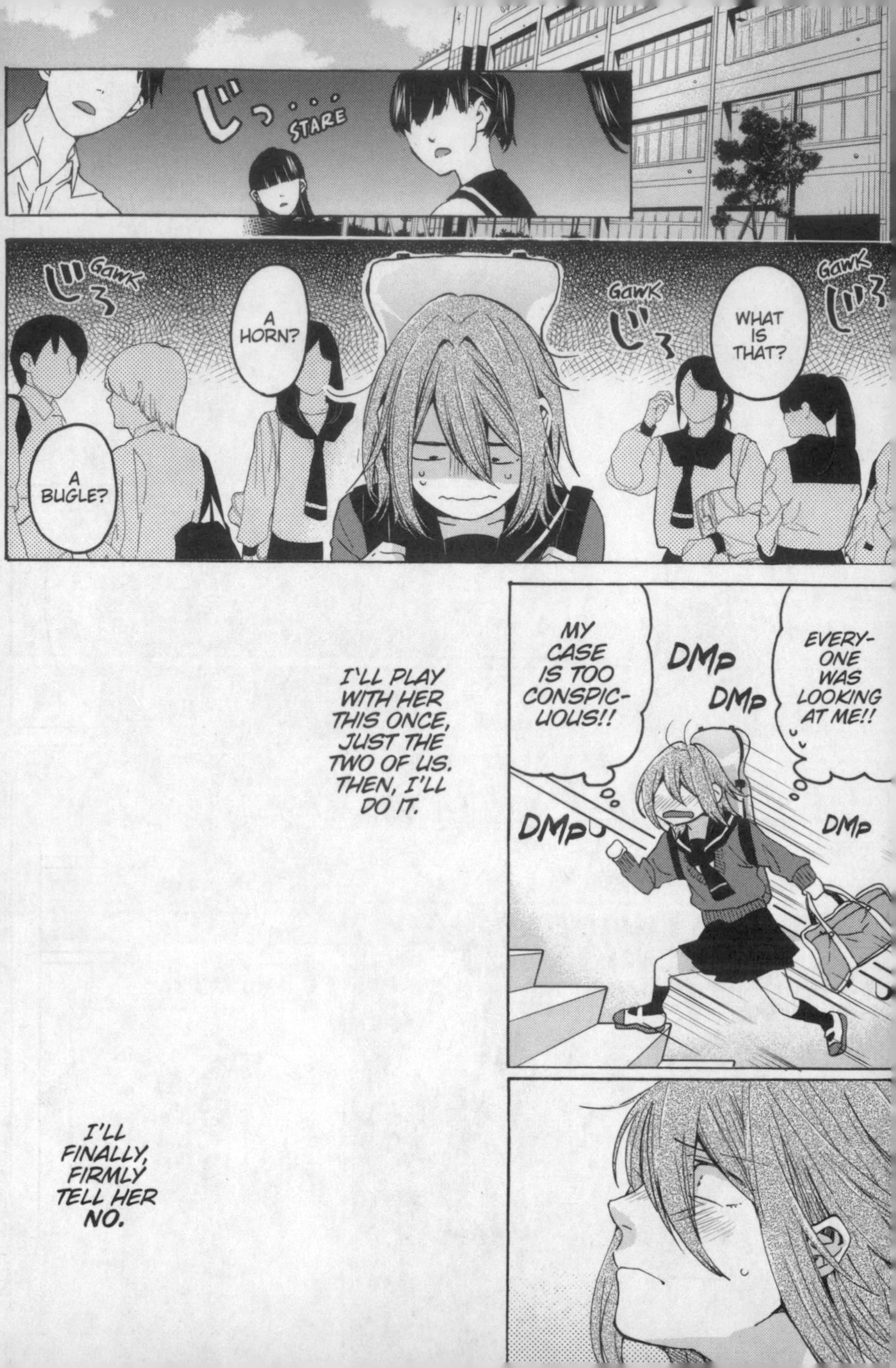
じっ...
STARE
Gawk
じろ
WHAT IS THAT?
Gawk
じろ
A HORN?
Gawk
じろ
A BUGLE?
EVERY-ONE WAS LOOKING AT ME!!
MY CASE IS TOO CONSPIC-UOUS!!
DMp
DMp
DMp
DMp
I'LL PLAY WITH HER THIS ONCE, JUST THE TWO OF US. THEN, I'LL DO IT.
I'LL FINALLY, FIRMLY TELL HER NO.

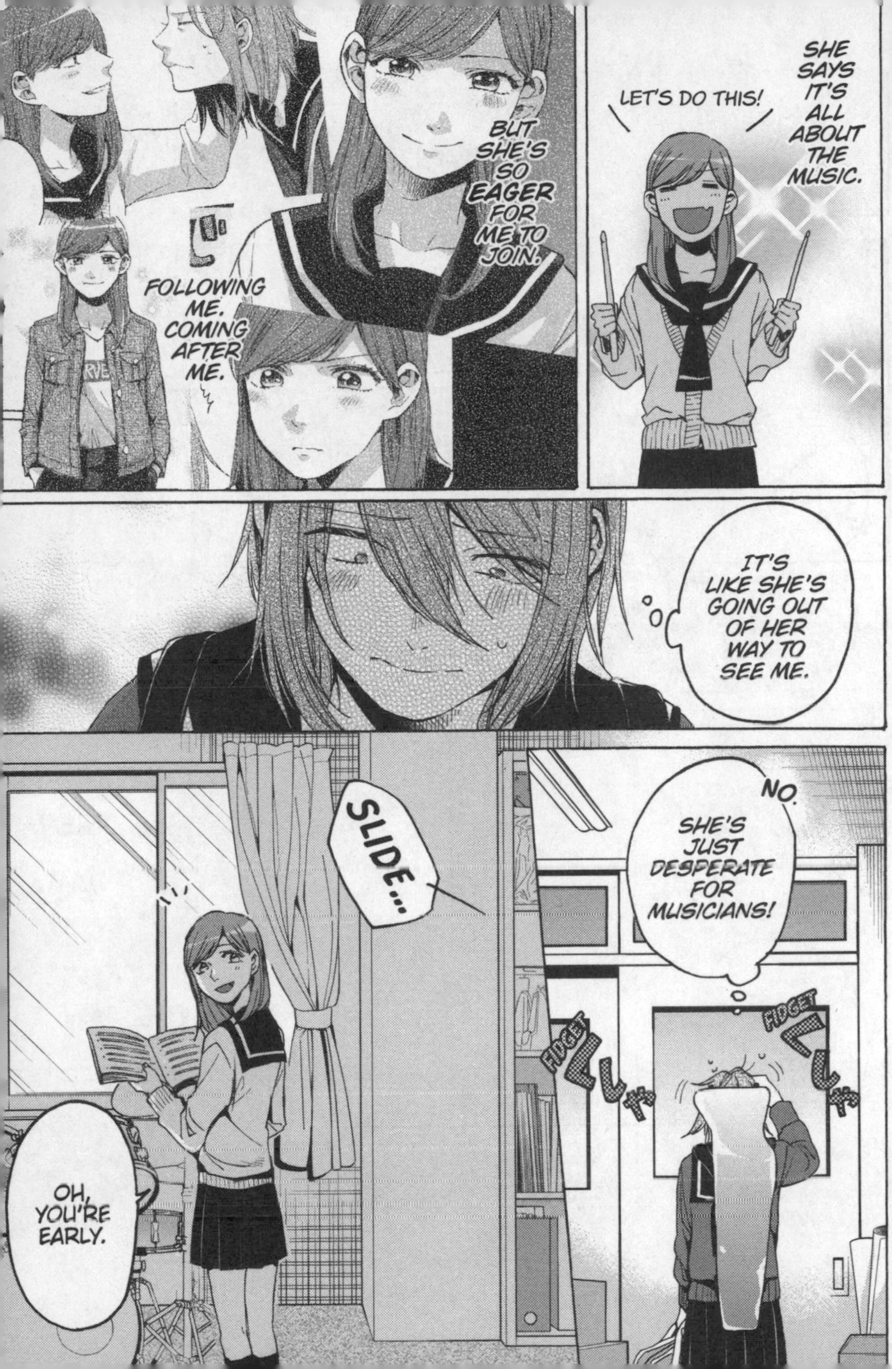
SHE SAYS IT'S ALL ABOUT THE MUSIC.
LET'S DO THIS!
BUT SHE'S SO EAGER FOR ME TO JOIN.
FOLLOWING ME. COMING AFTER ME.
IT'S LIKE SHE'S GOING OUT OF HER WAY TO SEE ME.
NO.
SHE'S JUST DESPERATE FOR MUSICIANS!
FIDGET
FIDGET
SLIDE...
OH, YOU'RE EARLY.

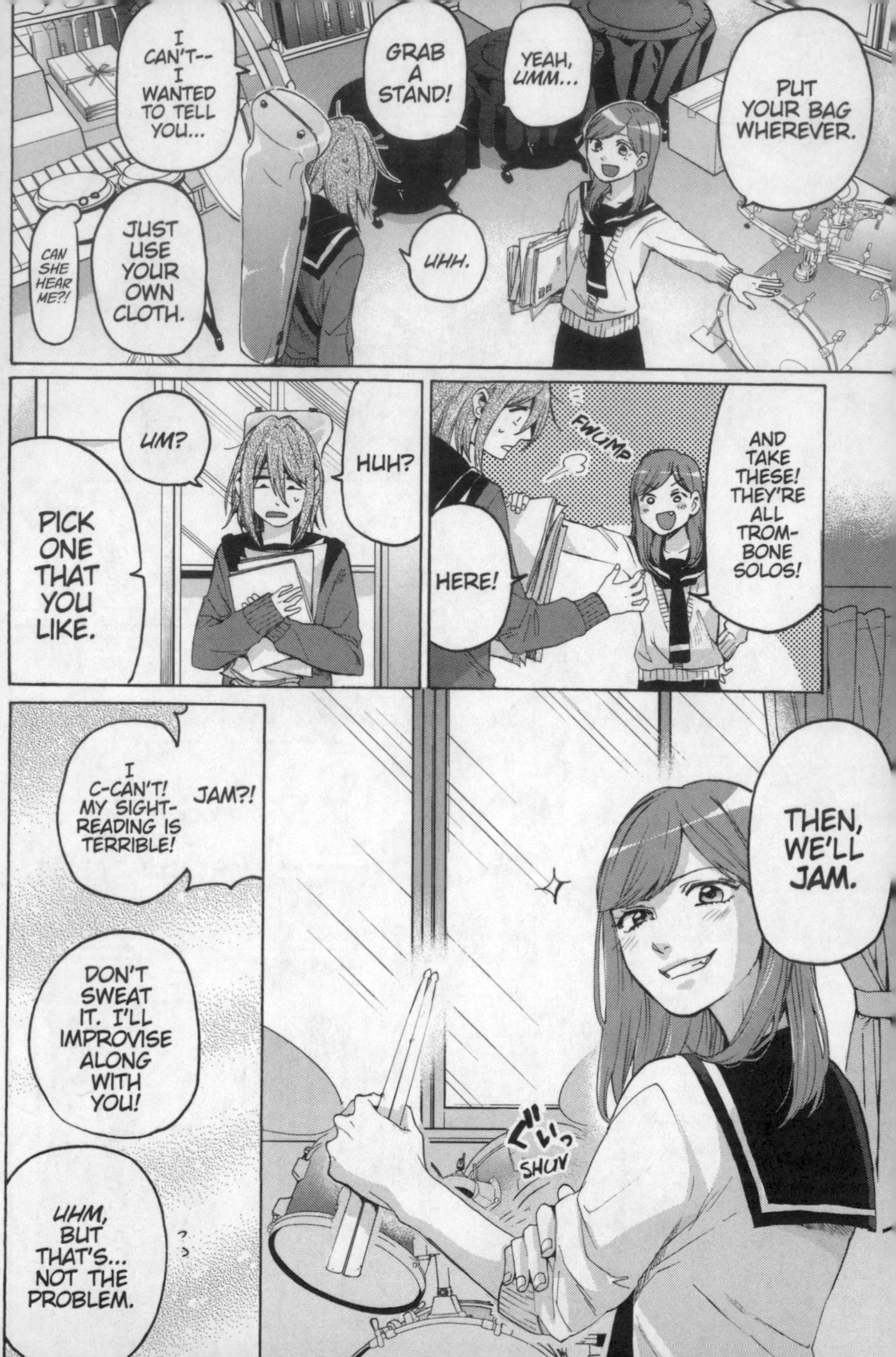
PUT YOUR BAG WHEREVER.
YEAH, UMM...
GRAB A STAND!
I CAN'T-- I WANTED TO TELL YOU...
UHH.
JUST USE YOUR OWN CLOTH.
CAN SHE HEAR ME?!
AND TAKE THESE! THEY'RE ALL TROM-BONE SOLOS!
FWUMP
HERE!
HUH?
UM?
PICK ONE THAT YOU LIKE.
THEN, WE'LL JAM.
SHUV
JAM?!
I C-CAN'T! MY SIGHT-READING IS TERRIBLE!
DON'T SWEAT IT. I'LL IMPROVISE ALONG WITH YOU!
UHM, BUT THAT'S... NOT THE PROBLEM.

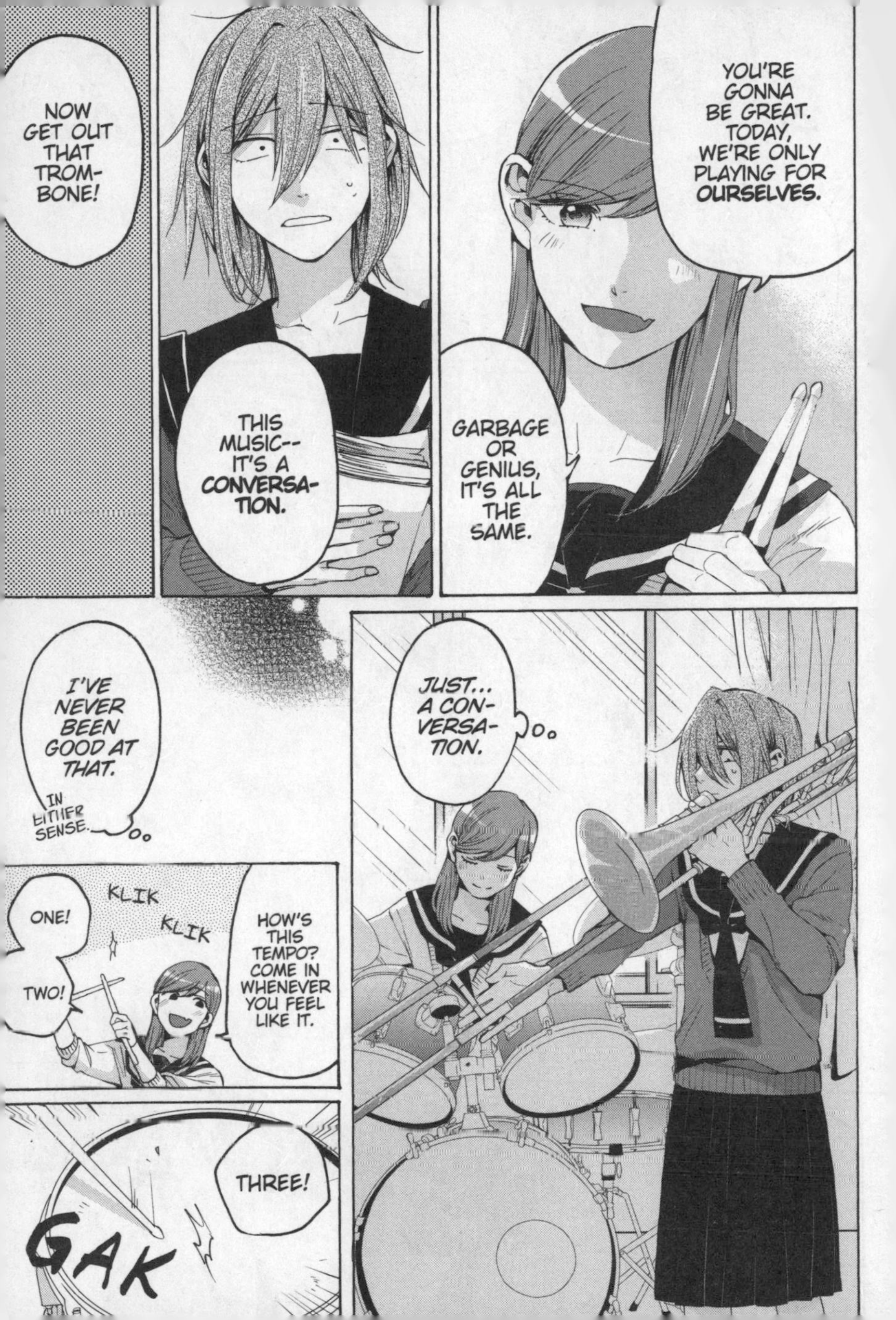
YOU'RE GONNA BE GREAT. TODAY, WE'RE ONLY PLAYING FOR **OURSELVES.**
GARBAGE OR GENIUS, IT'S ALL THE SAME.
NOW GET OUT THAT TROM-BONE!
THIS MUSIC-- IT'S A **CONVERSA-TION.**
JUST... A CON-VERSA-TION.
I'VE NEVER BEEN GOOD AT THAT.
IN EITHER SENSE.
HOW'S THIS TEMPO? COME IN WHENEVER YOU FEEL LIKE IT.
KLIK
KLIK
ONE!
TWO!
THREE!
GAK

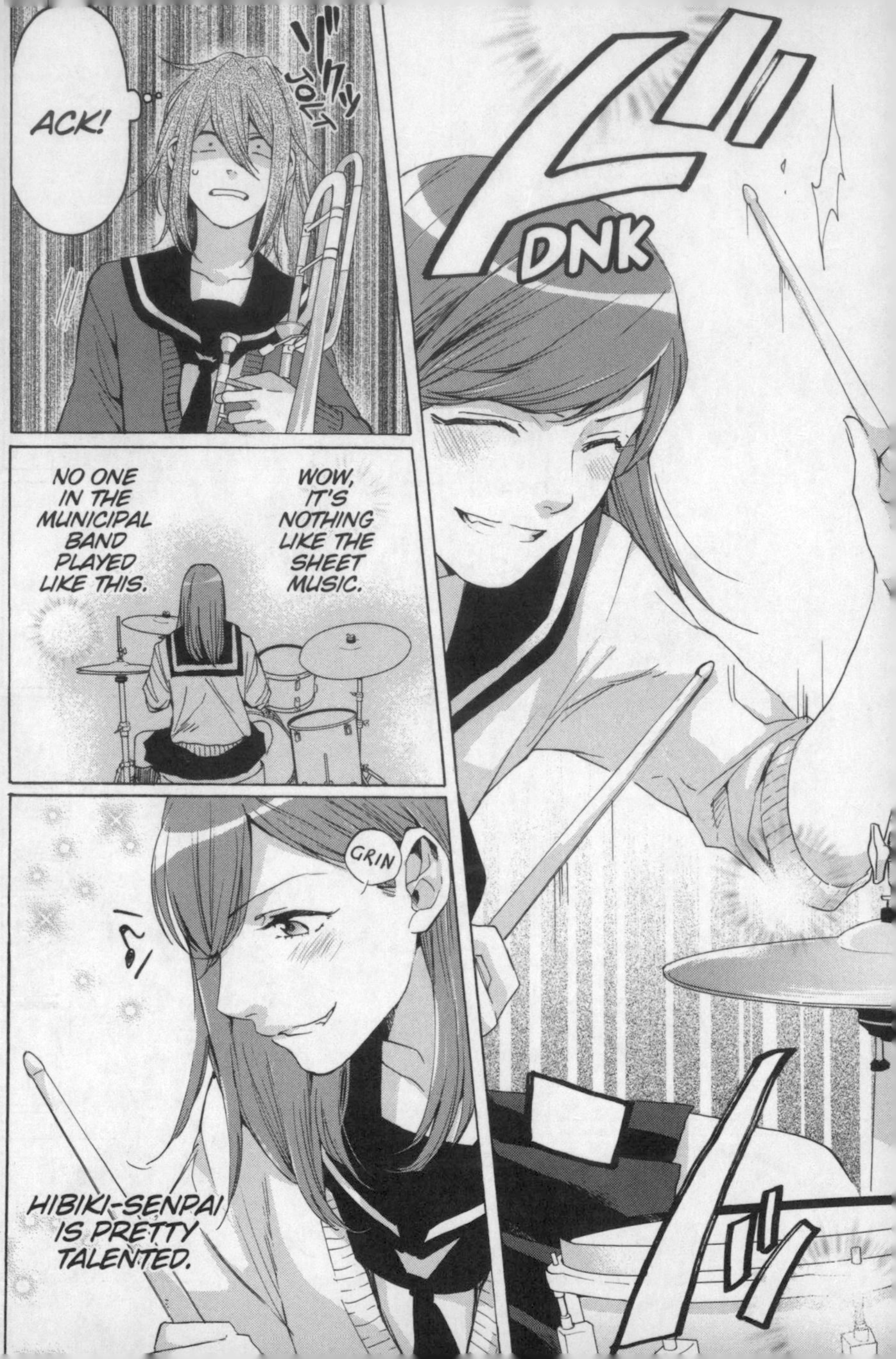
DNK
ACK!
JOLT
WOW, IT'S NOTHING LIKE THE SHEET MUSIC.
NO ONE IN THE MUNICIPAL BAND PLAYED LIKE THIS.
GRIN
HIBIKI-SENPAI IS PRETTY TALENTED.

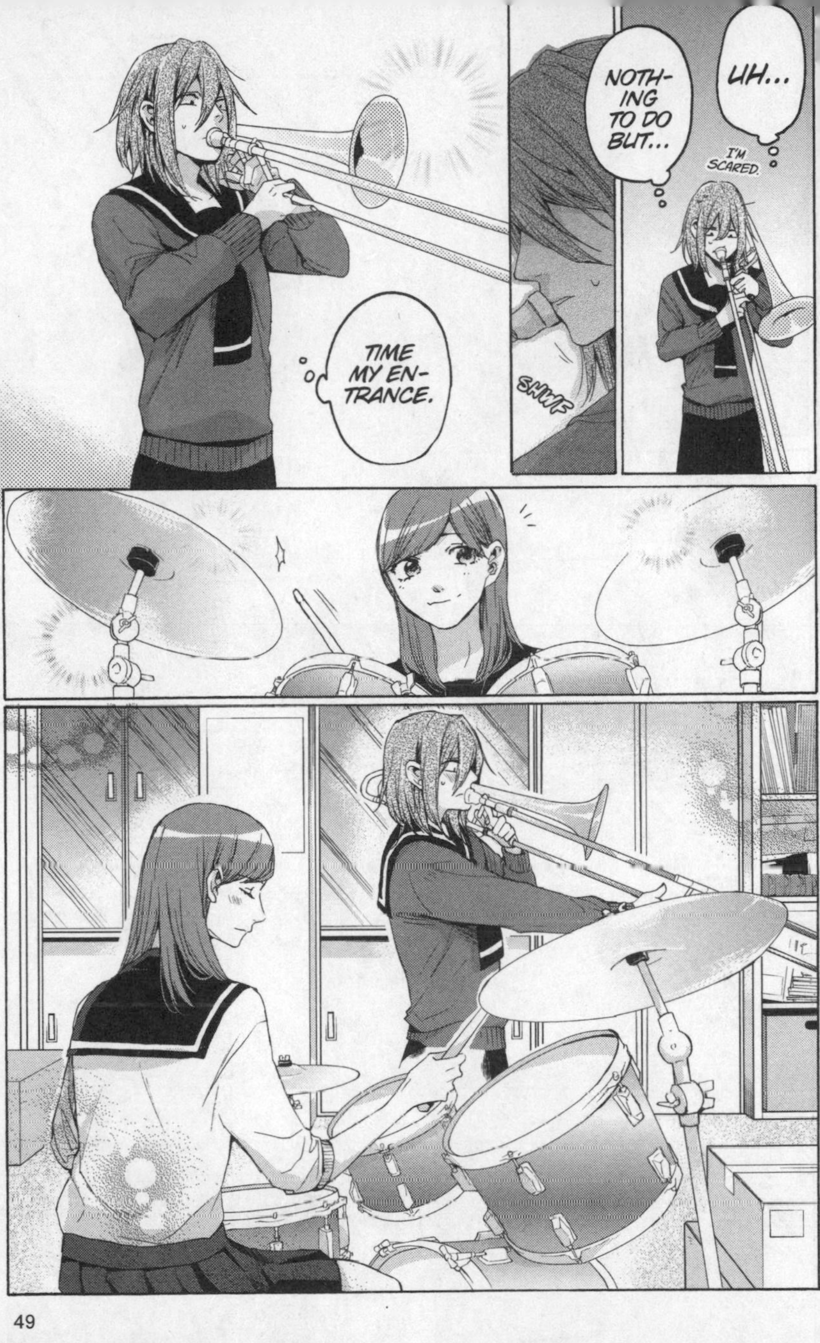
UH...
I'M SCARED.
NOTHING TO DO BUT...
SHWF
TIME MY EN-TRANCE.

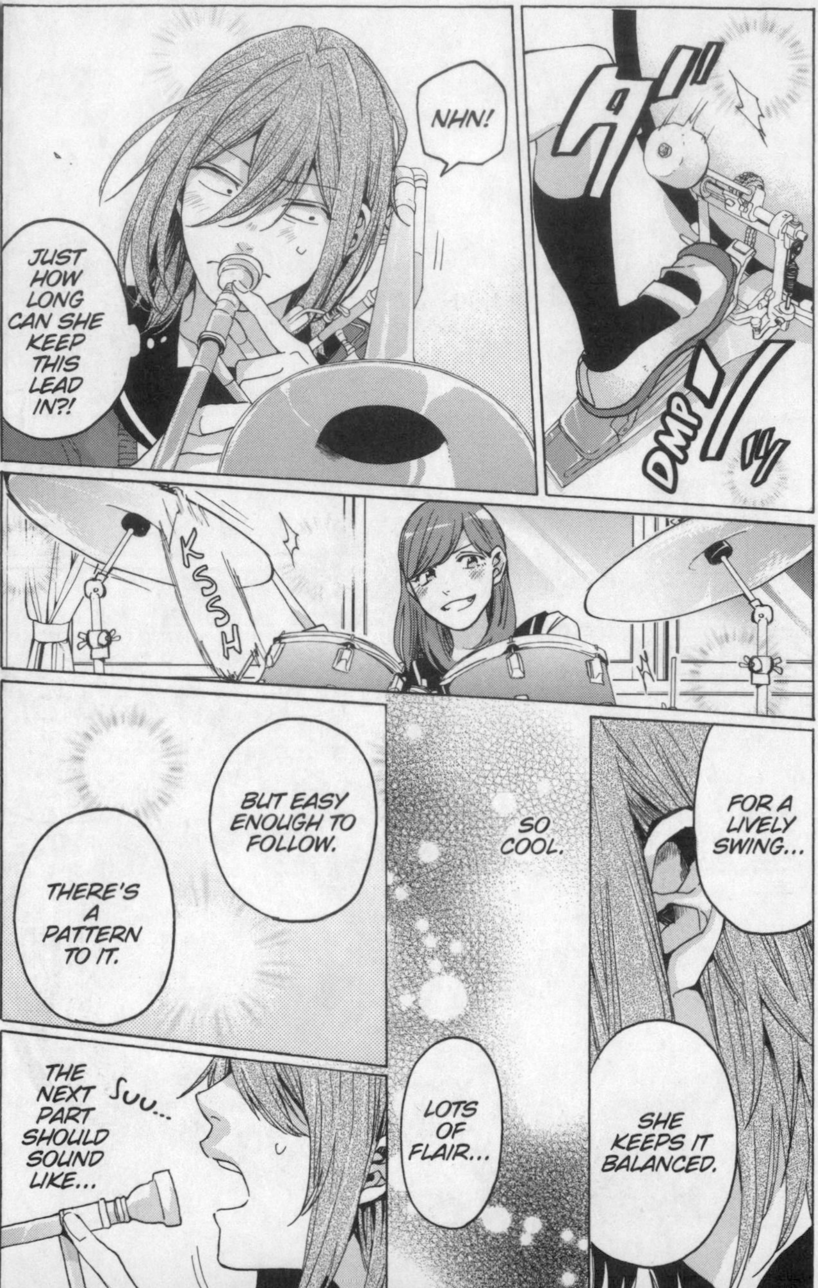
DMP
NHN!
JUST HOW LONG CAN SHE KEEP THIS LEAD IN?!
KSSSH
FOR A LIVELY SWING...
SHE KEEPS IT BALANCED.
SO COOL.
LOTS OF FLAIR...
BUT EASY ENOUGH TO FOLLOW.
THERE'S A PATTERN TO IT.
SUU...
THE NEXT PART SHOULD SOUND LIKE...

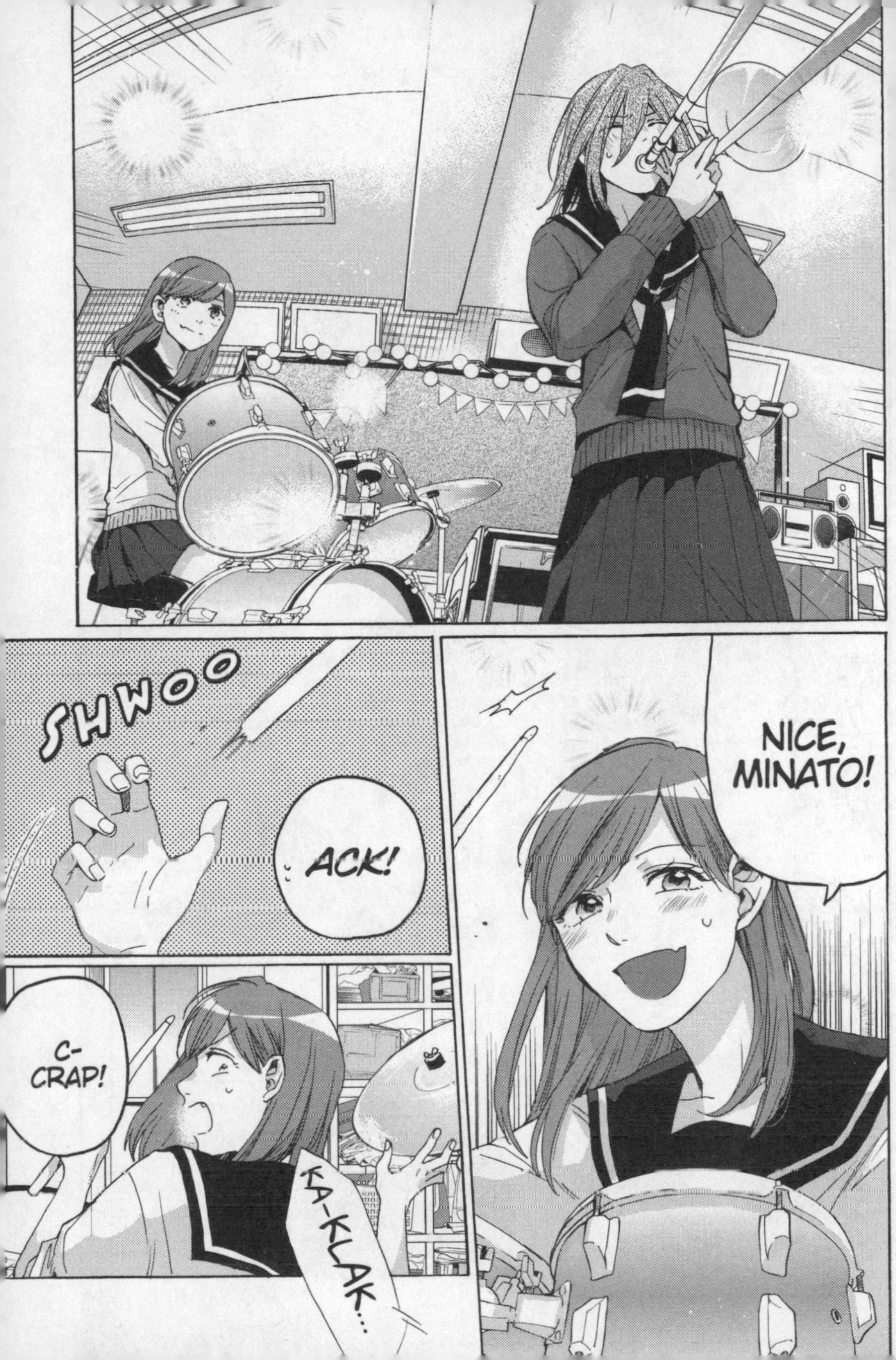
NICE, MINATO!
SHWOO
ACK!
C-CRAP!
KA-KLAK...

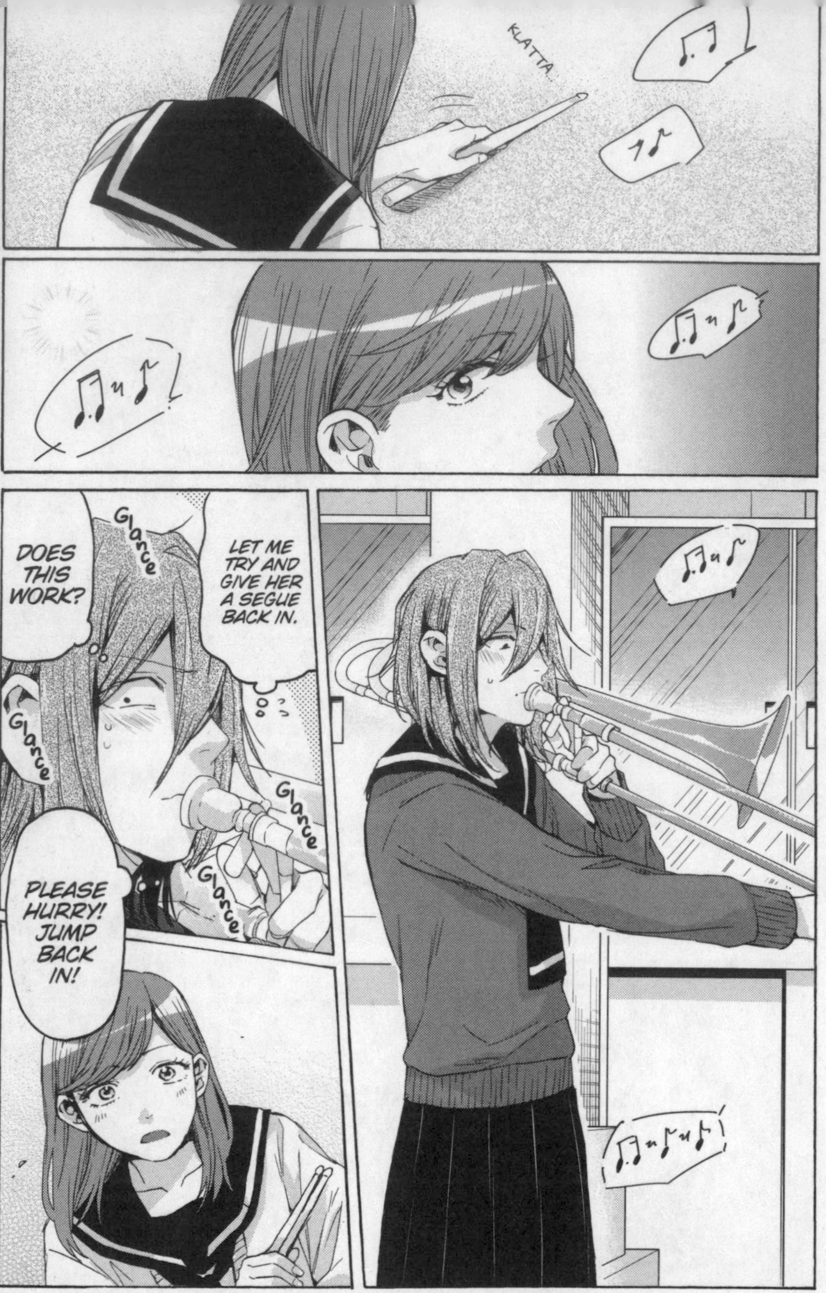
KLATTA...
LET ME TRY AND GIVE HER A SEGUE BACK IN.
Glance
DOES THIS WORK?
Glance
Glance
Glance
Glance
PLEASE HURRY! JUMP BACK IN!

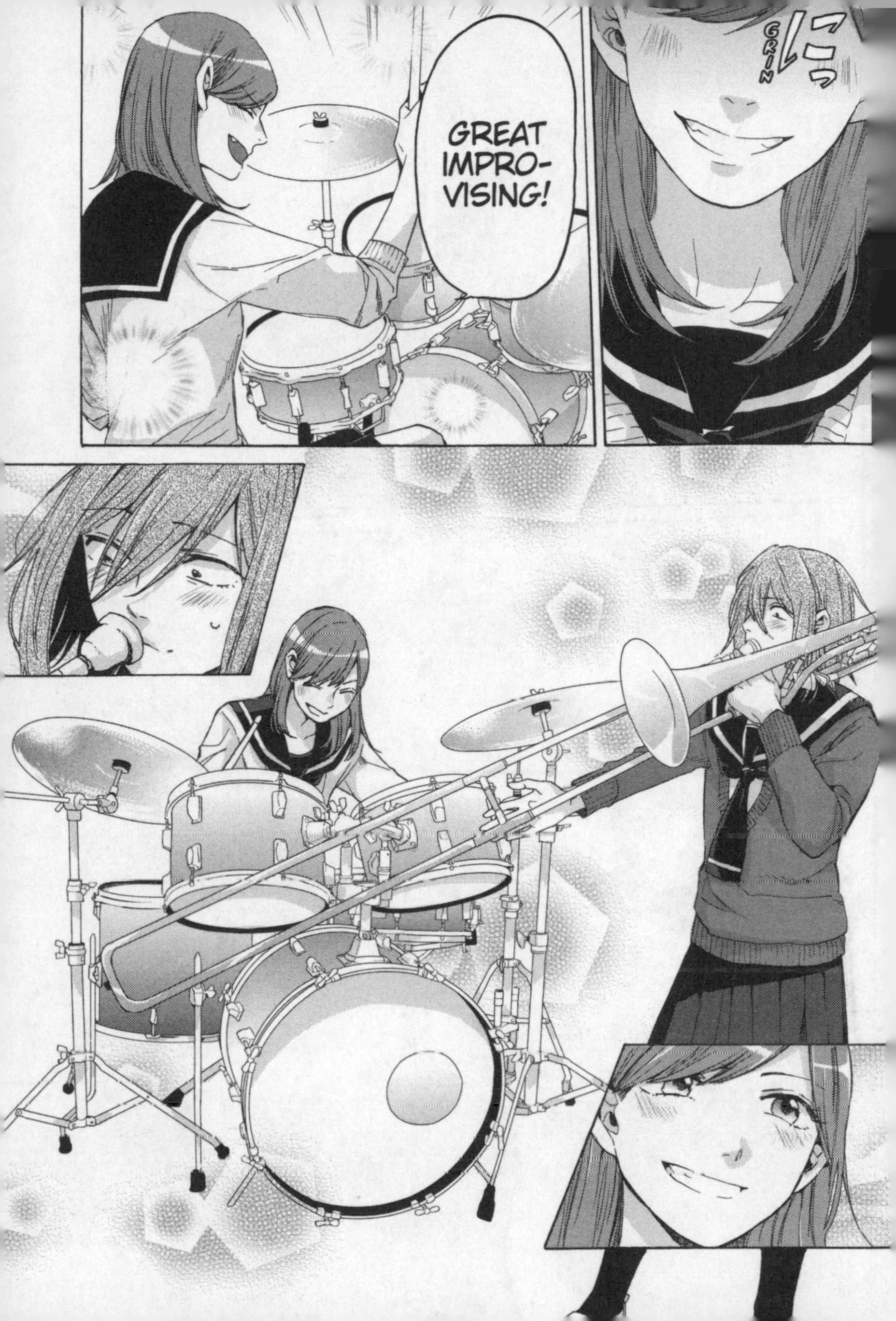

GRIN
GREAT IMPRO-VISING!

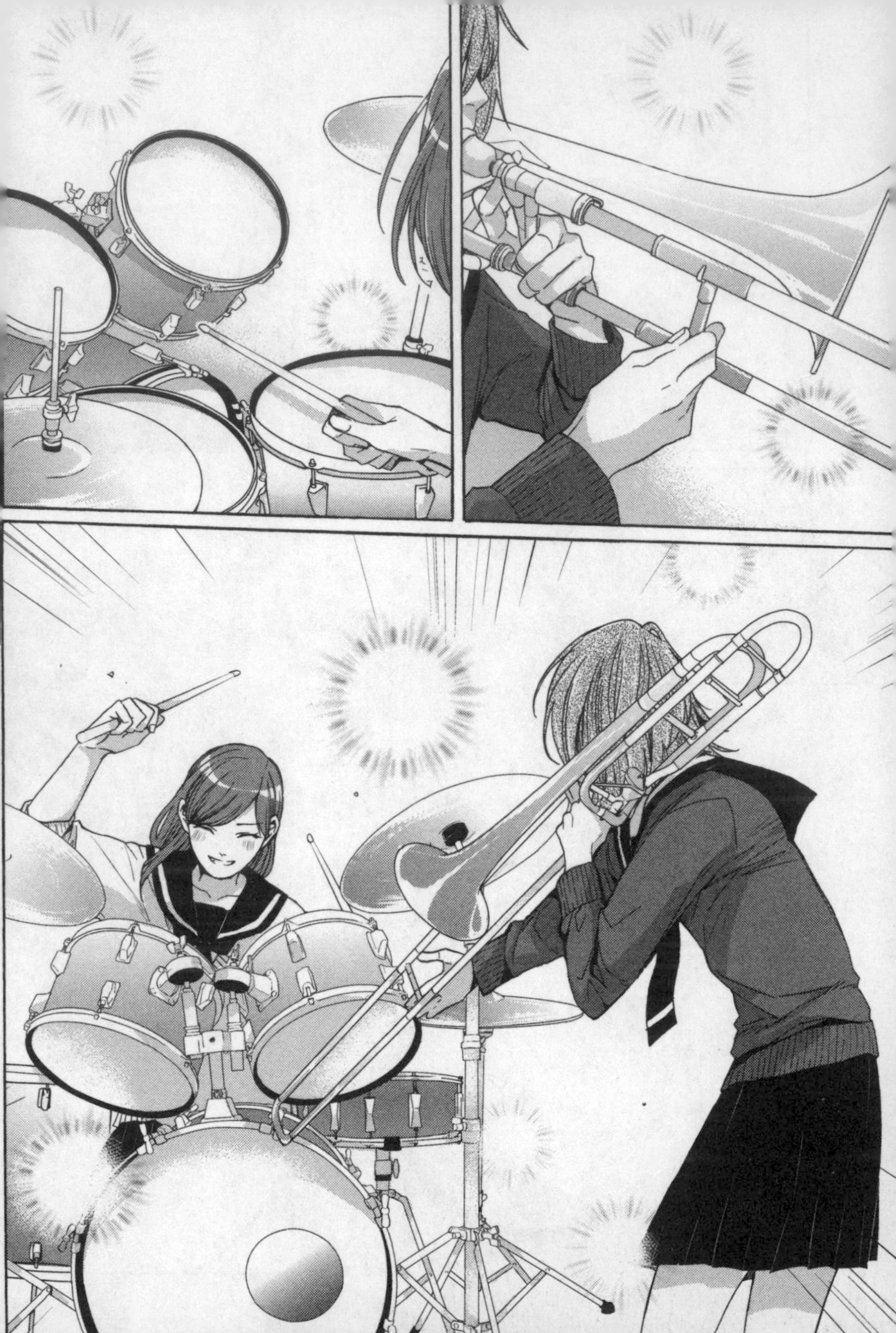

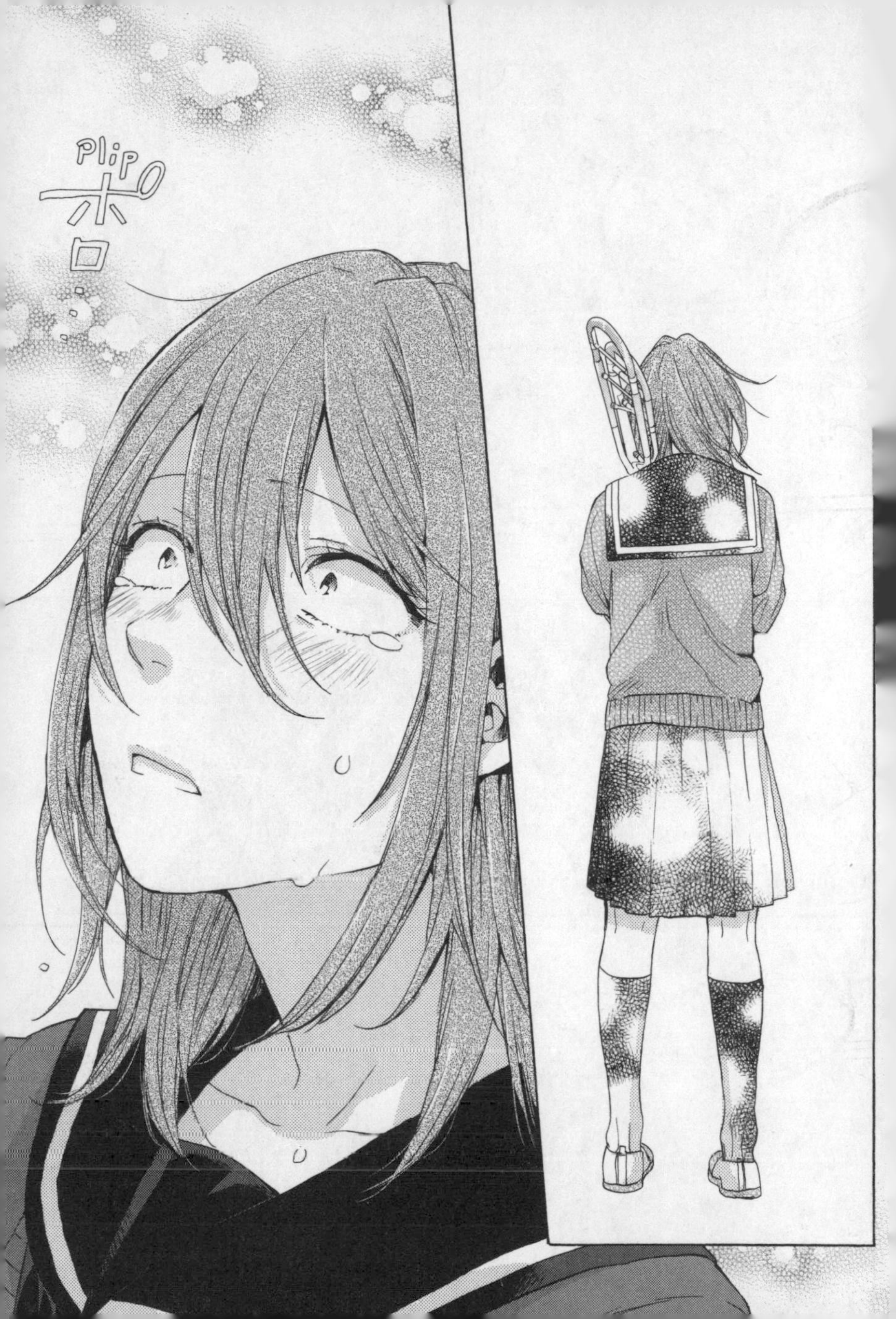
Plip
ホロ...

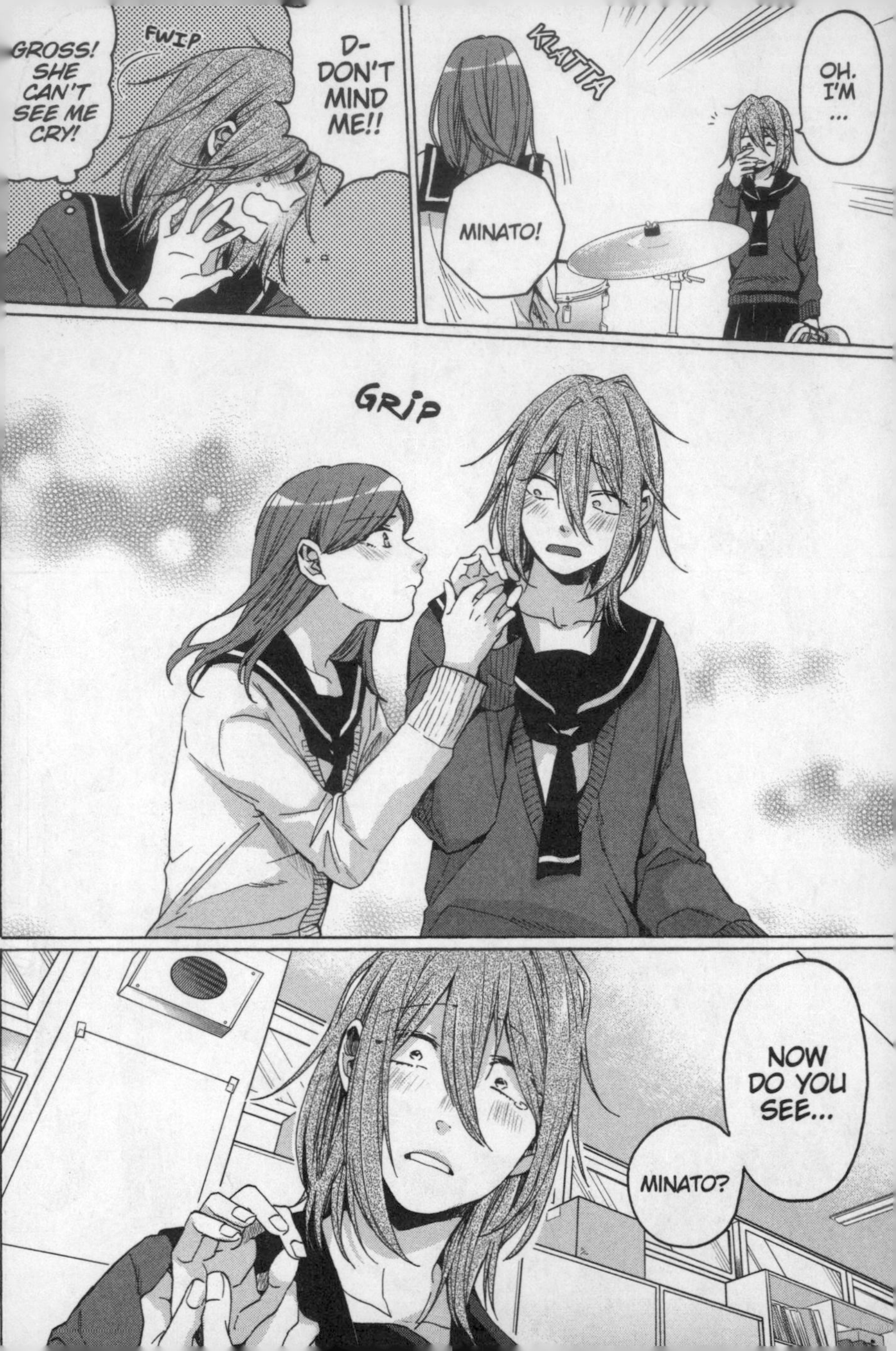
OH. I'M ...
KLATTA
MINATO!
D-DON'T MIND ME!!
FWIP
GROSS! SHE CAN'T SEE ME CRY!
GRIP
NOW DO YOU SEE...
MINATO?

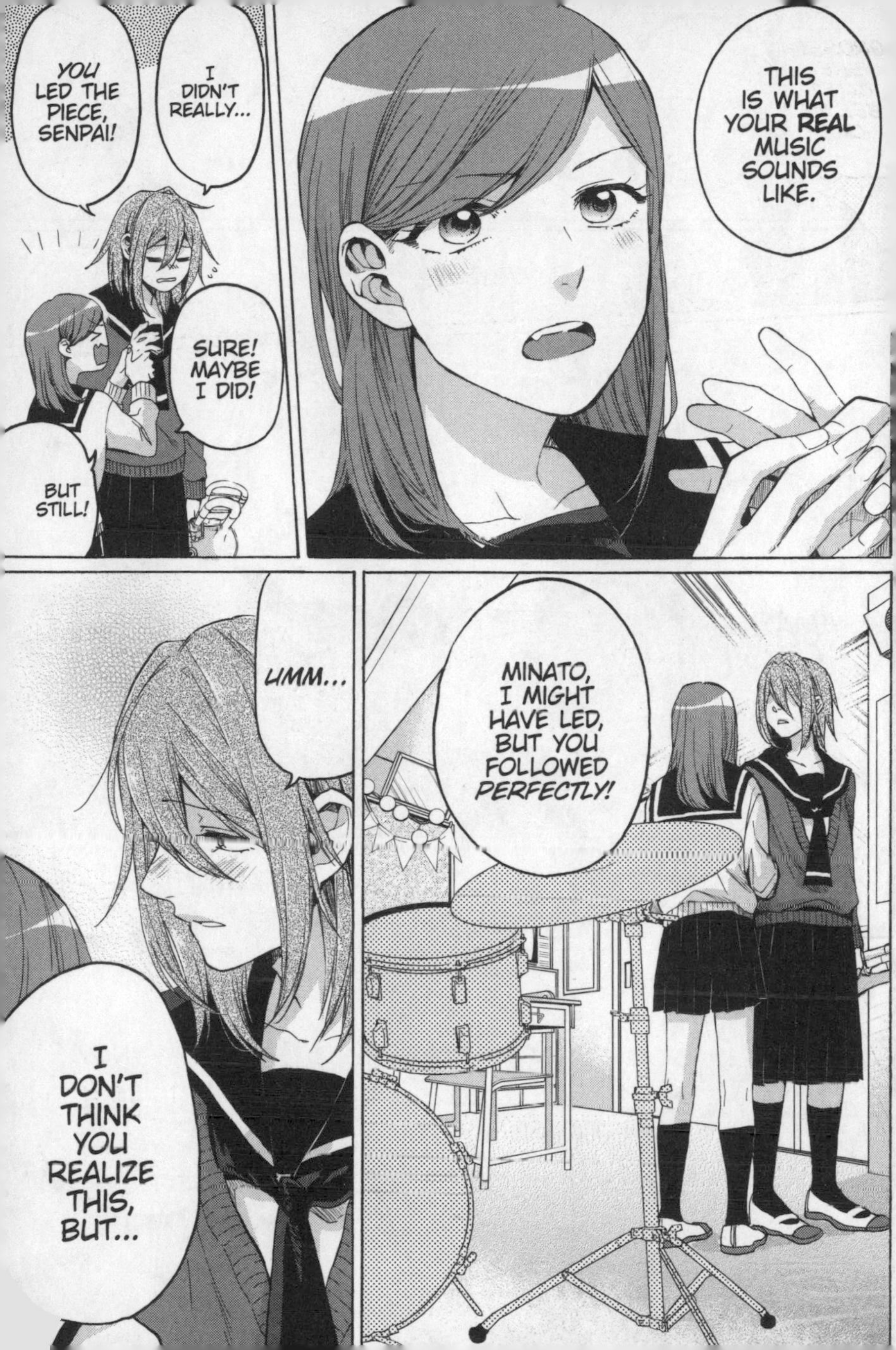
THIS IS WHAT YOUR REAL MUSIC SOUNDS LIKE.
I DIDN'T REALLY...
YOU LED THE PIECE, SENPAI!
SURE! MAYBE I DID!
BUT STILL!
MINATO, I MIGHT HAVE LED, BUT YOU FOLLOWED PERFECTLY!
UMM...
I DON'T THINK YOU REALIZE THIS, BUT...

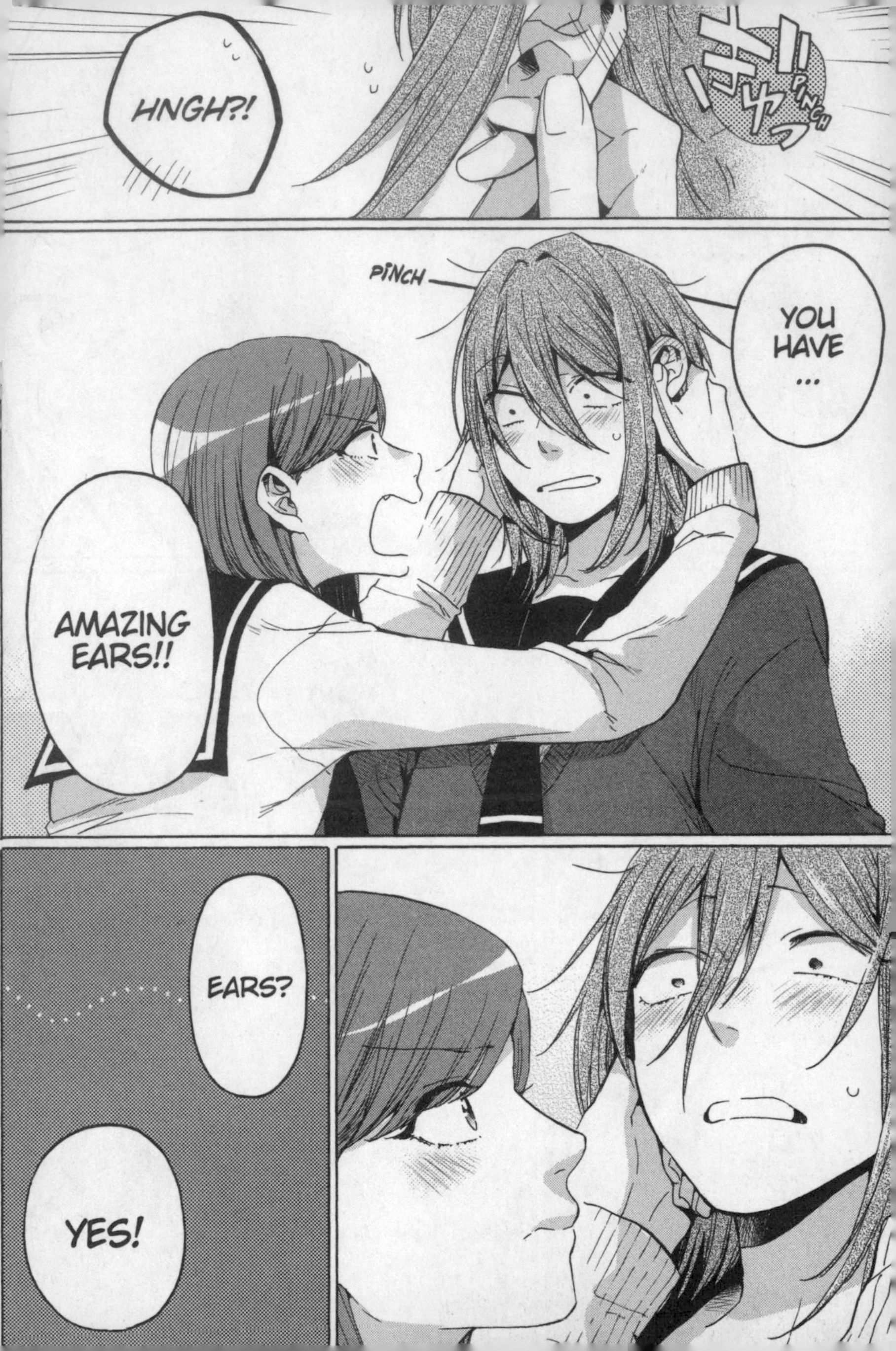

ギュッ
PINCH
HNGH?!
PINCH
YOU HAVE ...
AMAZING EARS!!
EARS?
YES!

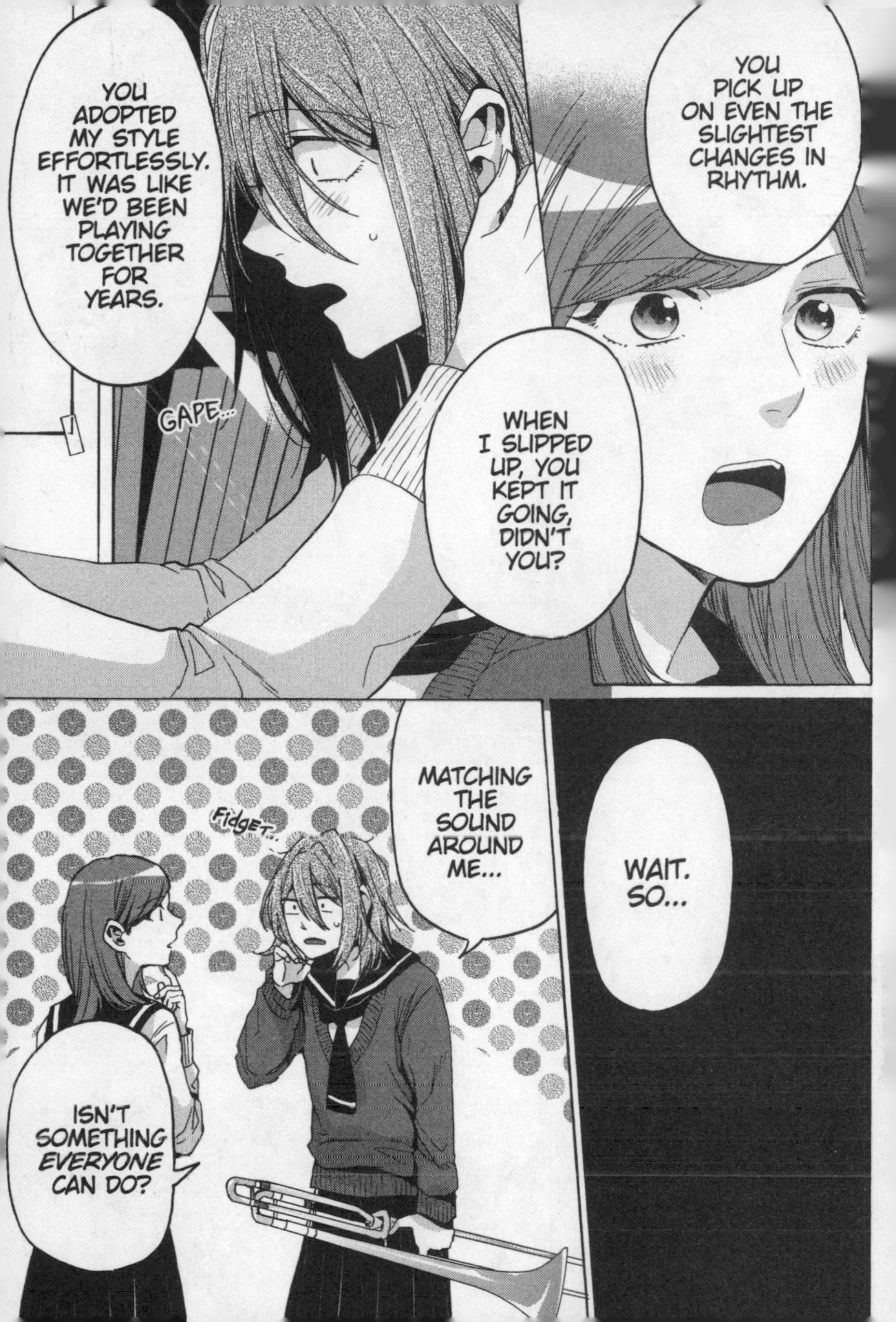
YOU PICK UP ON EVEN THE SLIGHTEST CHANGES IN RHYTHM.
WHEN I SLIPPED UP, YOU KEPT IT GOING, DIDN'T YOU?
YOU ADOPTED MY STYLE EFFORTLESSLY. IT WAS LIKE WE'D BEEN PLAYING TOGETHER FOR YEARS.
GAPE...
WAIT. SO...
MATCHING THE SOUND AROUND ME...
Fidget...
ISN'T SOMETHING *EVERYONE* CAN DO?

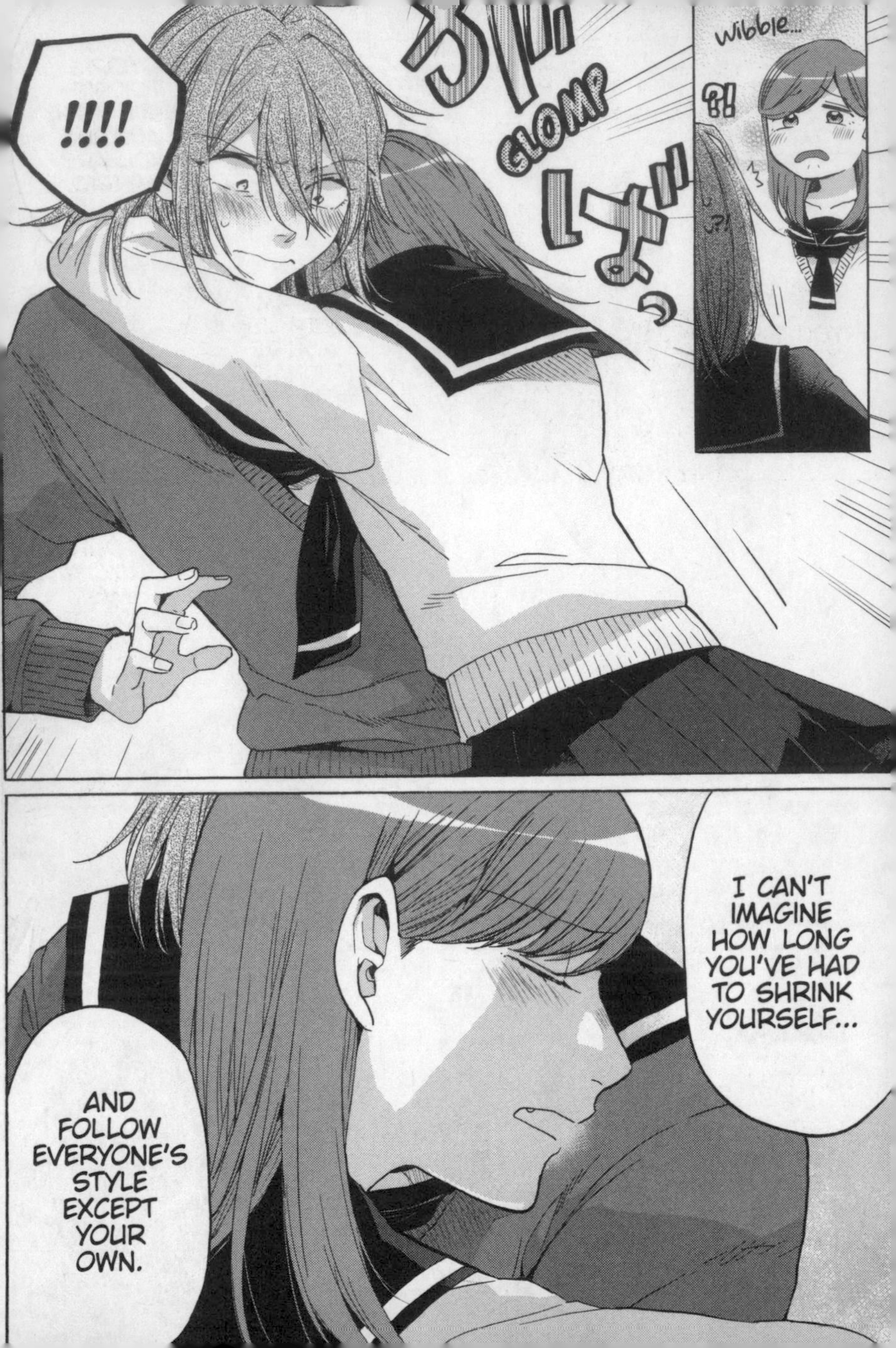
wibble...
?!
!!!!
GLOMP
I CAN'T IMAGINE HOW LONG YOU'VE HAD TO SHRINK YOURSELF...
AND FOLLOW EVERYONE'S STYLE EXCEPT YOUR OWN.

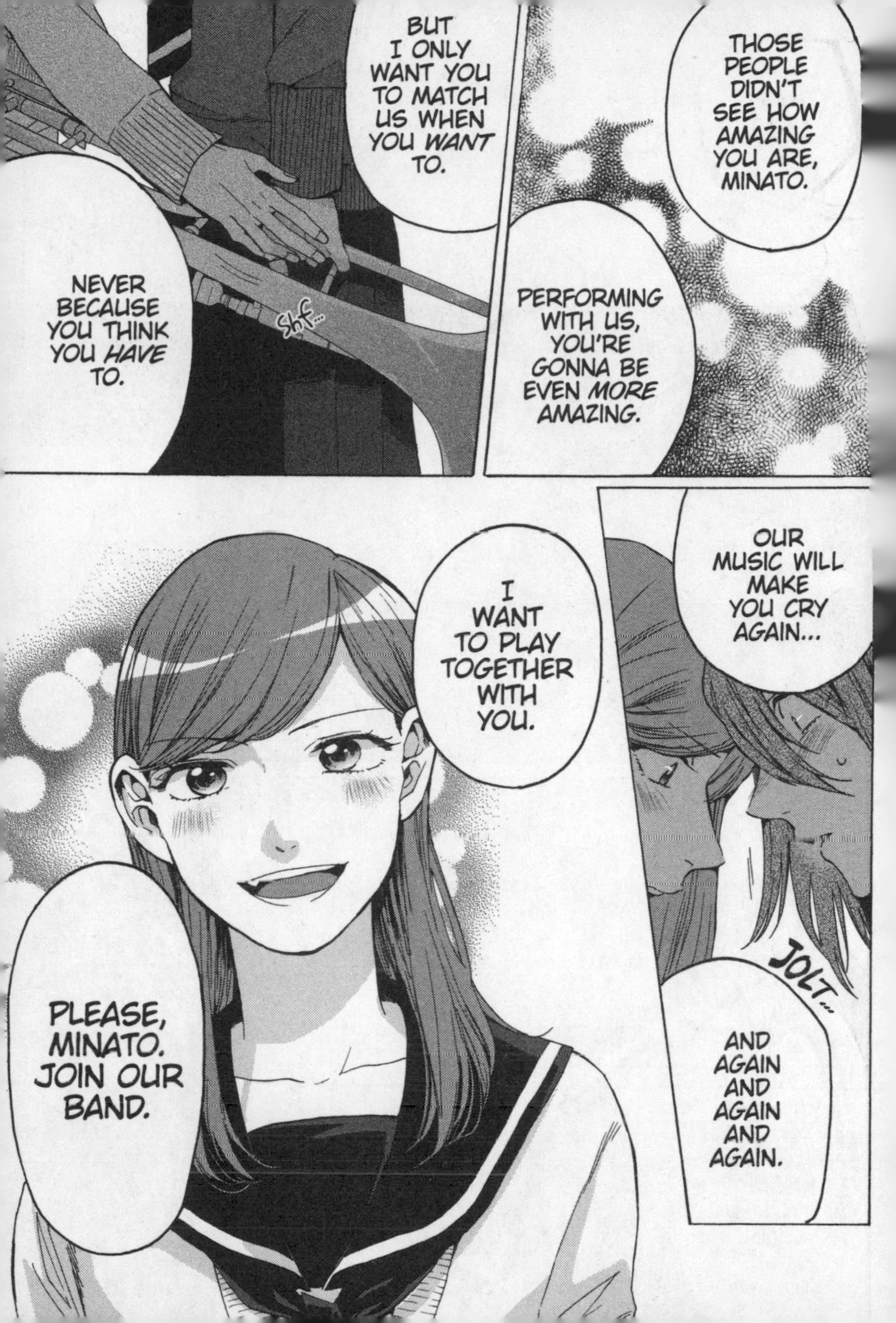
THOSE PEOPLE DIDN'T SEE HOW AMAZING YOU ARE, MINATO.
PERFORMING WITH US, YOU'RE GONNA BE EVEN *MORE* AMAZING.
BUT I ONLY WANT YOU TO MATCH US WHEN YOU *WANT* TO.
Shf...
NEVER BECAUSE YOU THINK YOU *HAVE* TO.
OUR MUSIC WILL MAKE YOU CRY AGAIN...
JOLT...
AND AGAIN AND AGAIN AND AGAIN.
I WANT TO PLAY TOGETHER WITH YOU.
PLEASE, MINATO. JOIN OUR BAND.

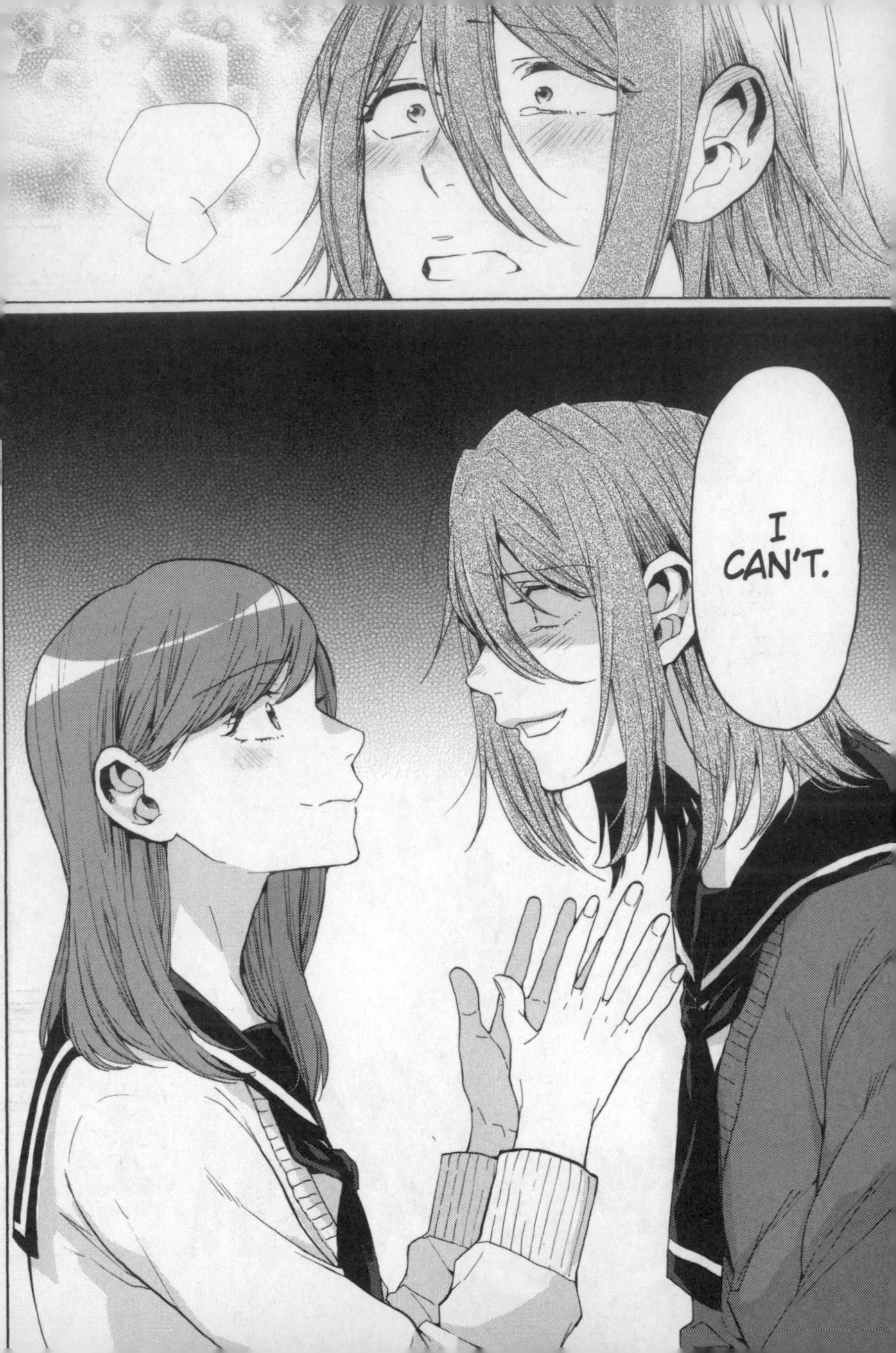
I CAN'T.

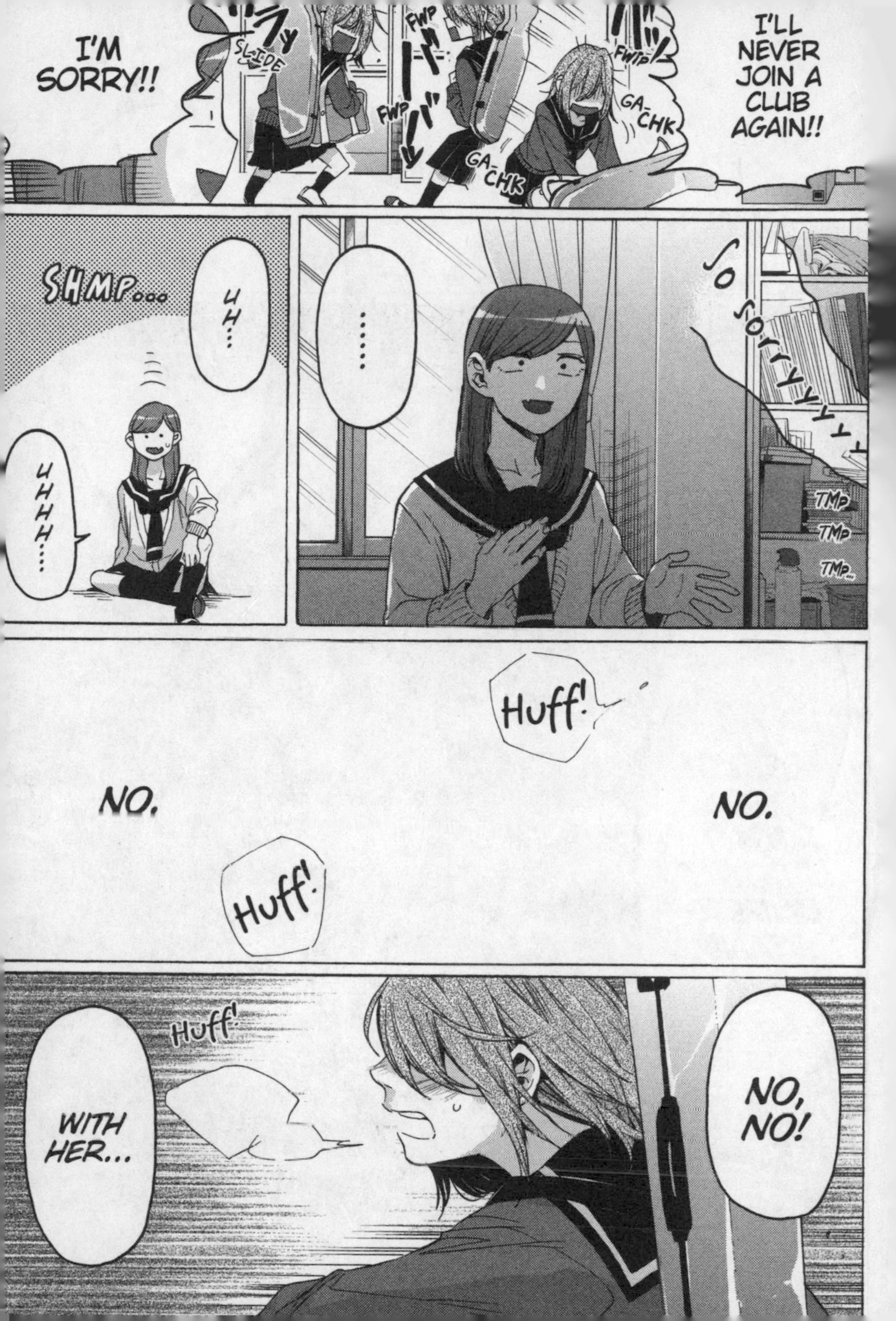
I'LL NEVER JOIN A CLUB AGAIN!!
FWIP
GA-CHK
GA-CHK
FWP
FWP
SLIDE
I'M SORRY!!
So sorryyyyy
TMP
TMP
TMP...
......
UH...
SHMP...
UHHH....
Huff!
NO.
NO.
Huff!
NO, NO!
Huff!
WITH HER...

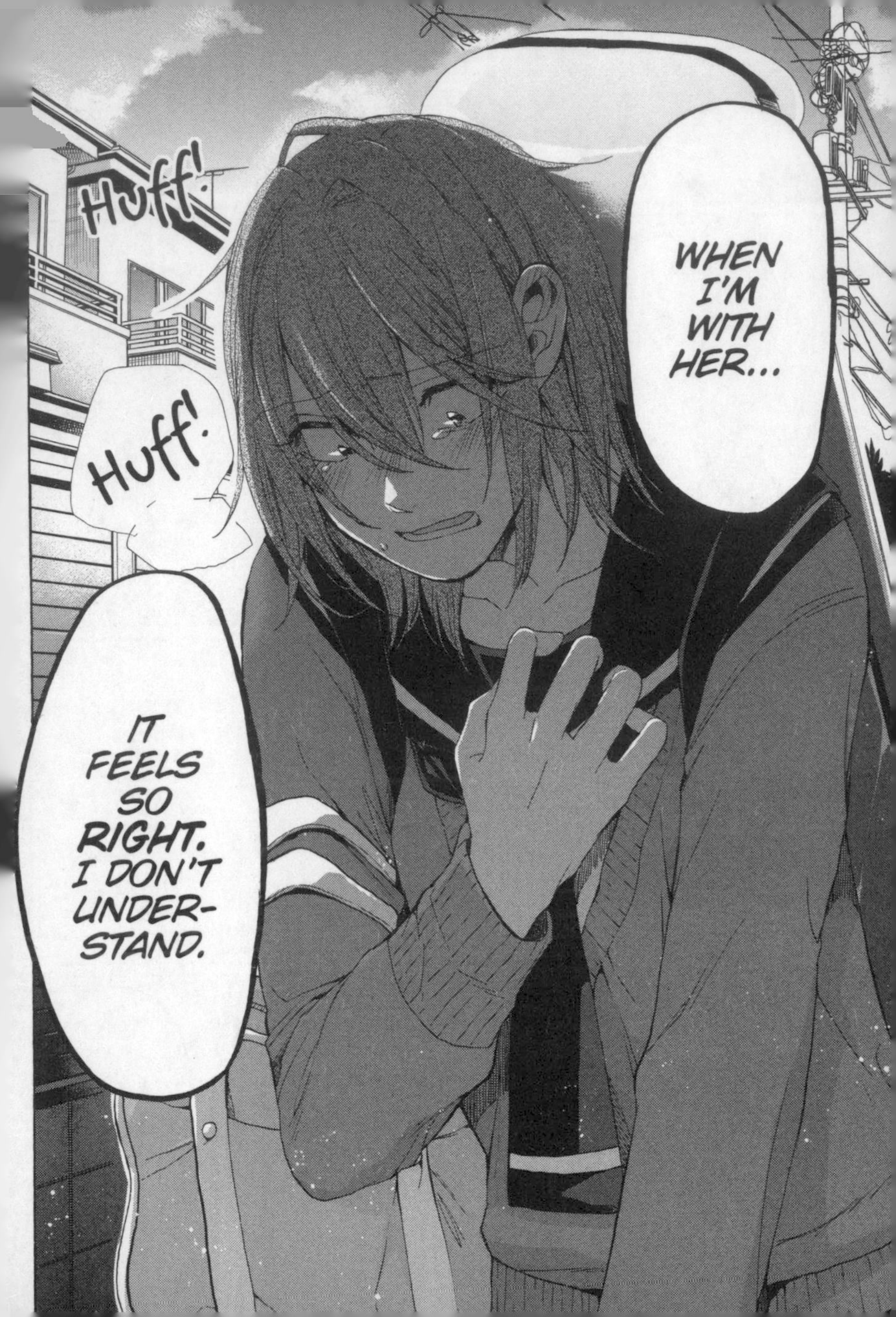
WHEN I'M WITH HER...
HUFF!
HUFF!
IT FEELS SO RIGHT. I DON'T UNDER-STAND.

Hello, Melancholic!

WE SOUNDED GREAT. I WAS SURE IT WAS GONNA WORK OUT.
A TOUGH ONE TO CRACK...
Stunned

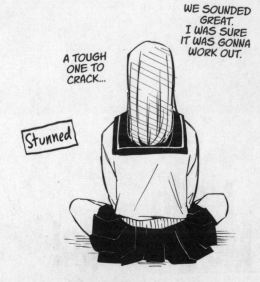

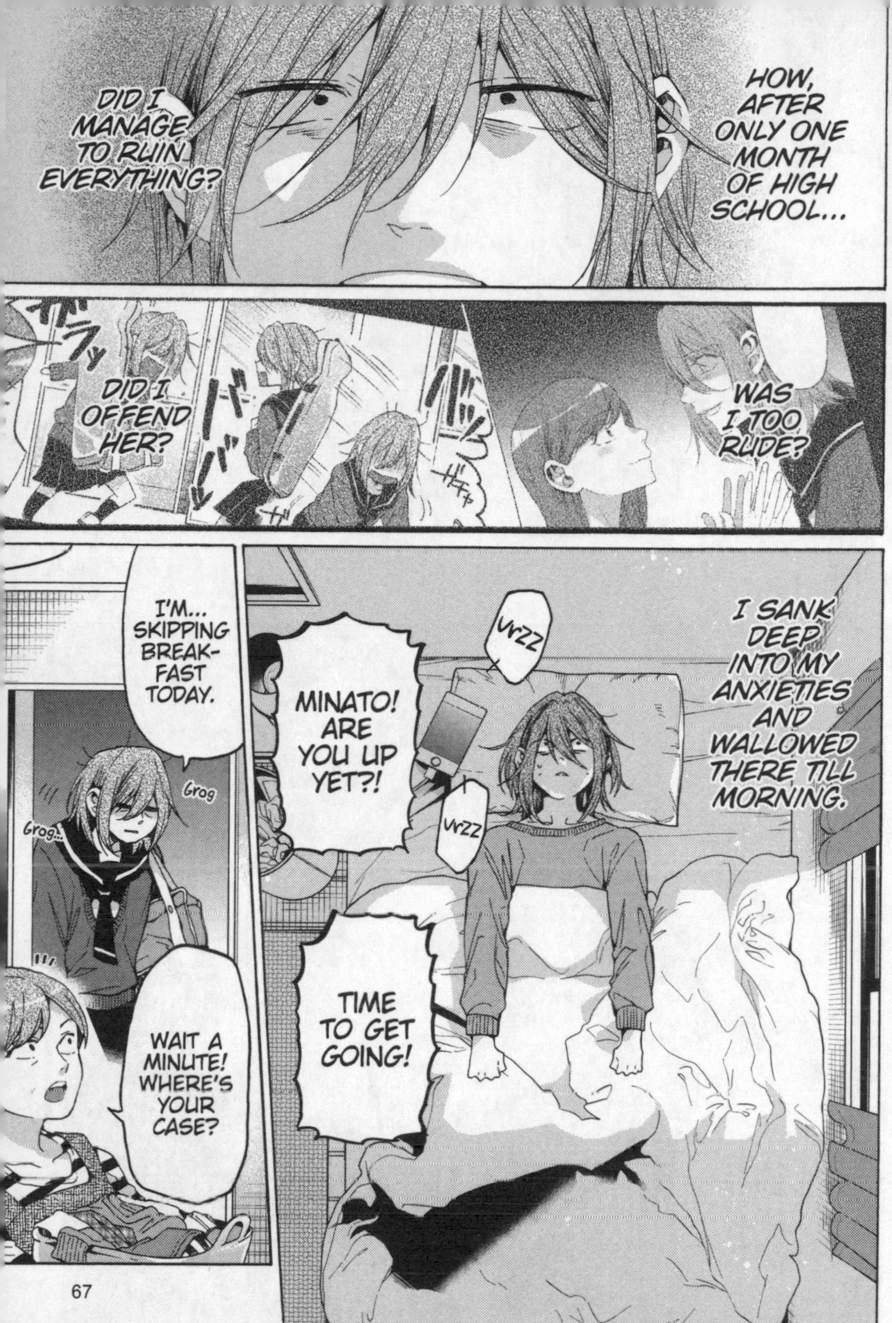
HOW, AFTER ONLY ONE MONTH OF HIGH SCHOOL...
DID I MANAGE TO RUIN EVERYTHING?
WAS I TOO RUDE?
DID I OFFEND HER?
I SANK DEEP INTO MY ANXIETIES AND WALLOWED THERE TILL MORNING.
Vrzz
Vrzz
MINATO! ARE YOU UP YET?!
TIME TO GET GOING!
I'M... SKIPPING BREAK-FAST TODAY.
Grog
Grog...
WAIT A MINUTE! WHERE'S YOUR CASE?

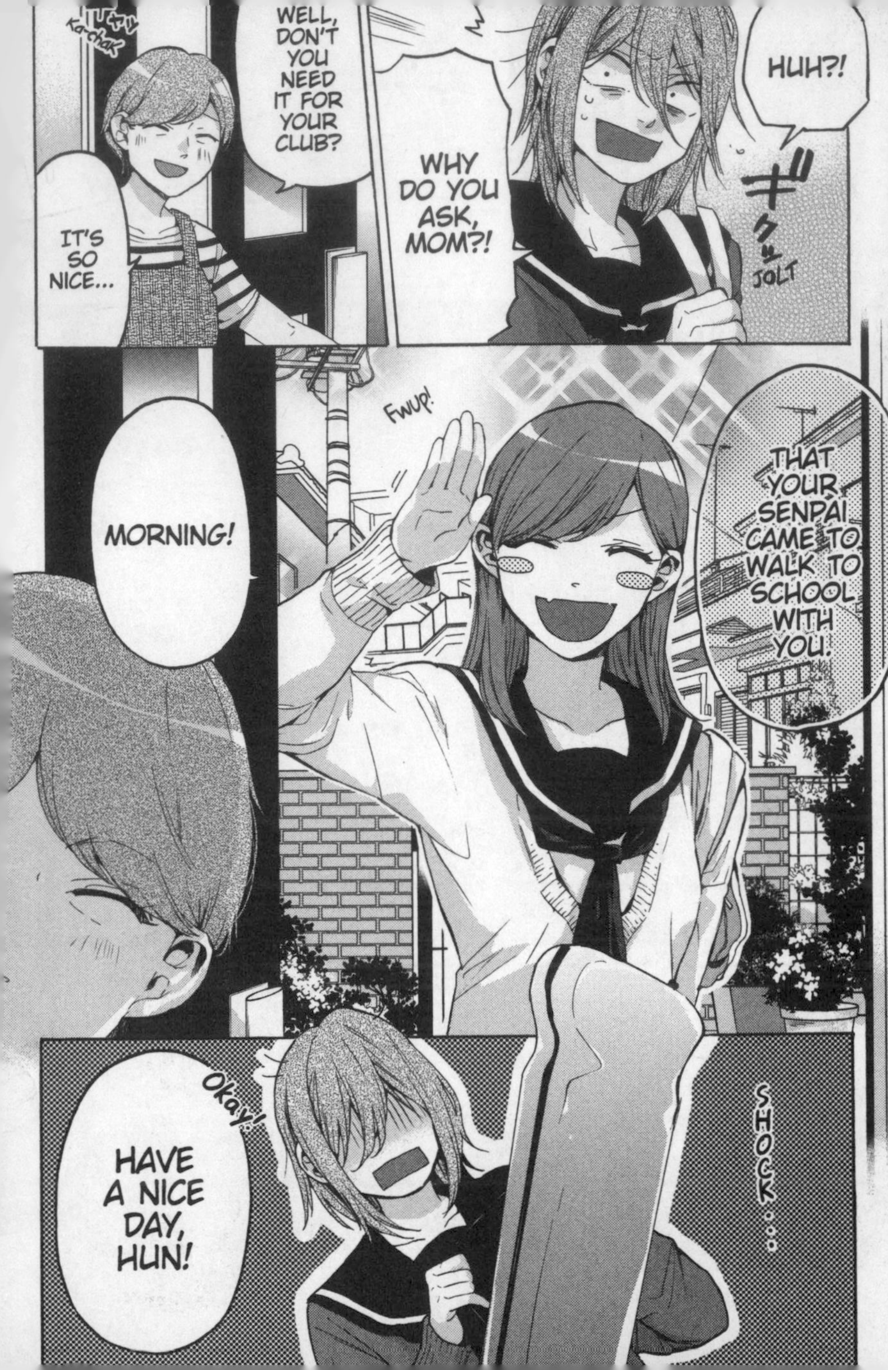
HUH?!
ギクッ
JOLT
WHY DO YOU ASK, MOM?!
WELL, DON'T YOU NEED IT FOR YOUR CLUB?
Ka-chak
IT'S SO NICE...
THAT YOUR SENPAI CAME TO WALK TO SCHOOL WITH YOU.
FWUP!
MORNING!
SHOCK...
Okay!
HAVE A NICE DAY, HUN!

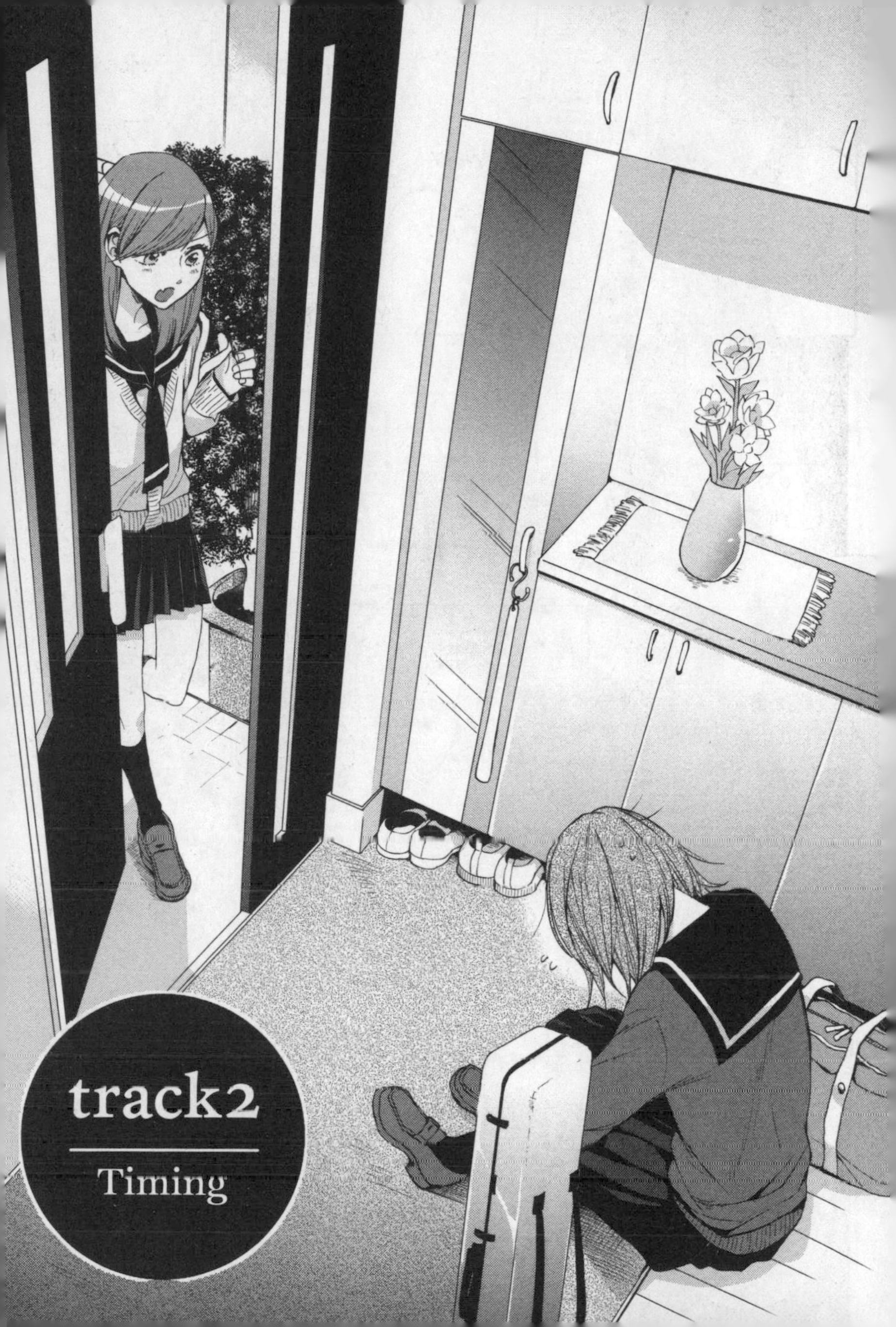
track2
Timing

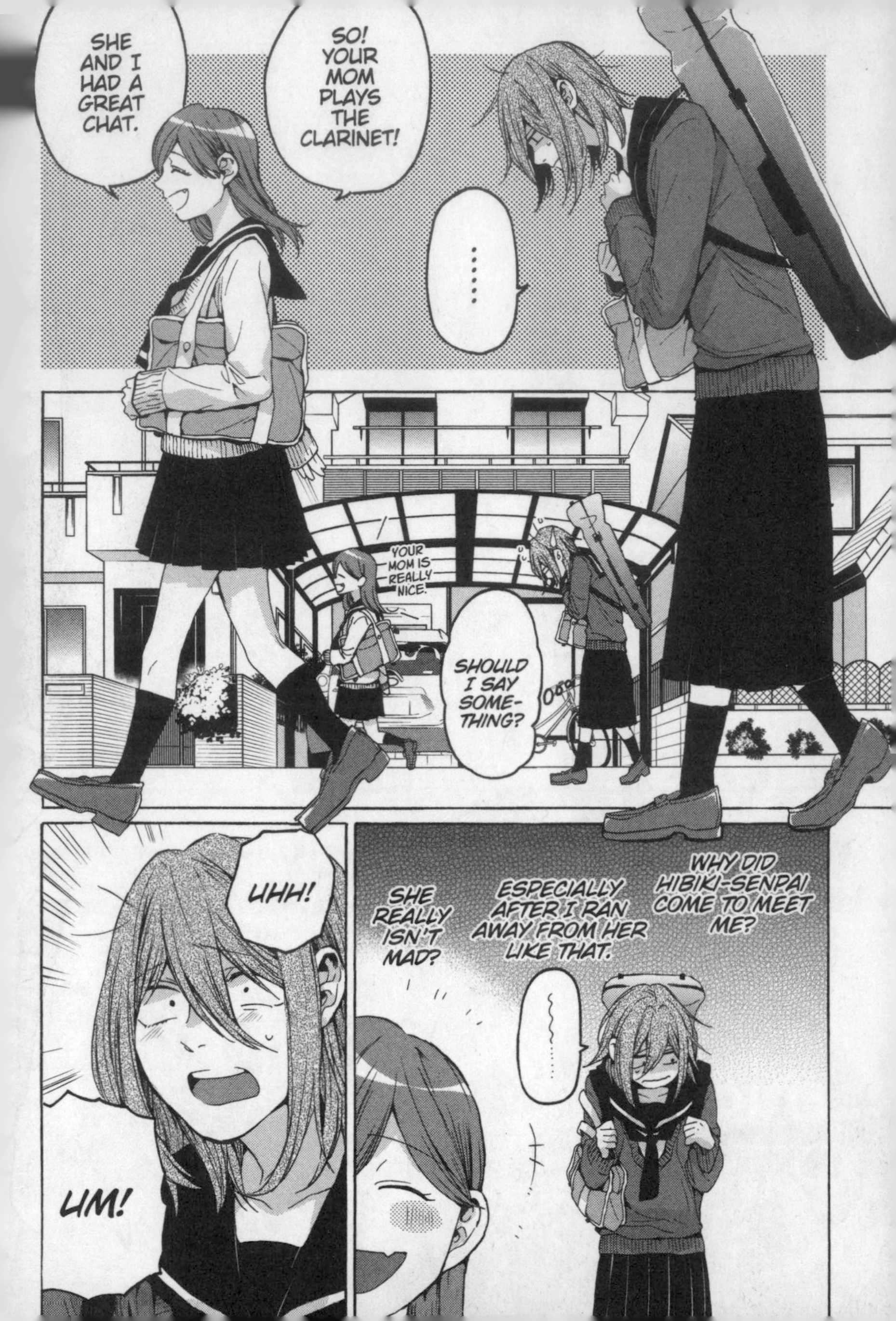
SO! YOUR MOM PLAYS THE CLARINET!
SHE AND I HAD A GREAT CHAT.
......
SHOULD I SAY SOME-THING?
YOUR MOM IS REALLY NICE.
WHY DID HIBIKI-SENPAI COME TO MEET ME?
ESPECIALLY AFTER I RAN AWAY FROM HER LIKE THAT.
SHE REALLY ISN'T MAD?
~......
UHH!
UM!

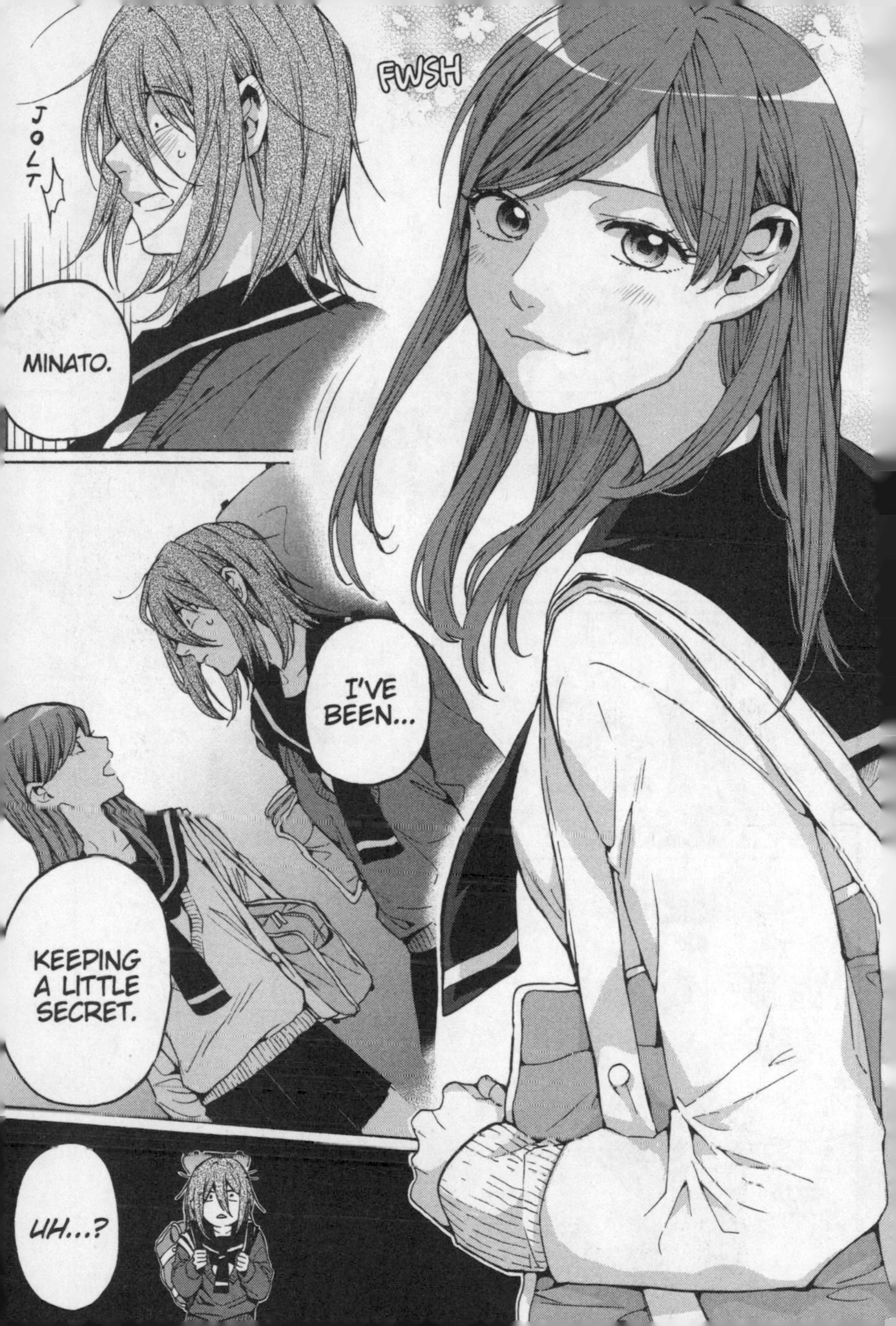
FWSH
JOLT
MINATO.
I'VE BEEN...
KEEPING A LITTLE SECRET.
UH...?

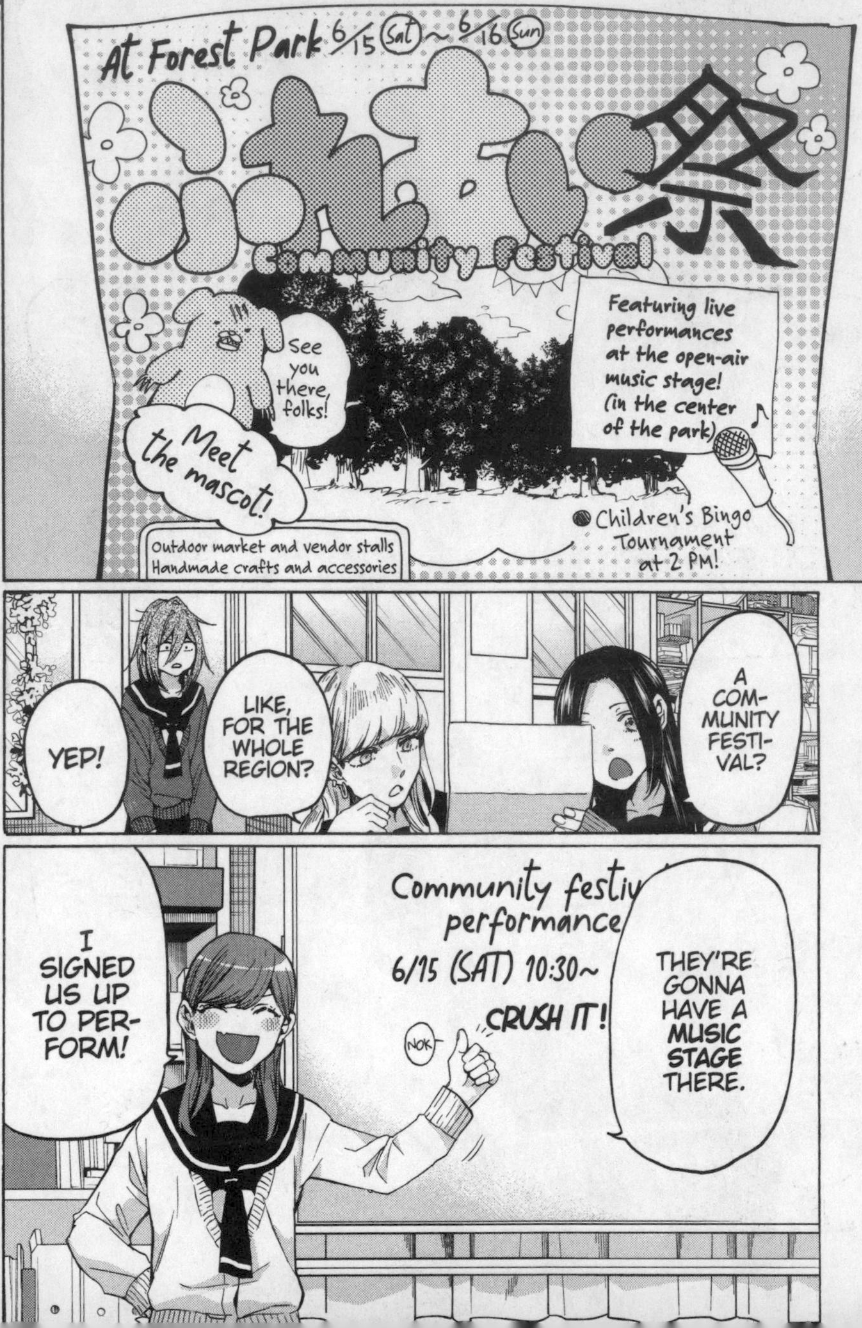
At Forest Park 6/15 (Sat) ~ 6/16 (Sun)
祭
Community Festival
See you there, folks!
Meet the mascot!
Featuring live performances at the open-air music stage! (in the center of the park)
Children's Bingo Tournament at 2 PM!
Outdoor market and vendor stalls
Handmade crafts and accessories
A COMMUNITY FESTIVAL?
LIKE, FOR THE WHOLE REGION?
YEP!
THEY'RE GONNA HAVE A MUSIC STAGE THERE.
Community festiv
performance
6/15 (SAT) 10:30~
CRUSH IT!
NOK
I SIGNED US UP TO PERFORM!

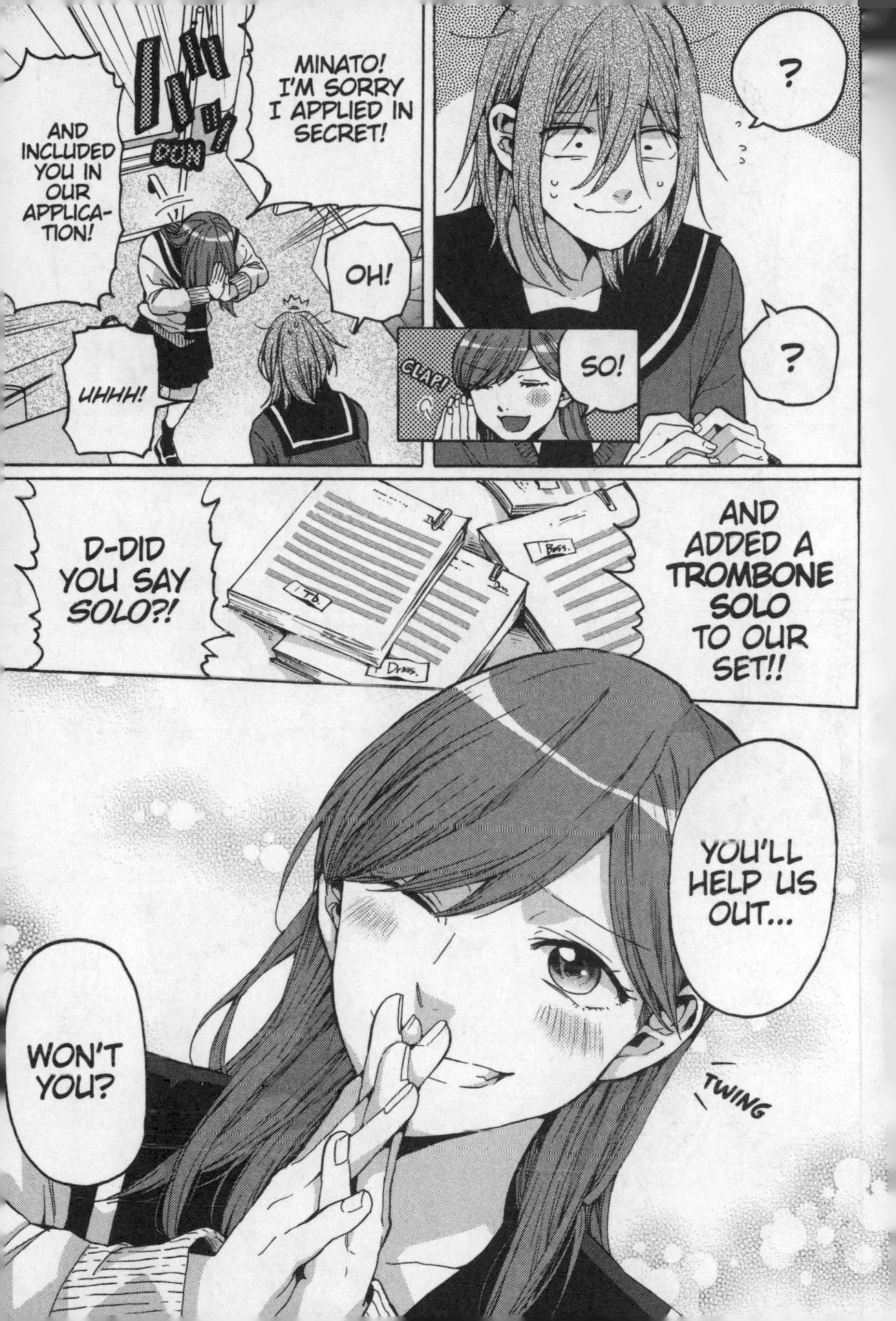
?
CLAP!
SO!
?
MINATO! I'M SORRY I APPLIED IN SECRET!
AND INCLUDED YOU IN OUR APPLICA-TION!
DON
OH!
UHHH!
AND ADDED A TROMBONE SOLO TO OUR SET!!
D-DID YOU SAY SOLO?!
YOU'LL HELP US OUT...
TWING
WON'T YOU?

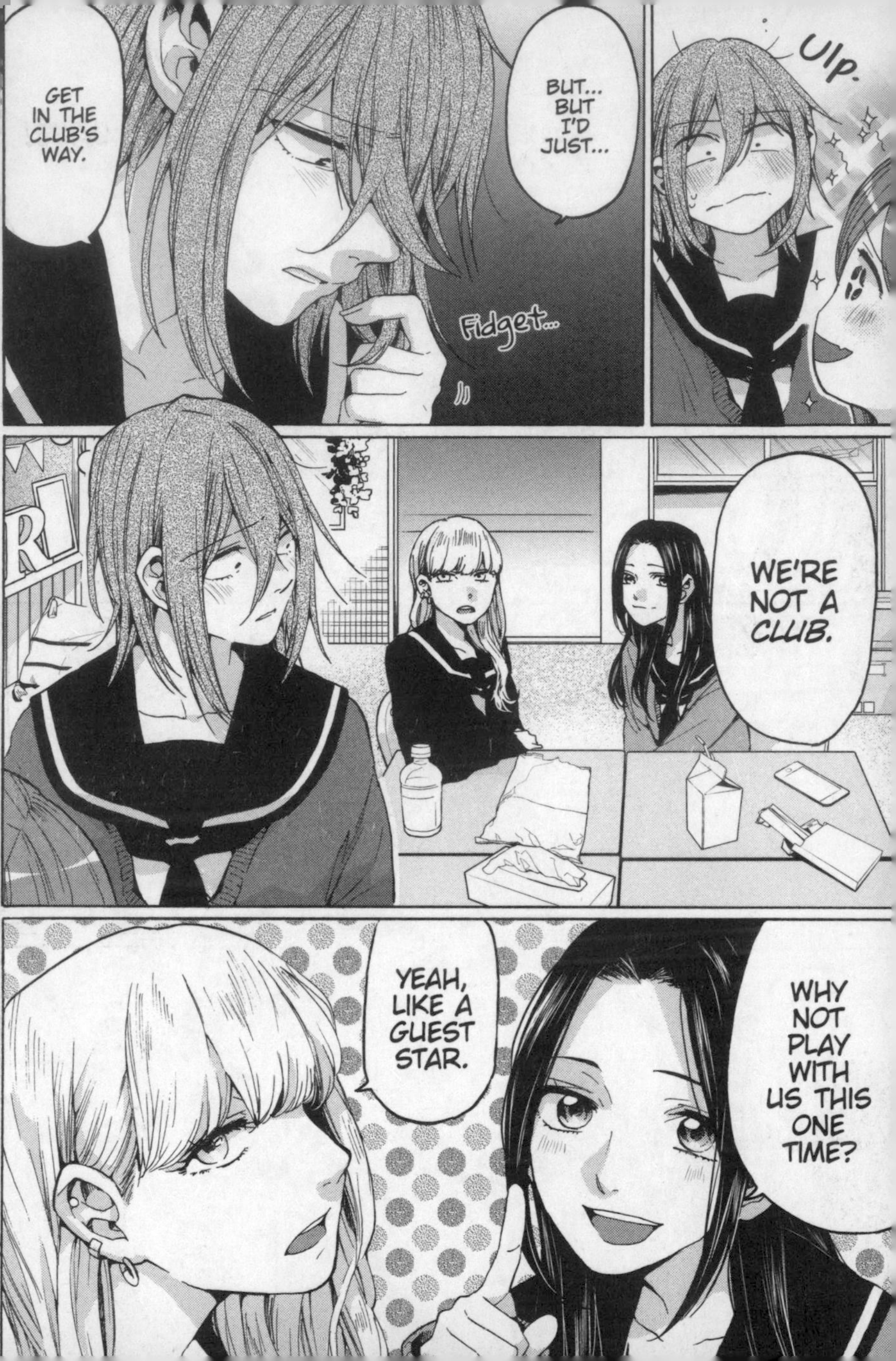
Ulp.
BUT... BUT I'D JUST...
Fidget...
GET IN THE CLUB'S WAY.
WE'RE NOT A CLUB.
WHY NOT PLAY WITH US THIS ONE TIME?
YEAH, LIKE A GUEST STAR.

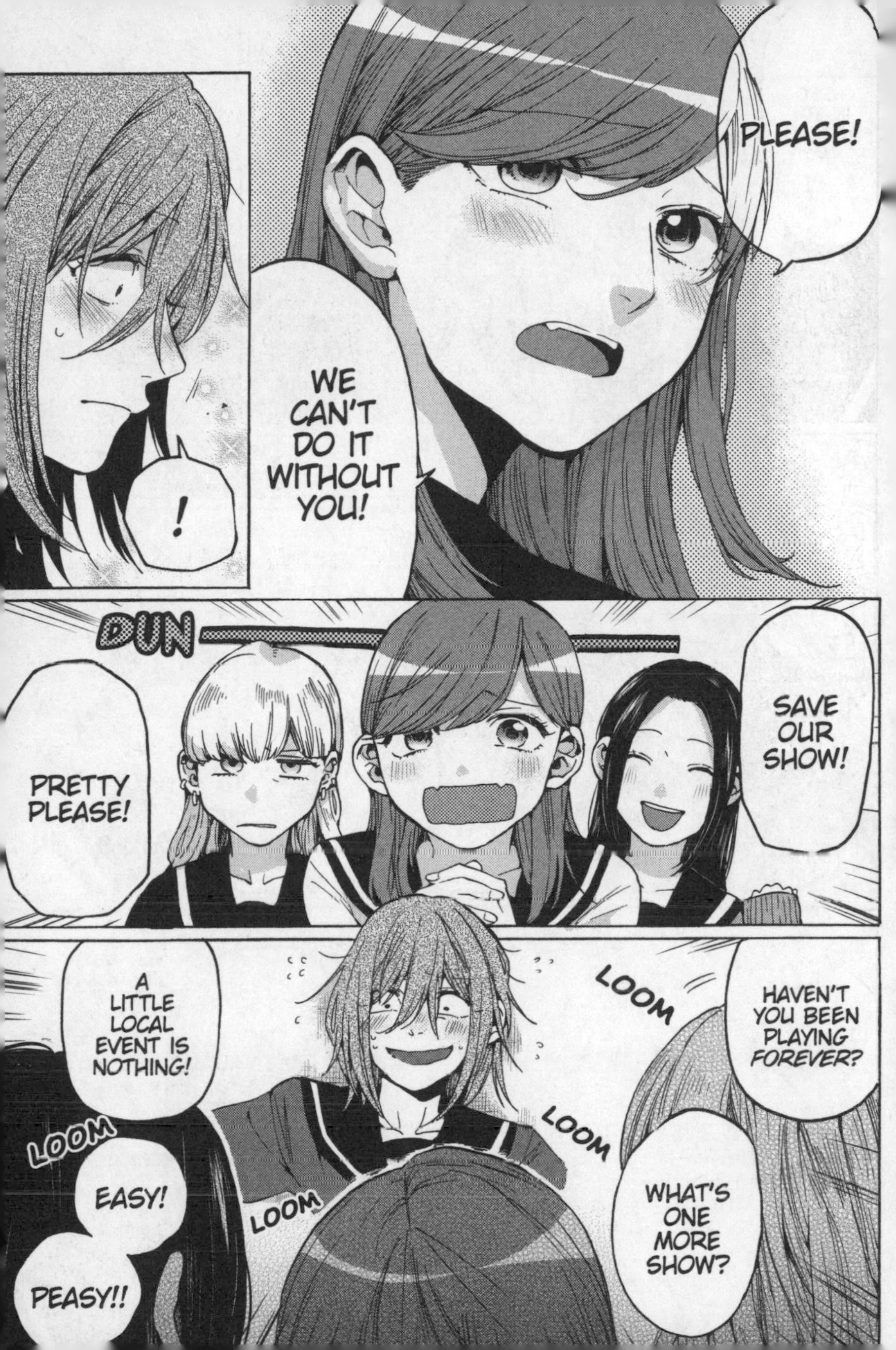
PLEASE!
WE CAN'T DO IT WITHOUT YOU!
!
SAVE OUR SHOW!
DUN
PRETTY PLEASE!
HAVEN'T YOU BEEN PLAYING FOREVER?
LOOM
WHAT'S ONE MORE SHOW?
LOOM
A LITTLE LOCAL EVENT IS NOTHING!
LOOM
LOOM
EASY!
PEASY!!

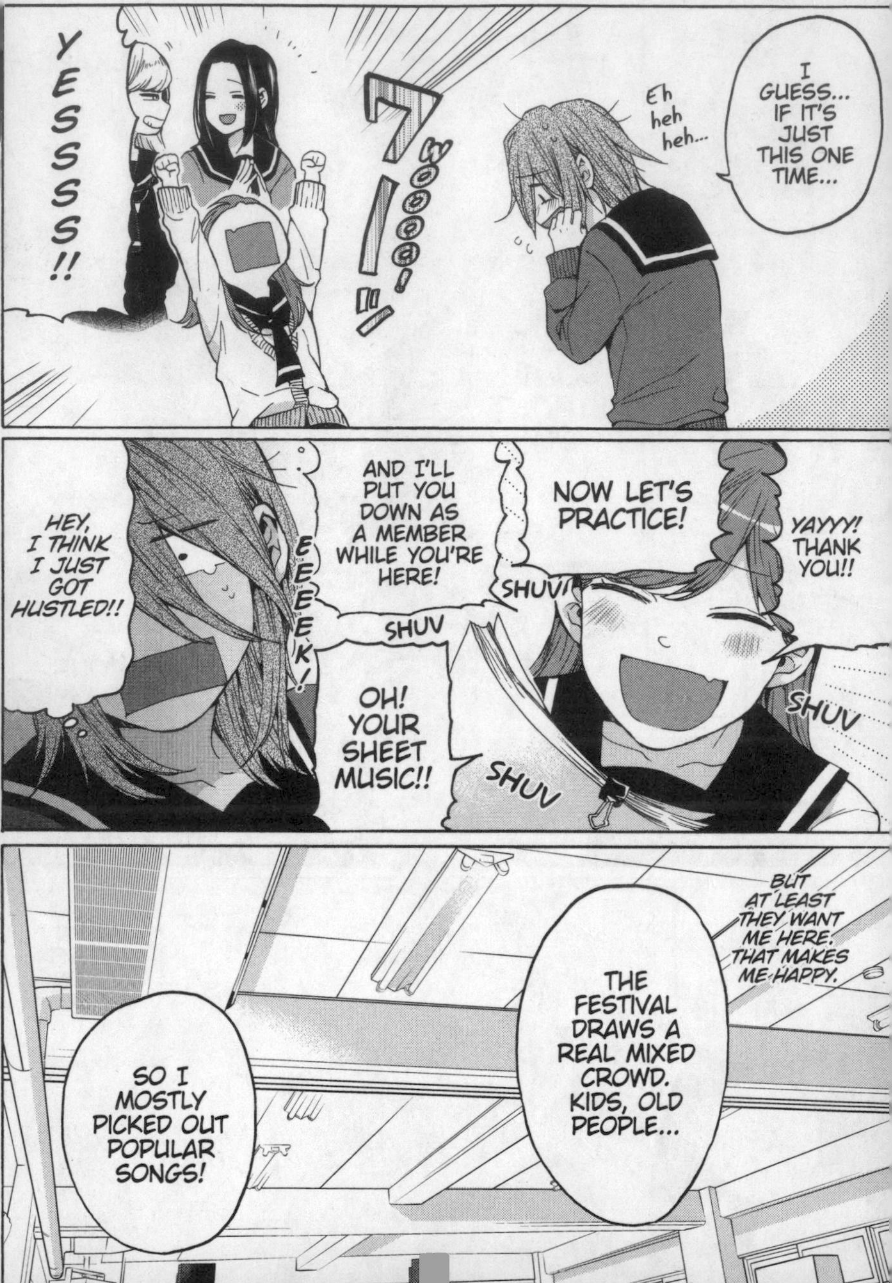
I GUESS... IF IT'S JUST THIS ONE TIME...
Eh heh heh...
YESSSS!!
YAYYY! THANK YOU!!
NOW LET'S PRACTICE!
SHUV
AND I'LL PUT YOU DOWN AS A MEMBER WHILE YOU'RE HERE!
SHUV
SHUV
OH! YOUR SHEET MUSIC!!
SHUV
EEEEEK!
HEY, I THINK I JUST GOT HUSTLED!!
BUT AT LEAST THEY WANT ME HERE. THAT MAKES ME HAPPY.
THE FESTIVAL DRAWS A REAL MIXED CROWD. KIDS, OLD PEOPLE...
SO I MOSTLY PICKED OUT POPULAR SONGS!

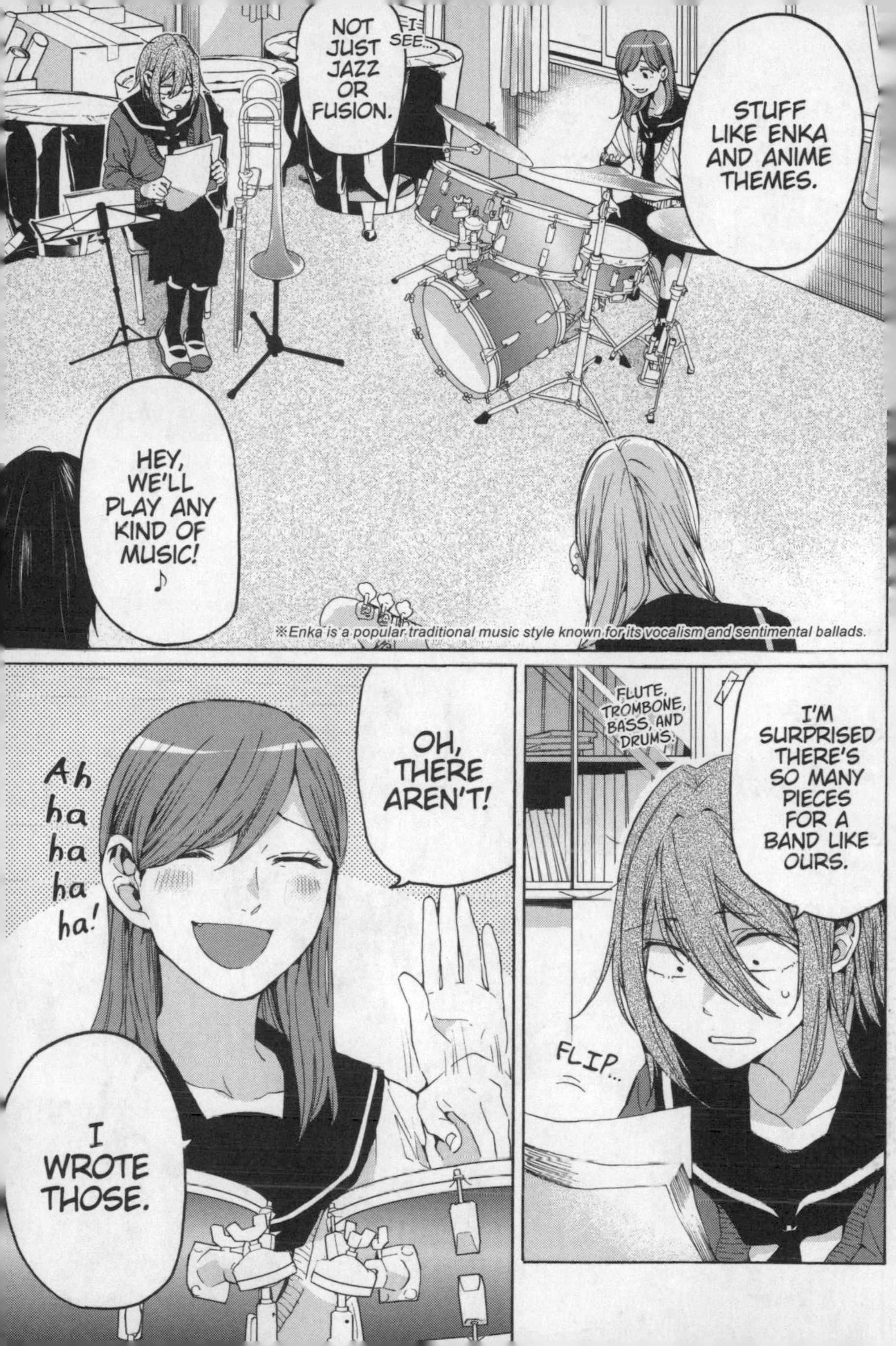
STUFF LIKE ENKA AND ANIME THEMES.
I SEE...
NOT JUST JAZZ OR FUSION.
HEY, WE'LL PLAY ANY KIND OF MUSIC! ♪
I'M SURPRISED THERE'S SO MANY PIECES FOR A BAND LIKE OURS.
FLUTE, TROMBONE, BASS, AND DRUMS.
FLIP...
OH, THERE AREN'T!
Ahhahahaha!
I WROTE THOSE.
※Enka is a popular traditional music style known for its vocalism and sentimental ballads.

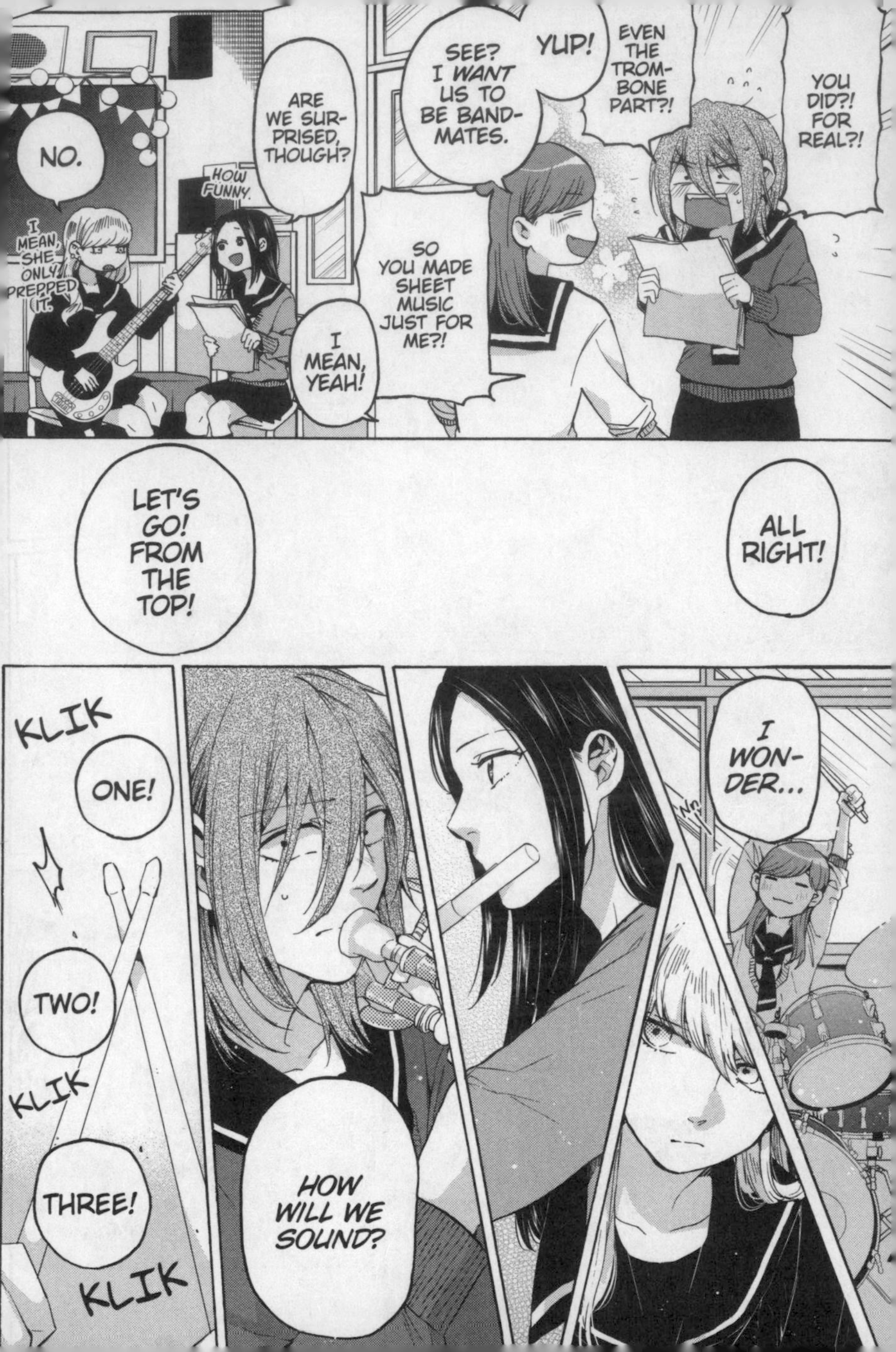
YOU DID?! FOR REAL?!
EVEN THE TROMBONE PART?!
YUP!
SEE? I *WANT* US TO BE BANDMATES.
SO YOU MADE SHEET MUSIC JUST FOR ME?!
I MEAN, YEAH!
ARE WE SURPRISED, THOUGH?
HOW FUNNY.
NO.
I MEAN, SHE ONLY PREPPED IT.
ALL RIGHT!
LET'S GO! FROM THE TOP!
I WONDER...
HOW WILL WE SOUND?
KLIK
ONE!
TWO!
KLIK
THREE!
KLIK

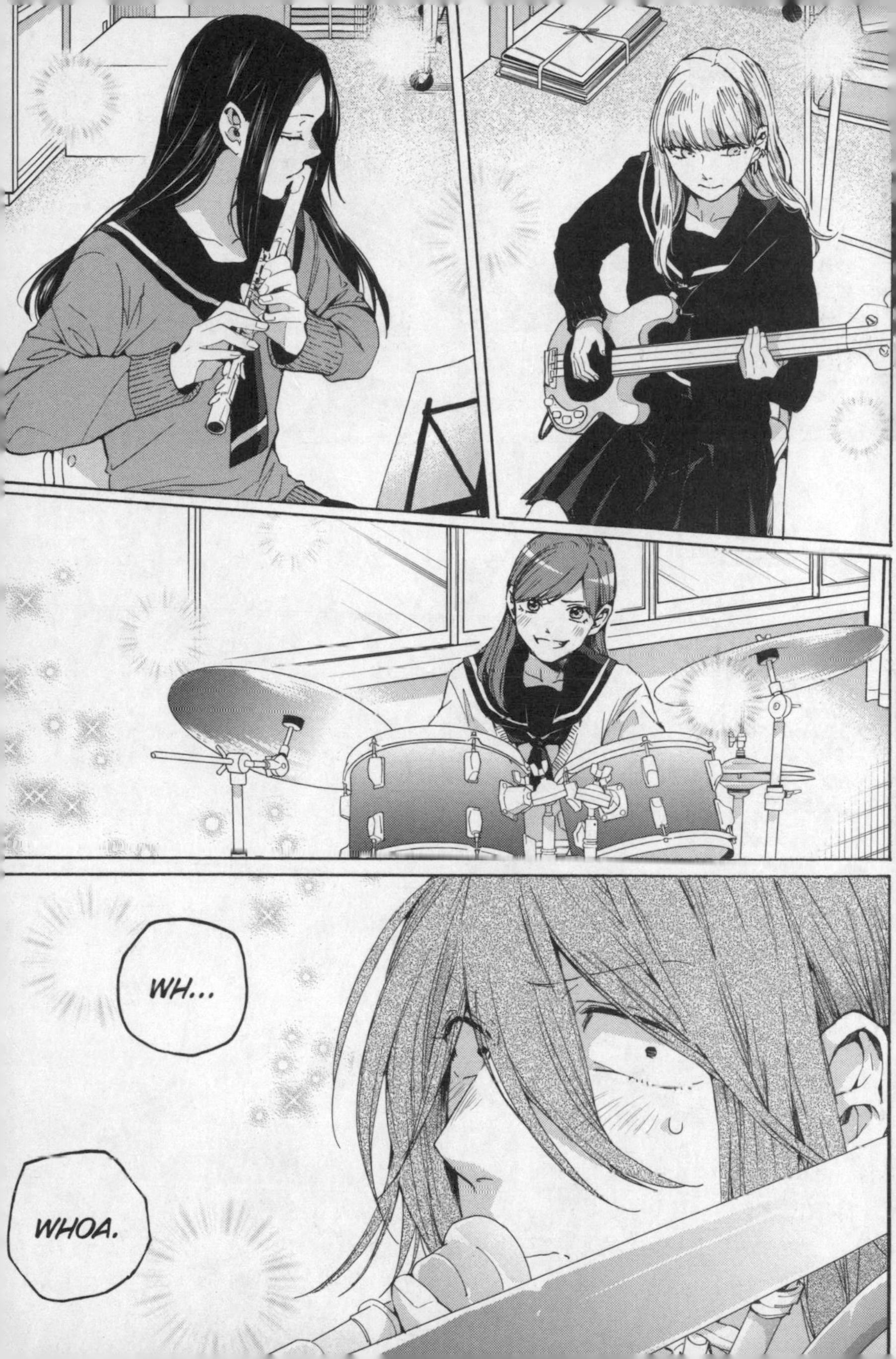
WH...
WHOA.

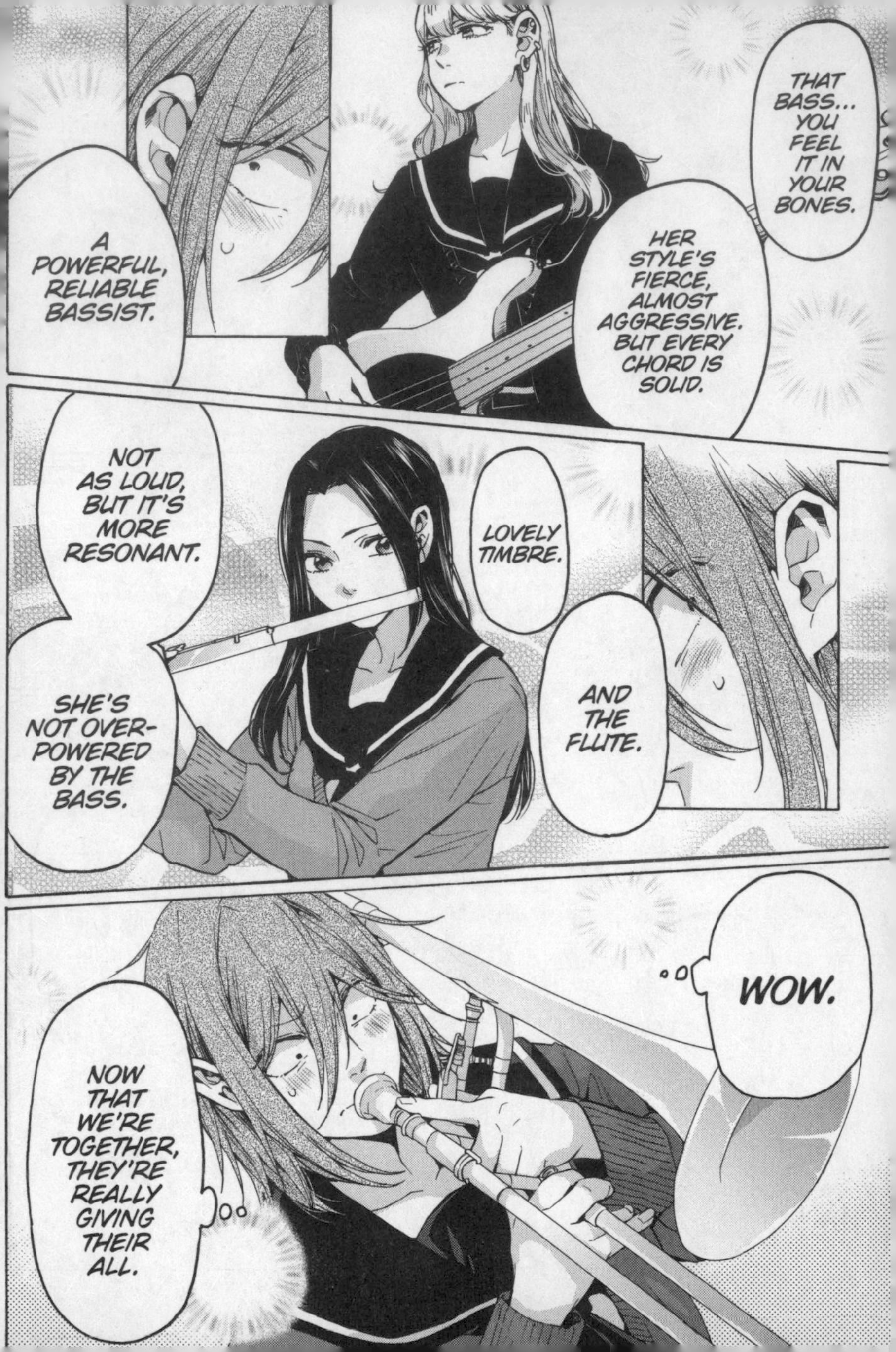
THAT BASS... YOU FEEL IT IN YOUR BONES.
HER STYLE'S FIERCE, ALMOST AGGRESSIVE. BUT EVERY CHORD IS SOLID.
A POWERFUL, RELIABLE BASSIST.
AND THE FLUTE.
LOVELY TIMBRE.
NOT AS LOUD, BUT IT'S MORE RESONANT.
SHE'S NOT OVER-POWERED BY THE BASS.
WOW.
NOW THAT WE'RE TOGETHER, THEY'RE REALLY GIVING THEIR ALL.

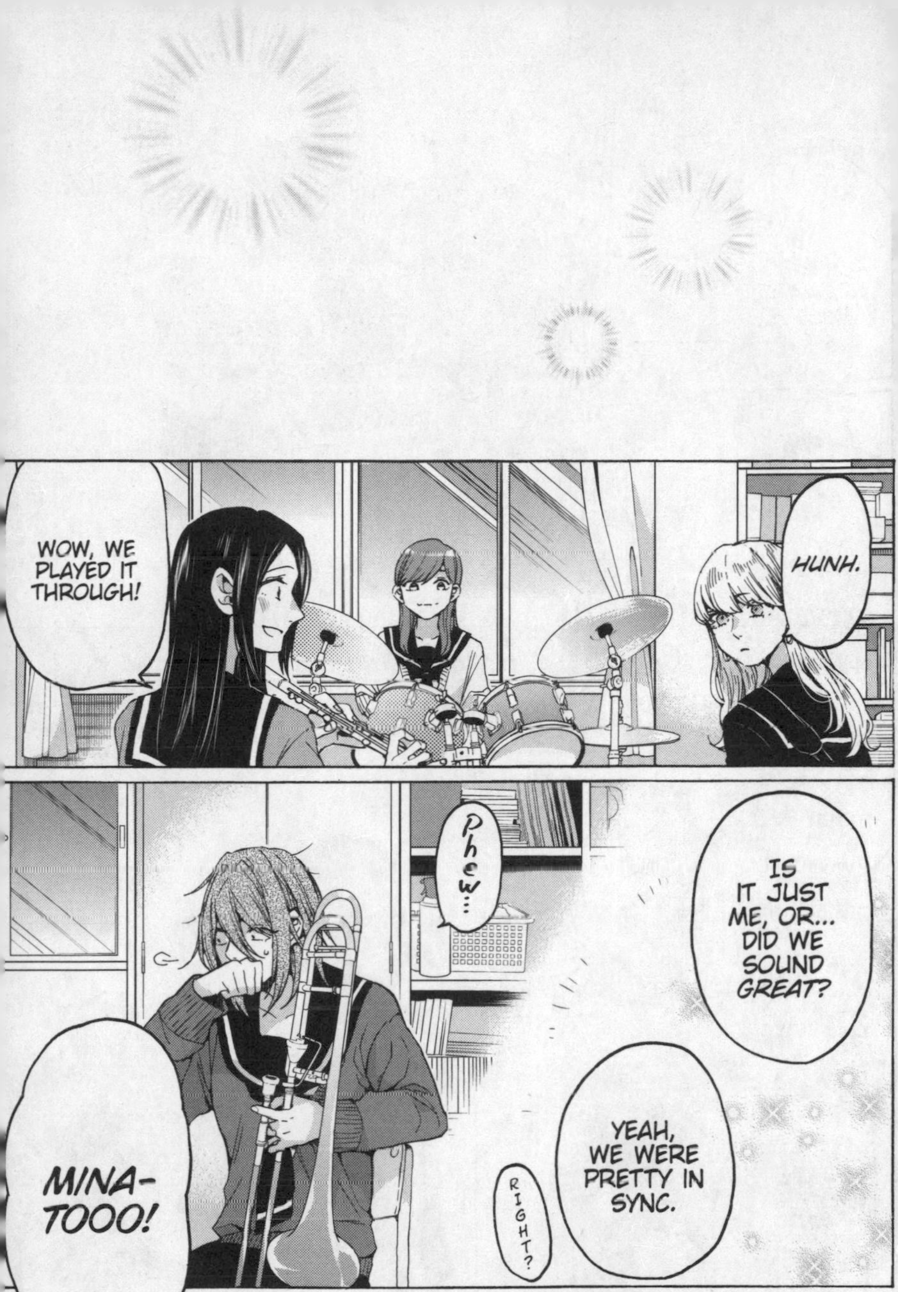
HUNH.
WOW, WE PLAYED IT THROUGH!
IS IT JUST ME, OR... DID WE SOUND GREAT?
Phew...
YEAH, WE WERE PRETTY IN SYNC.
RIGHT?
MINA-TOOO!

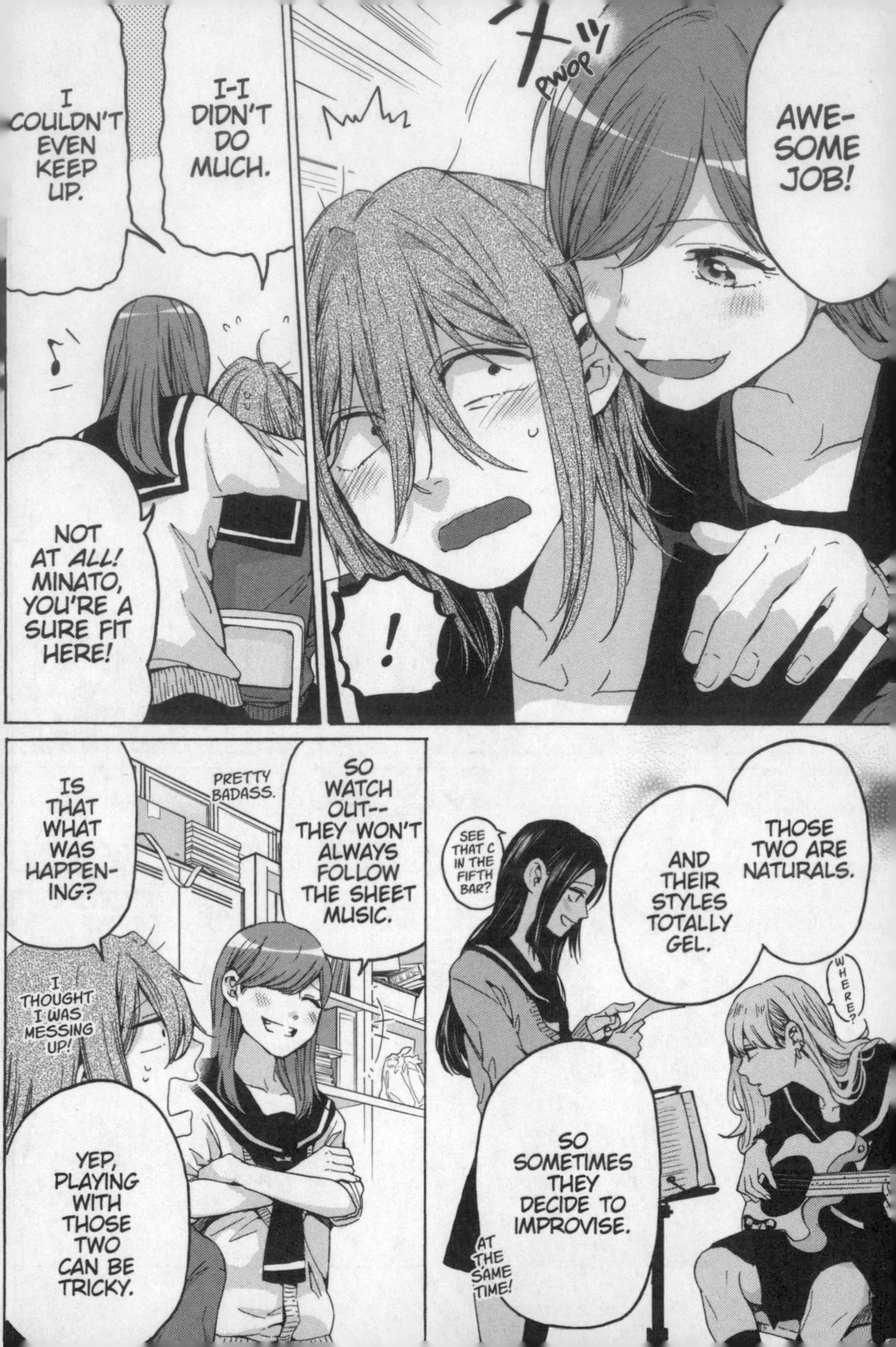
PWOP
AWESOME JOB!
!
I-I DIDN'T DO MUCH.
I COULDN'T EVEN KEEP UP.
NOT AT ALL! MINATO, YOU'RE A SURE FIT HERE!
THOSE TWO ARE NATURALS.
AND THEIR STYLES TOTALLY GEL.
SEE THAT C IN THE FIFTH BAR?
WHERE?
SO SOMETIMES THEY DECIDE TO IMPROVISE.
AT THE SAME TIME!
SO WATCH OUT-- THEY WON'T ALWAYS FOLLOW THE SHEET MUSIC.
PRETTY BADASS.
IS THAT WHAT WAS HAPPENING?
I THOUGHT I WAS MESSING UP!
YEP, PLAYING WITH THOSE TWO CAN BE TRICKY.

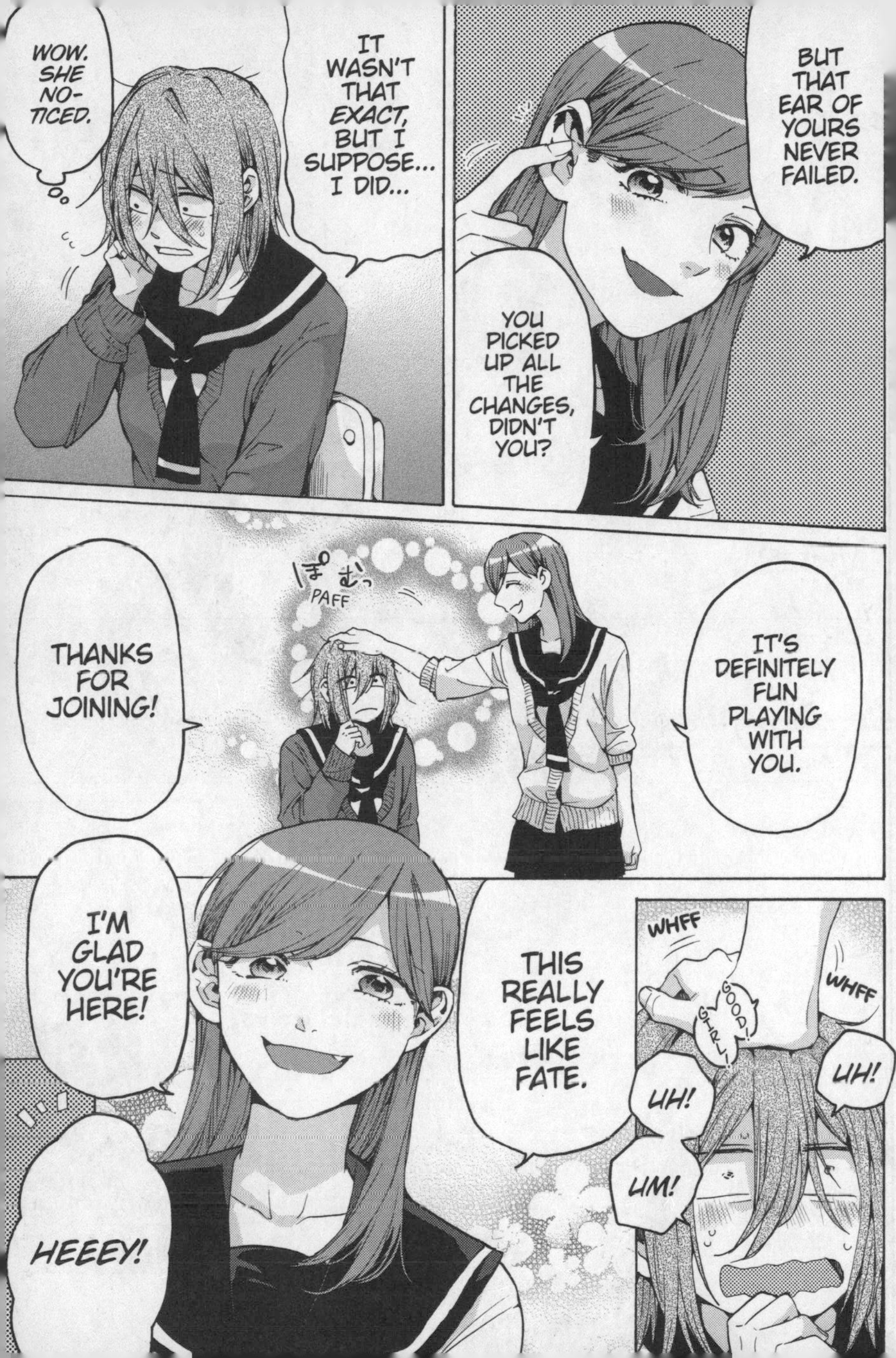
BUT THAT EAR OF YOURS NEVER FAILED.
YOU PICKED UP ALL THE CHANGES, DIDN'T YOU?
IT WASN'T THAT *EXACT*, BUT I SUPPOSE... I DID...
WOW. SHE NO-TICED.
IT'S DEFINITELY FUN PLAYING WITH YOU.
ぽむっ
PAFF
THANKS FOR JOINING!
WHFF
WHFF
GOOD GIRL!
UH!
UH!
UM!
THIS REALLY FEELS LIKE FATE.
I'M GLAD YOU'RE HERE!
HEEEY!

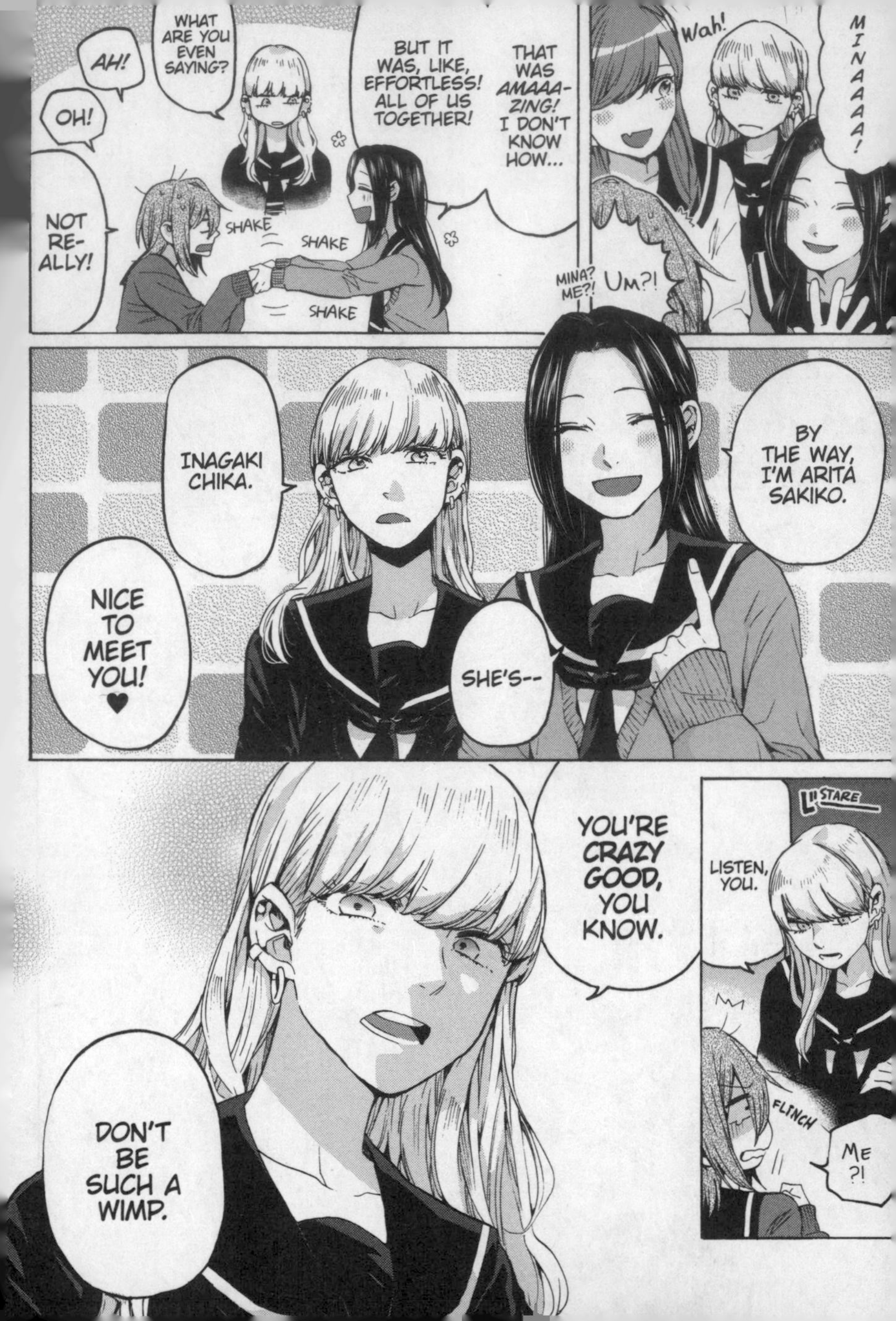
MINAAAAA!
Wah!
UM?!
MINA? ME?!
THAT WAS AMAAAA-ZING! I DON'T KNOW HOW...
BUT IT WAS, LIKE, EFFORTLESS! ALL OF US TOGETHER!
WHAT ARE YOU EVEN SAYING?
AH!
OH!
NOT RE-ALLY!
SHAKE
SHAKE
SHAKE
BY THE WAY, I'M ARITA SAKIKO.
SHE'S--
INAGAKI CHIKA.
NICE TO MEET YOU! ♥
STARE
LISTEN, YOU.
ME ?!
FLINCH
YOU'RE CRAZY GOOD, YOU KNOW.
DON'T BE SUCH A WIMP.

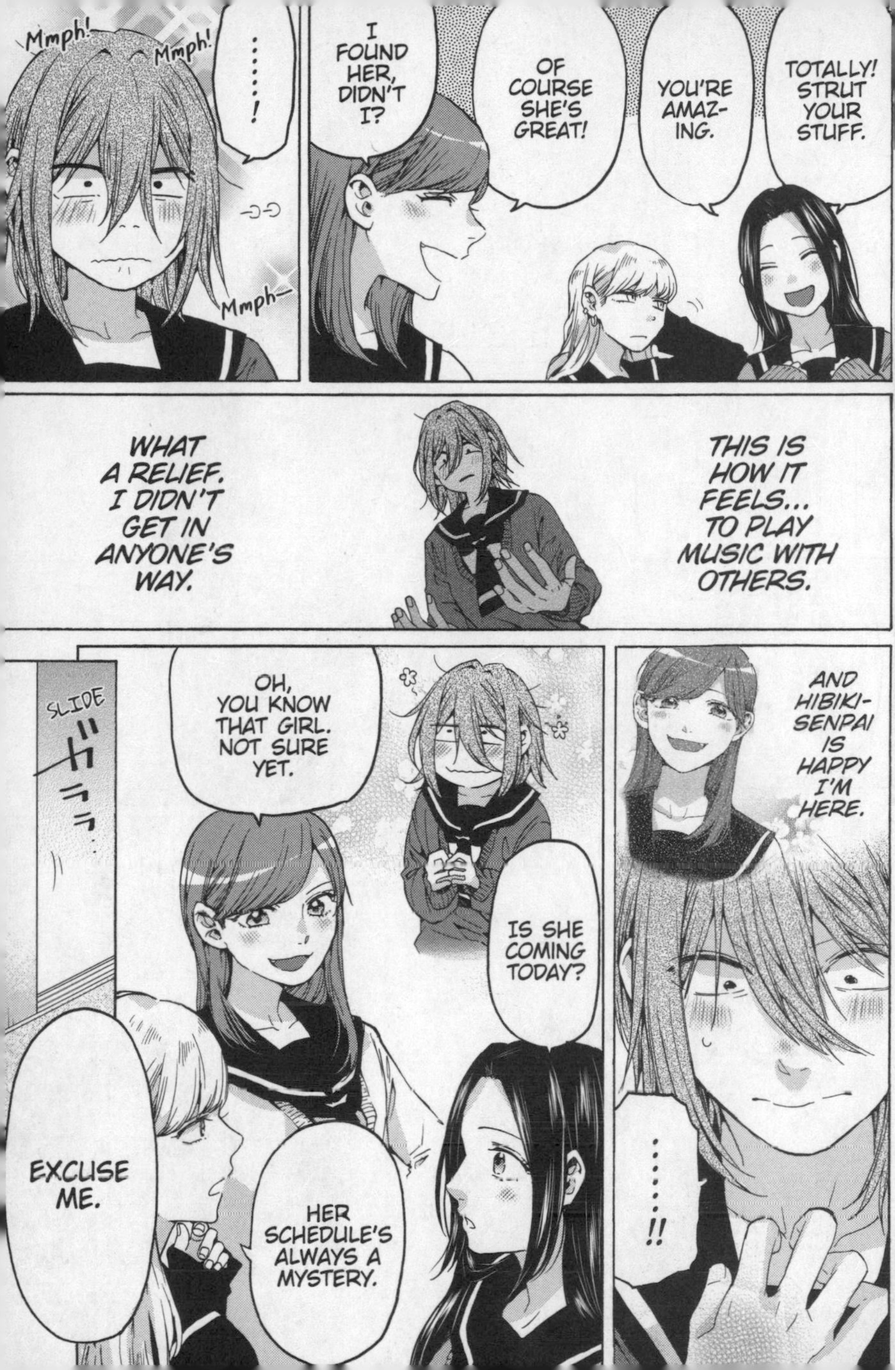
TOTALLY! STRUT YOUR STUFF.
YOU'RE AMAZ-ING.
OF COURSE SHE'S GREAT!
I FOUND HER, DIDN'T I?
Mmph!
......!
Mmph!
Mmph—
THIS IS HOW IT FEELS... TO PLAY MUSIC WITH OTHERS.
WHAT A RELIEF. I DIDN'T GET IN ANYONE'S WAY.
AND HIBIKI-SENPAI IS HAPPY I'M HERE.
......!!
IS SHE COMING TODAY?
OH, YOU KNOW THAT GIRL. NOT SURE YET.
HER SCHEDULE'S ALWAYS A MYSTERY.
SLIDE
EXCUSE ME.

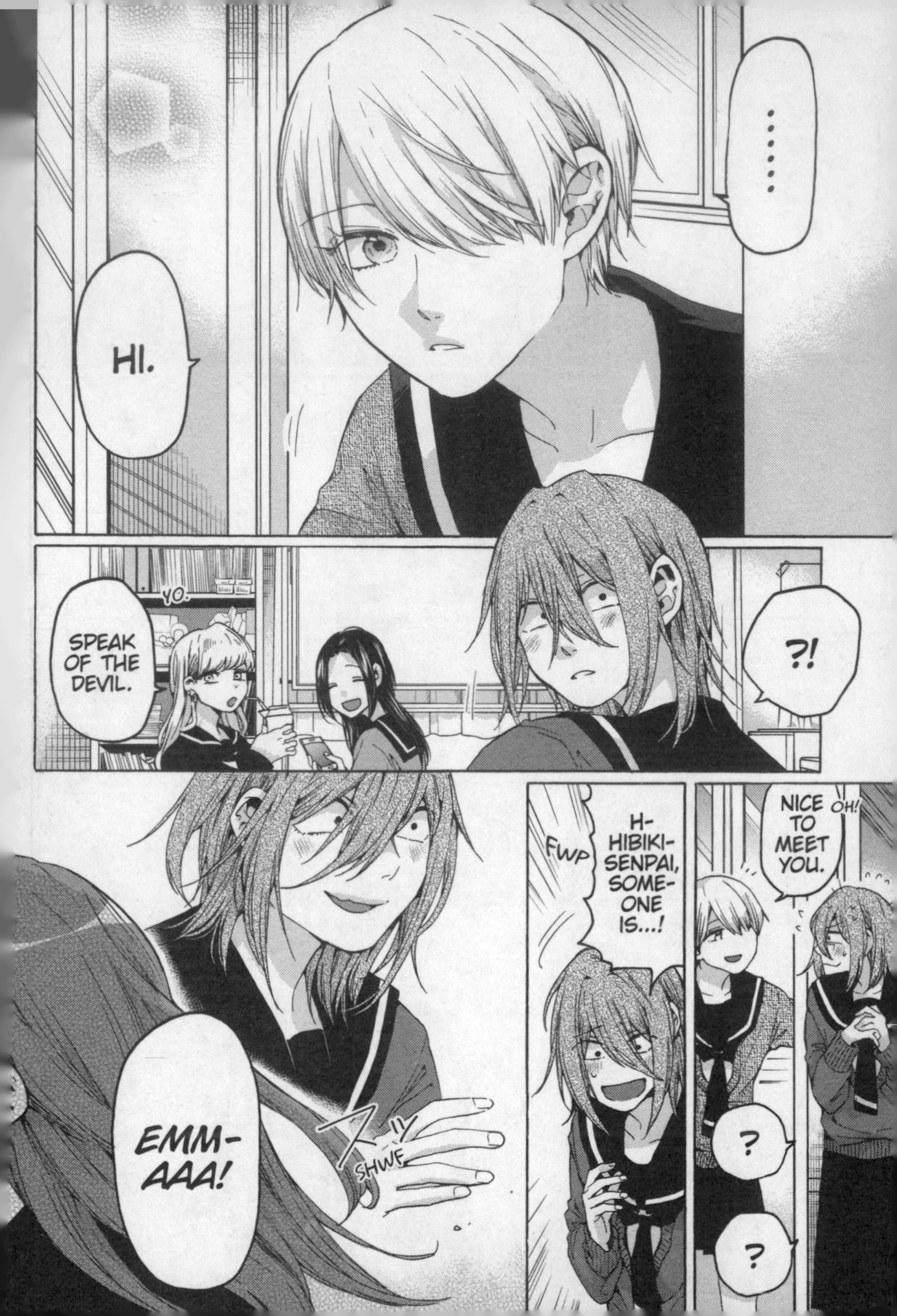
......
HI.
?!
YO.
SPEAK OF THE DEVIL.
OH!
NICE TO MEET YOU.
?
?
FWP
H-HIBIKI-SENPAI, SOMEONE IS...!
EMM-AAA!
SHWF

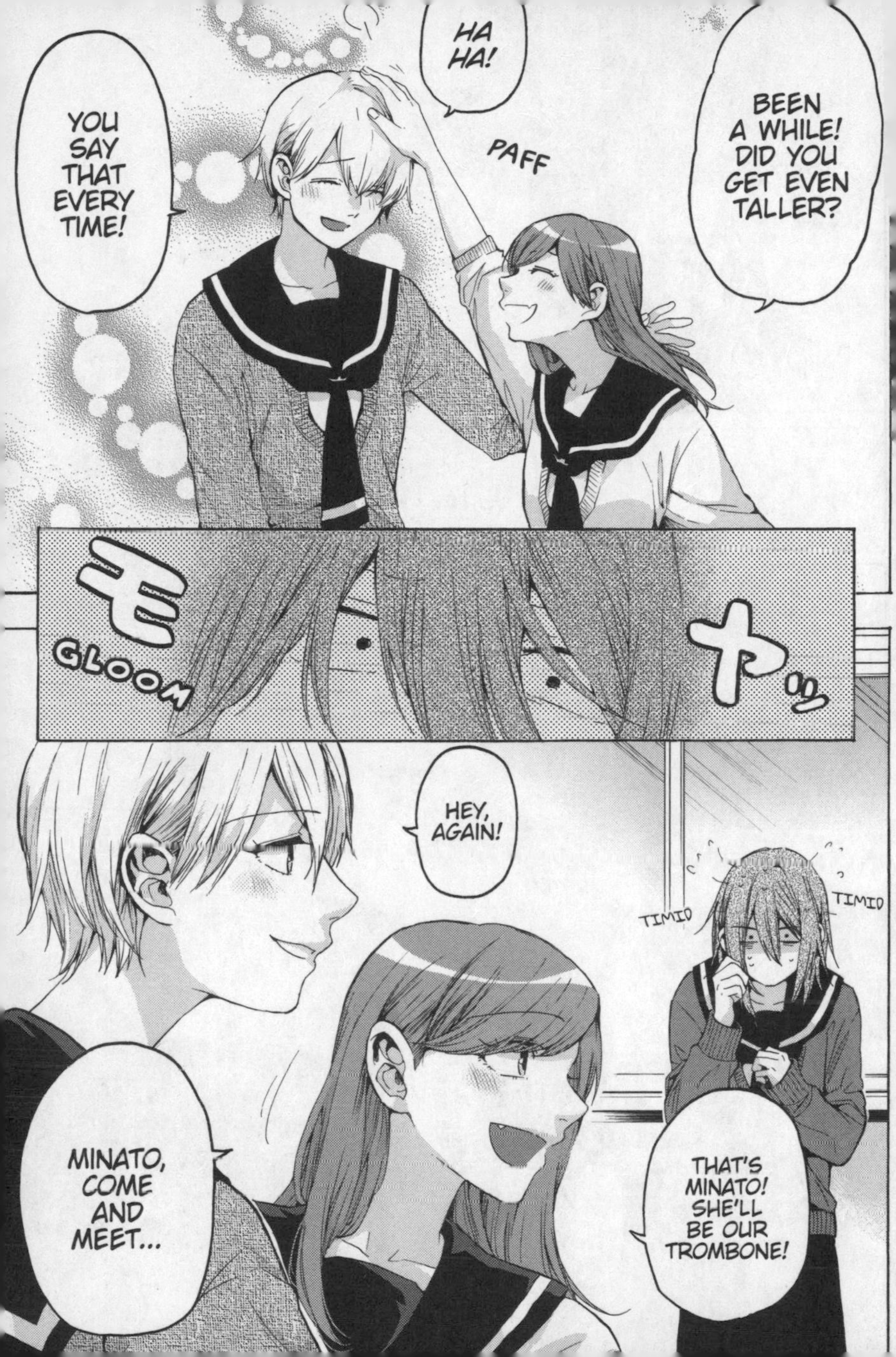
BEEN A WHILE! DID YOU GET EVEN TALLER?
HA HA!
PAFF
YOU SAY THAT EVERY TIME!
モ
ヤッ
GLOOM
HEY, AGAIN!
TIMID
TIMID
THAT'S MINATO! SHE'LL BE OUR TROMBONE!
MINATO, COME AND MEET...

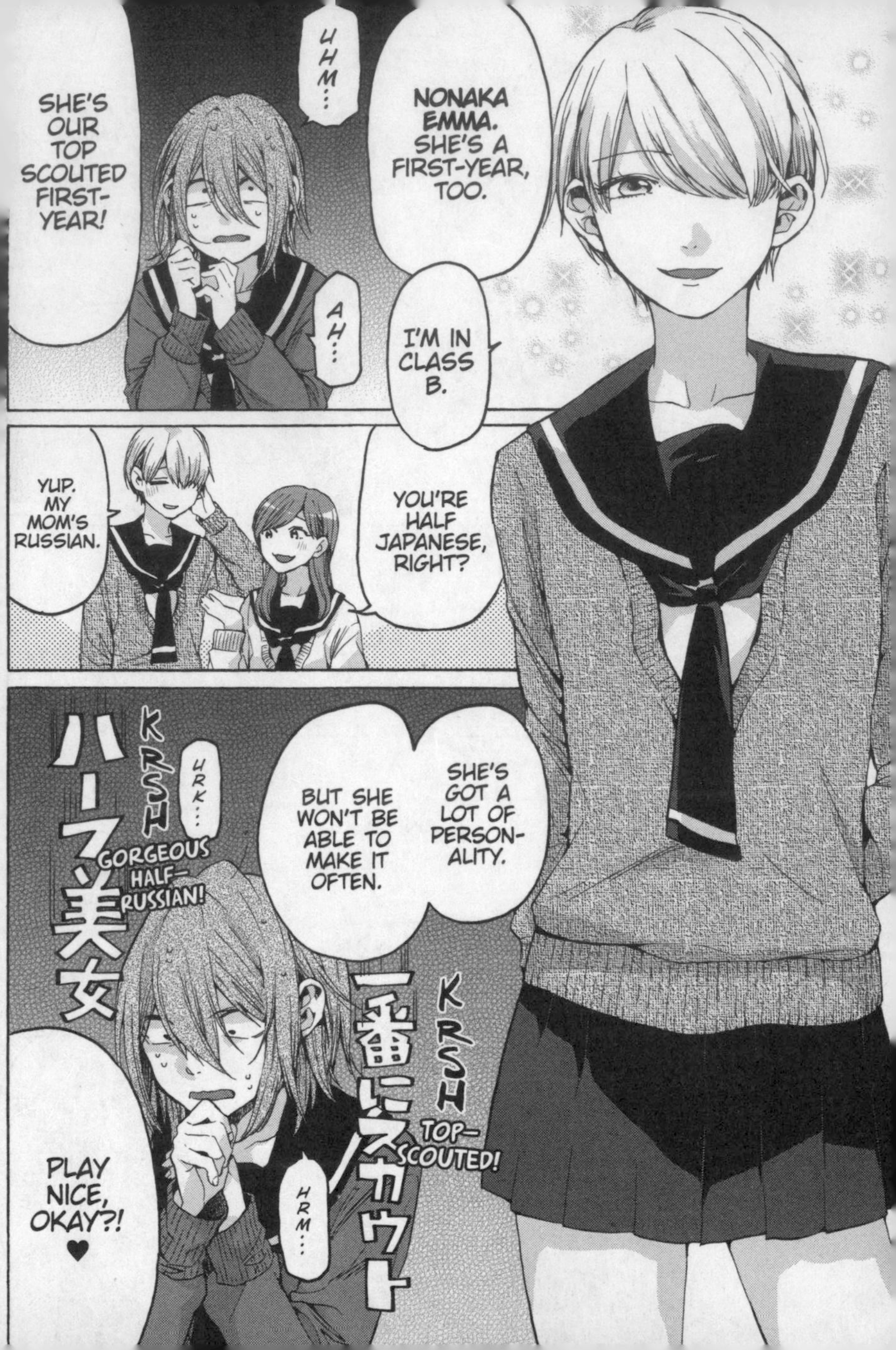
NONAKA EMMA. SHE'S A FIRST-YEAR, TOO.
I'M IN CLASS B.
UHM...
AH...
SHE'S OUR TOP SCOUTED FIRST-YEAR!
YOU'RE HALF JAPANESE, RIGHT?
YUP. MY MOM'S RUSSIAN.
SHE'S GOT A LOT OF PERSON-ALITY.
BUT SHE WON'T BE ABLE TO MAKE IT OFTEN.
KRSH
一番にスカウト
TOP-SCOUTED!
KRSH
ハーフ美女
GORGEOUS HALF-RUSSIAN!
URK...
HRM...
PLAY NICE, OKAY?! ♥

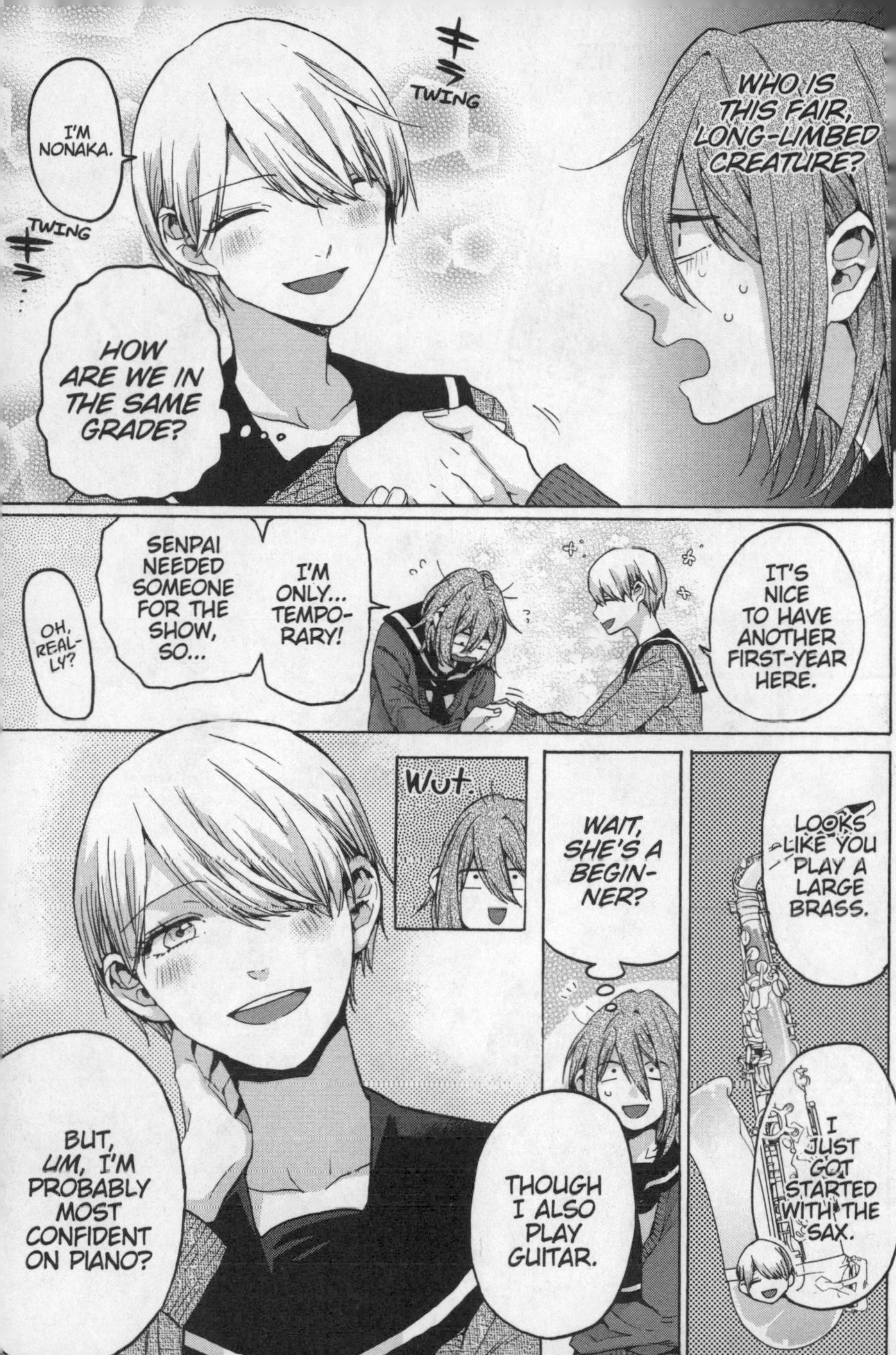
WHO IS THIS FAIR, LONG-LIMBED CREATURE?
TWING
I'M NONAKA.
TWING
HOW ARE WE IN THE SAME GRADE?
IT'S NICE TO HAVE ANOTHER FIRST-YEAR HERE.
I'M ONLY... TEMPO-RARY!
SENPAI NEEDED SOMEONE FOR THE SHOW, SO...
OH, REAL-LY?
LOOKS LIKE YOU PLAY A LARGE BRASS.
I JUST GOT STARTED WITH THE SAX.
WAIT, SHE'S A BEGIN-NER?
WUT.
THOUGH I ALSO PLAY GUITAR.
BUT, UM, I'M PROBABLY MOST CONFIDENT ON PIANO?

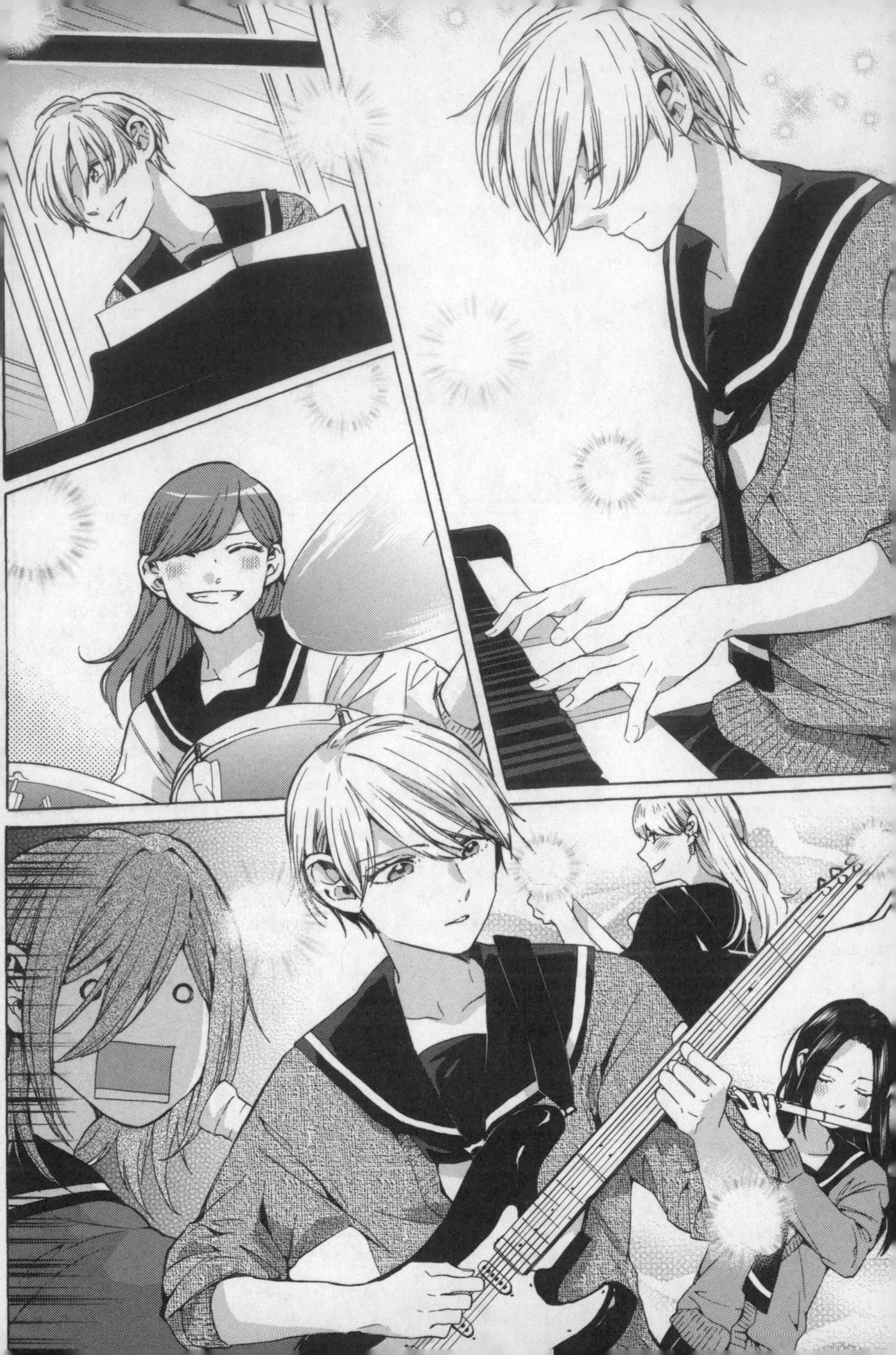

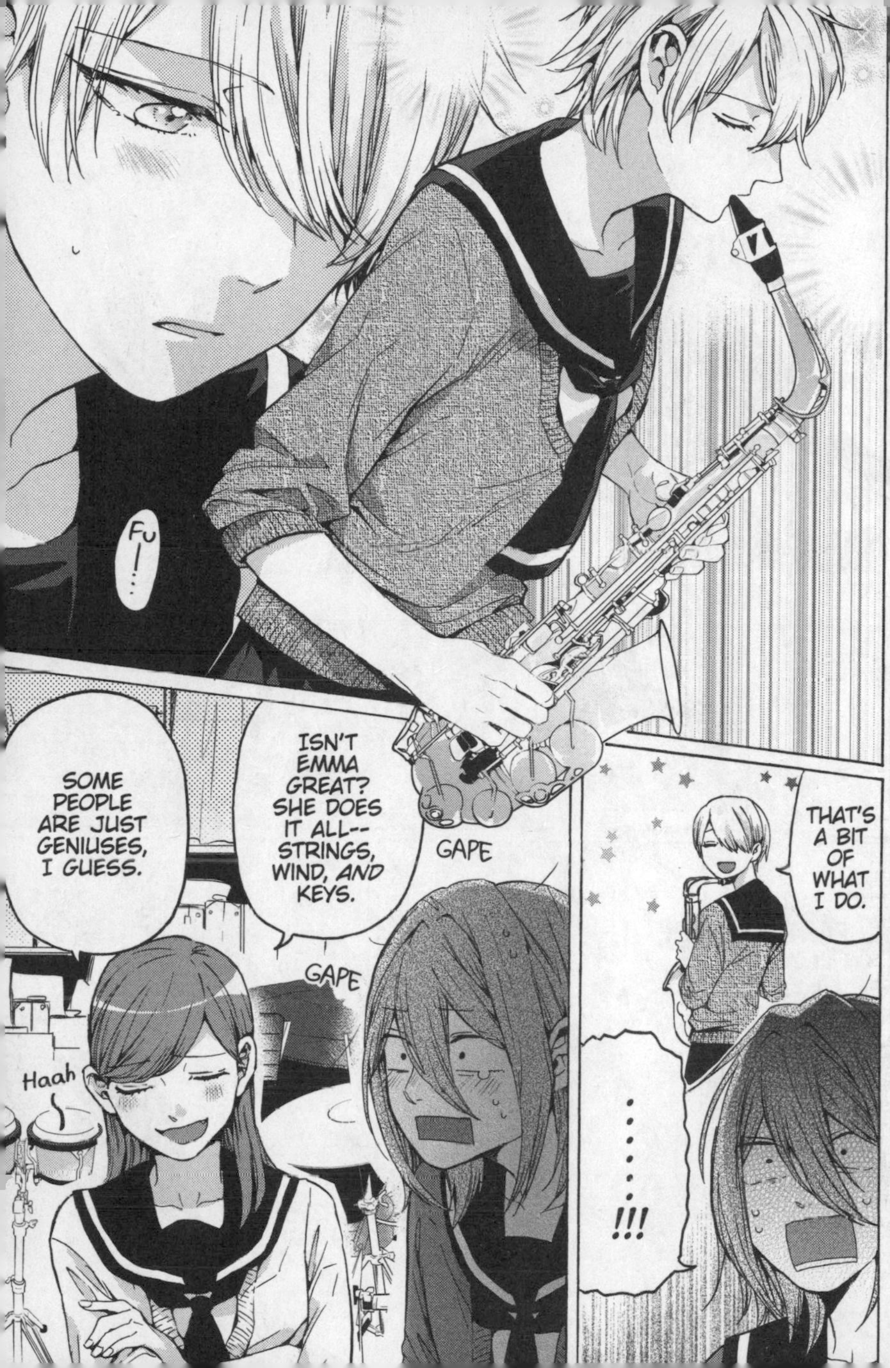
Fu!...
THAT'S A BIT OF WHAT I DO.
......!!!
GAPE
ISN'T EMMA GREAT? SHE DOES IT ALL-- STRINGS, WIND, AND KEYS.
SOME PEOPLE ARE JUST GENIUSES, I GUESS.
GAPE
Haah

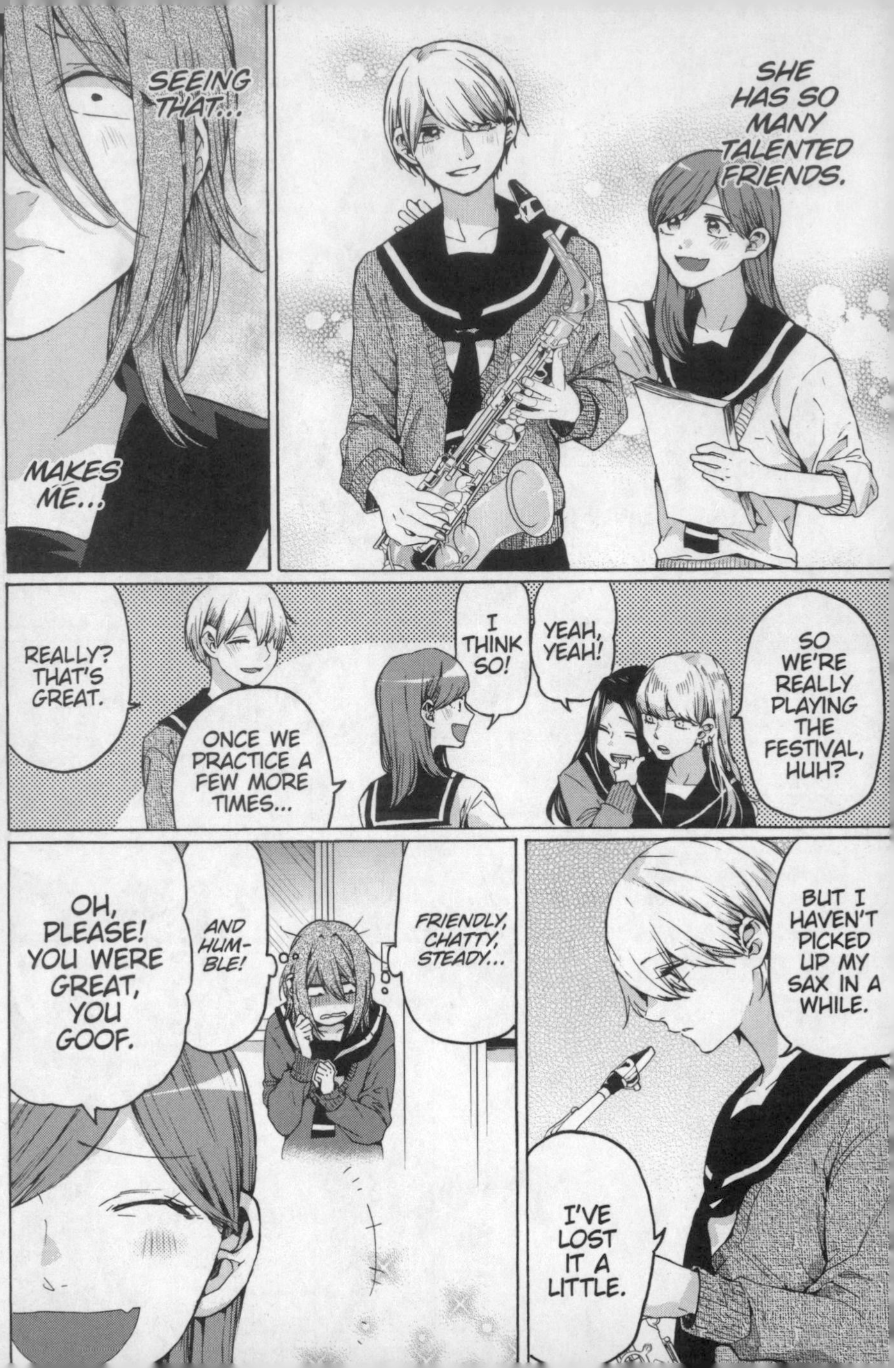
SHE HAS SO MANY TALENTED FRIENDS.
SEEING THAT...
MAKES ME...
SO WE'RE REALLY PLAYING THE FESTIVAL, HUH?
YEAH, YEAH!
I THINK SO!
ONCE WE PRACTICE A FEW MORE TIMES...
REALLY? THAT'S GREAT.
BUT I HAVEN'T PICKED UP MY SAX IN A WHILE.
I'VE LOST IT A LITTLE.
FRIENDLY, CHATTY, STEADY...
AND HUM-BLE!
OH, PLEASE! YOU WERE GREAT, YOU GOOF.

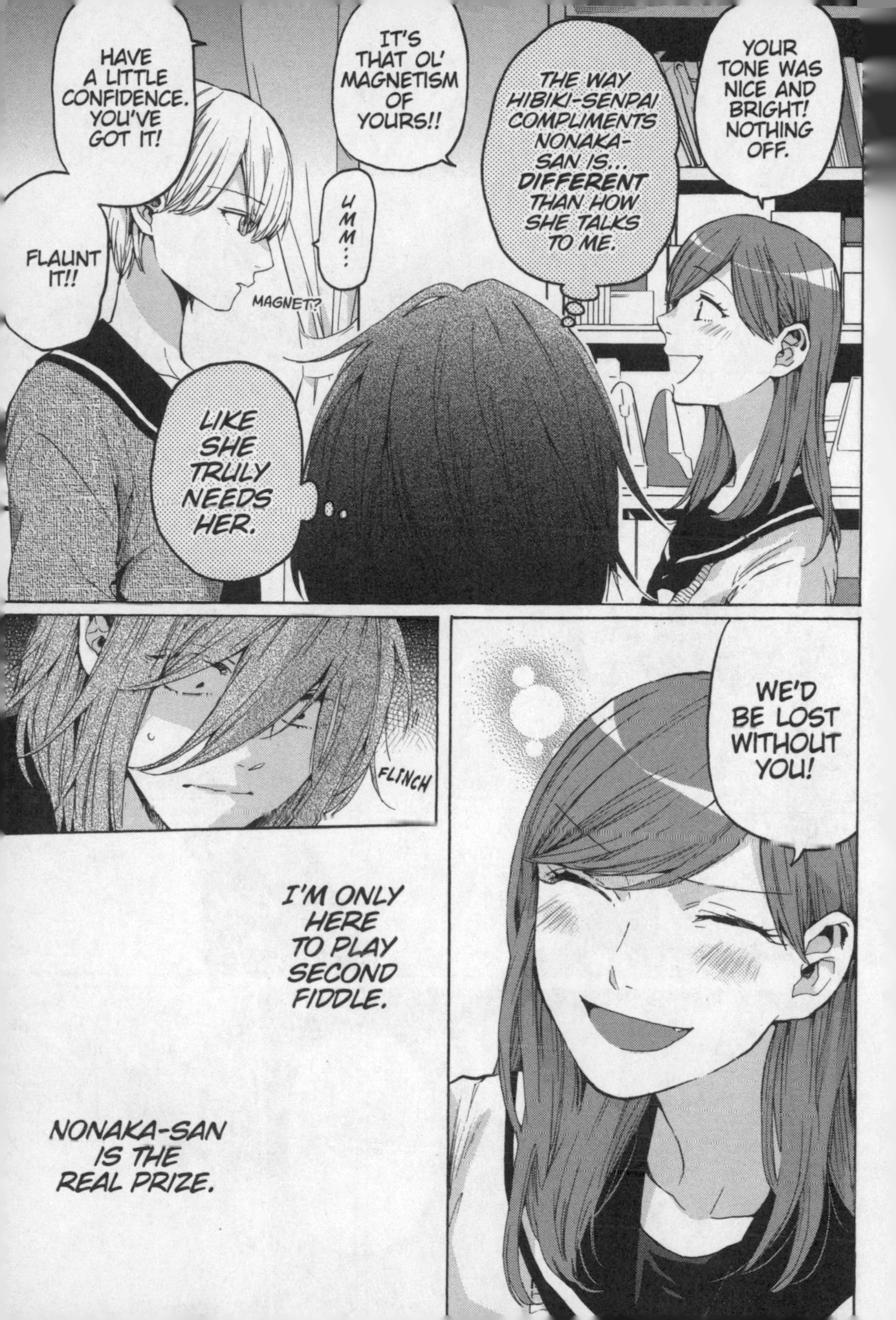
YOUR TONE WAS NICE AND BRIGHT! NOTHING OFF.
THE WAY HIBIKI-SENPAI COMPLIMENTS NONAKA-SAN IS... DIFFERENT THAN HOW SHE TALKS TO ME.
IT'S THAT OL' MAGNETISM OF YOURS!!
UMM...
MAGNET?
HAVE A LITTLE CONFIDENCE. YOU'VE GOT IT!
FLAUNT IT!!
LIKE SHE TRULY NEEDS HER.
WE'D BE LOST WITHOUT YOU!
FLINCH
I'M ONLY HERE TO PLAY SECOND FIDDLE.
NONAKA-SAN IS THE REAL PRIZE.

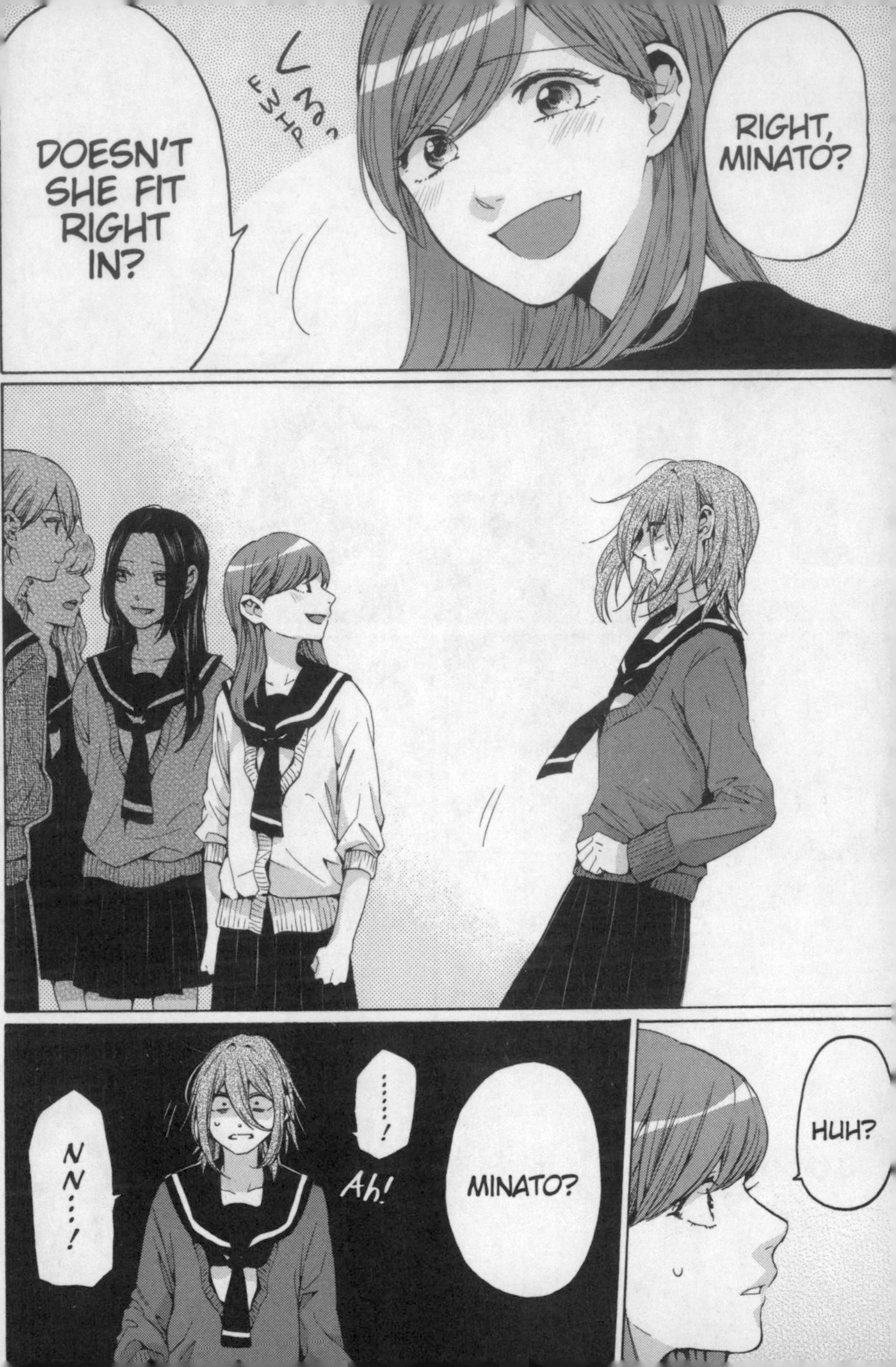
RIGHT, MINATO?
FWSHP
DOESN'T SHE FIT RIGHT IN?
HUH?
MINATO?
......!
Ah!
NN...!

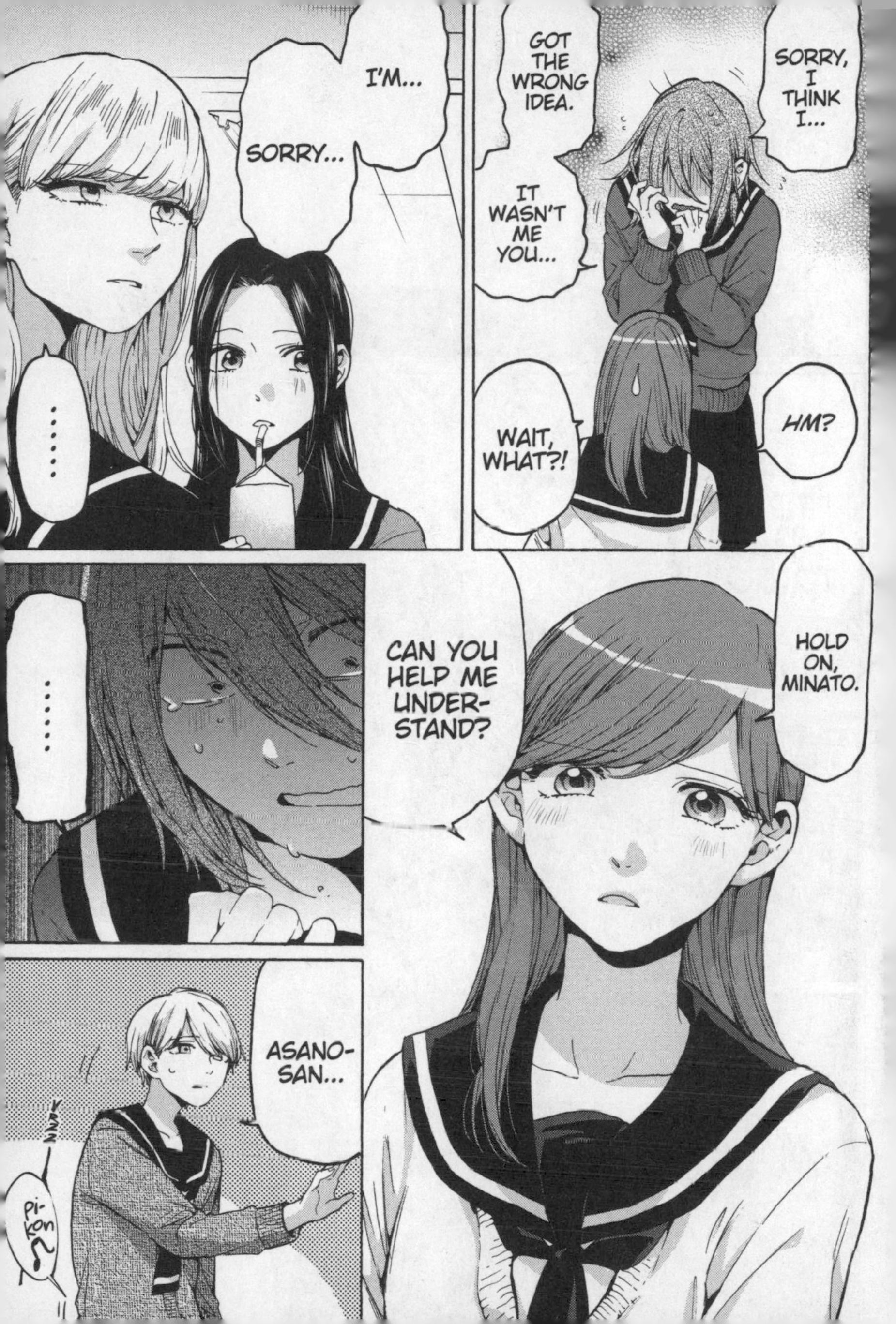
SORRY, I THINK I...
GOT THE WRONG IDEA.
IT WASN'T ME YOU...
HM?
WAIT, WHAT?!
I'M...
SORRY...
......
HOLD ON, MINATO.
CAN YOU HELP ME UNDERSTAND?
......
ASANO-SAN...
VRZZ
pi-kon♪

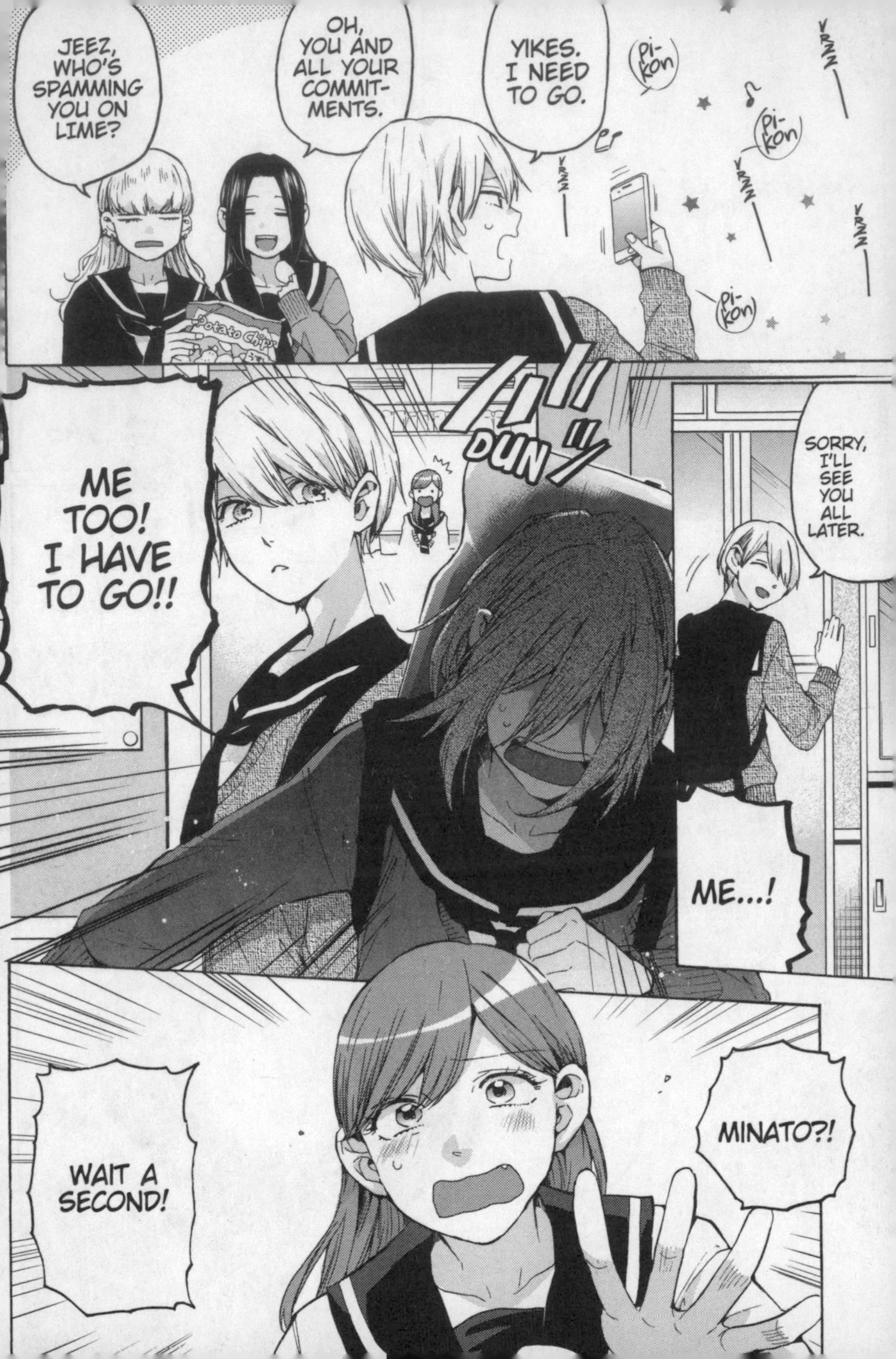

VRZZ
pi-kon
pi-kon
VRZZ
VRZZ
pi-kon
YIKES. I NEED TO GO.
OH, YOU AND ALL YOUR COMMIT-MENTS.
JEEZ, WHO'S SPAMMING YOU ON LIME?
Potato Chips
SORRY, I'LL SEE YOU ALL LATER.
DUN
ME...!
ME TOO! I HAVE TO GO!!
MINATO?!
WAIT A SECOND!

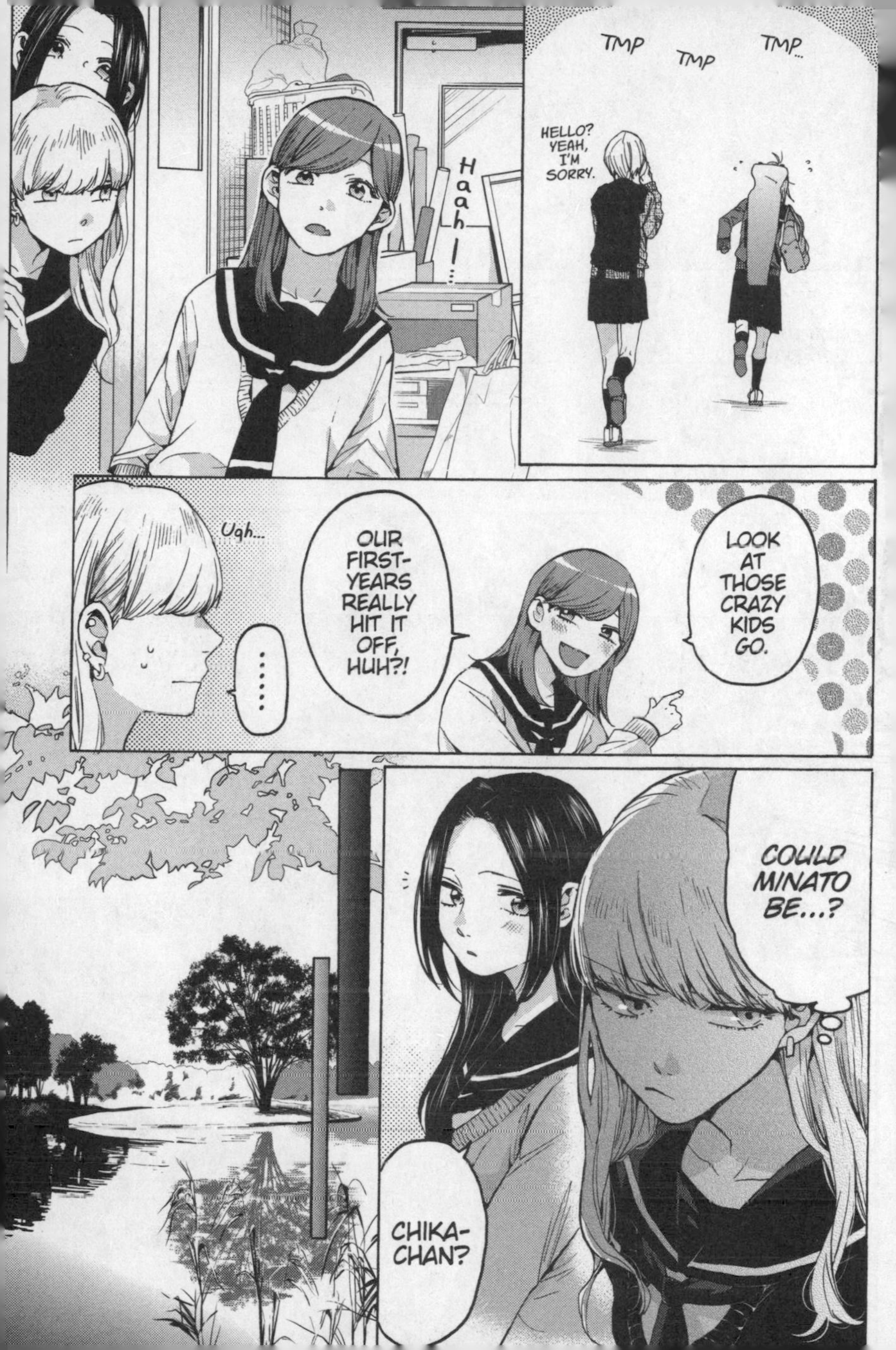
TMP...
TMP
TMP
HELLO? YEAH, I'M SORRY.
Haah!...
LOOK AT THOSE CRAZY KIDS GO.
OUR FIRST-YEARS REALLY HIT IT OFF, HUH?!
Ugh...
......
COULD MINATO BE...?
CHIKA-CHAN?

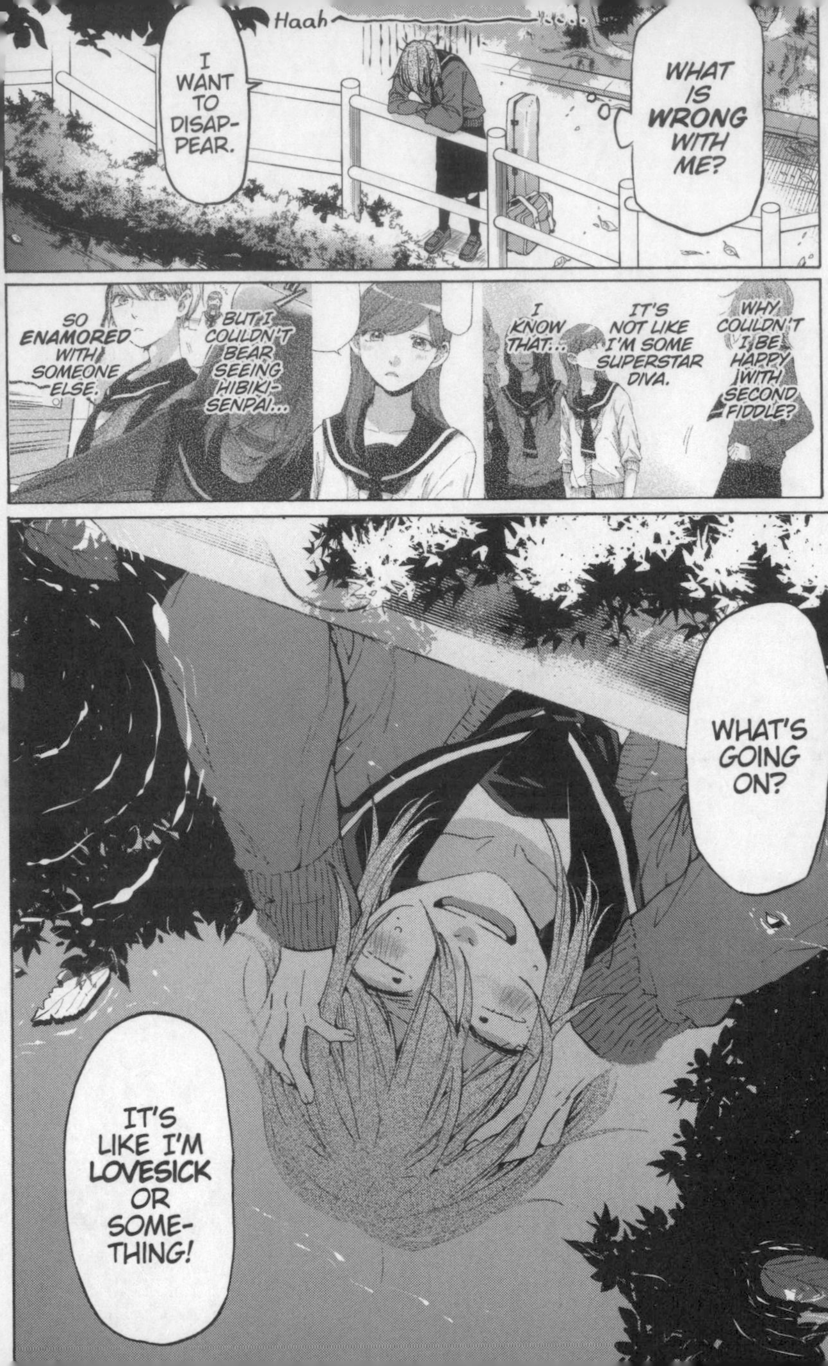
WHAT IS WRONG WITH ME?
Haah
I WANT TO DISAPPEAR.
WHY COULDN'T I BE HAPPY WITH SECOND FIDDLE?
IT'S NOT LIKE I'M SOME SUPERSTAR DIVA.
I KNOW THAT...
BUT I COULDN'T BEAR SEEING HIBIKI-SENPAI...
SO ENAMORED WITH SOMEONE ELSE.
WHAT'S GOING ON?
IT'S LIKE I'M LOVESICK OR SOMETHING!

Hello,
Melancholic!

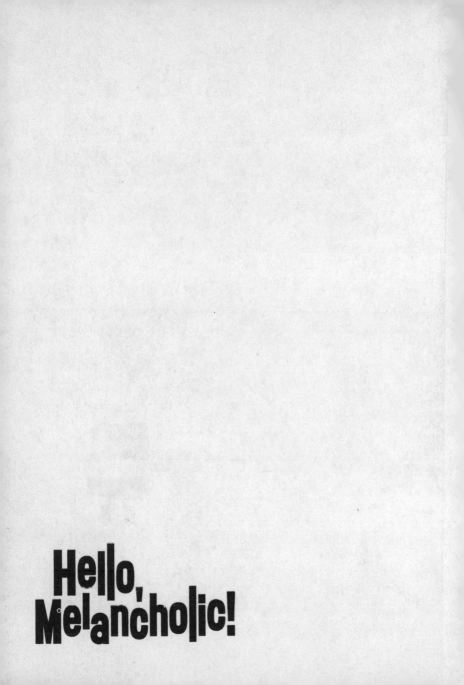

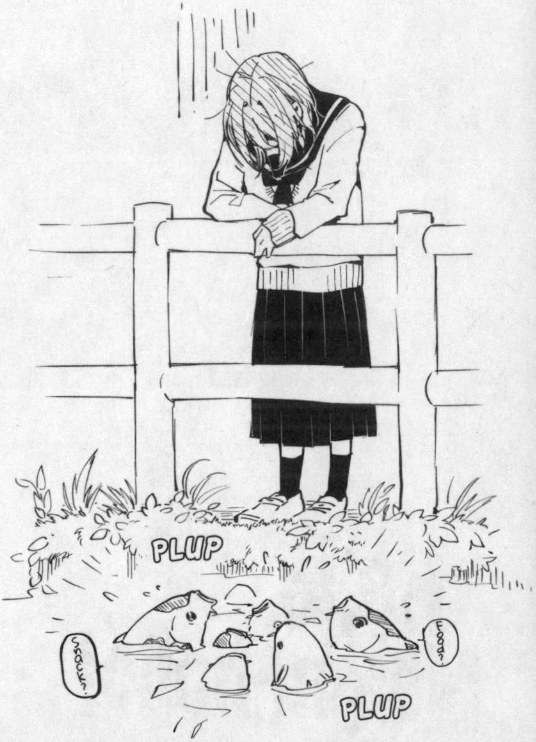
PLUP
Food?
Snack?
PLUP

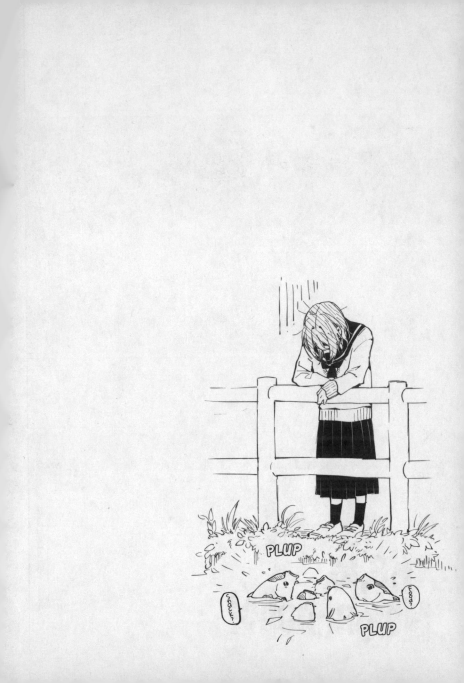

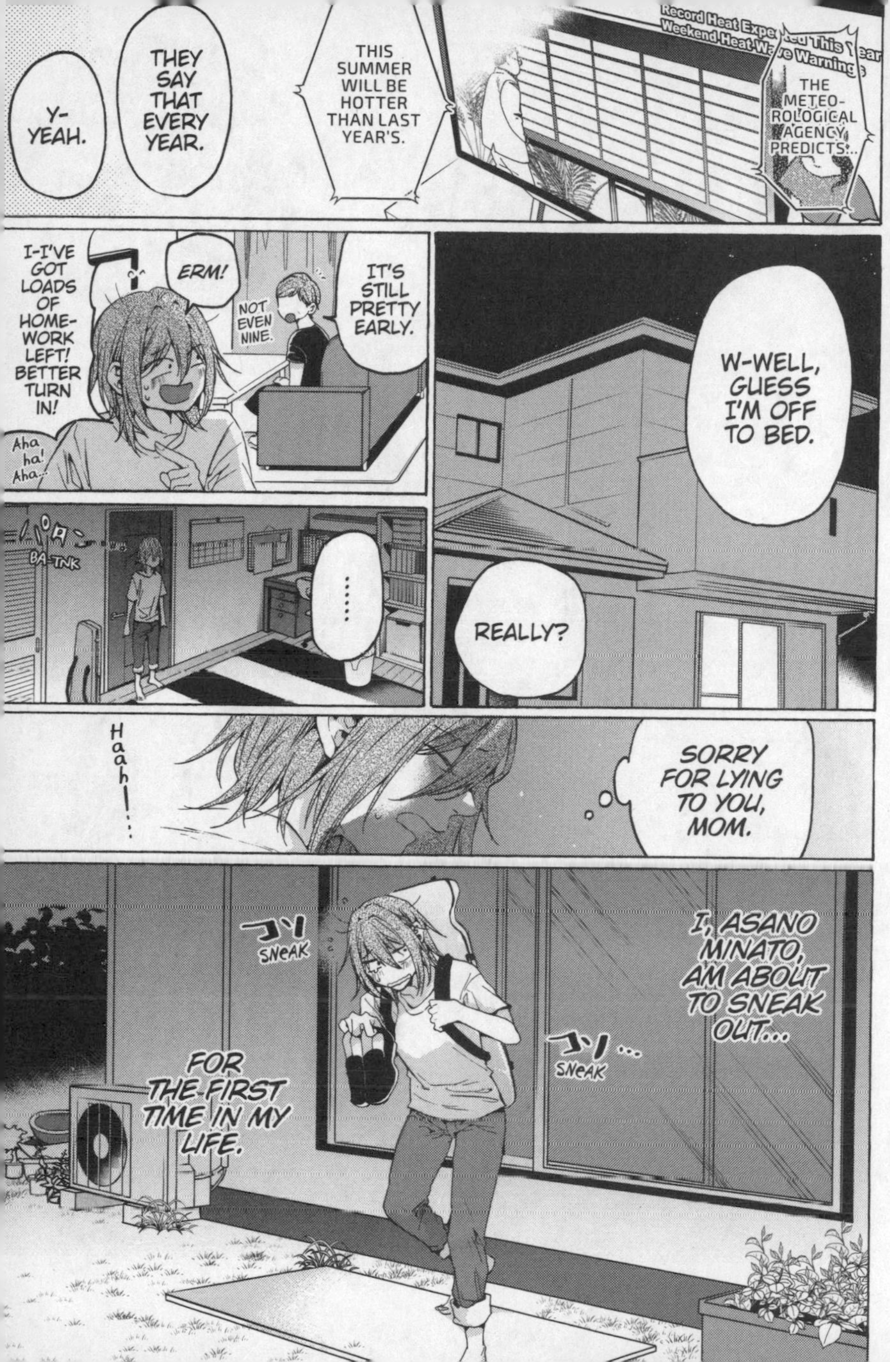
Record Heat Expected This Year
Weekend Heat Wave Warning
THE METEOROLOGICAL AGENCY PREDICTS...
THIS SUMMER WILL BE HOTTER THAN LAST YEAR'S.
THEY SAY THAT EVERY YEAR.
Y-YEAH.
W-WELL, GUESS I'M OFF TO BED.
REALLY?
IT'S STILL PRETTY EARLY.
NOT EVEN NINE.
ERM!
I-I'VE GOT LOADS OF HOMEWORK LEFT! BETTER TURN IN!
Aha ha! Aha...
......
BA-TNK
SORRY FOR LYING TO YOU, MOM.
Haaah...
I, ASANO MINATO, AM ABOUT TO SNEAK OUT...
SNEAK
SNEAK
FOR THE FIRST TIME IN MY LIFE.

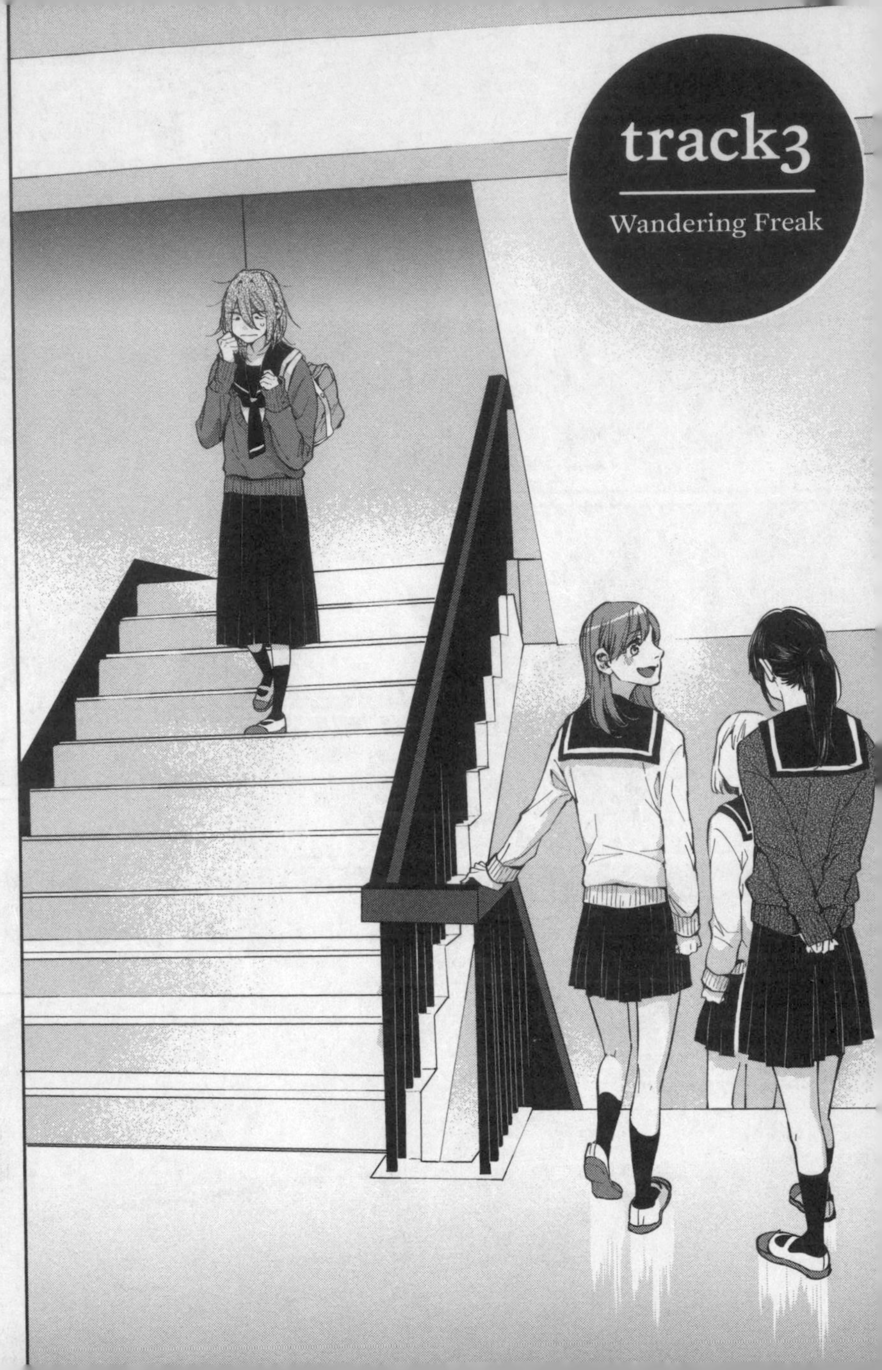
track3
Wandering Freak

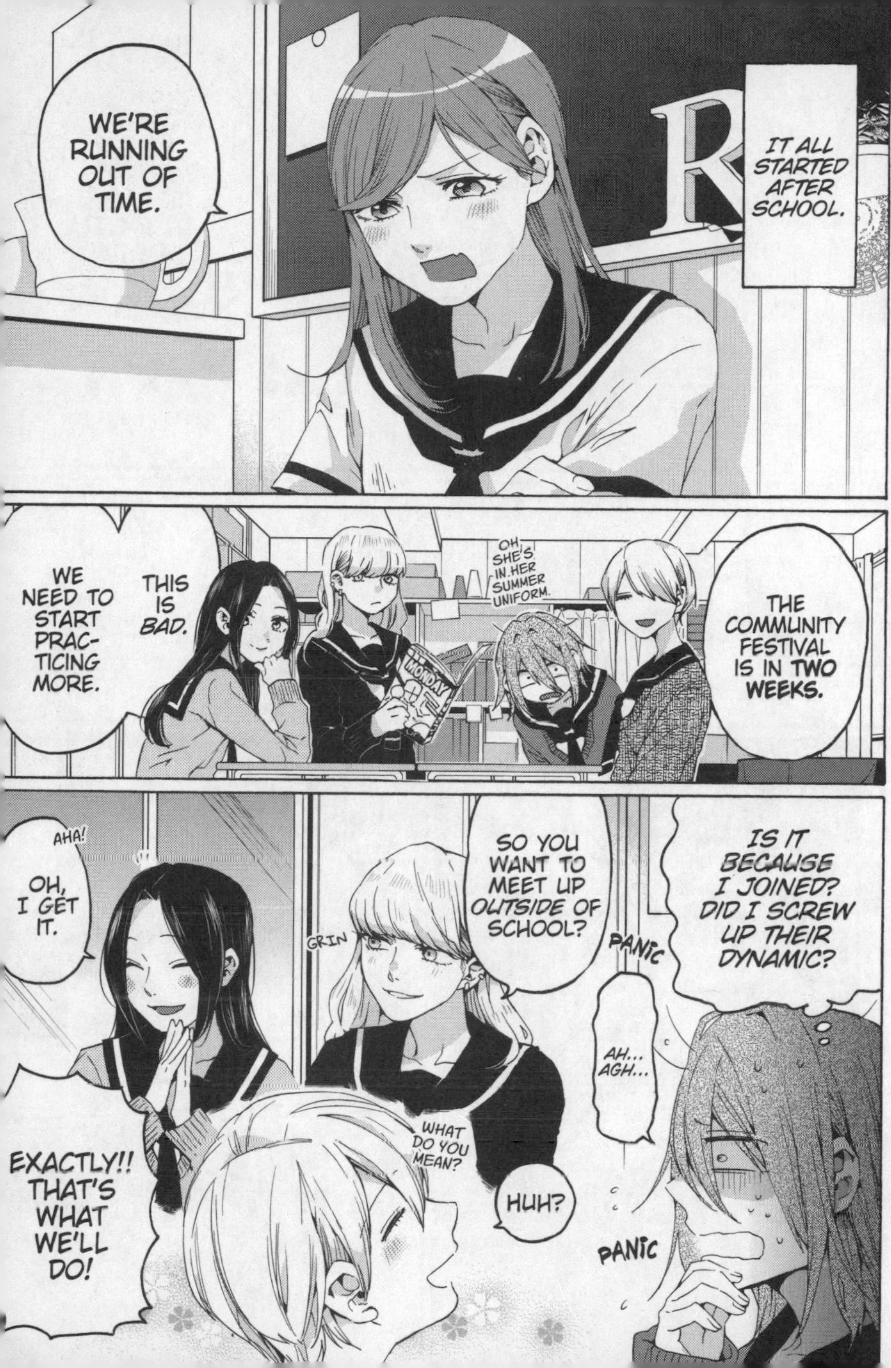
IT ALL STARTED AFTER SCHOOL.
WE'RE RUNNING OUT OF TIME.
THE COMMUNITY FESTIVAL IS IN TWO WEEKS.
OH, SHE'S IN HER SUMMER UNIFORM.
THIS IS BAD.
WE NEED TO START PRAC-TICING MORE.
IS IT BECAUSE I JOINED? DID I SCREW UP THEIR DYNAMIC?
PANIC
AH... AGH...
SO YOU WANT TO MEET UP OUTSIDE OF SCHOOL?
GRIN
AHA!
OH, I GET IT.
WHAT DO YOU MEAN?
HUH?
PANIC
EXACTLY!! THAT'S WHAT WE'LL DO!

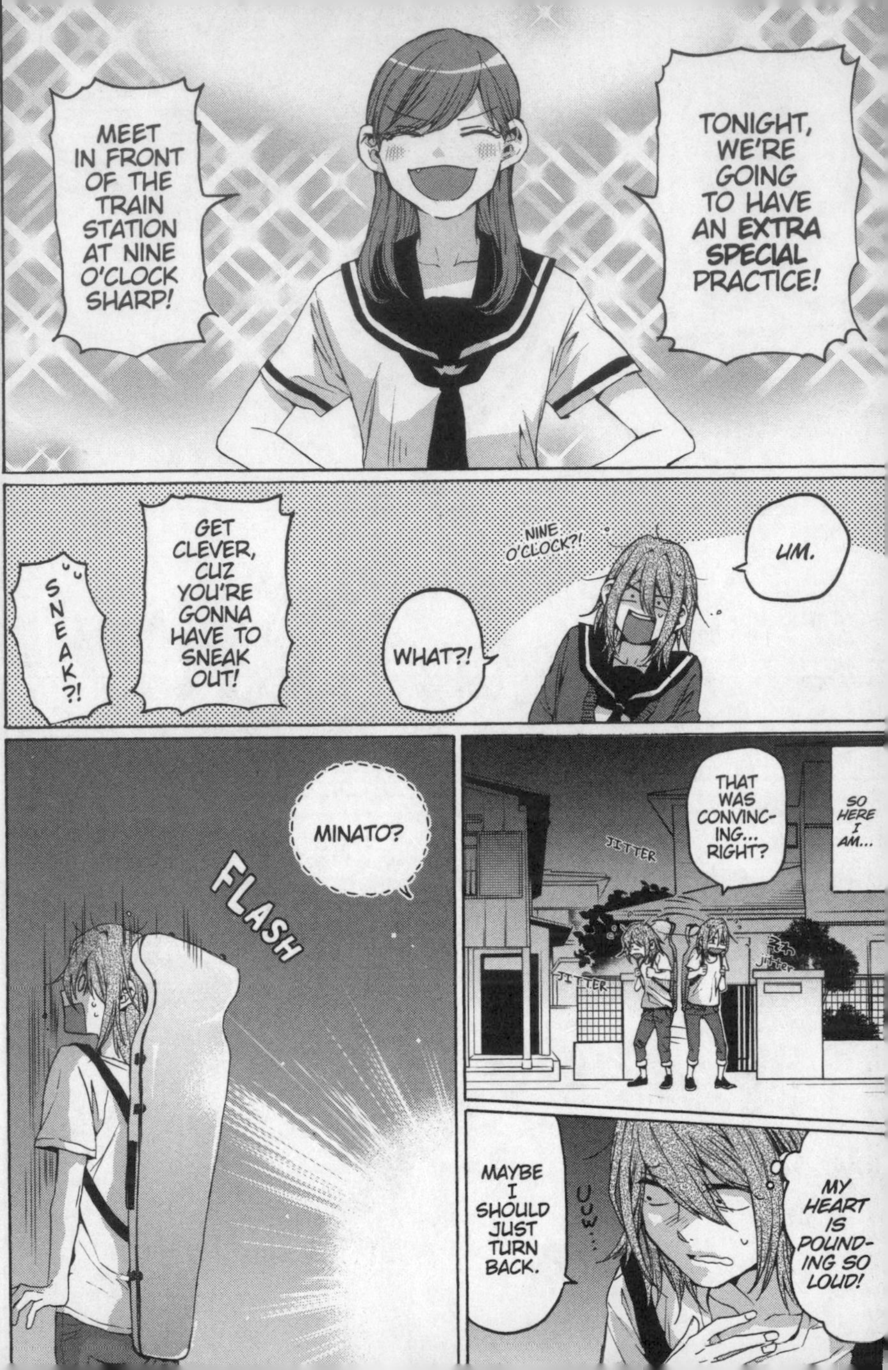
TONIGHT, WE'RE GOING TO HAVE AN EXTRA SPECIAL PRACTICE!
MEET IN FRONT OF THE TRAIN STATION AT NINE O'CLOCK SHARP!
UM.
NINE O'CLOCK?!
WHAT?!
GET CLEVER, CUZ YOU'RE GONNA HAVE TO SNEAK OUT!
SNEAK?!
SO HERE I AM...
THAT WAS CONVINCING... RIGHT?
JITTER
JITTER
jitter
MY HEART IS POUNDING SO LOUD!
UUW...
MAYBE I SHOULD JUST TURN BACK.
MINATO?
FLASH

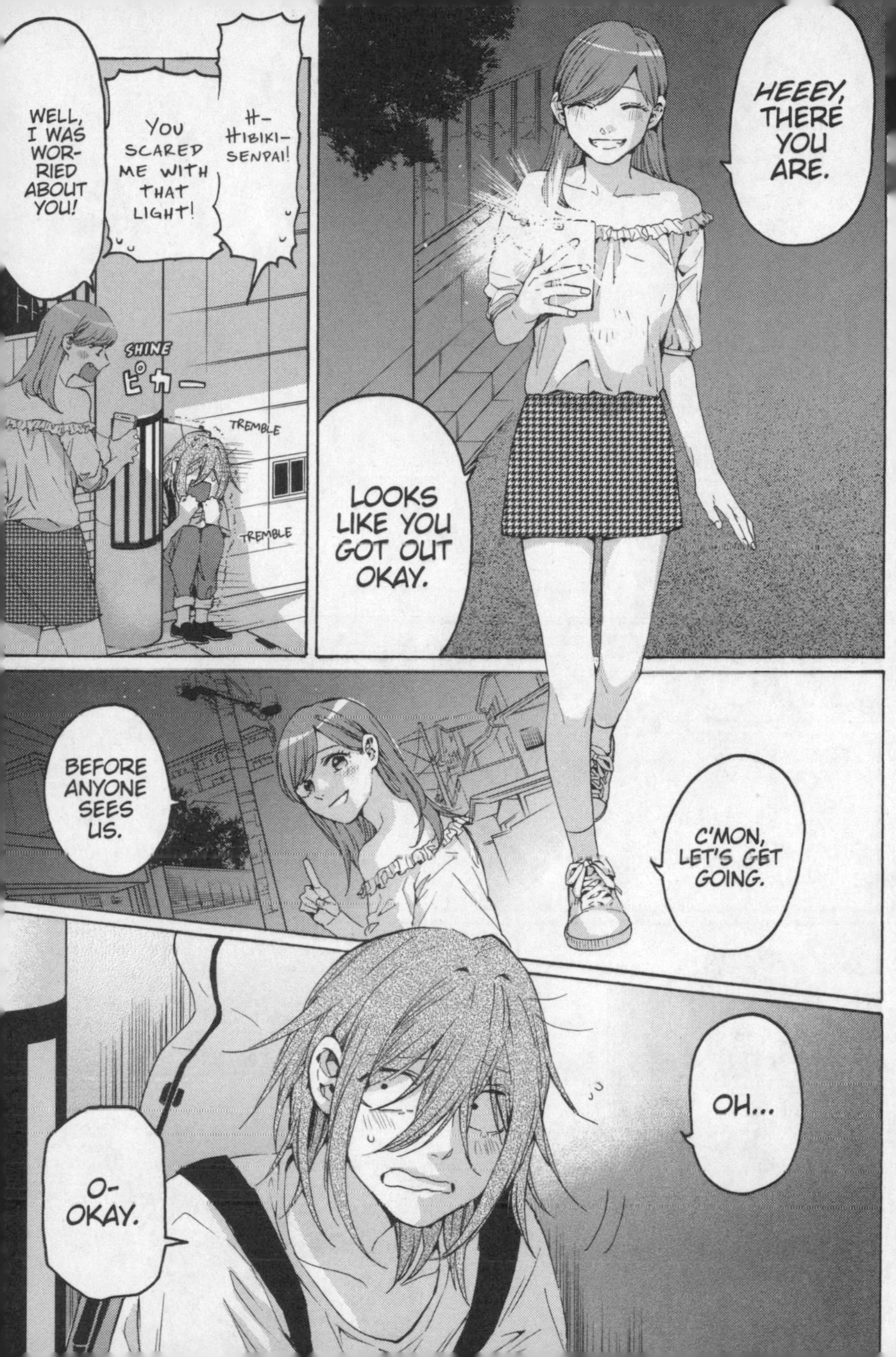
HEEEY, THERE YOU ARE.
LOOKS LIKE YOU GOT OUT OKAY.
H-HIBIKI-SENPAI!
YOU SCARED ME WITH THAT LIGHT!
WELL, I WAS WORRIED ABOUT YOU!
SHINE
ピカー
TREMBLE
TREMBLE
C'MON, LET'S GET GOING.
BEFORE ANYONE SEES US.
OH...
O-OKAY.

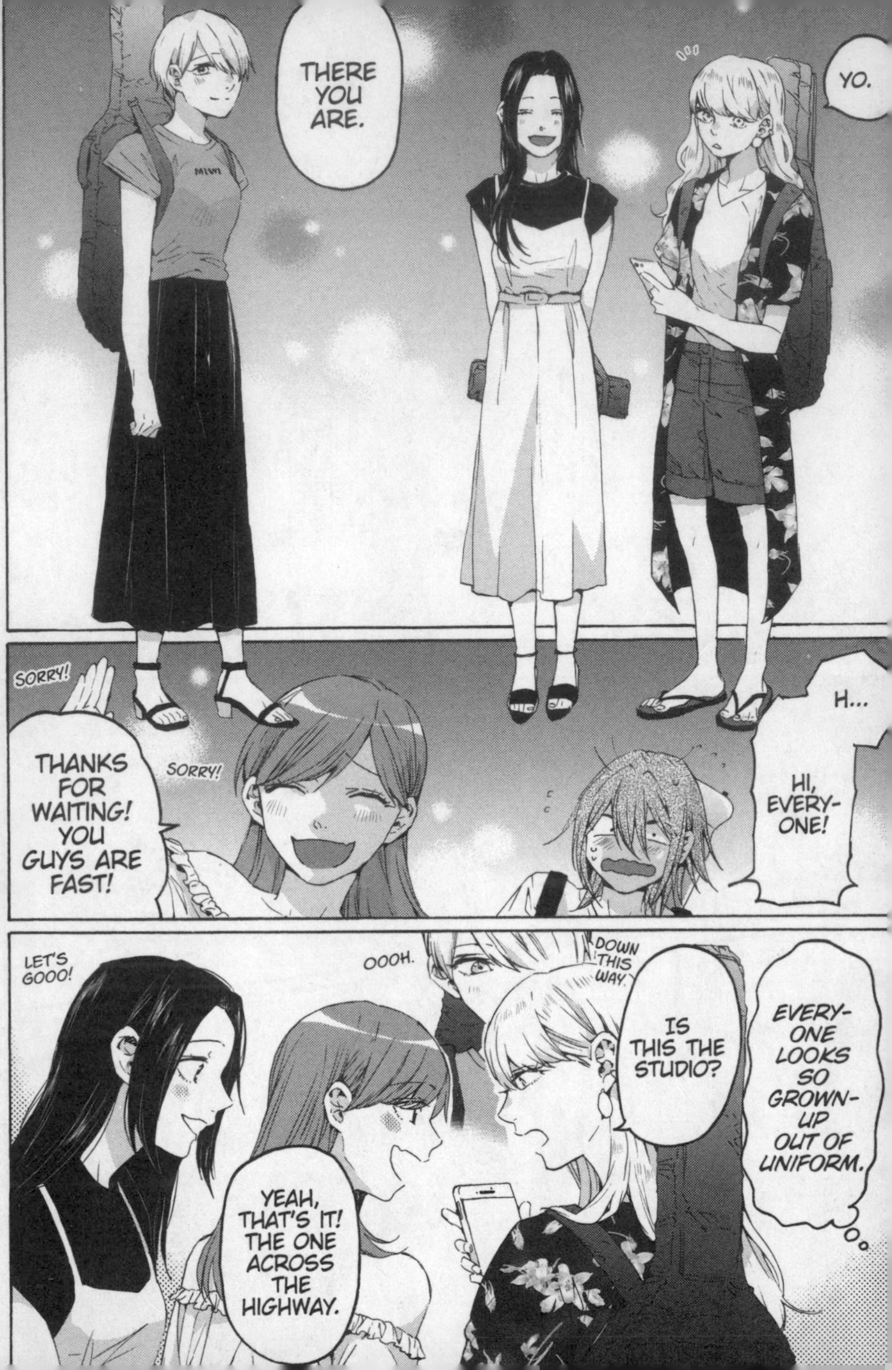
YO.
THERE YOU ARE.
H...
HI, EVERYONE!
SORRY!
SORRY!
THANKS FOR WAITING! YOU GUYS ARE FAST!
EVERYONE LOOKS SO GROWN-UP OUT OF UNIFORM.
IS THIS THE STUDIO?
DOWN THIS WAY.
OOOH.
YEAH, THAT'S IT! THE ONE ACROSS THE HIGHWAY.
LET'S GOOO!

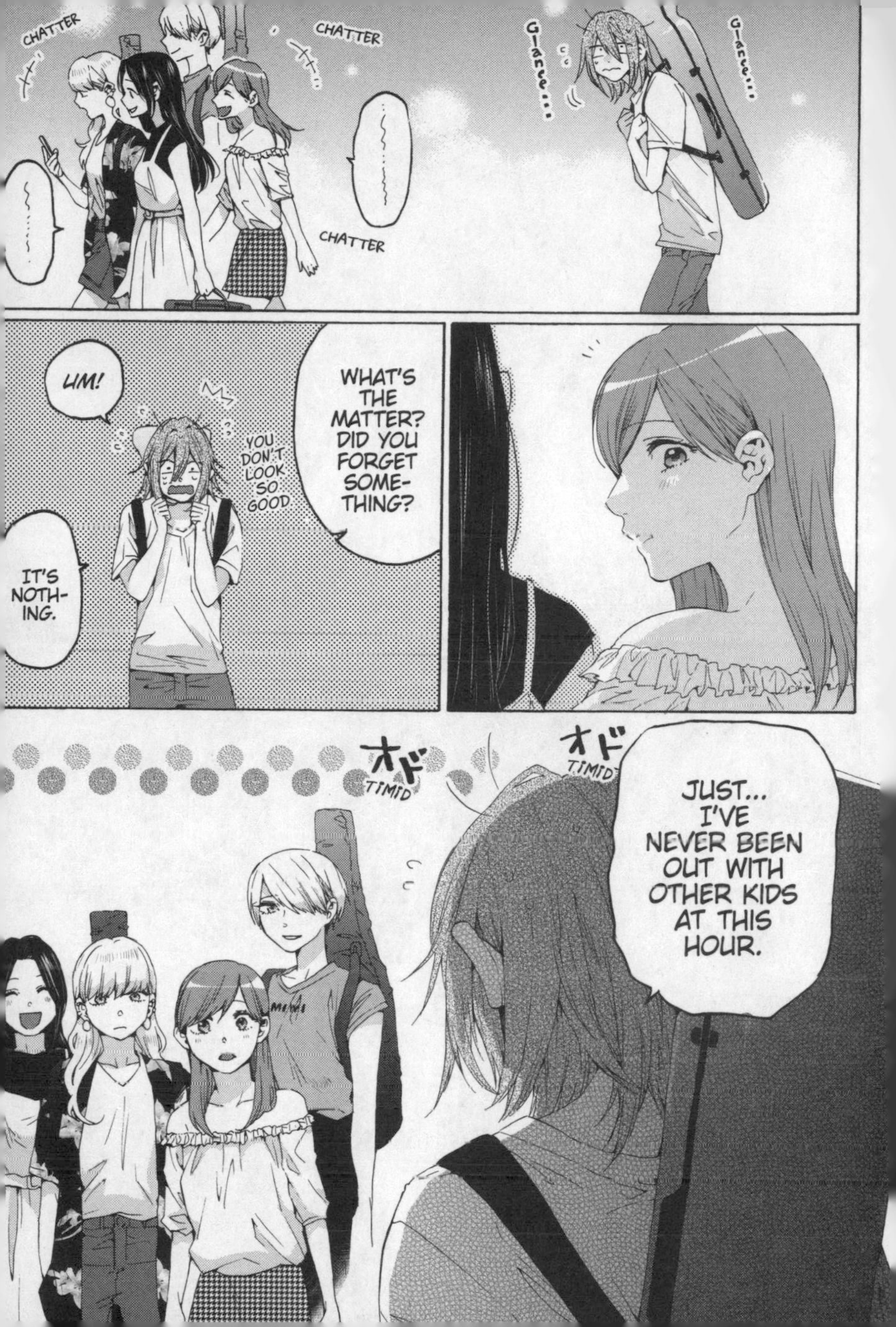
Glance...
Glance...
CHATTER
CHATTER
CHATTER
WHAT'S THE MATTER? DID YOU FORGET SOME-THING?
UM!
YOU DON'T LOOK SO GOOD
IT'S NOTH-ING.
オド TIMID
オド TIMID
JUST... I'VE NEVER BEEN OUT WITH OTHER KIDS AT THIS HOUR.

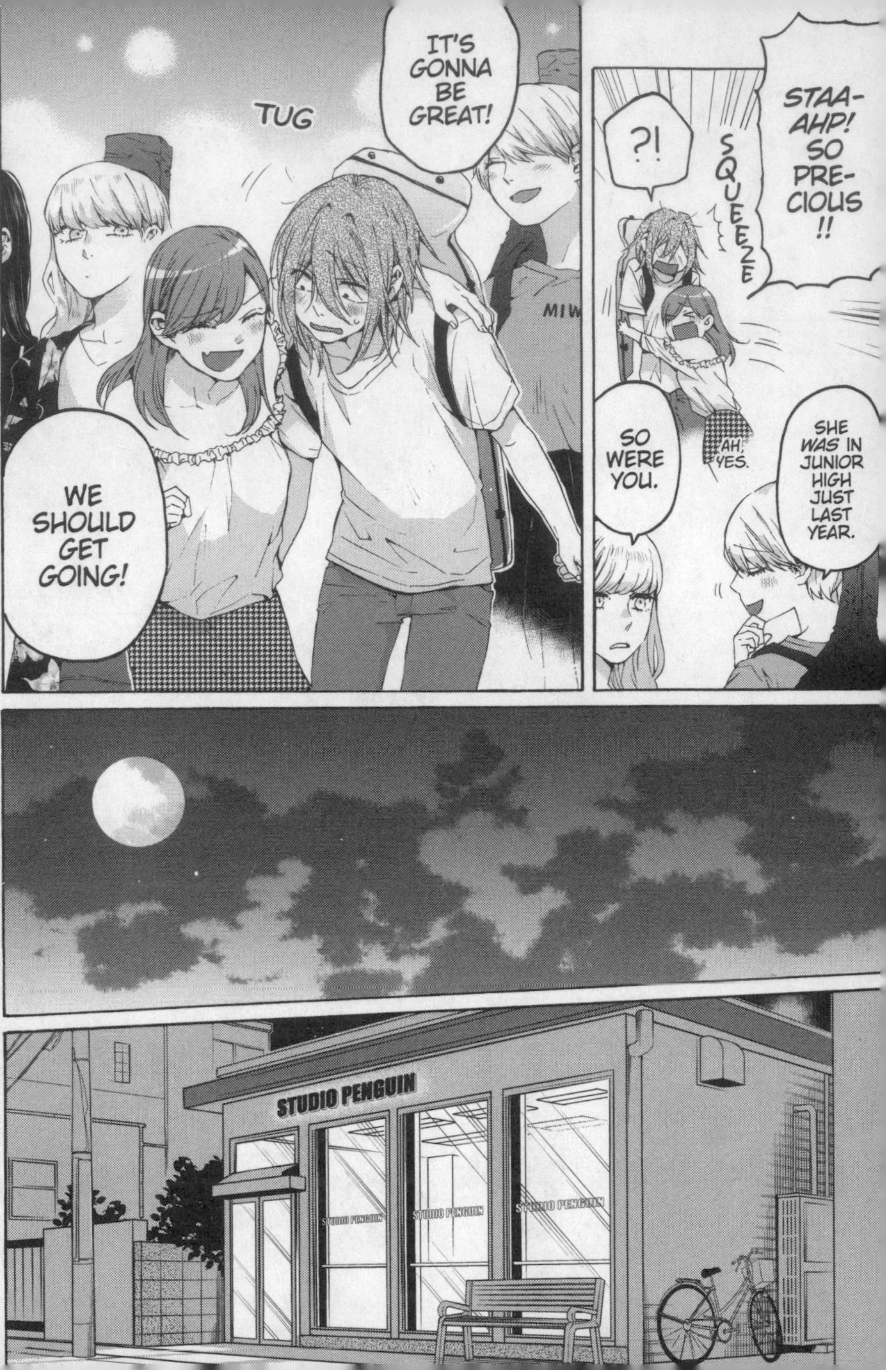
STAA-AHP! SO PRE-CIOUS!!
?!
SQUEEZE
SHE WAS IN JUNIOR HIGH JUST LAST YEAR.
AH, YES.
SO WERE YOU.
IT'S GONNA BE GREAT!
TUG
MIW
WE SHOULD GET GOING!
STUDIO PENGUIN
STUDIO PENGUIN
STUDIO PENGUIN
STUDIO PENGUIN

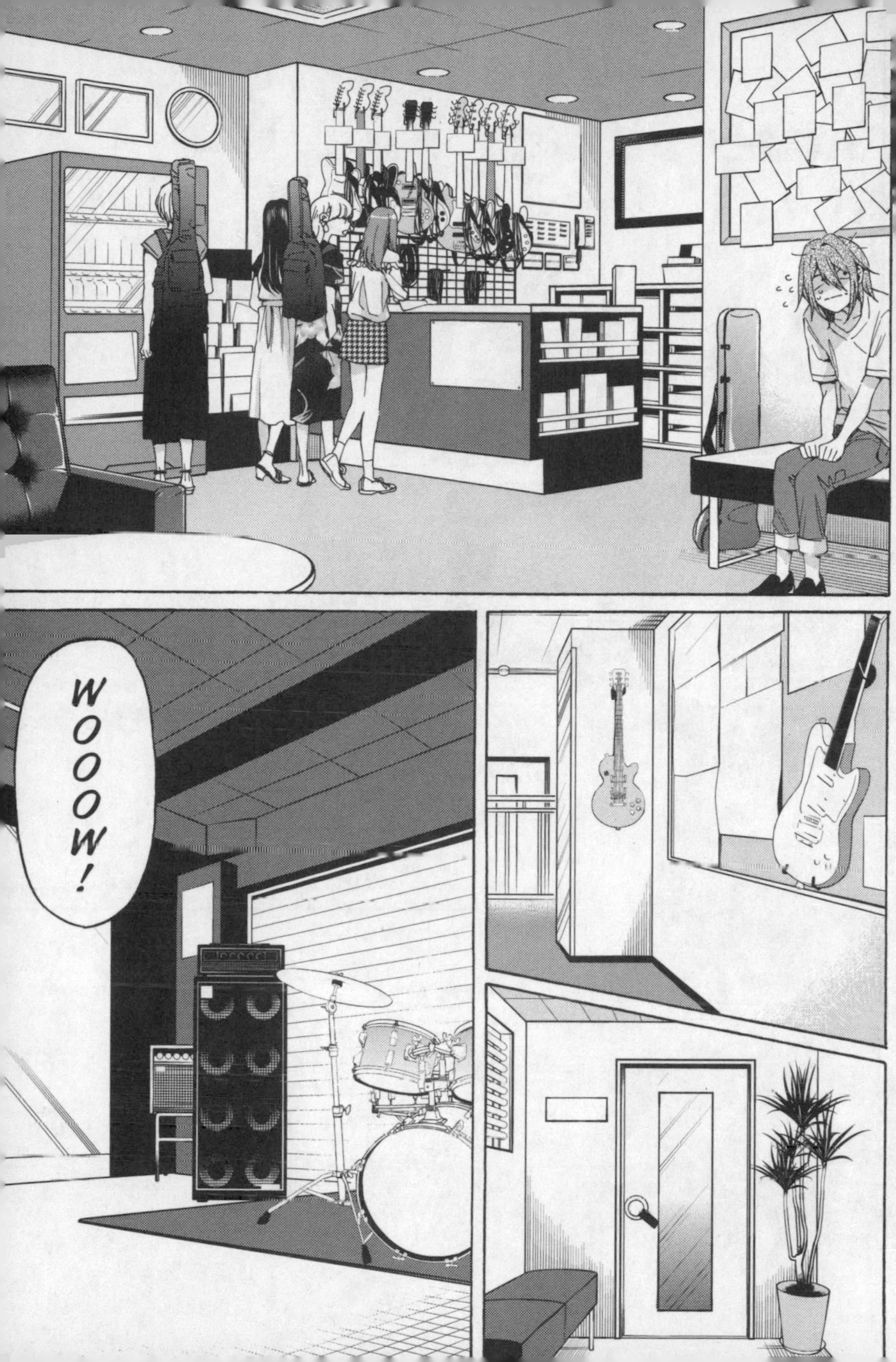
WOOOW!

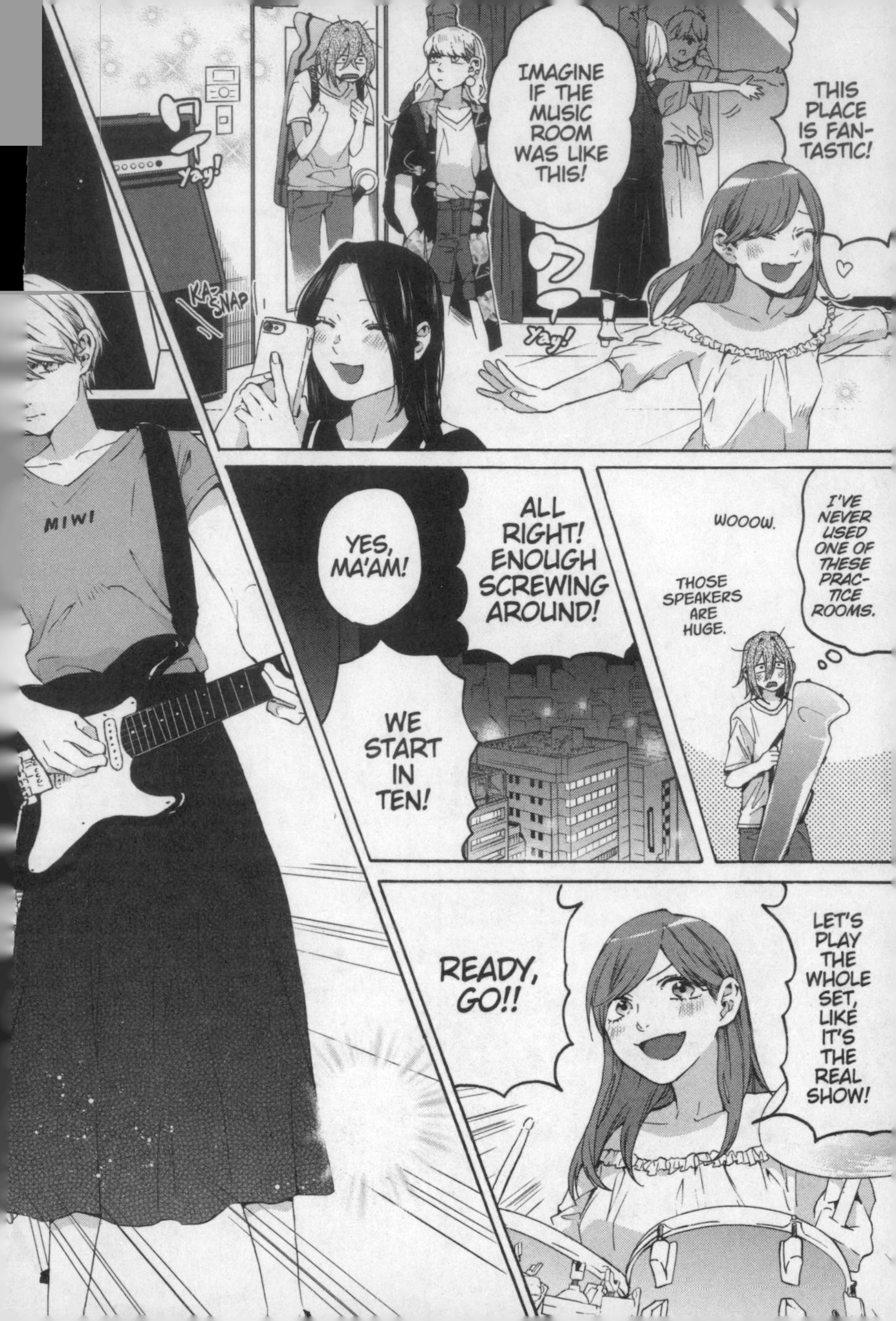
THIS PLACE IS FANTASTIC!
Yay!
IMAGINE IF THE MUSIC ROOM WAS LIKE THIS!
Yay!
KA-SNAP
I'VE NEVER USED ONE OF THESE PRACTICE ROOMS.
WOOOW.
THOSE SPEAKERS ARE HUGE.
ALL RIGHT! ENOUGH SCREWING AROUND!
YES, MA'AM!
WE START IN TEN!
LET'S PLAY THE WHOLE SET, LIKE IT'S THE REAL SHOW!
READY, GO!!
MIWI

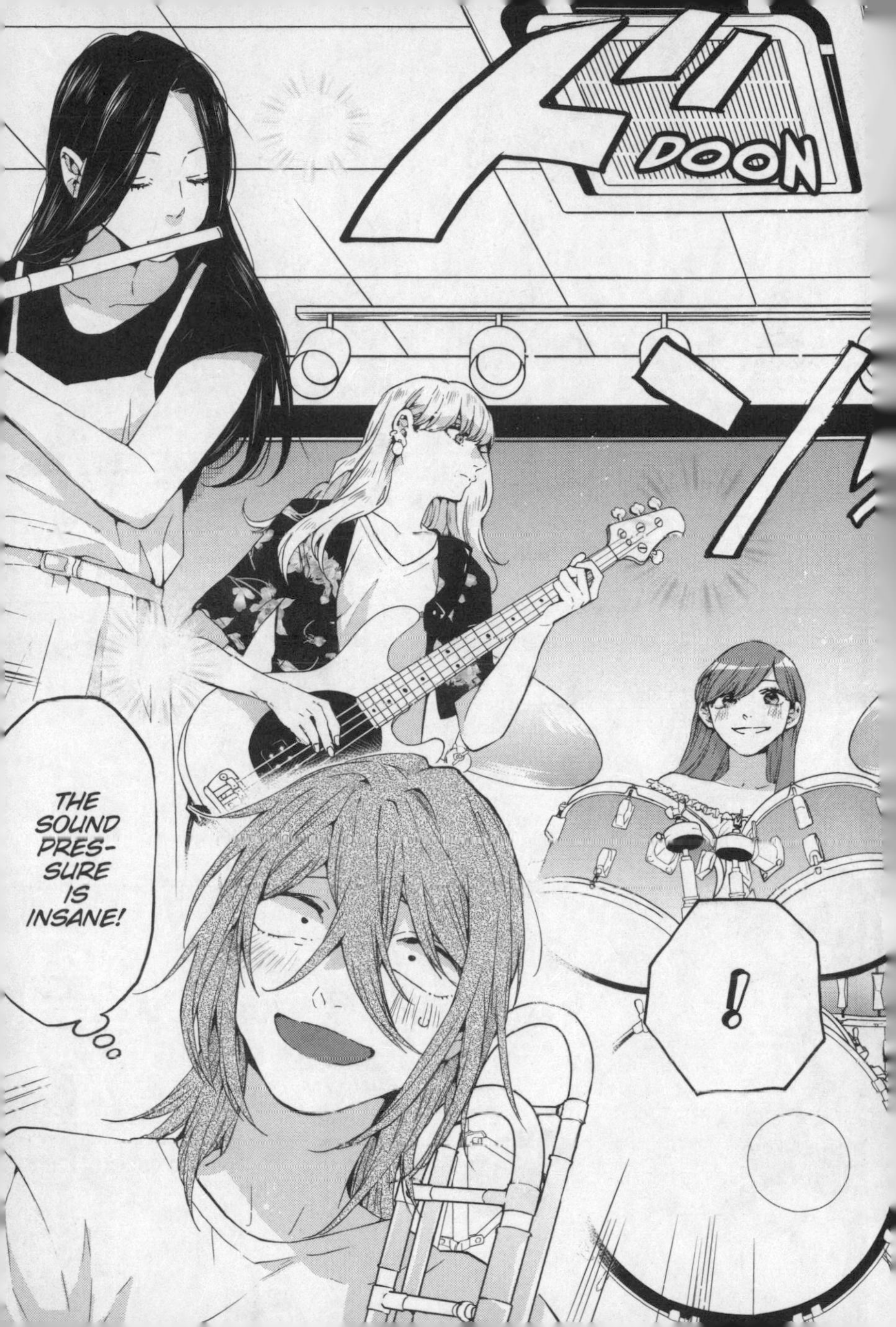
DOON
THE SOUND PRES-SURE IS INSANE!
!

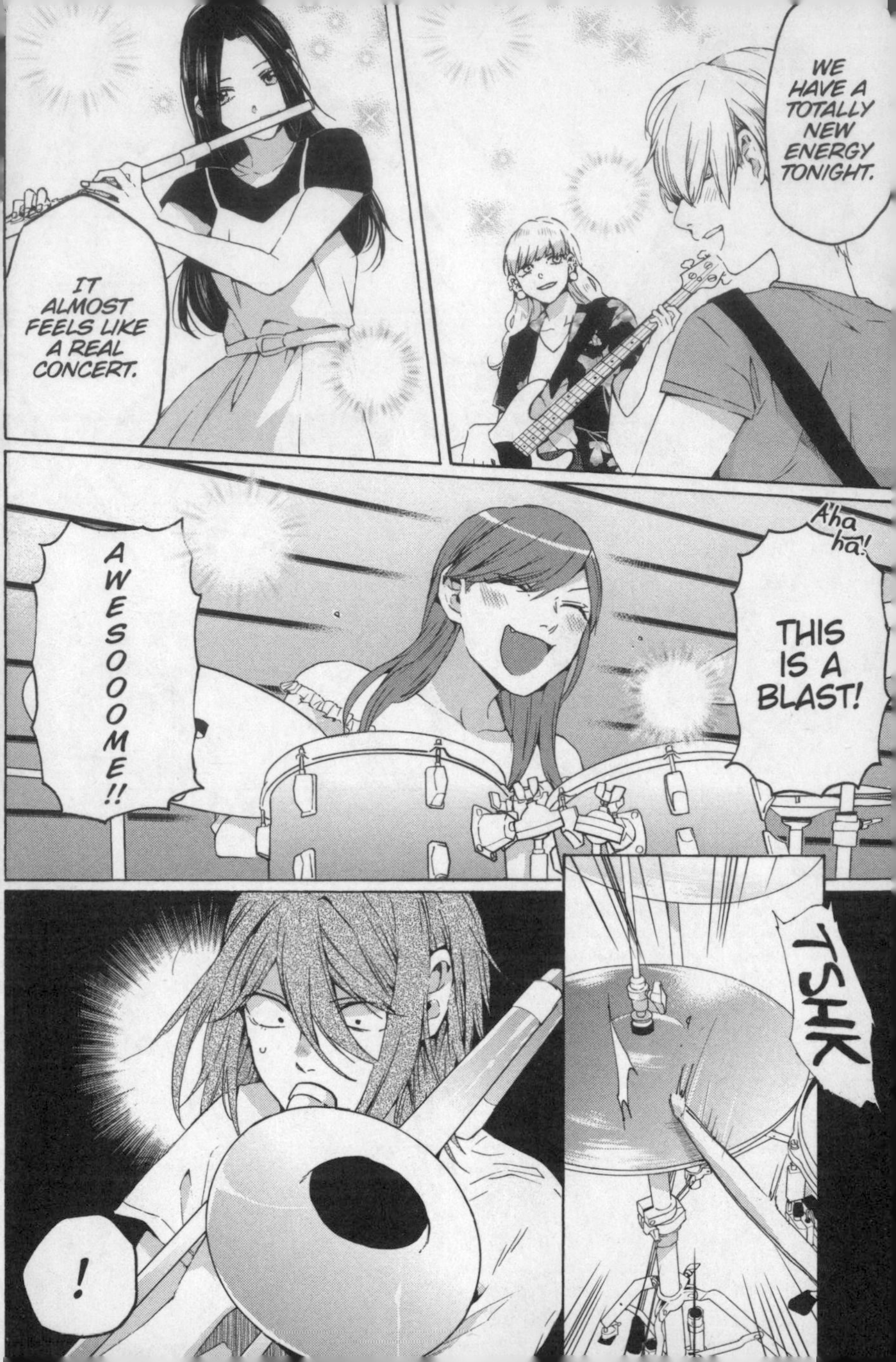
WE HAVE A TOTALLY NEW ENERGY TONIGHT.
IT ALMOST FEELS LIKE A REAL CONCERT.
A'ha ha!
THIS IS A BLAST!
AWESOOOOME!!
TSHK
!

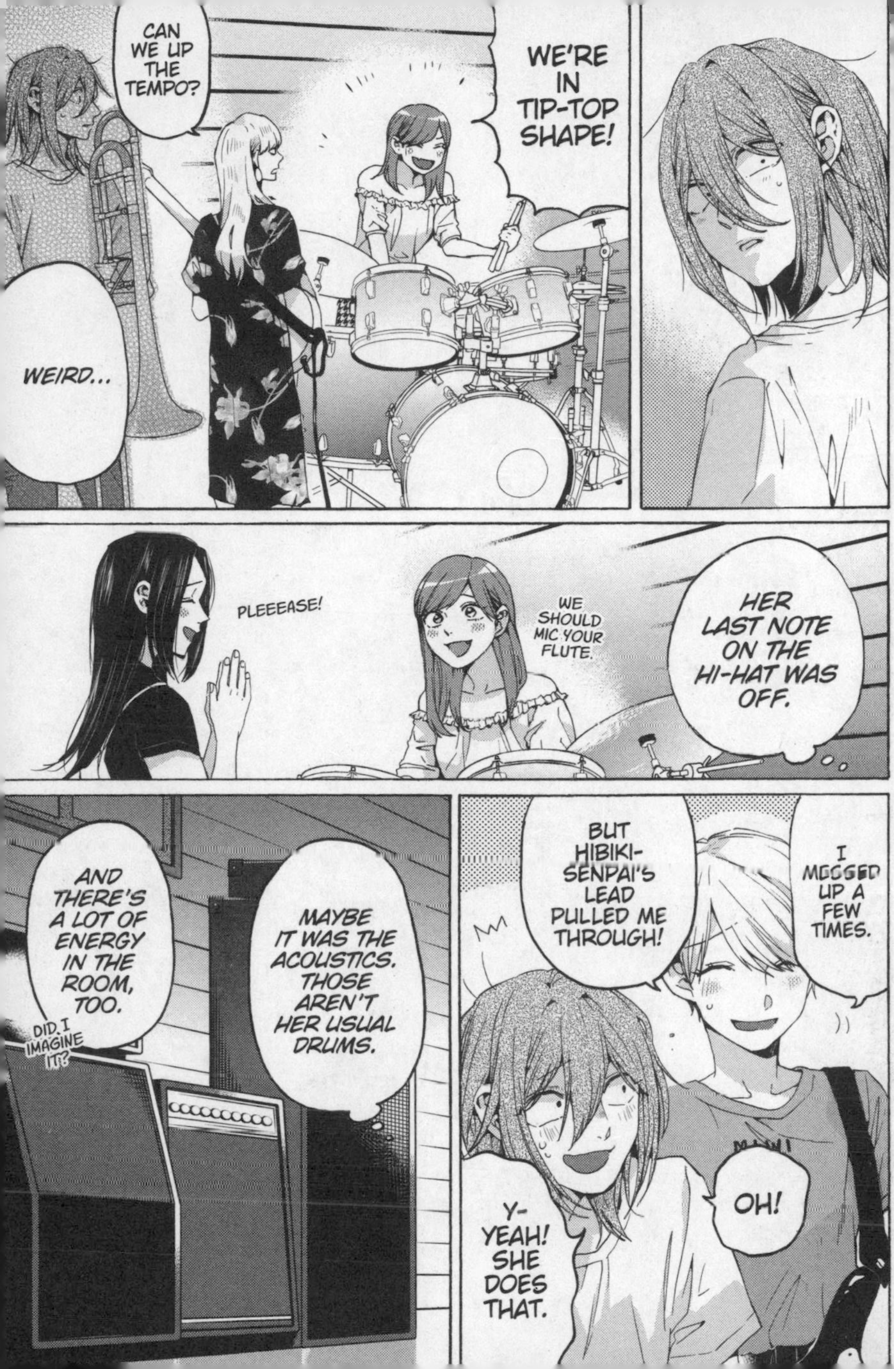
WE'RE IN TIP-TOP SHAPE!
CAN WE UP THE TEMPO?
WEIRD...
HER LAST NOTE ON THE HI-HAT WAS OFF.
WE SHOULD MIC YOUR FLUTE.
PLEEEASE!
I MESSED UP A FEW TIMES.
BUT HIBIKI-SENPAI'S LEAD PULLED ME THROUGH!
OH!
Y-YEAH! SHE DOES THAT.
MAYBE IT WAS THE ACOUSTICS. THOSE AREN'T HER USUAL DRUMS.
AND THERE'S A LOT OF ENERGY IN THE ROOM, TOO.
DID I IMAGINE IT?

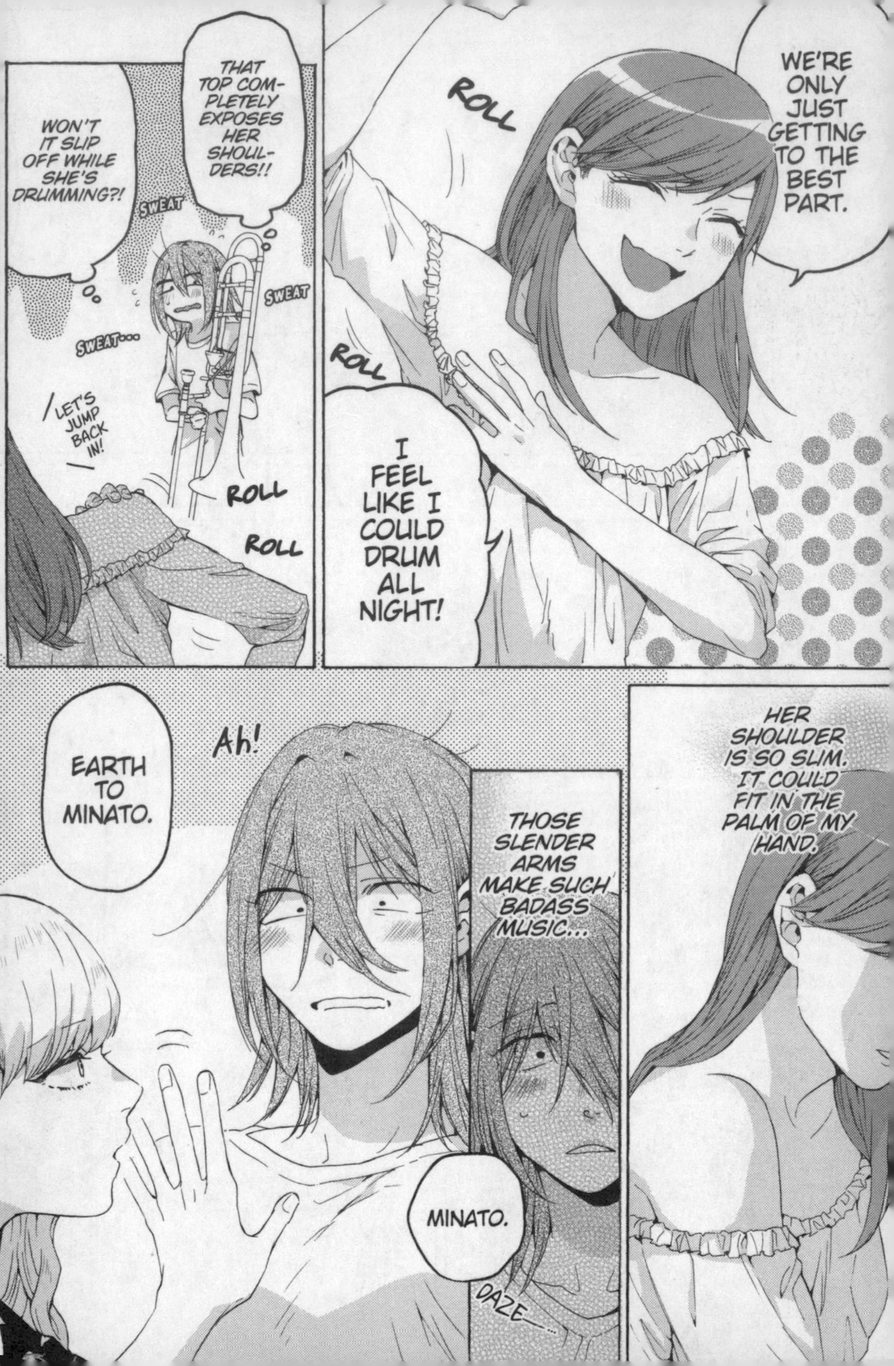
WE'RE ONLY JUST GETTING TO THE BEST PART.
ROLL
ROLL
I FEEL LIKE I COULD DRUM ALL NIGHT!
THAT TOP COMPLETELY EXPOSES HER SHOULDERS!!
WON'T IT SLIP OFF WHILE SHE'S DRUMMING?!
SWEAT
SWEAT
SWEAT...
LET'S JUMP BACK IN!
ROLL
ROLL
HER SHOULDER IS SO SLIM. IT COULD FIT IN THE PALM OF MY HAND.
THOSE SLENDER ARMS MAKE SUCH BADASS MUSIC...
MINATO.
DAZE...
Ah!
EARTH TO MINATO.

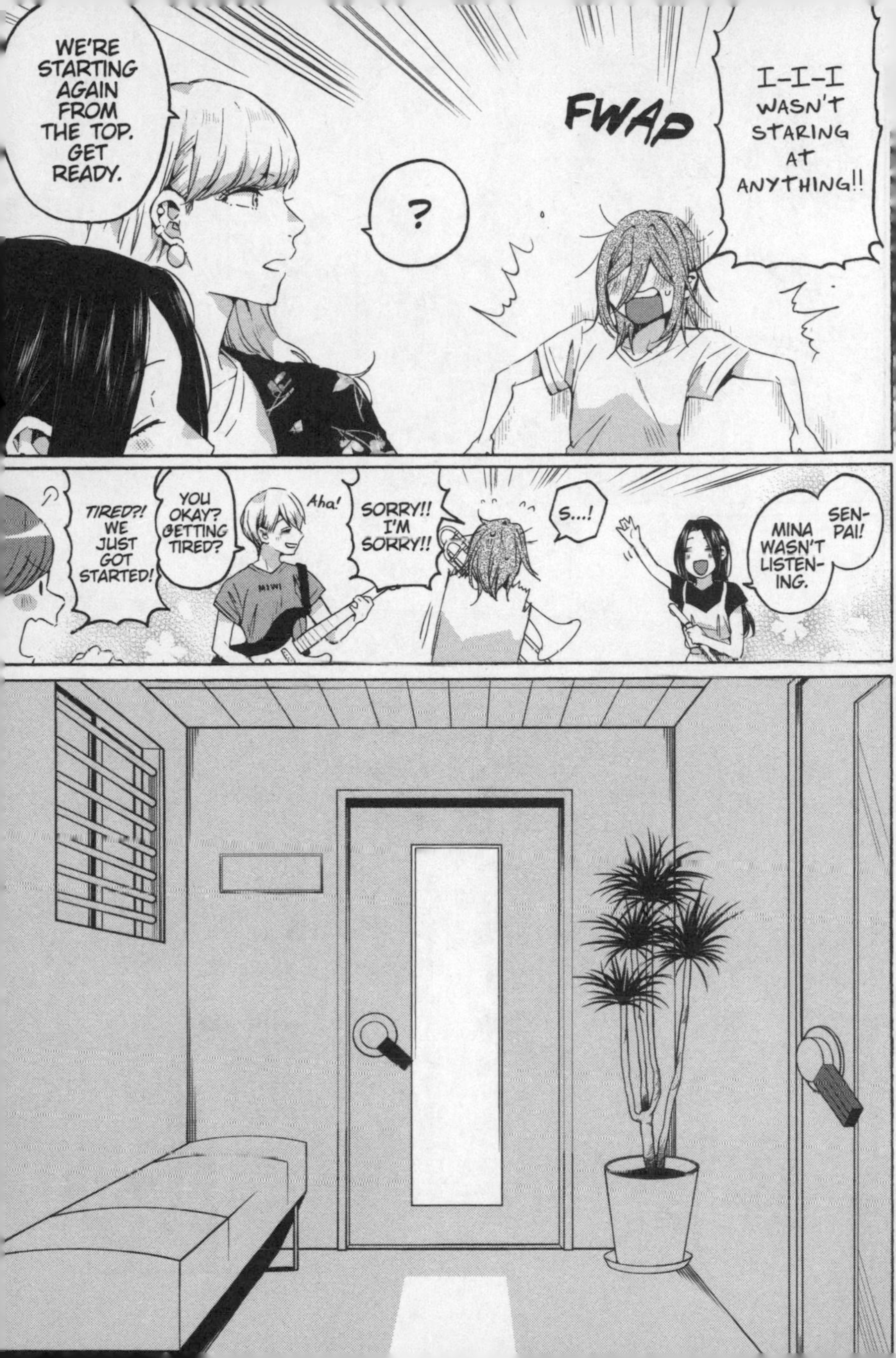

I-I-I WASN'T STARING AT ANYTHING!!
FWAP
?
WE'RE STARTING AGAIN FROM THE TOP. GET READY.
SEN-PAI! MINA WASN'T LISTEN-ING.
S...!
SORRY!! I'M SORRY!!
Aha!
YOU OKAY? GETTING TIRED?
TIRED?! WE JUST GOT STARTED!

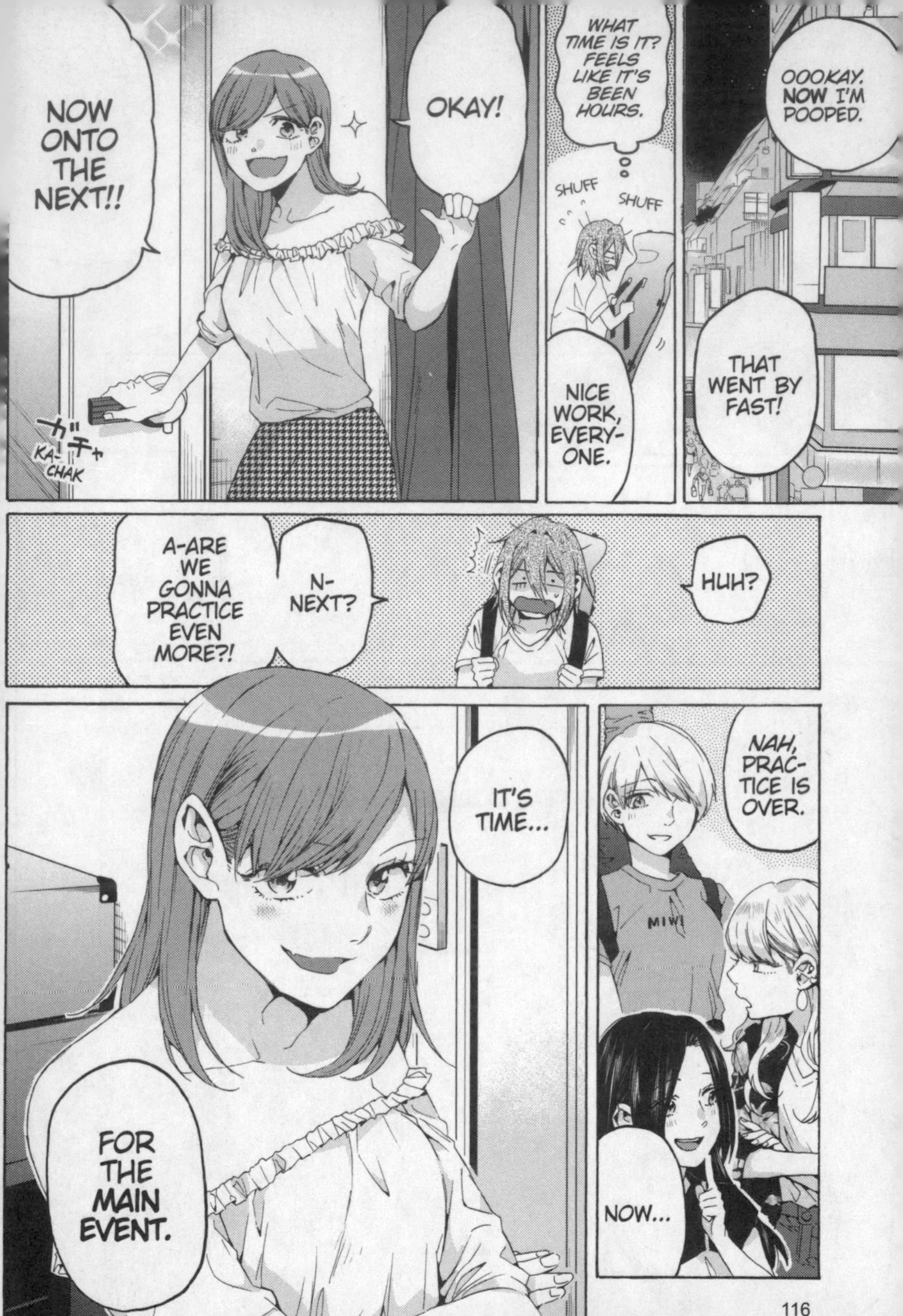
OOOKAY. NOW I'M POOPED.
THAT WENT BY FAST!
WHAT TIME IS IT? FEELS LIKE IT'S BEEN HOURS.
SHUFF
SHUFF
NICE WORK, EVERY-ONE.
OKAY!
NOW ONTO THE NEXT!!
ガチャ KA-CHAK
HUH?
N-NEXT?
A-ARE WE GONNA PRACTICE EVEN MORE?!
NAH, PRAC-TICE IS OVER.
NOW...
IT'S TIME...
FOR THE MAIN EVENT.
MIWI

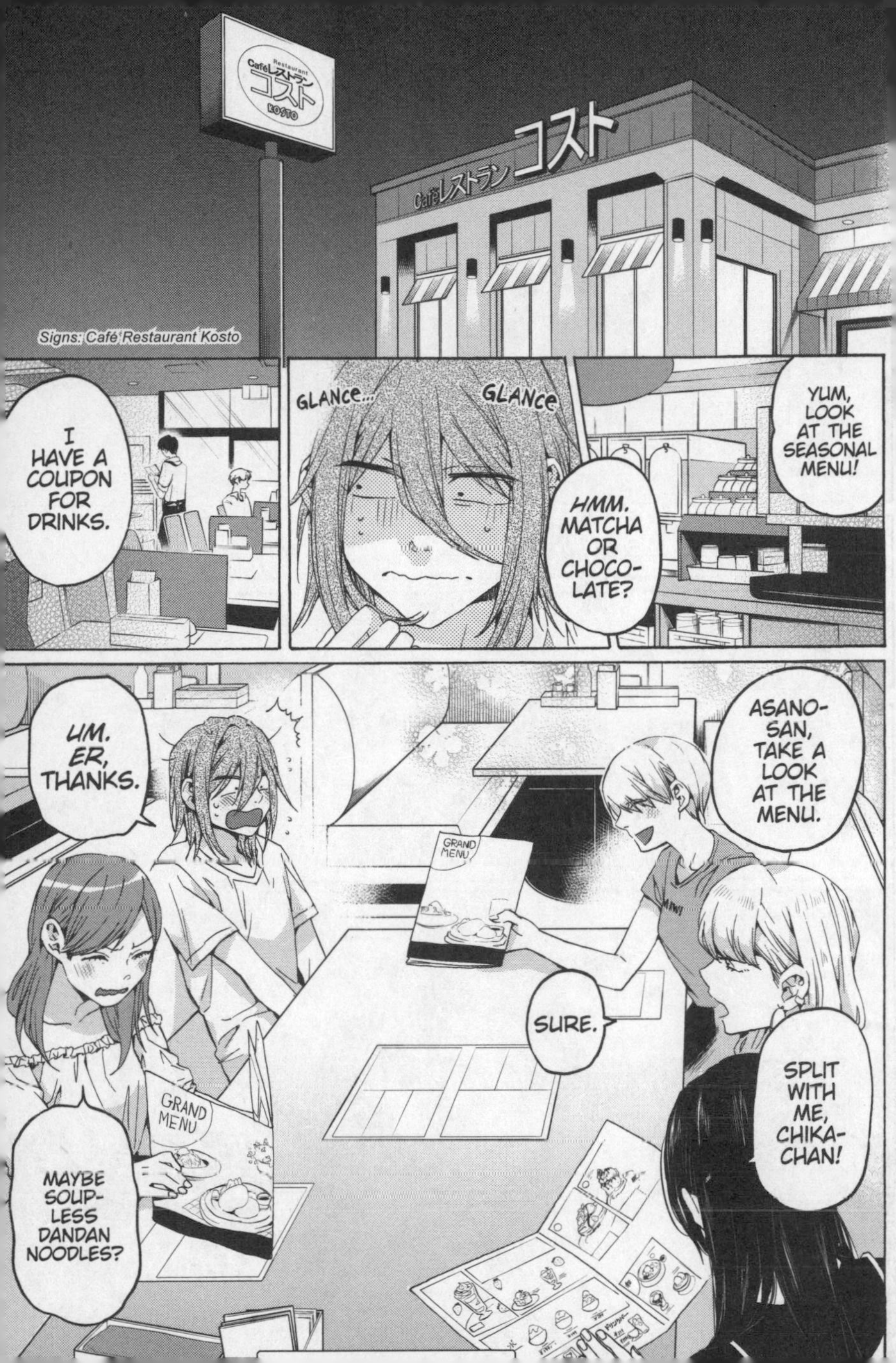
Restaurant
Caféレストラン
コスト
KOSTO
Caféレストランコスト
Signs: Café Restaurant Kosto
YUM, LOOK AT THE SEASONAL MENU!
GLANCE...
GLANCE
HMM. MATCHA OR CHOCO-LATE?
I HAVE A COUPON FOR DRINKS.
ASANO-SAN, TAKE A LOOK AT THE MENU.
UM. ER, THANKS.
GRAND MENU
SURE.
SPLIT WITH ME, CHIKA-CHAN!
GRAND MENU
MAYBE SOUP-LESS DANDAN NOODLES?

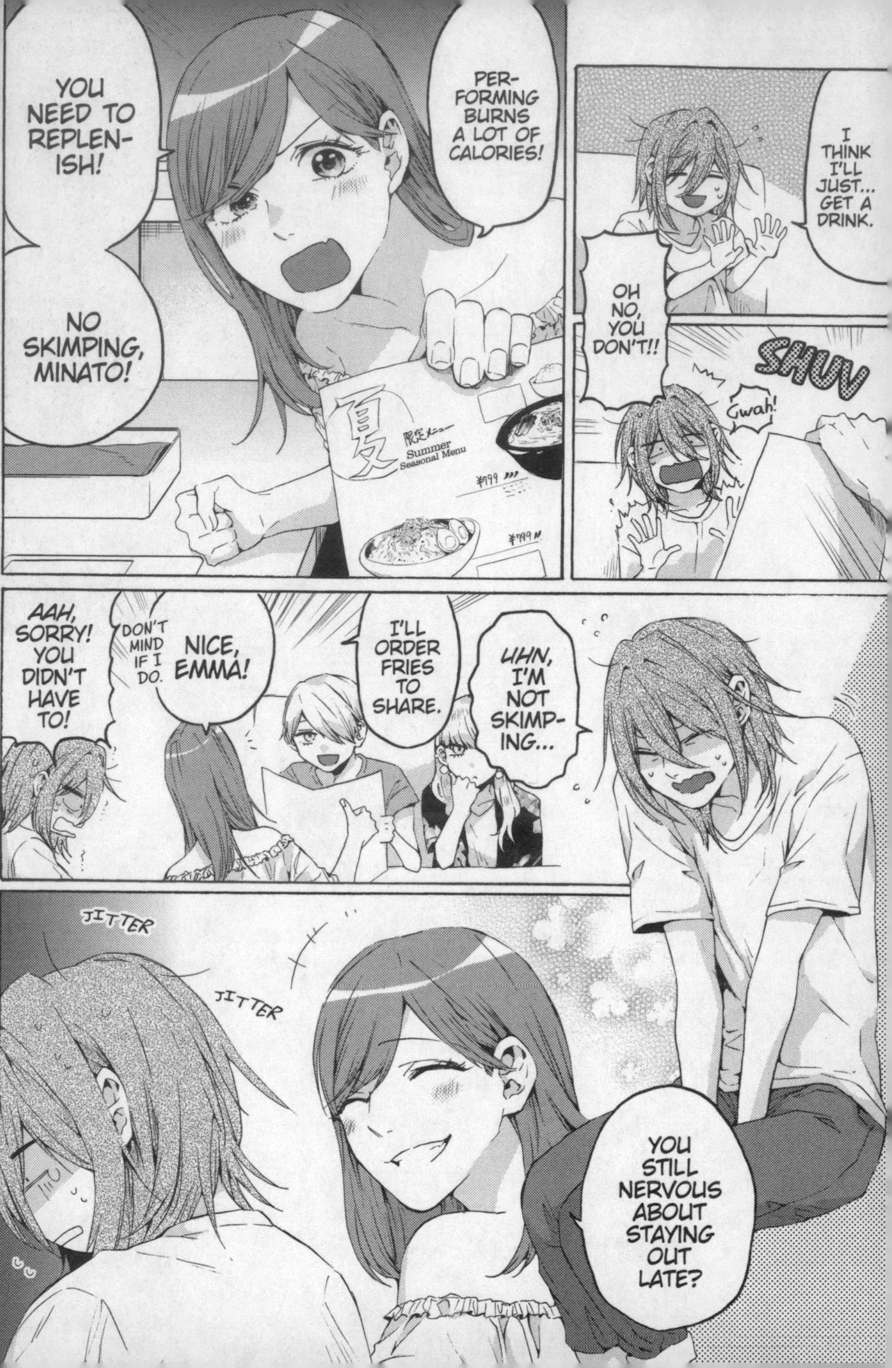
I THINK I'LL JUST... GET A DRINK.
OH NO, YOU DON'T!!
SHUV
Gwah!
PER-FORMING BURNS A LOT OF CALORIES!
YOU NEED TO REPLEN-ISH!
NO SKIMPING, MINATO!
夏
限定メニュー
Summer Seasonal Menu
¥799
¥799
UHN, I'M NOT SKIMP-ING...
I'LL ORDER FRIES TO SHARE.
NICE, EMMA!
DON'T MIND IF I DO.
AAH, SORRY! YOU DIDN'T HAVE TO!
JITTER
JITTER
YOU STILL NERVOUS ABOUT STAYING OUT LATE?

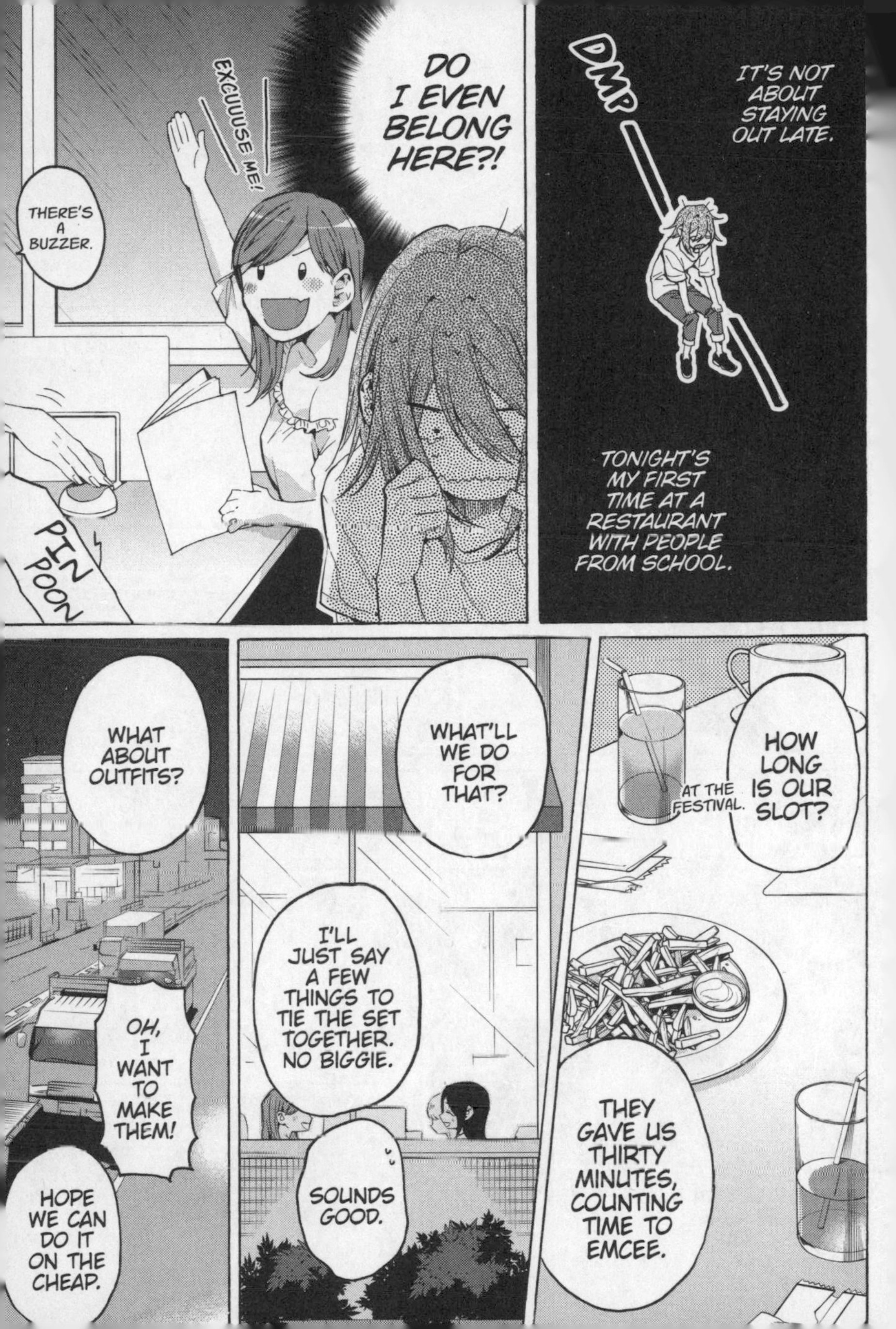
DMP
IT'S NOT ABOUT STAYING OUT LATE.
TONIGHT'S MY FIRST TIME AT A RESTAURANT WITH PEOPLE FROM SCHOOL.
DO I EVEN BELONG HERE?!
EXCUUUSE ME!
THERE'S A BUZZER.
PIN POON
HOW LONG IS OUR SLOT?
AT THE FESTIVAL.
THEY GAVE US THIRTY MINUTES, COUNTING TIME TO EMCEE.
WHAT'LL WE DO FOR THAT?
I'LL JUST SAY A FEW THINGS TO TIE THE SET TOGETHER. NO BIGGIE.
SOUNDS GOOD.
WHAT ABOUT OUTFITS?
OH, I WANT TO MAKE THEM!
HOPE WE CAN DO IT ON THE CHEAP.

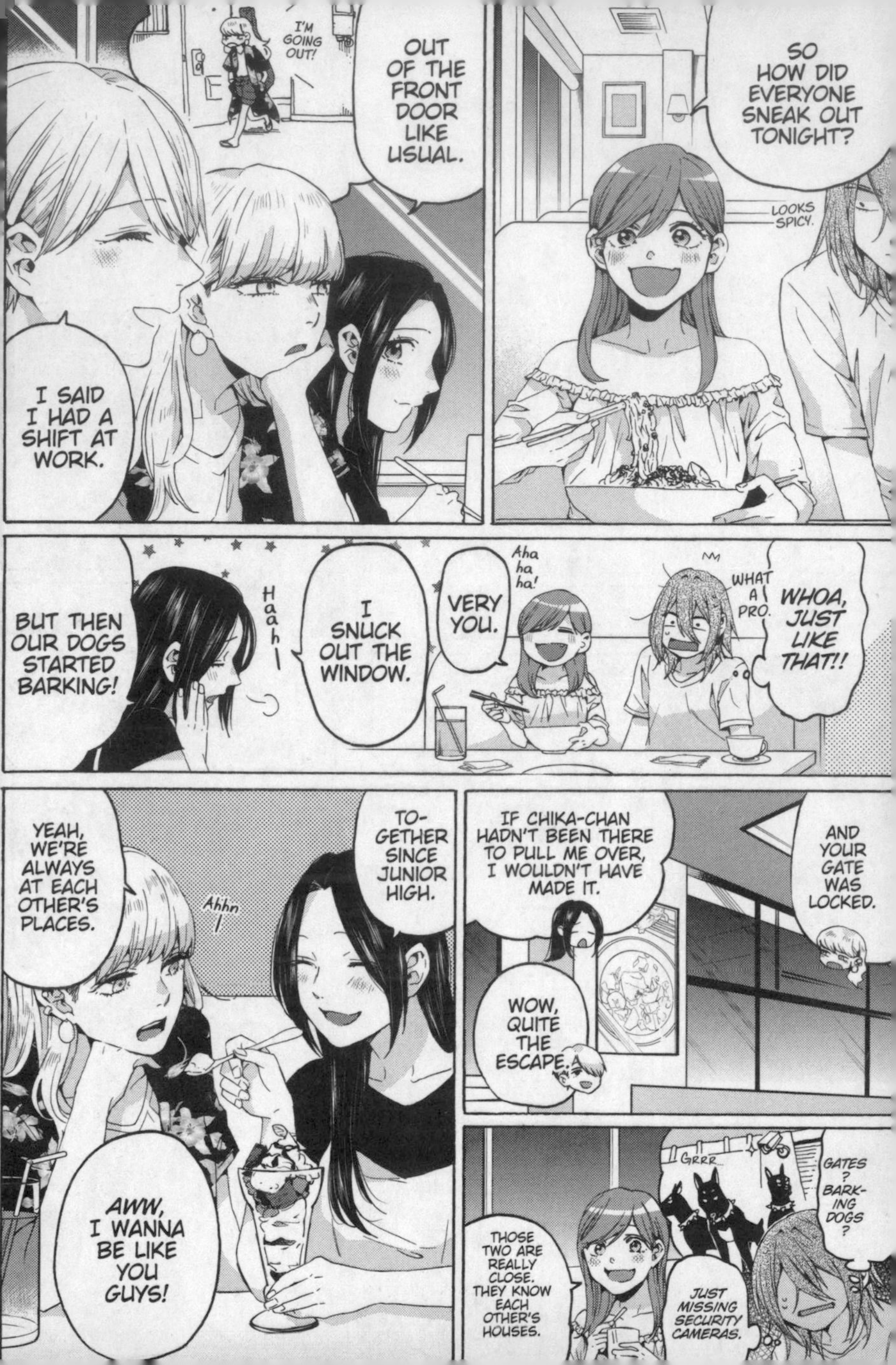
SO HOW DID EVERYONE SNEAK OUT TONIGHT?
LOOKS SPICY.
OUT OF THE FRONT DOOR LIKE USUAL.
I'M GOING OUT!
I SAID I HAD A SHIFT AT WORK.
WHOA, JUST LIKE THAT!!
WHAT A PRO.
Aha ha ha!
VERY YOU.
I SNUCK OUT THE WINDOW.
Haah!
BUT THEN OUR DOGS STARTED BARKING!
AND YOUR GATE WAS LOCKED.
IF CHIKA-CHAN HADN'T BEEN THERE TO PULL ME OVER, I WOULDN'T HAVE MADE IT.
WOW, QUITE THE ESCAPE.
GATES? BARKING-DOGS?
GRRR
JUST MISSING SECURITY CAMERAS.
THOSE TWO ARE REALLY CLOSE. THEY KNOW EACH OTHER'S HOUSES.
TO-GETHER SINCE JUNIOR HIGH.
YEAH, WE'RE ALWAYS AT EACH OTHER'S PLACES.
Ahhn!
AWW, I WANNA BE LIKE YOU GUYS!

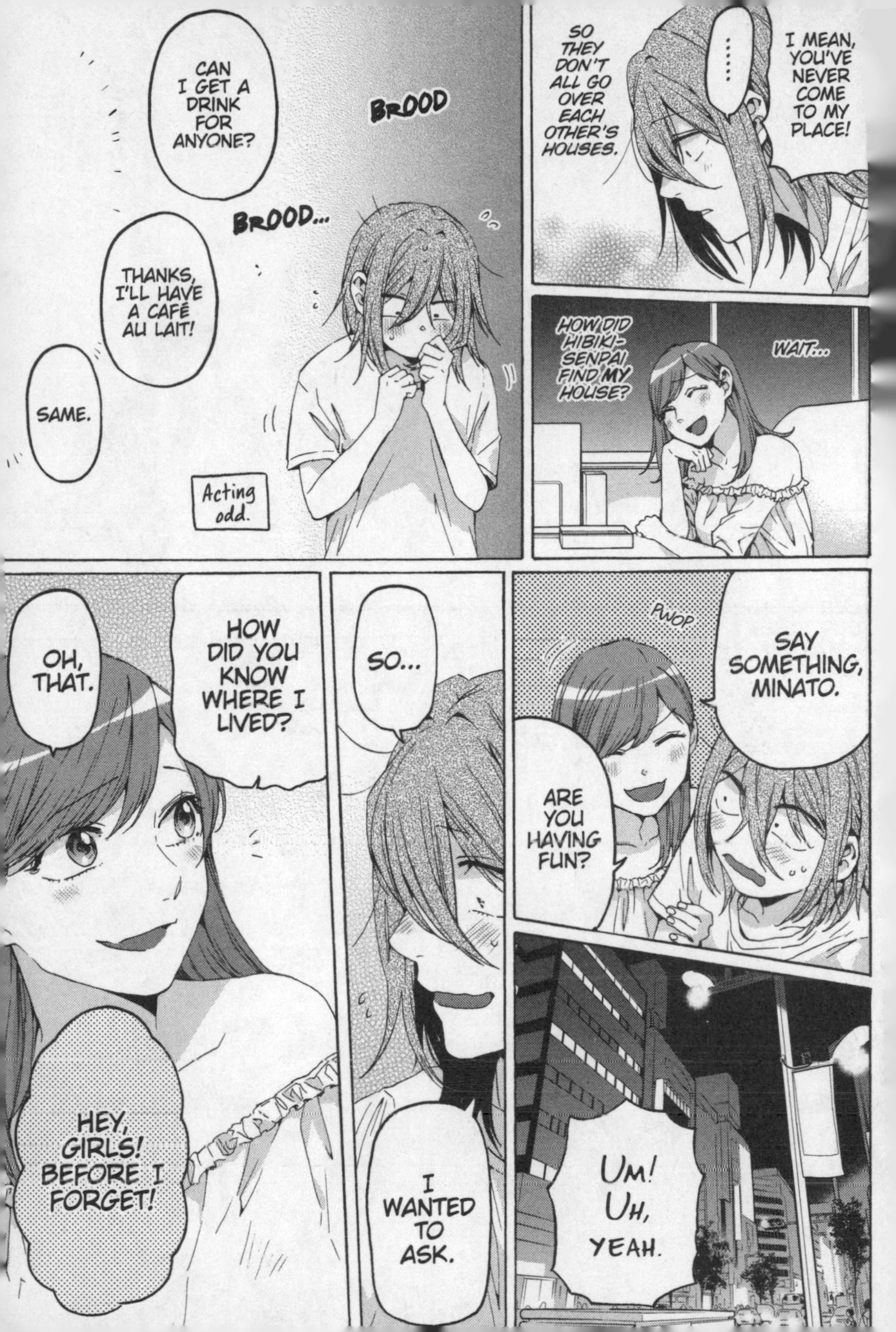
I MEAN, YOU'VE NEVER COME TO MY PLACE!
......
SO THEY DON'T ALL GO OVER EACH OTHER'S HOUSES.
WAIT...
HOW DID HIBIKI-SENPAI FIND MY HOUSE?
CAN I GET A DRINK FOR ANYONE?
BROOD
BROOD...
THANKS, I'LL HAVE A CAFÉ AU LAIT!
SAME.
Acting odd.
PWOP
SAY SOMETHING, MINATO.
ARE YOU HAVING FUN?
UM! UH, YEAH.
SO...
I WANTED TO ASK.
HOW DID YOU KNOW WHERE I LIVED?
OH, THAT.
HEY, GIRLS! BEFORE I FORGET!

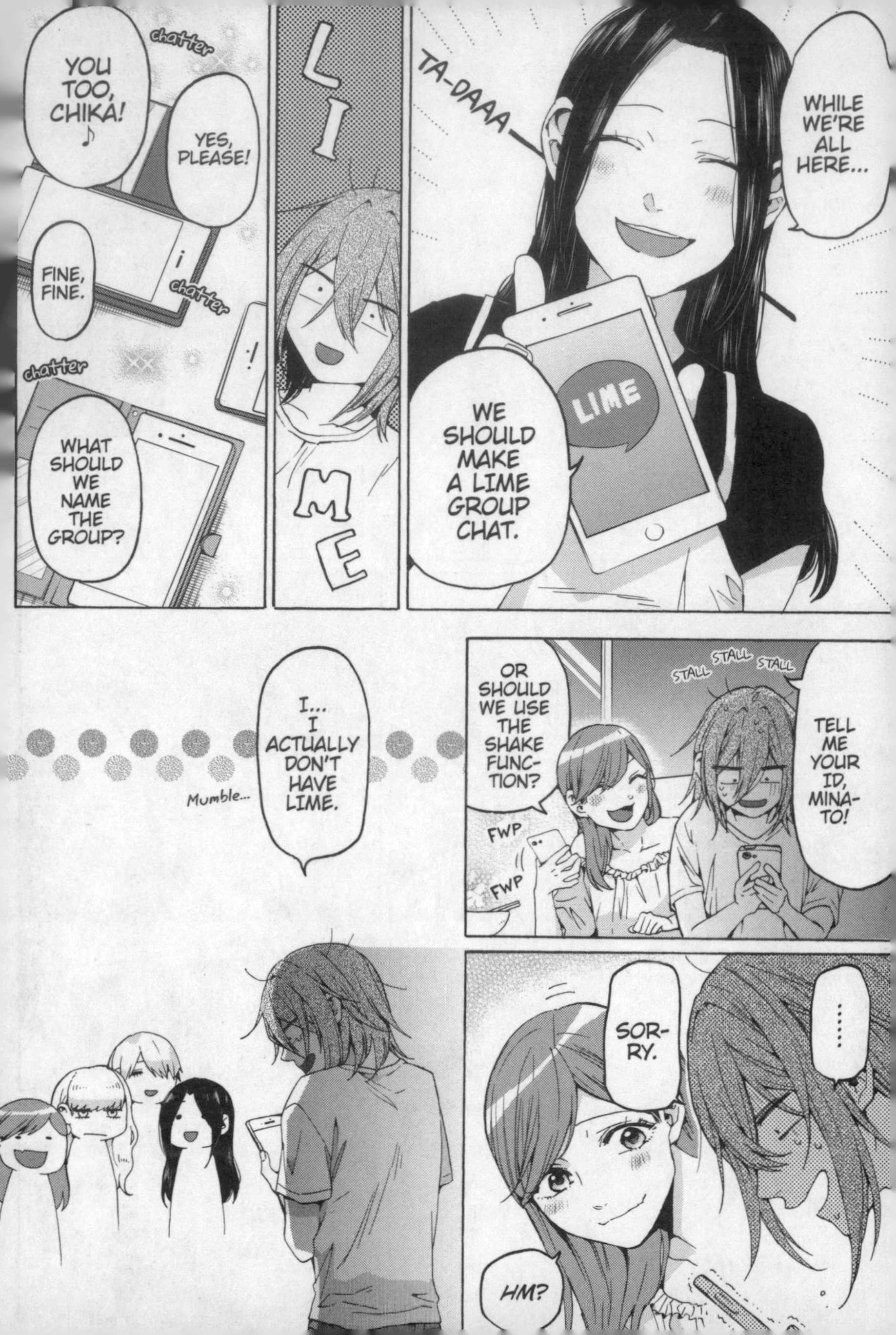
WHILE WE'RE ALL HERE...
TA-DAAAA—
WE SHOULD MAKE A LIME GROUP CHAT.
LIME
LIME
chatter
YES, PLEASE!
YOU TOO, CHIKA! ♪
FINE, FINE.
chatter
chatter
WHAT SHOULD WE NAME THE GROUP?
TELL ME YOUR ID, MINATO!
STALL STALL STALL
OR SHOULD WE USE THE SHAKE FUNCTION?
FWP
FWP
I... I ACTUALLY DON'T HAVE LIME.
Mumble...
......
SORRY.
HM?

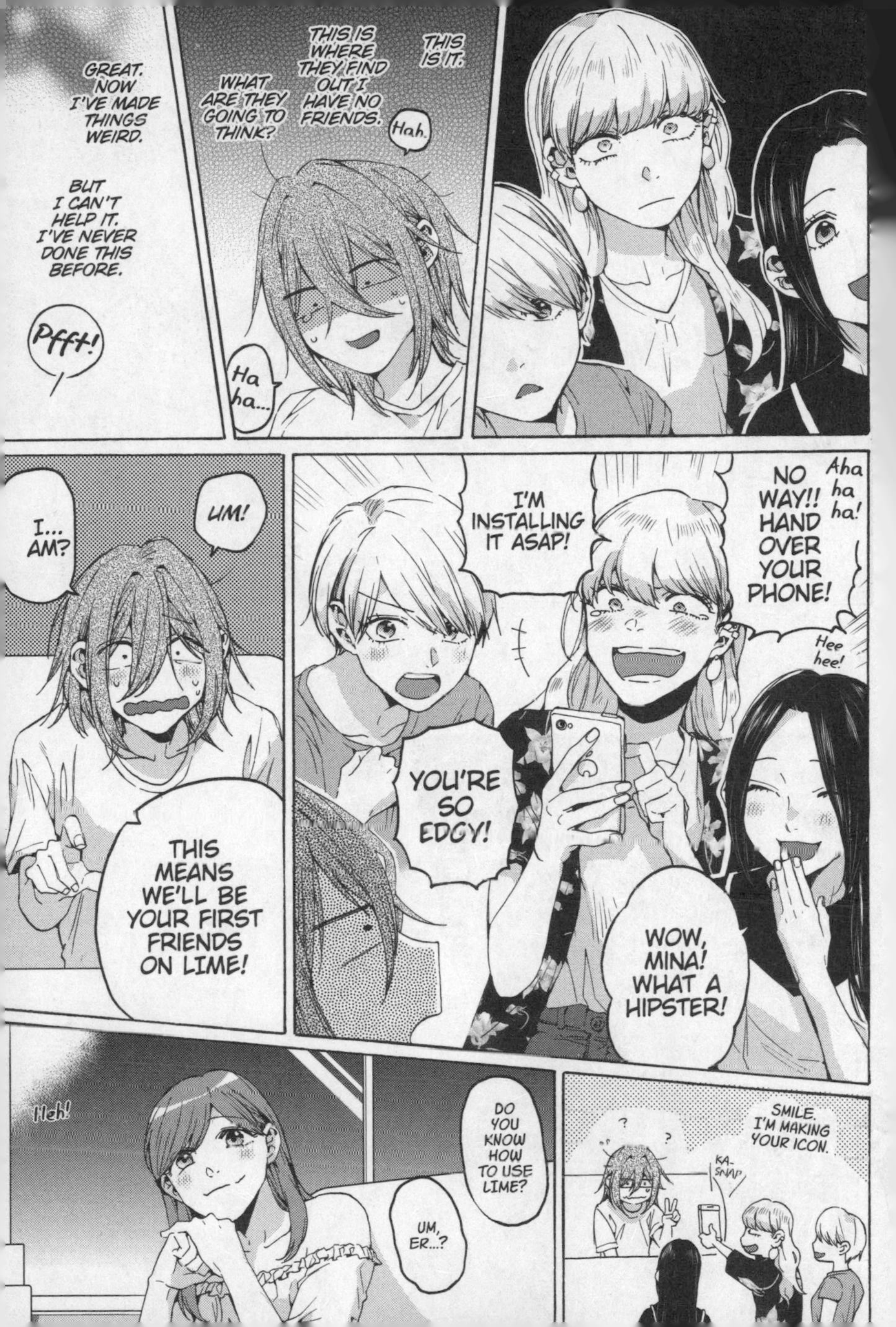
THIS IS IT.
THIS IS WHERE THEY FIND OUT I HAVE NO FRIENDS.
WHAT ARE THEY GOING TO THINK?
Hah.
Ha ha...
GREAT. NOW I'VE MADE THINGS WEIRD.
BUT I CAN'T HELP IT. I'VE NEVER DONE THIS BEFORE.
Pffft!
Aha ha ha!
NO WAY!! HAND OVER YOUR PHONE!
I'M INSTALLING IT ASAP!
Hee hee!
YOU'RE SO EDGY!
WOW, MINA! WHAT A HIPSTER!
UM!
I... AM?
THIS MEANS WE'LL BE YOUR FIRST FRIENDS ON LIME!
SMILE. I'M MAKING YOUR ICON.
KA-SNAP
DO YOU KNOW HOW TO USE LIME?
UM, ER...?
Heh!

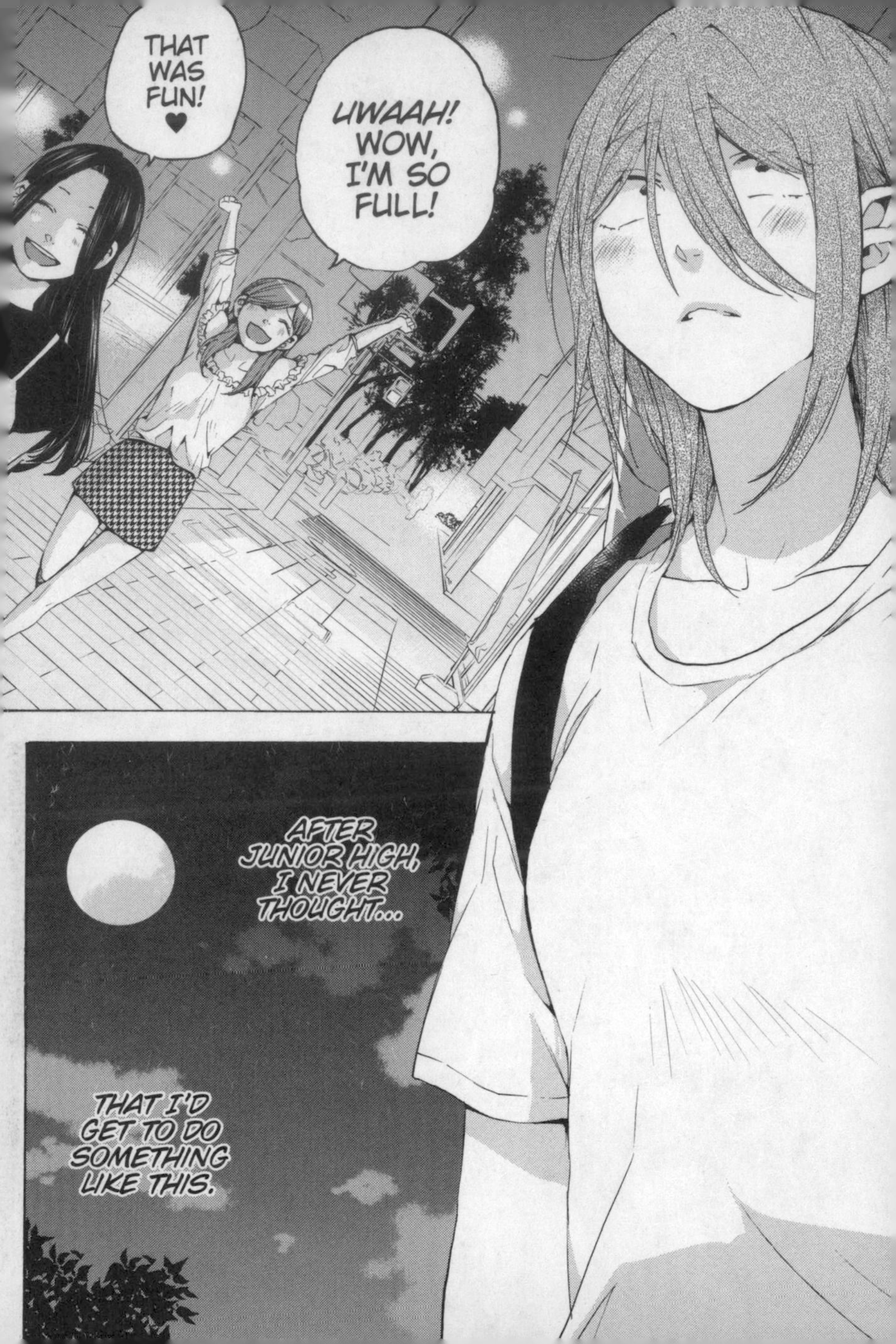
UWAAH! WOW, I'M SO FULL!
THAT WAS FUN! ♥
AFTER JUNIOR HIGH, I NEVER THOUGHT...
THAT I'D GET TO DO SOMETHING LIKE THIS.

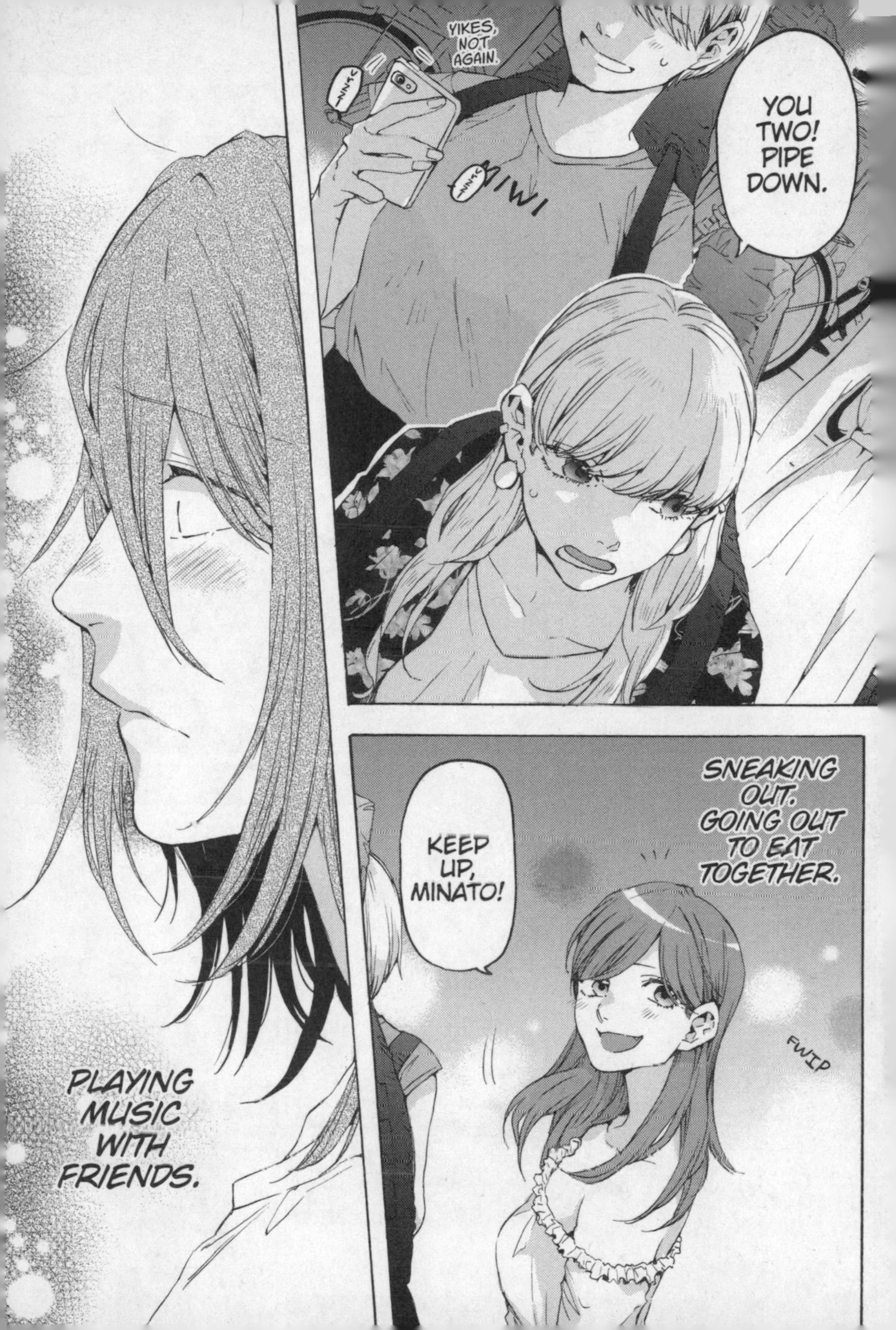
YOU TWO! PIPE DOWN.
YIKES, NOT AGAIN.
SNEAKING OUT. GOING OUT TO EAT TOGETHER.
KEEP UP, MINATO!
FWIP
PLAYING MUSIC WITH FRIENDS.

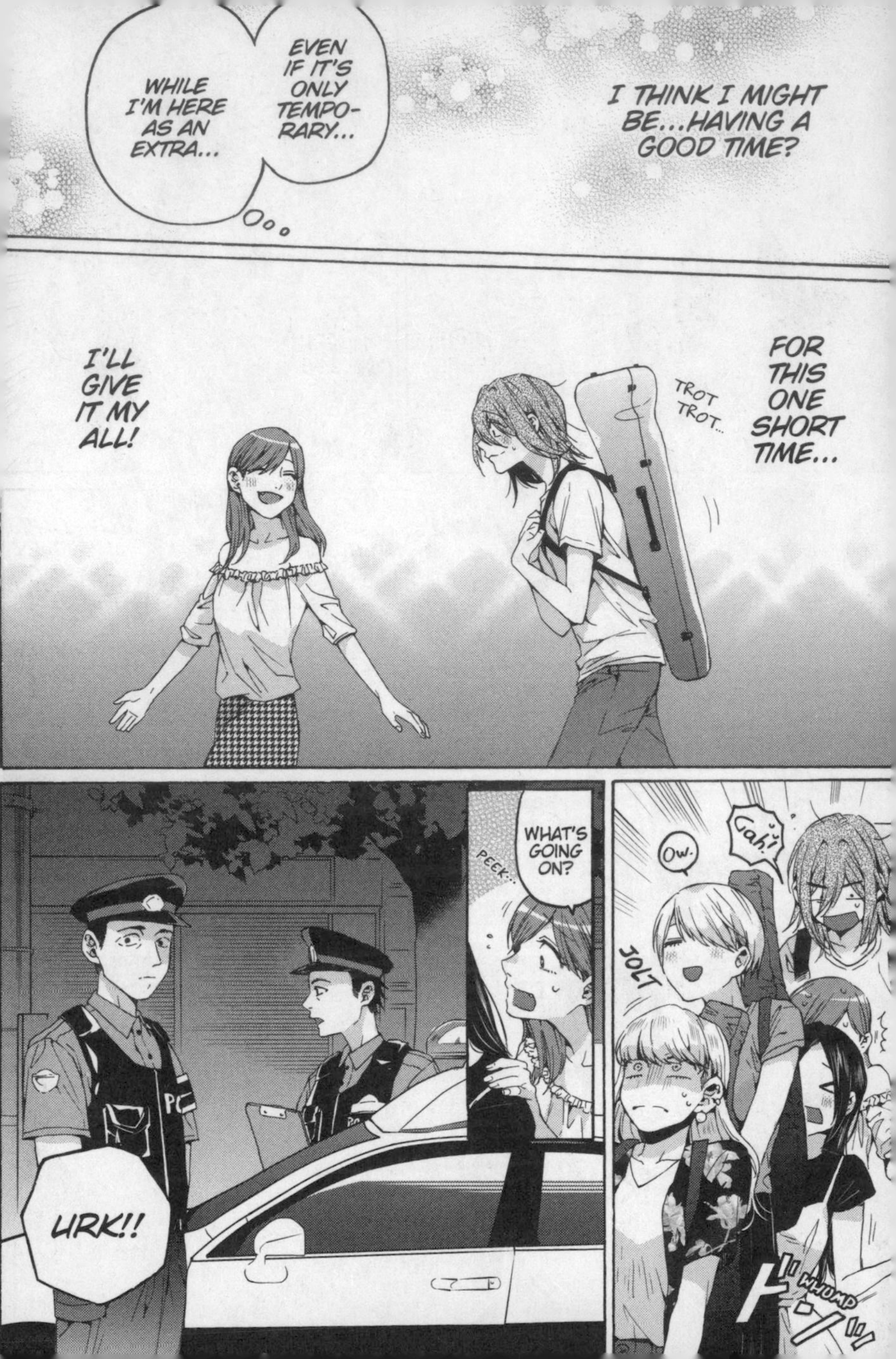
I THINK I MIGHT BE...HAVING A GOOD TIME?
EVEN IF IT'S ONLY TEMPO-RARY...
WHILE I'M HERE AS AN EXTRA...
FOR THIS ONE SHORT TIME...
TROT TROT...
I'LL GIVE IT MY ALL!
Gah!
Ow.
JOLT
WHUMP
WHAT'S GOING ON?
PEEK...
URK!!

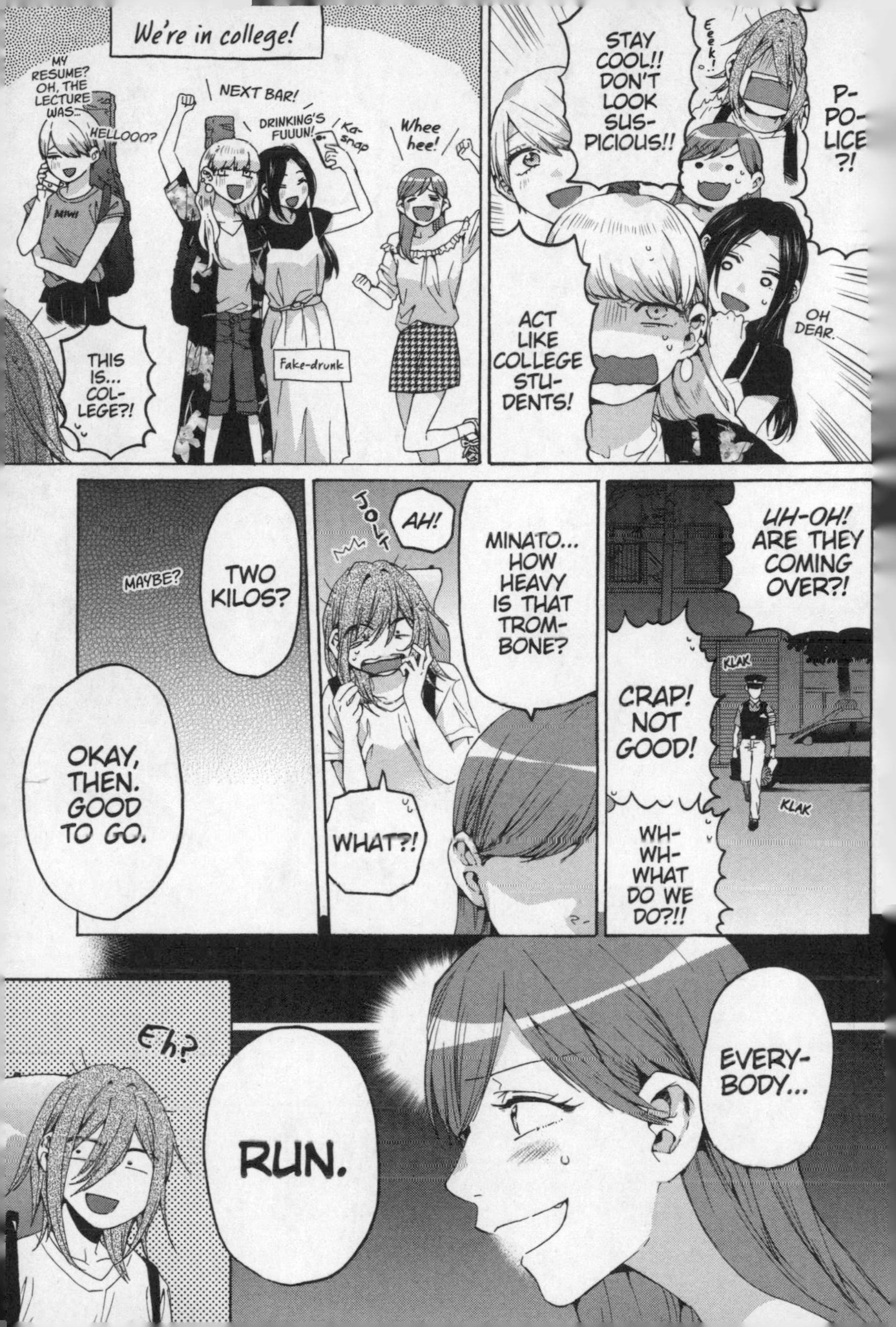
P-PO-LICE?!
Eeek!
STAY COOL!! DON'T LOOK SUS-PICIOUS!!
ACT LIKE COLLEGE STU-DENTS!
OH DEAR.
We're in college!
MY RESUME? OH, THE LECTURE WAS...
HELLOOO?
NEXT BAR!
DRINKING'S FUUUN!
Ka-snap
Whee hee!
THIS IS... COL-LEGE?!
Fake-drunk
UH-OH! ARE THEY COMING OVER?!
KLAK
CRAP! NOT GOOD!
KLAK
WH-WH-WHAT DO WE DO?!!
MINATO... HOW HEAVY IS THAT TROM-BONE?
AH!
JOLT
WHAT?!
TWO KILOS?
MAYBE?
OKAY, THEN. GOOD TO GO.
EVERY-BODY...
RUN.
Eh?

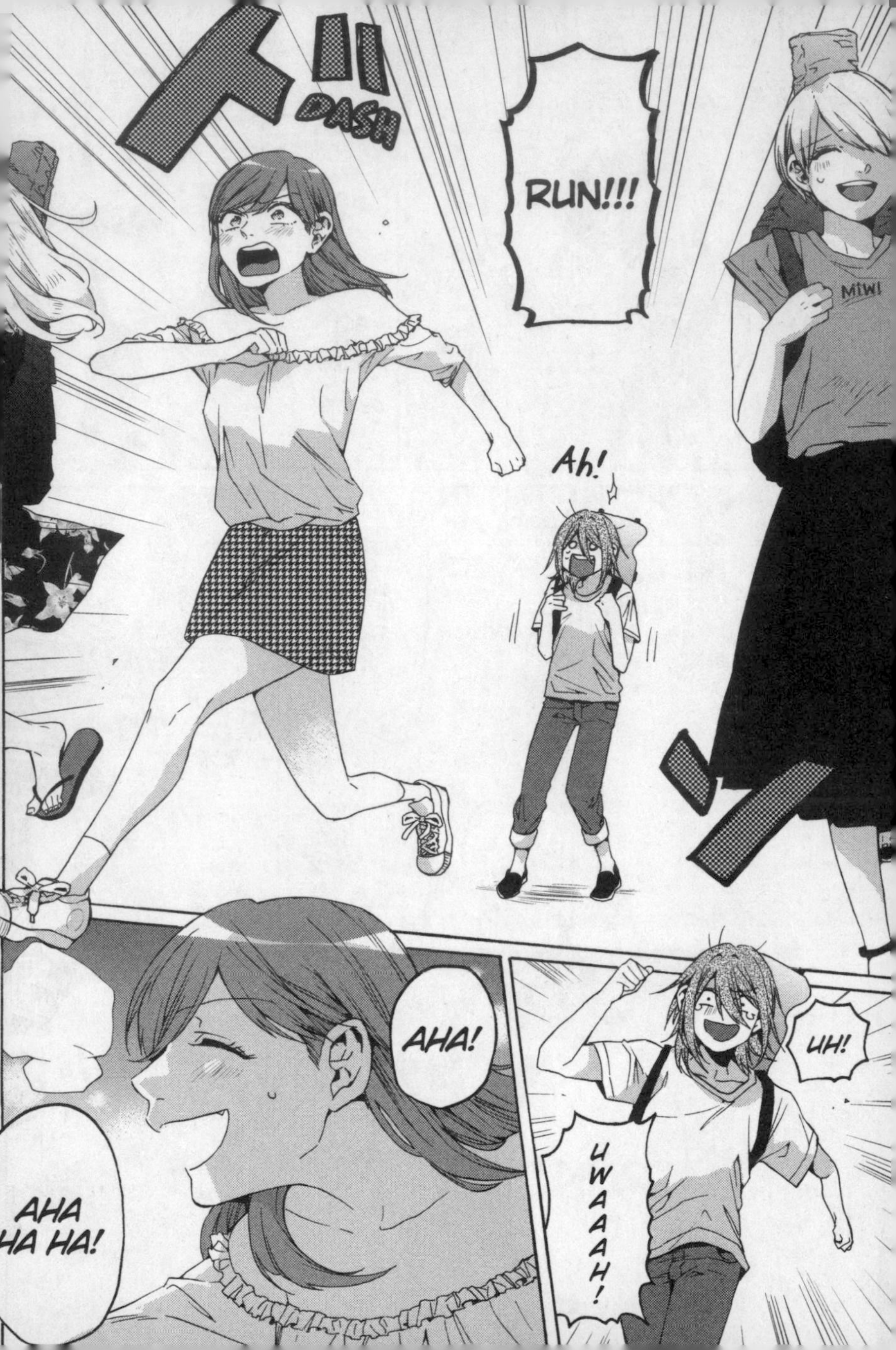
MIWI
RUN!!!
DASH
Ah!
UH!
UWAAAAH!
AHA!
AHA HA HA!

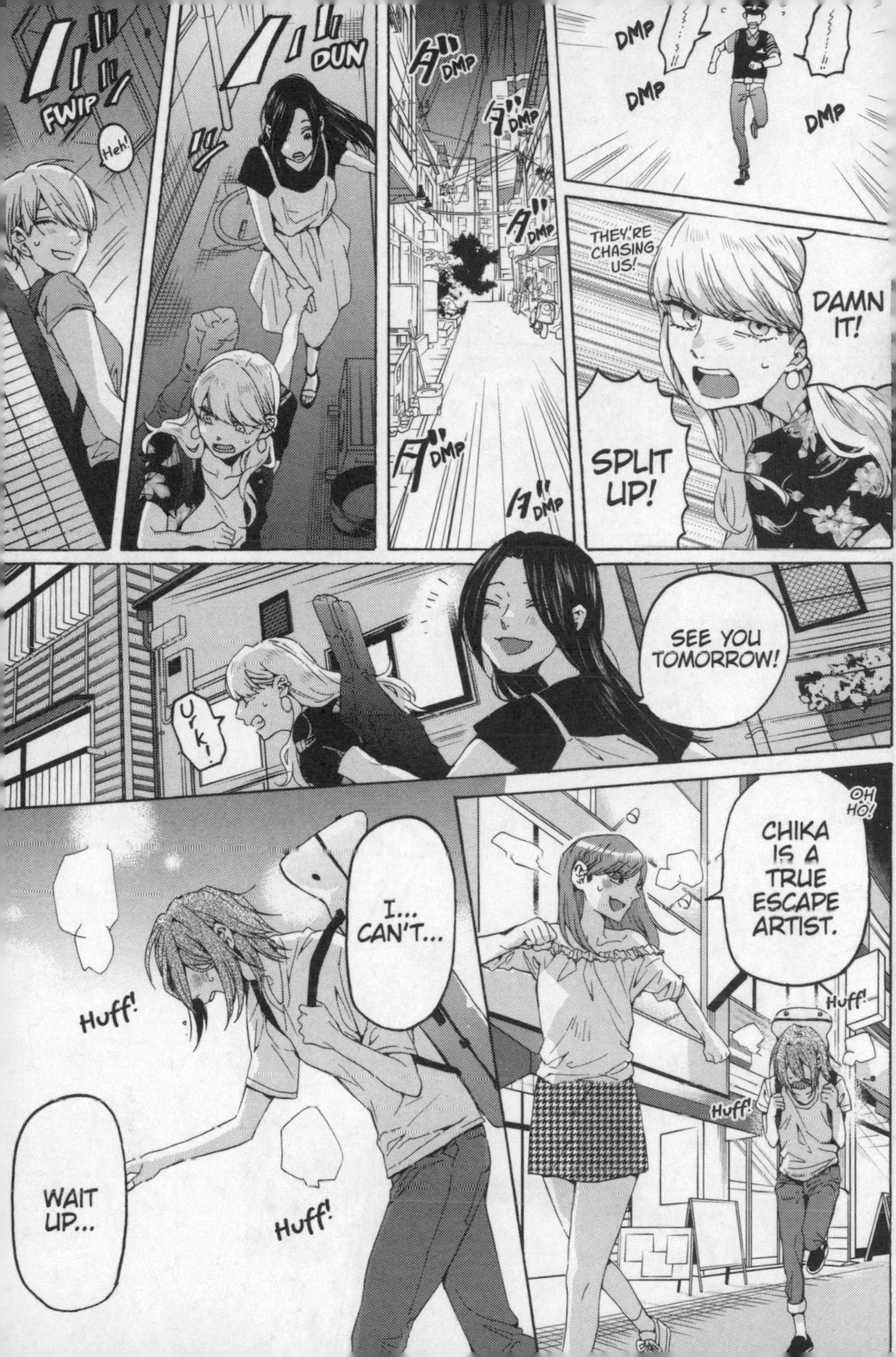
DMP
DMP
DMP
THEY'RE CHASING US!
DAMN IT!
SPLIT UP!
DMP
DMP
DMP
DMP
DMP
DUN
FWIP
Heh!
SEE YOU TOMORROW!
Urk!
OH HO!
CHIKA IS A TRUE ESCAPE ARTIST.
Huff!
Huff!
I... CAN'T...
Huff!
WAIT UP...
Huff!

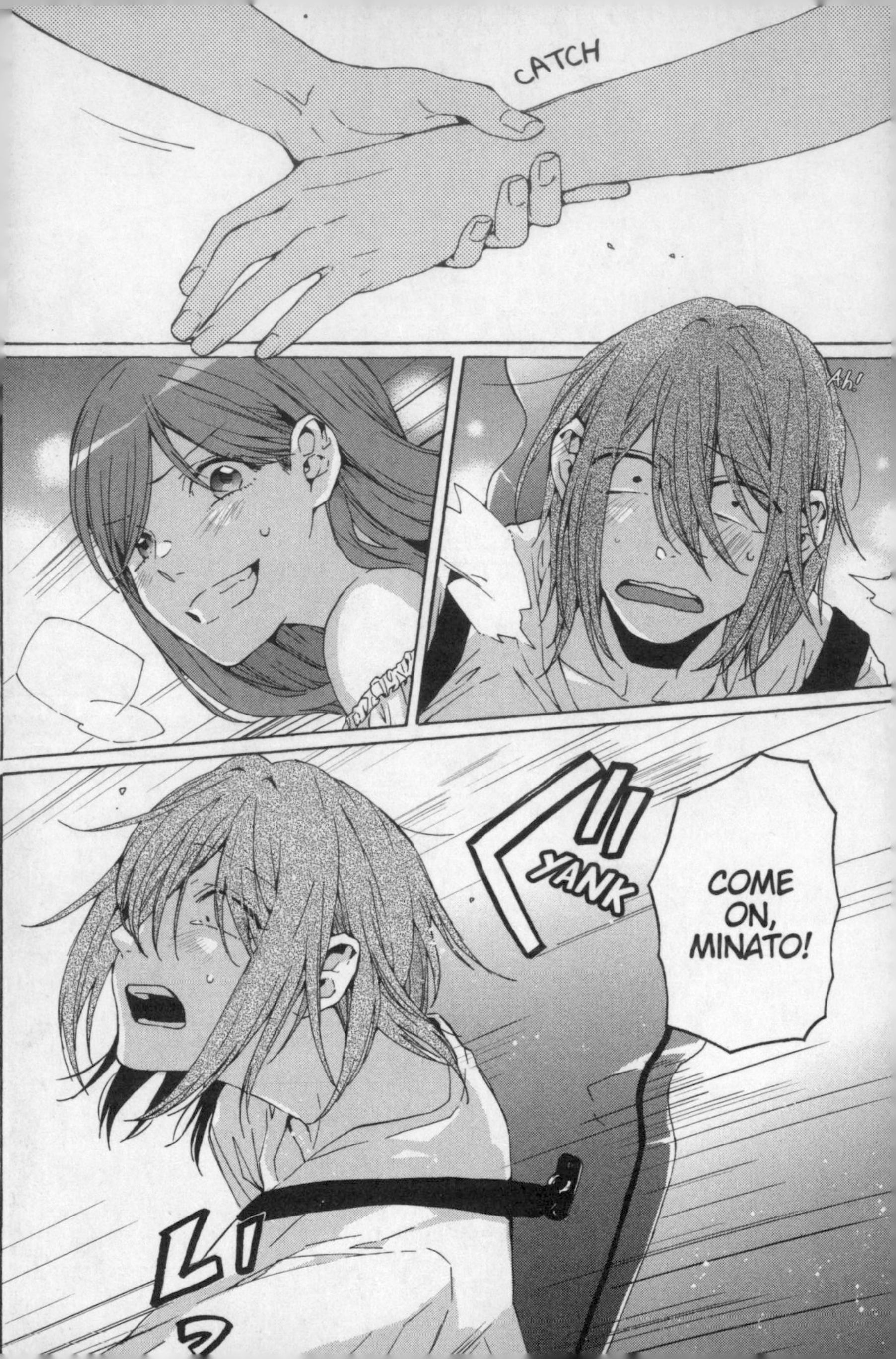
CATCH
Ah!
YANK
COME ON, MINATO!

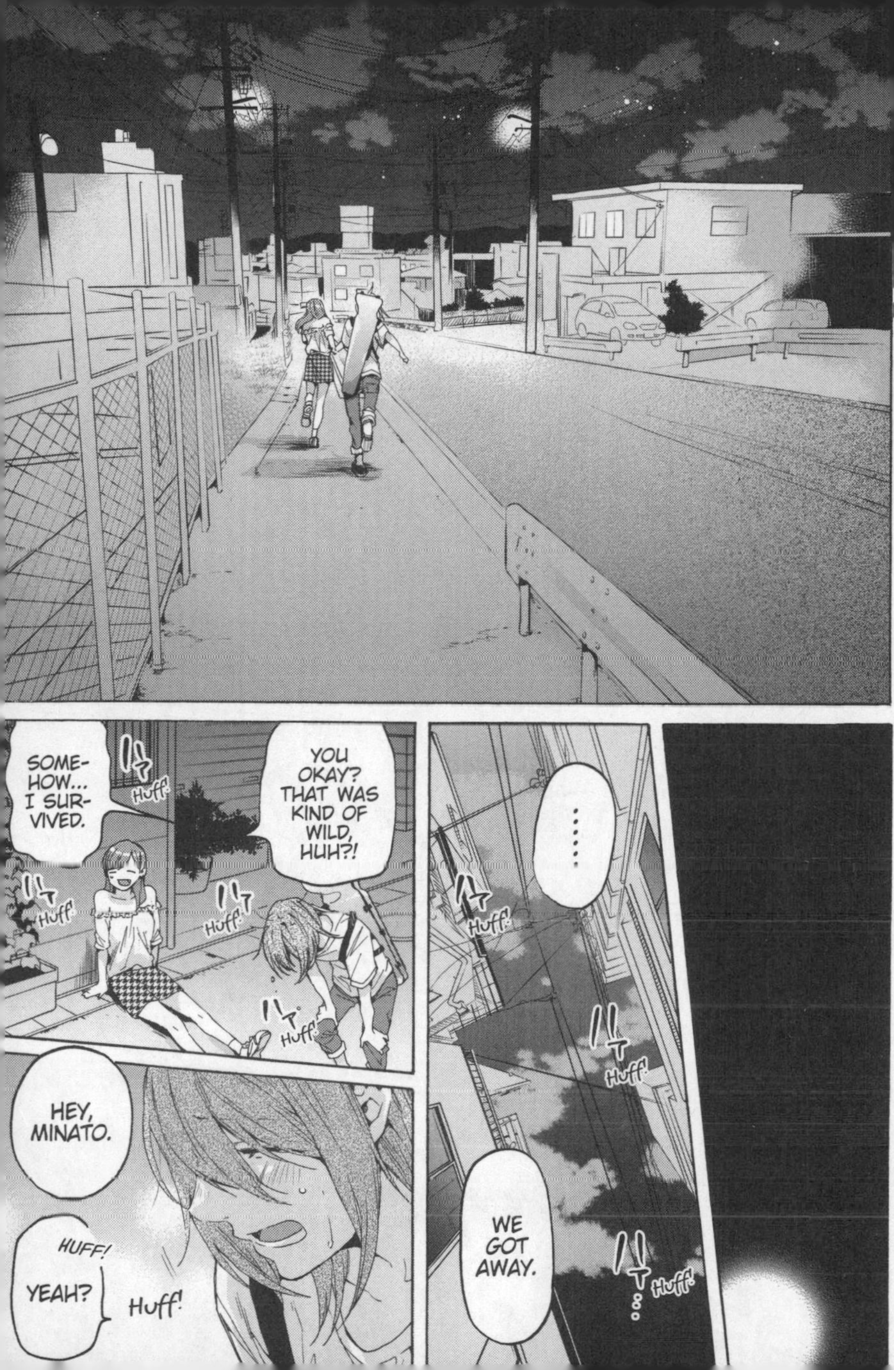
......
ハァ Huff!
ハァ Huff!
WE GOT AWAY.
ハァ... Huff!
YOU OKAY? THAT WAS KIND OF WILD, HUH?!
SOME-HOW... I SUR-VIVED.
ハァ Huff!
ハァ Huff!
ハァ Huff!
ハァ Huff!
HEY, MINATO.
HUFF!
YEAH?
Huff!

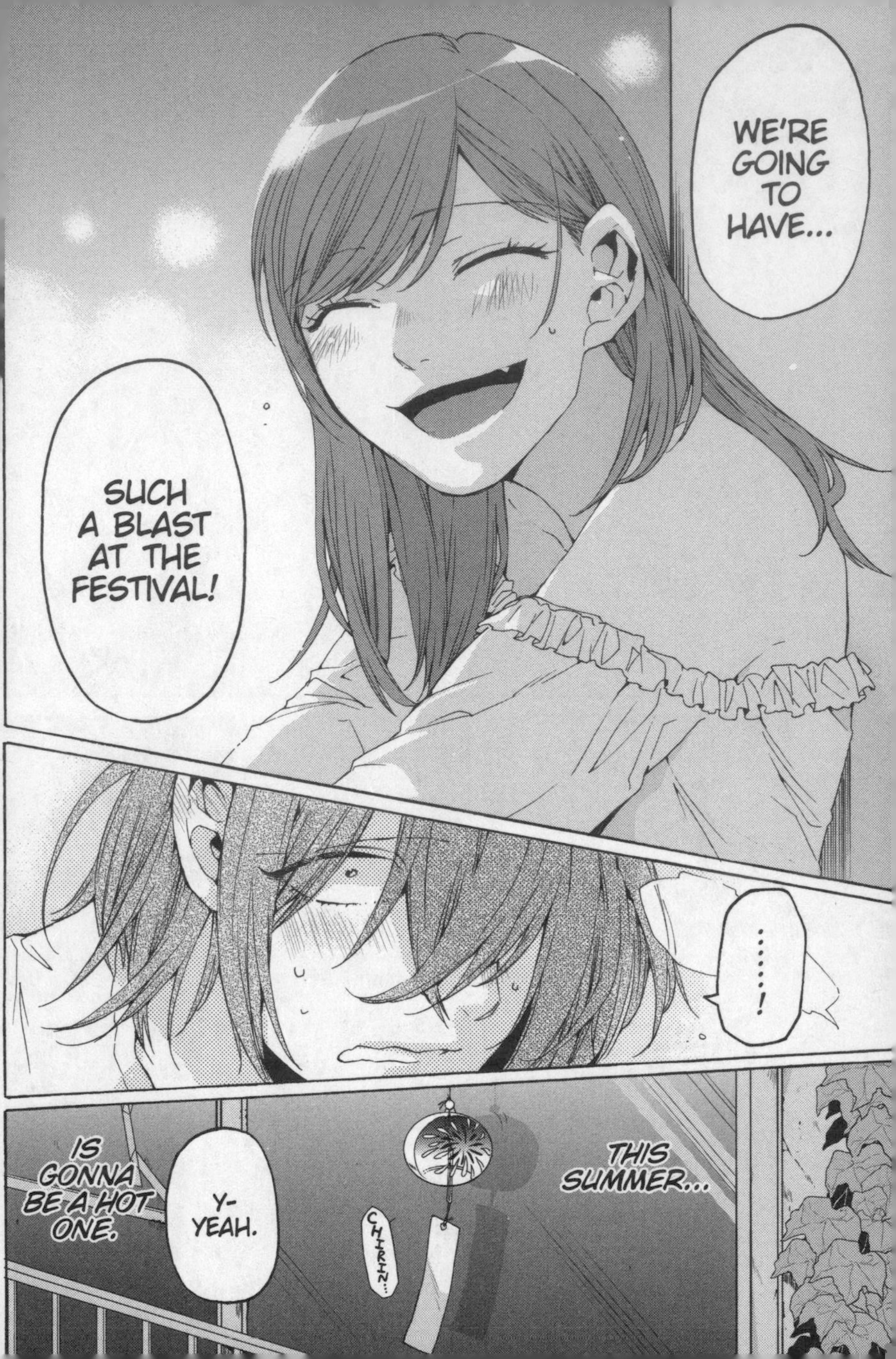
WE'RE GOING TO HAVE...
SUCH A BLAST AT THE FESTIVAL!
......!
THIS SUMMER...
CHIRIN...
Y-YEAH.
IS GONNA BE A HOT ONE.

Hello, Melancholic!

NEXT-DAY SORENESS

RUNNING AROUND WITH TWO KILOS ON MY BACK... THAT WAS ROUGH.

URRGH...

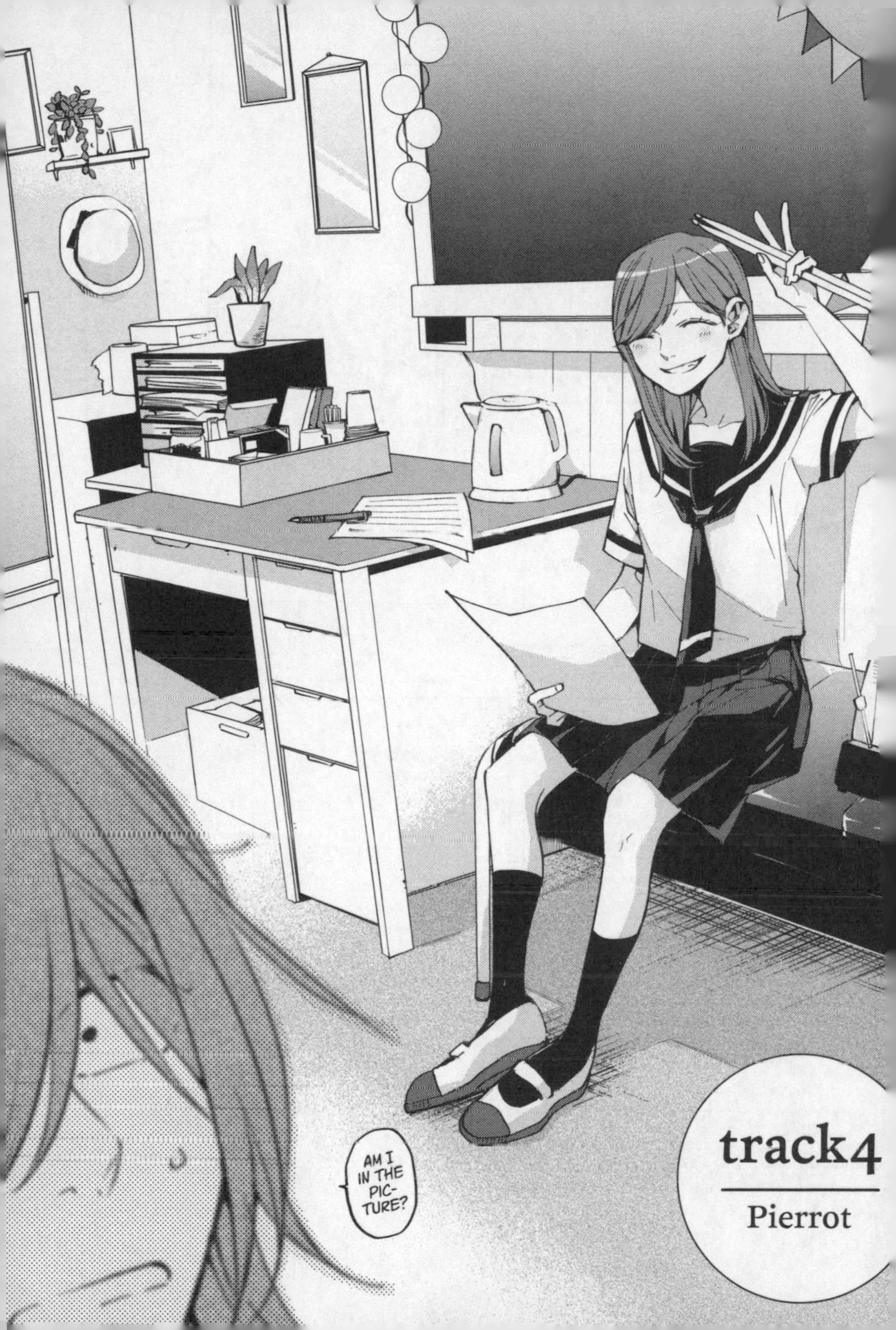
AM I IN THE PICTURE?
track4
Pierrot

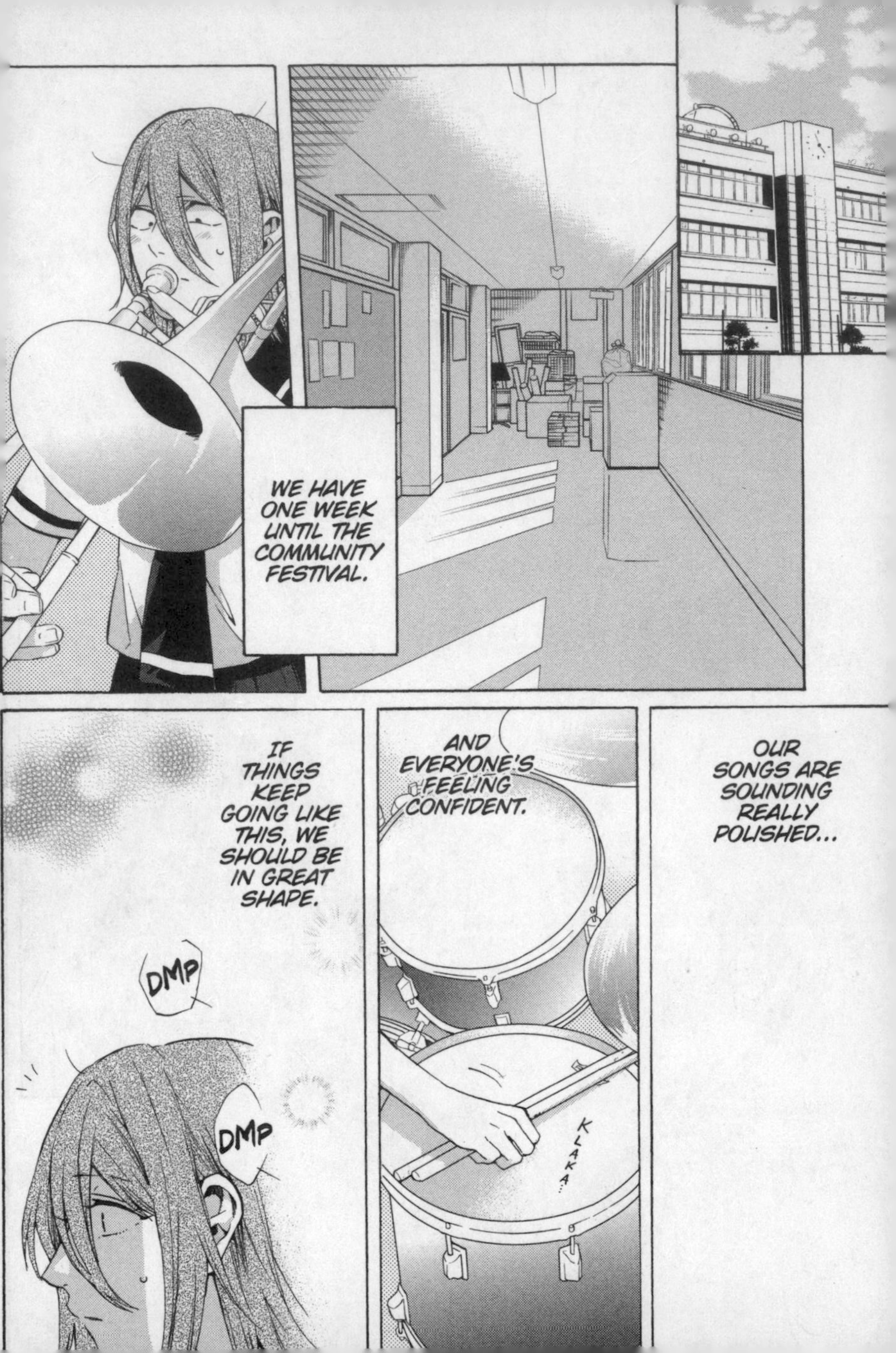
WE HAVE ONE WEEK UNTIL THE COMMUNITY FESTIVAL.
OUR SONGS ARE SOUNDING REALLY POLISHED...
AND EVERYONE'S FEELING CONFIDENT.
KLAKA...
IF THINGS KEEP GOING LIKE THIS, WE SHOULD BE IN GREAT SHAPE.
DMP
DMP

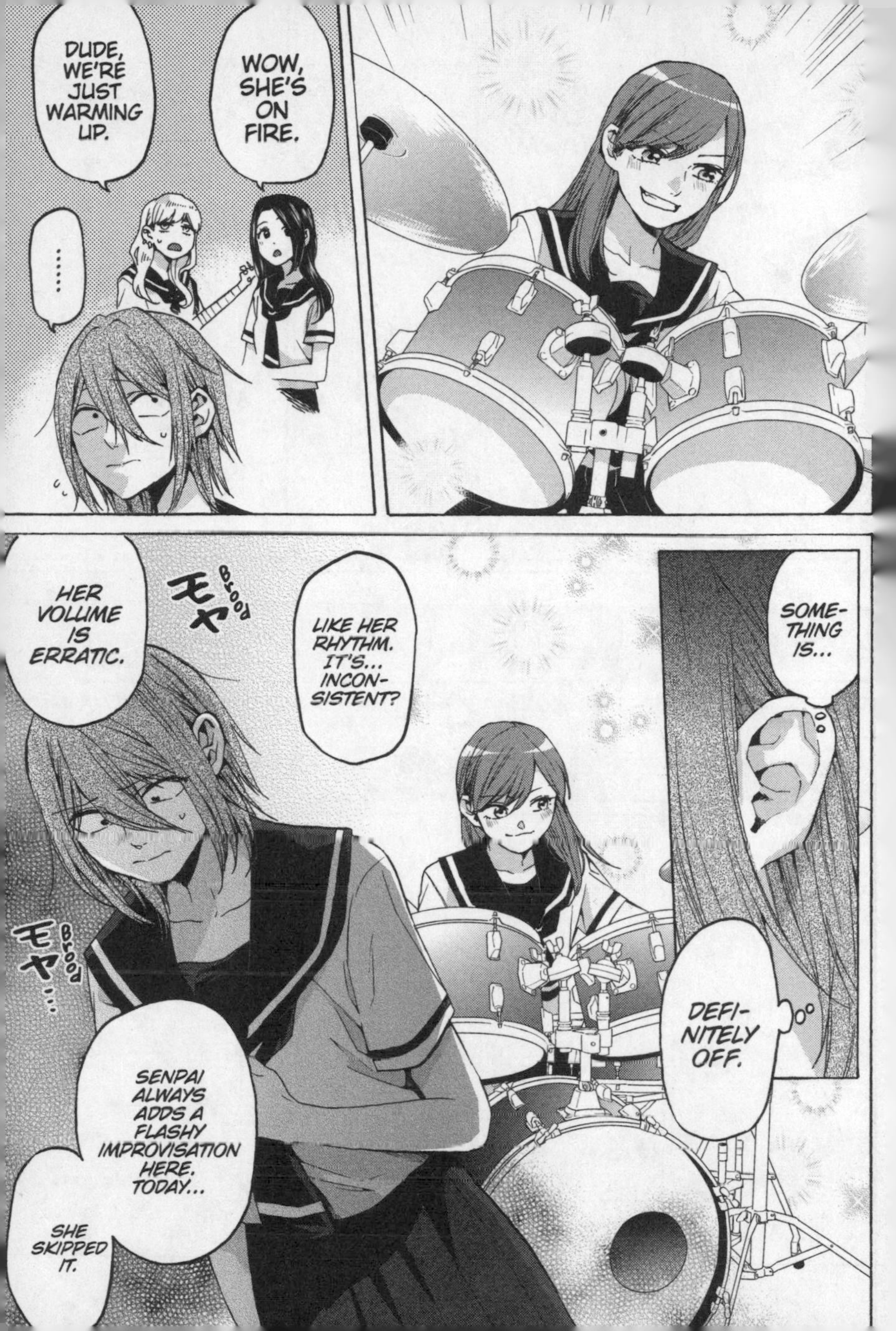
WOW, SHE'S ON FIRE.
DUDE, WE'RE JUST WARMING UP.
......
SOMETHING IS...
LIKE HER RHYTHM. IT'S... INCONSISTENT?
モヤ Brood
HER VOLUME IS ERRATIC.
DEFINITELY OFF.
モヤ... Brood
SENPAI ALWAYS ADDS A FLASHY IMPROVISATION HERE. TODAY...
SHE SKIPPED IT.

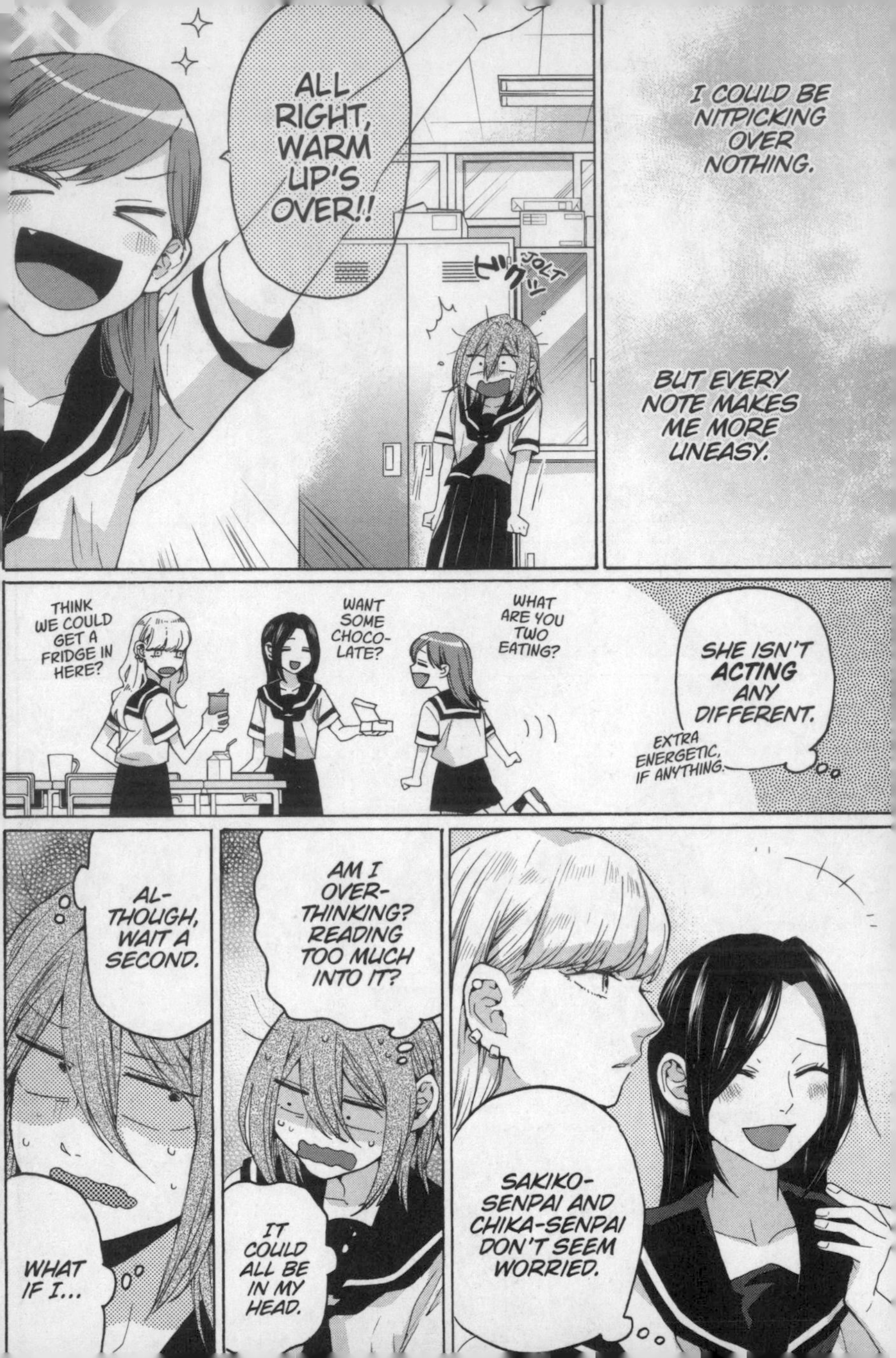
I COULD BE NITPICKING OVER NOTHING.
BUT EVERY NOTE MAKES ME MORE UNEASY.
ALL RIGHT, WARM UP'S OVER!!
JOLT
SHE ISN'T ACTING ANY DIFFERENT.
EXTRA ENERGETIC, IF ANYTHING.
WHAT ARE YOU TWO EATING?
WANT SOME CHOCO-LATE?
THINK WE COULD GET A FRIDGE IN HERE?
SAKIKO-SENPAI AND CHIKA-SENPAI DON'T SEEM WORRIED.
AM I OVER-THINKING? READING TOO MUCH INTO IT?
IT COULD ALL BE IN MY HEAD.
AL-THOUGH, WAIT A SECOND.
WHAT IF I...

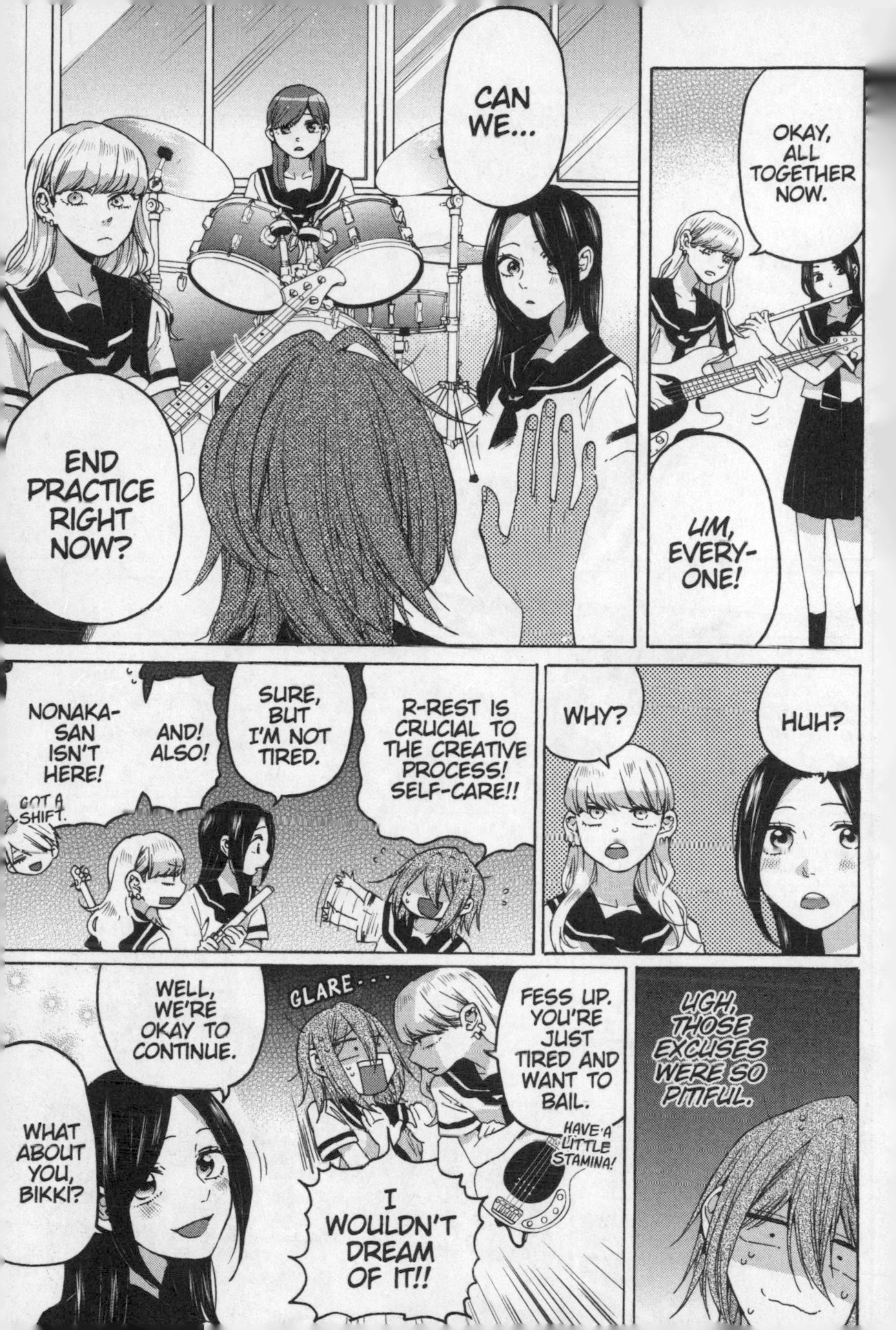

OKAY, ALL TOGETHER NOW.
UM, EVERY-ONE!
CAN WE...
END PRACTICE RIGHT NOW?
HUH?
WHY?
R-REST IS CRUCIAL TO THE CREATIVE PROCESS! SELF-CARE!!
SURE, BUT I'M NOT TIRED.
AND! ALSO!
NONAKA-SAN ISN'T HERE!
GOT A SHIFT.
UGH, THOSE EXCUSES WERE SO PITIFUL.
FESS UP. YOU'RE JUST TIRED AND WANT TO BAIL.
GLARE...
WELL, WE'RE OKAY TO CONTINUE.
HAVE A LITTLE STAMINA!
I WOULDN'T DREAM OF IT!!
WHAT ABOUT YOU, BIKKI?

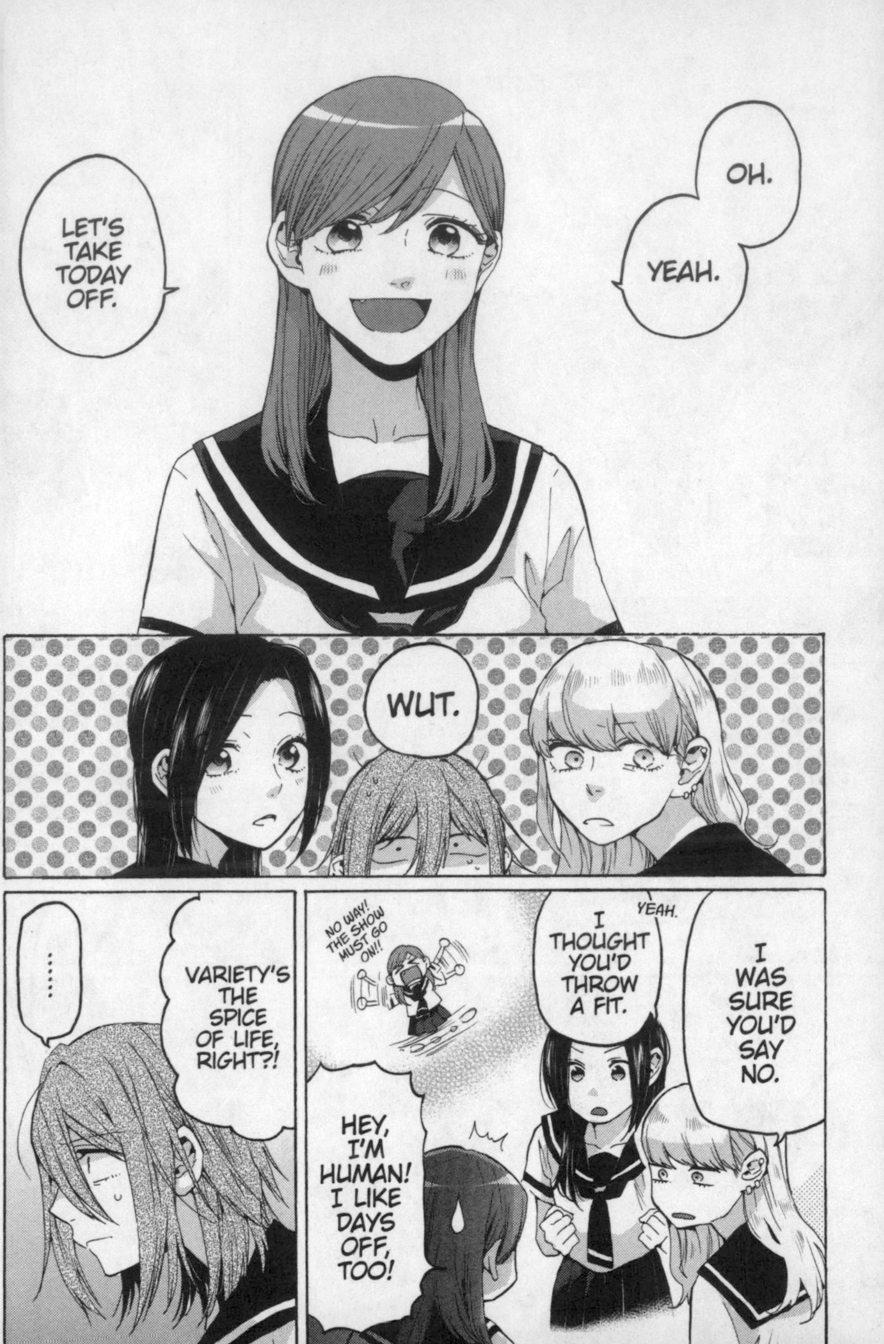
OH.
YEAH.
LET'S TAKE TODAY OFF.
WUT.
I WAS SURE YOU'D SAY NO.
YEAH.
I THOUGHT YOU'D THROW A FIT.
NO WAY! THE SHOW MUST GO ON!!
HEY, I'M HUMAN! I LIKE DAYS OFF, TOO!
VARIETY'S THE SPICE OF LIFE, RIGHT?!
......

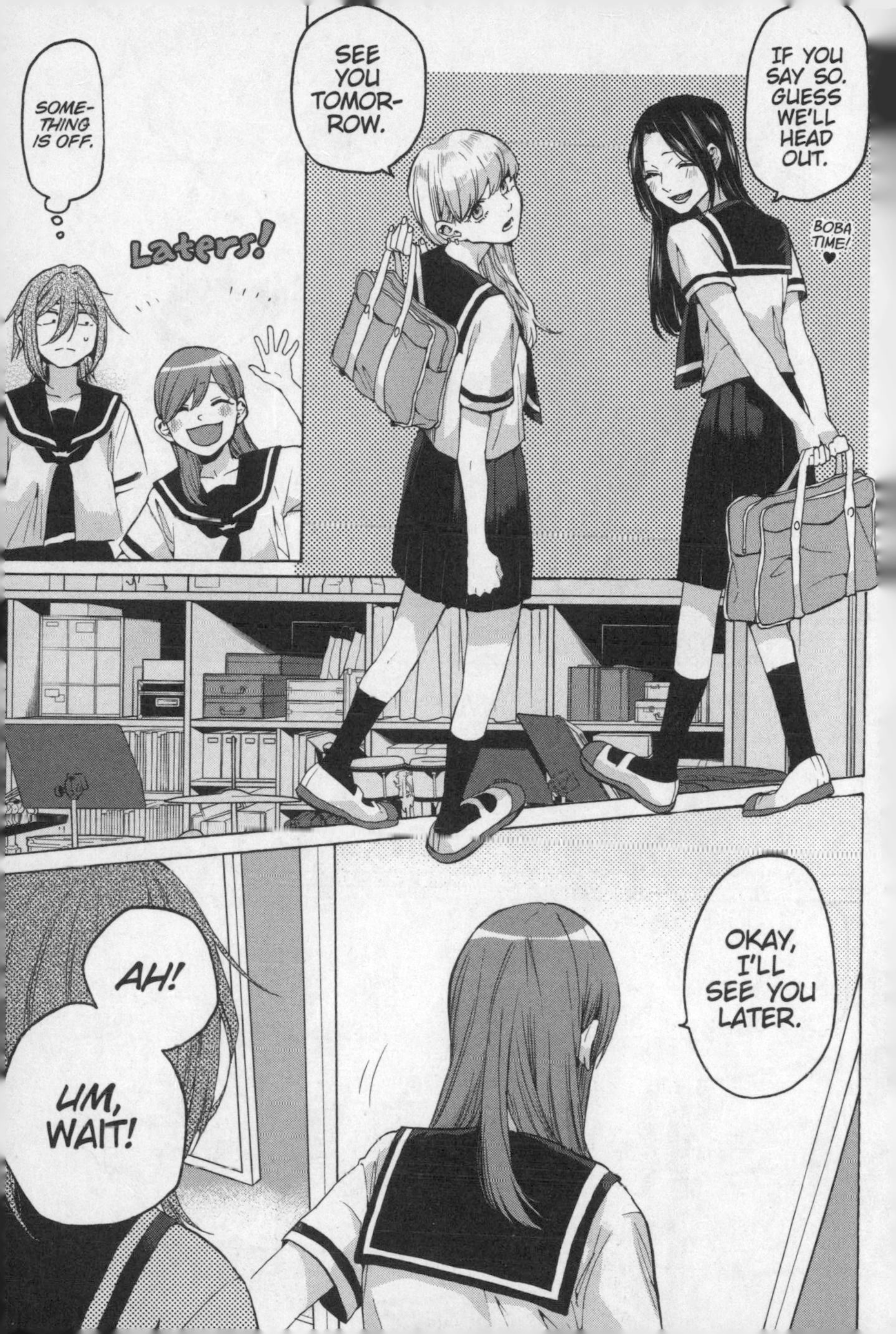
IF YOU SAY SO. GUESS WE'LL HEAD OUT.
BOBA TIME! ♥
SEE YOU TOMOR-ROW.
Laters!
SOME-THING IS OFF.
OKAY, I'LL SEE YOU LATER.
AH!
UM, WAIT!

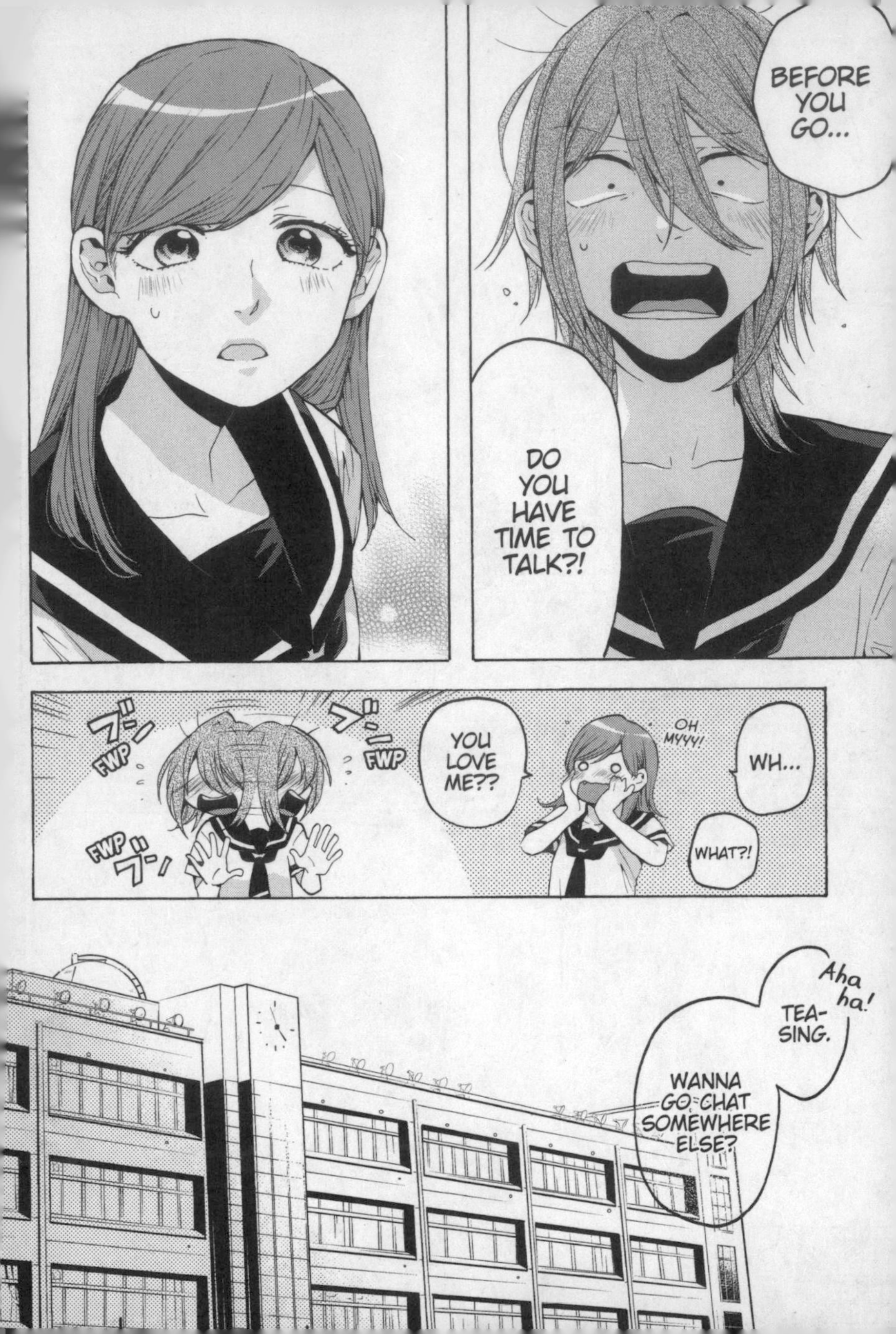
BEFORE YOU GO...
DO YOU HAVE TIME TO TALK?!
WH...
WHAT?!
OH MYYY!
YOU LOVE ME??
FWP
FWP
FWP
Aha ha!
TEA-SING.
WANNA GO CHAT SOMEWHERE ELSE?

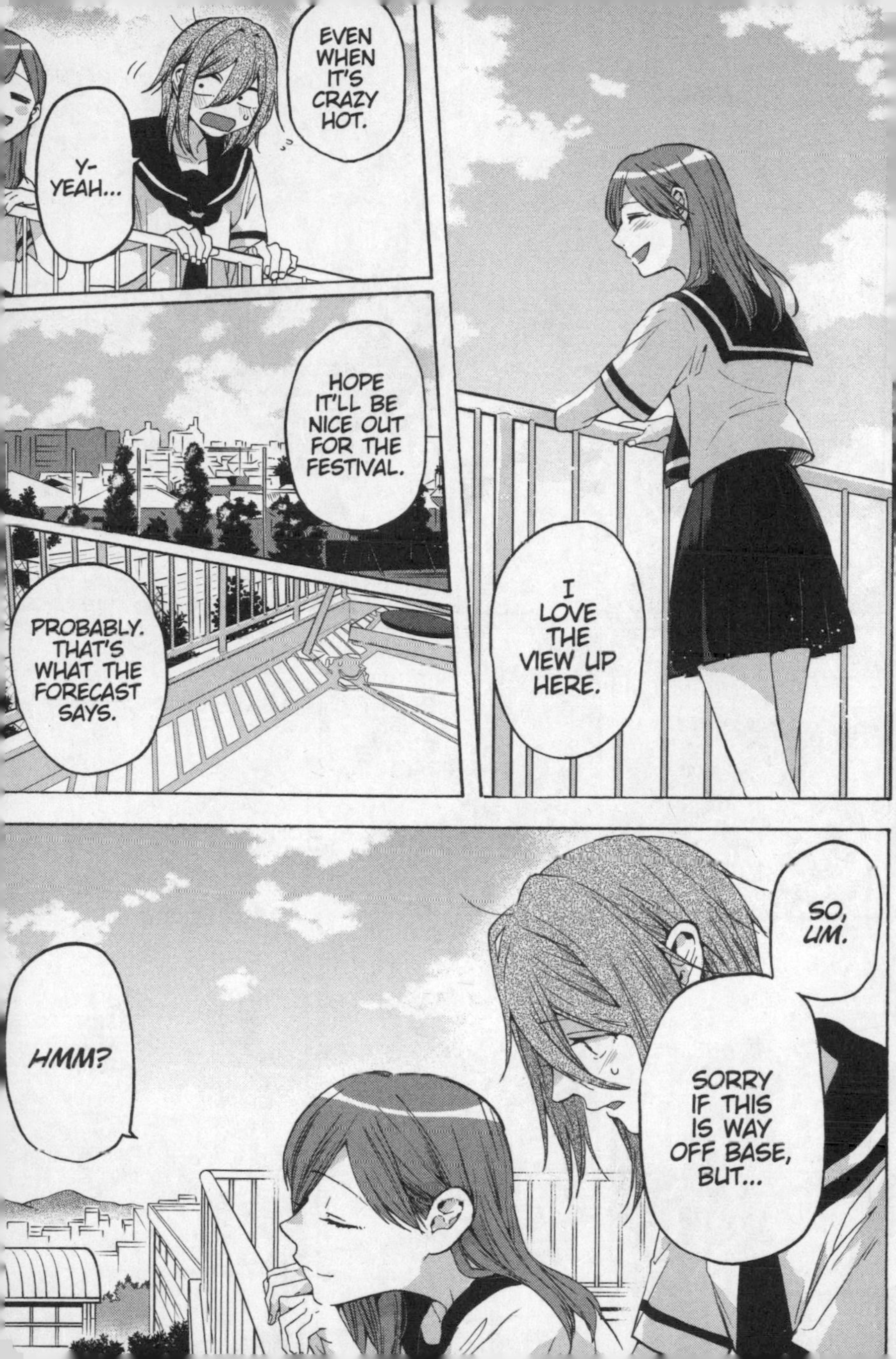
I LOVE THE VIEW UP HERE.
EVEN WHEN IT'S CRAZY HOT.
Y-YEAH...
HOPE IT'LL BE NICE OUT FOR THE FESTIVAL.
PROBABLY. THAT'S WHAT THE FORECAST SAYS.
SO, UM.
SORRY IF THIS IS WAY OFF BASE, BUT...
HMM?

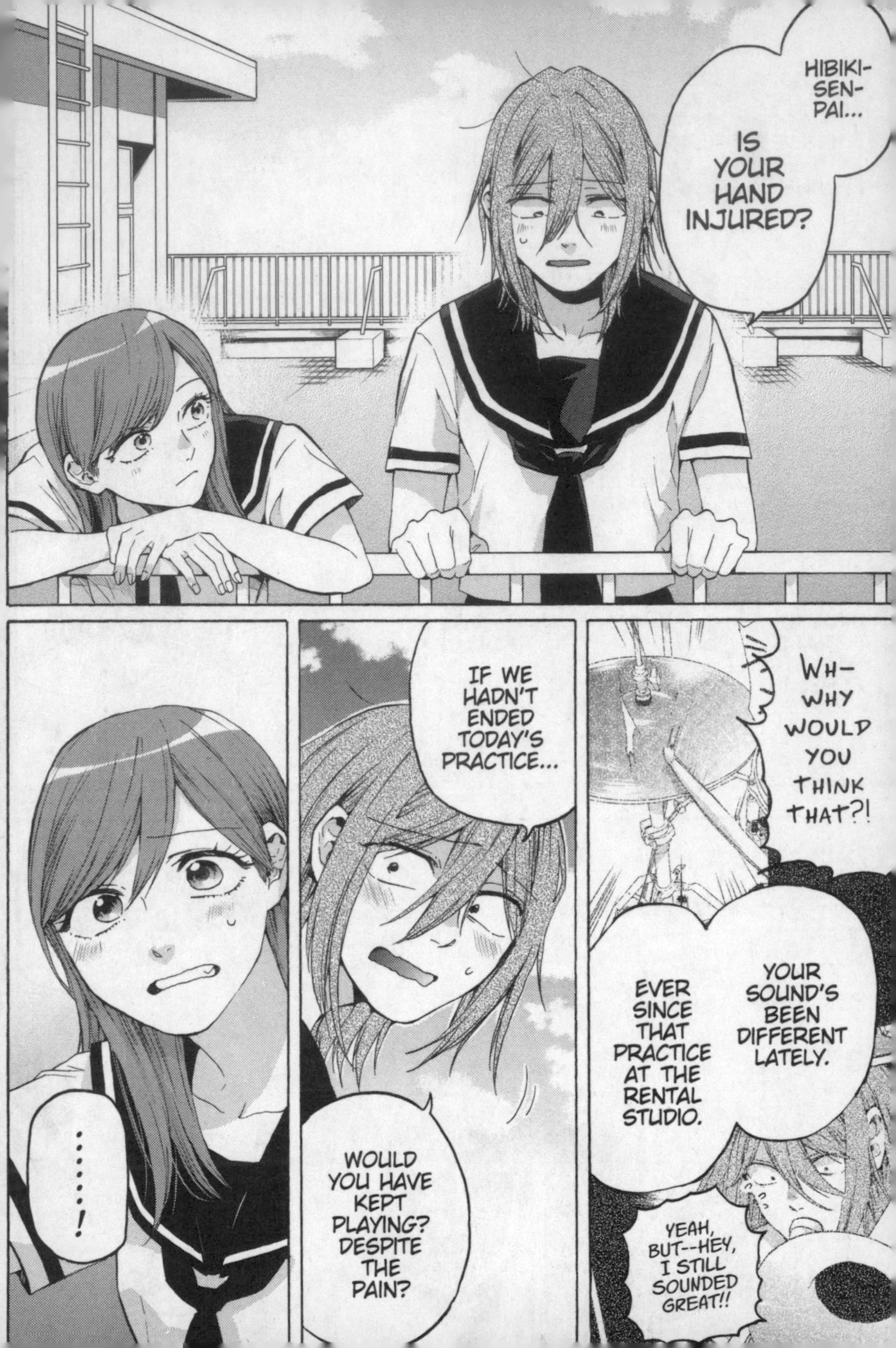

HIBIKI-SENPAI...
IS YOUR HAND INJURED?
WH-WHY WOULD YOU THINK THAT?!
YOUR SOUND'S BEEN DIFFERENT LATELY.
EVER SINCE THAT PRACTICE AT THE RENTAL STUDIO.
YEAH, BUT--HEY, I STILL SOUNDED GREAT!!
IF WE HADN'T ENDED TODAY'S PRACTICE...
WOULD YOU HAVE KEPT PLAYING? DESPITE THE PAIN?
......!

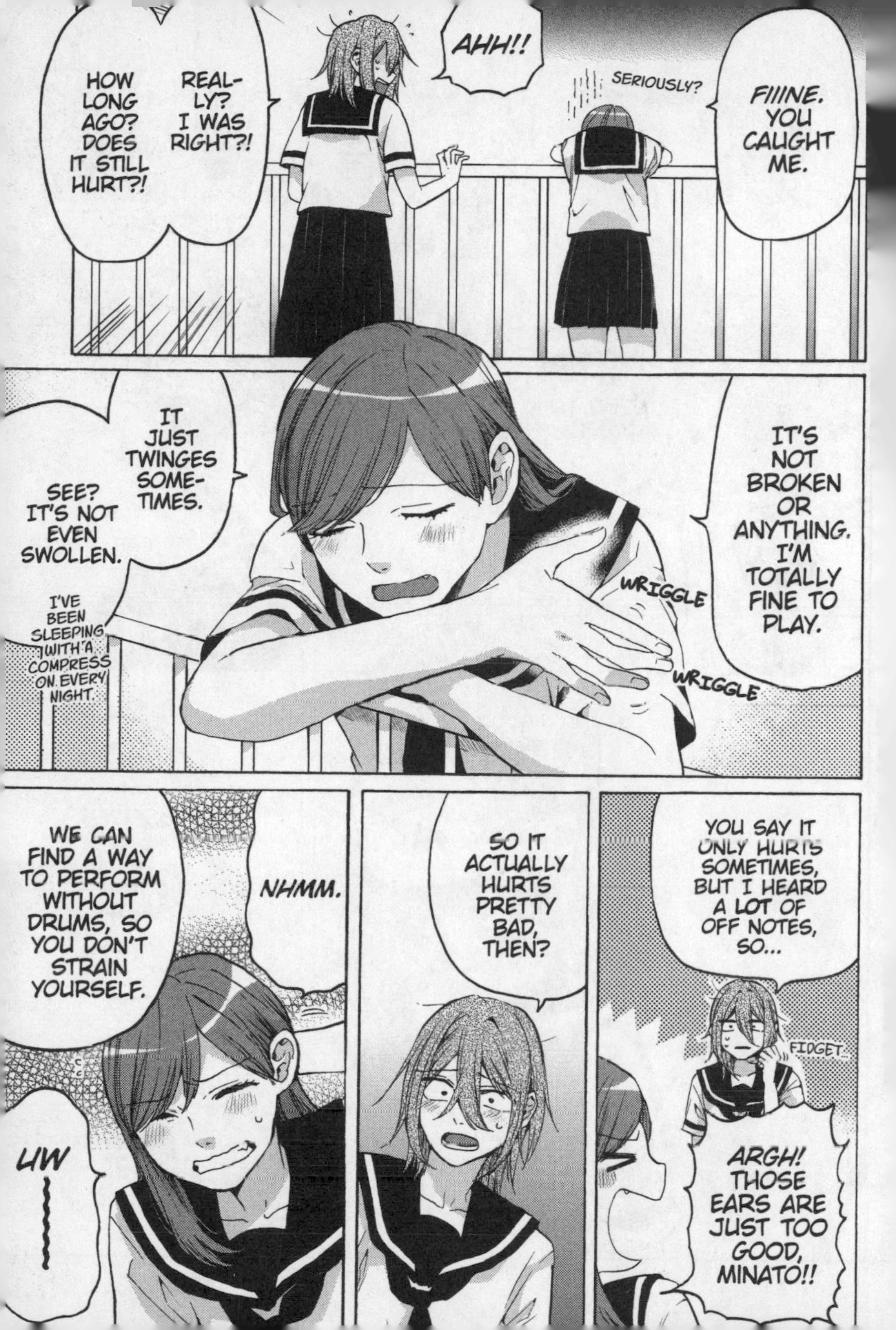
FIIINE. YOU CAUGHT ME.
SERIOUSLY?
AHH!!
REALLY? I WAS RIGHT?!
HOW LONG AGO? DOES IT STILL HURT?!
IT'S NOT BROKEN OR ANYTHING. I'M TOTALLY FINE TO PLAY.
WRIGGLE
WRIGGLE
IT JUST TWINGES SOMETIMES.
SEE? IT'S NOT EVEN SWOLLEN.
I'VE BEEN SLEEPING WITH A COMPRESS ON EVERY NIGHT.
YOU SAY IT ONLY HURTS SOMETIMES, BUT I HEARD A LOT OF OFF NOTES, SO...
FIDGET...
ARGH! THOSE EARS ARE JUST TOO GOOD, MINATO!!
SO IT ACTUALLY HURTS PRETTY BAD, THEN?
NHMM.
WE CAN FIND A WAY TO PERFORM WITHOUT DRUMS, SO YOU DON'T STRAIN YOURSELF.
UW—

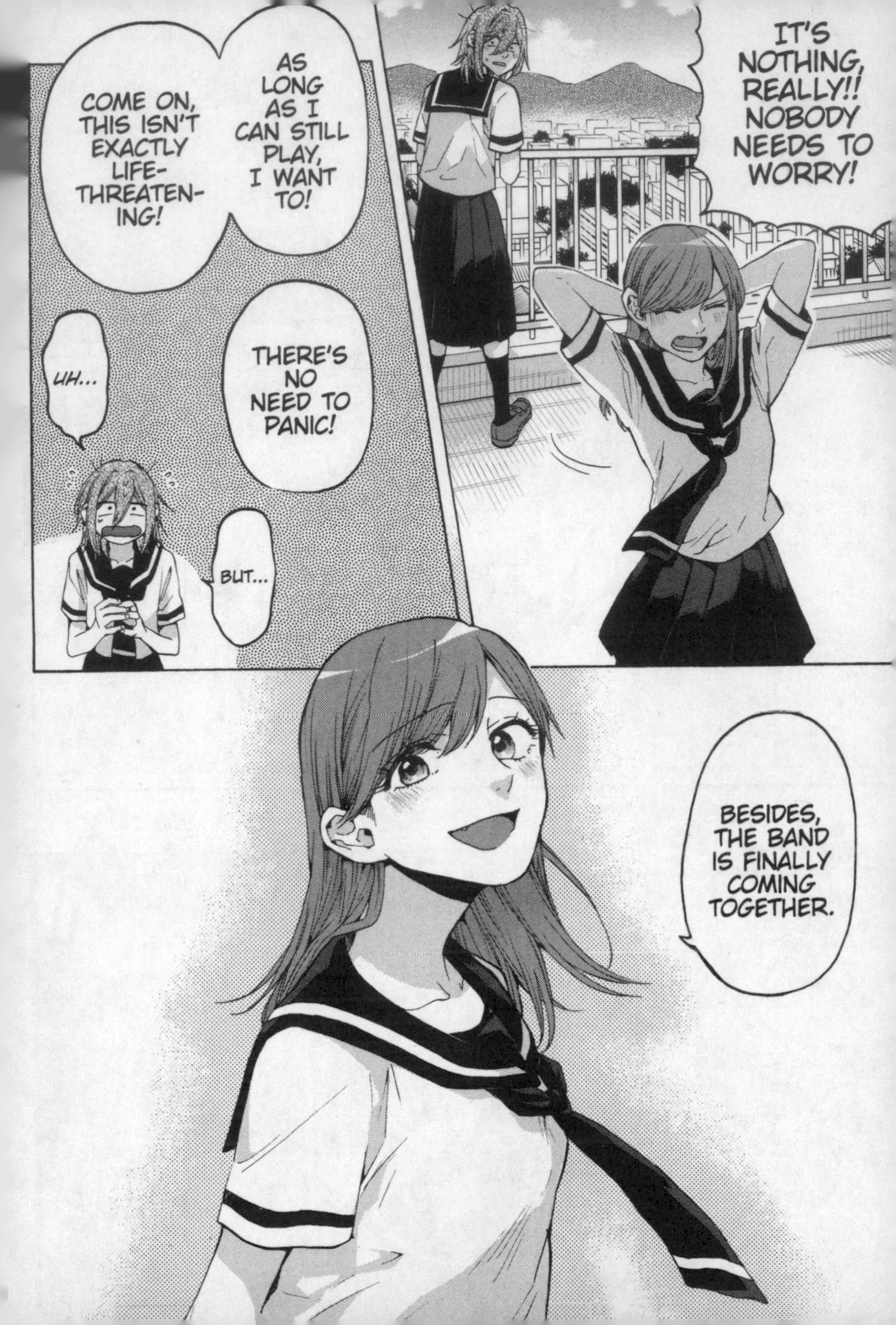
IT'S NOTHING, REALLY!! NOBODY NEEDS TO WORRY!
AS LONG AS I CAN STILL PLAY, I WANT TO!
COME ON, THIS ISN'T EXACTLY LIFE-THREATENING!
THERE'S NO NEED TO PANIC!
UH...
BUT...
BESIDES, THE BAND IS FINALLY COMING TOGETHER.

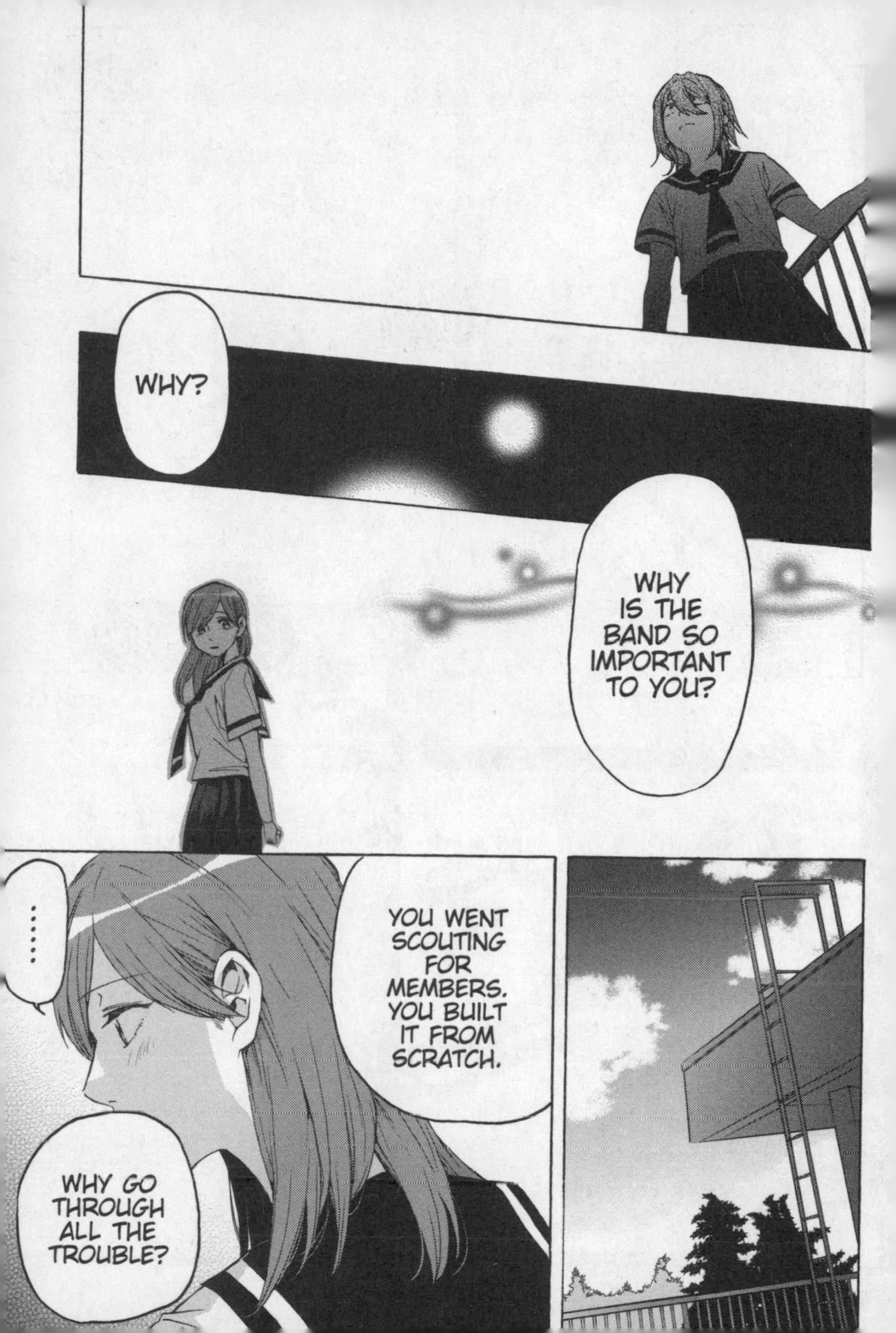
WHY?
WHY IS THE BAND SO IMPORTANT TO YOU?
YOU WENT SCOUTING FOR MEMBERS. YOU BUILT IT FROM SCRATCH.
......
WHY GO THROUGH ALL THE TROUBLE?

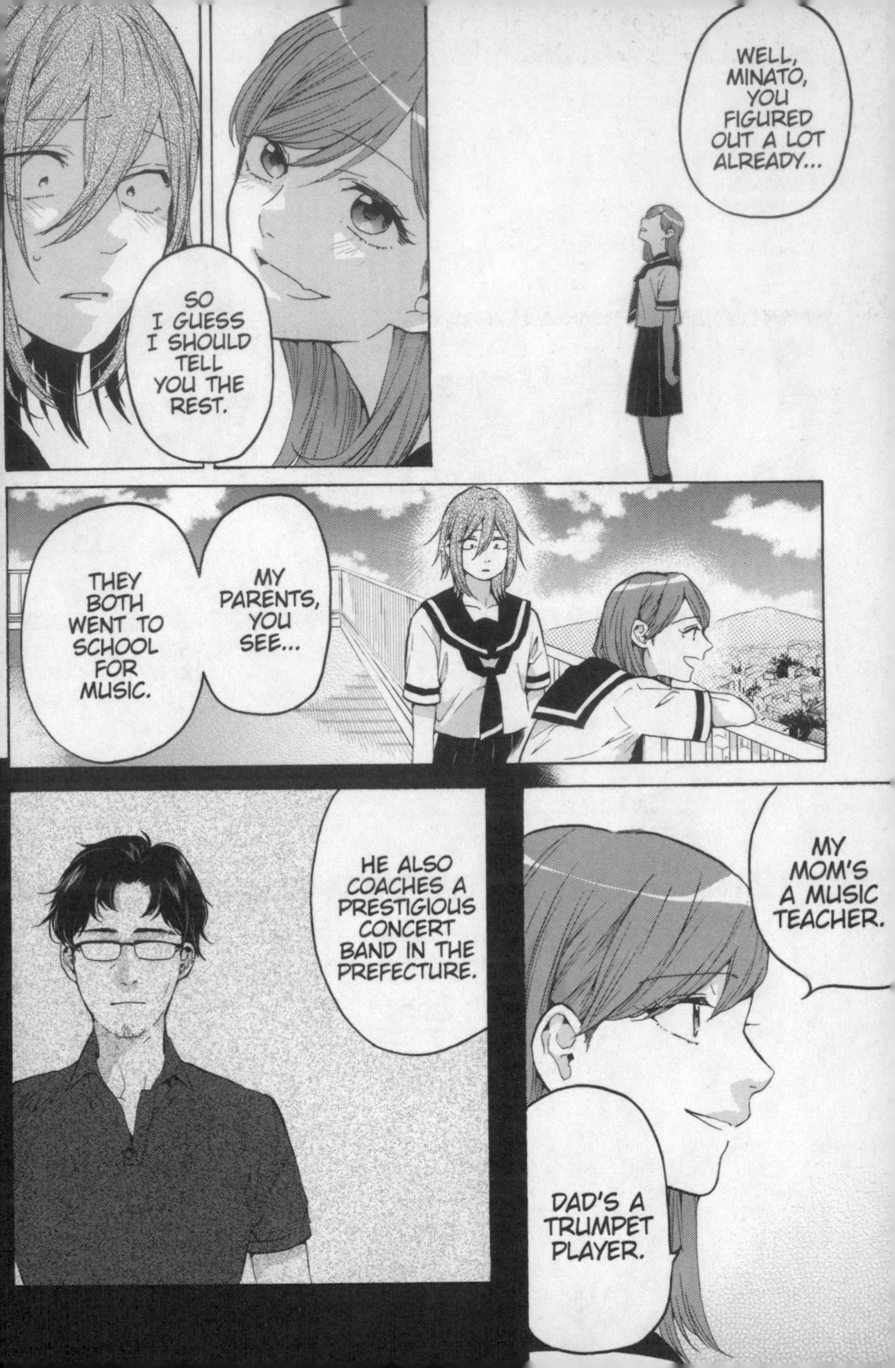
WELL, MINATO, YOU FIGURED OUT A LOT ALREADY...
SO I GUESS I SHOULD TELL YOU THE REST.
MY PARENTS, YOU SEE...
THEY BOTH WENT TO SCHOOL FOR MUSIC.
MY MOM'S A MUSIC TEACHER.
DAD'S A TRUMPET PLAYER.
HE ALSO COACHES A PRESTIGIOUS CONCERT BAND IN THE PREFECTURE.

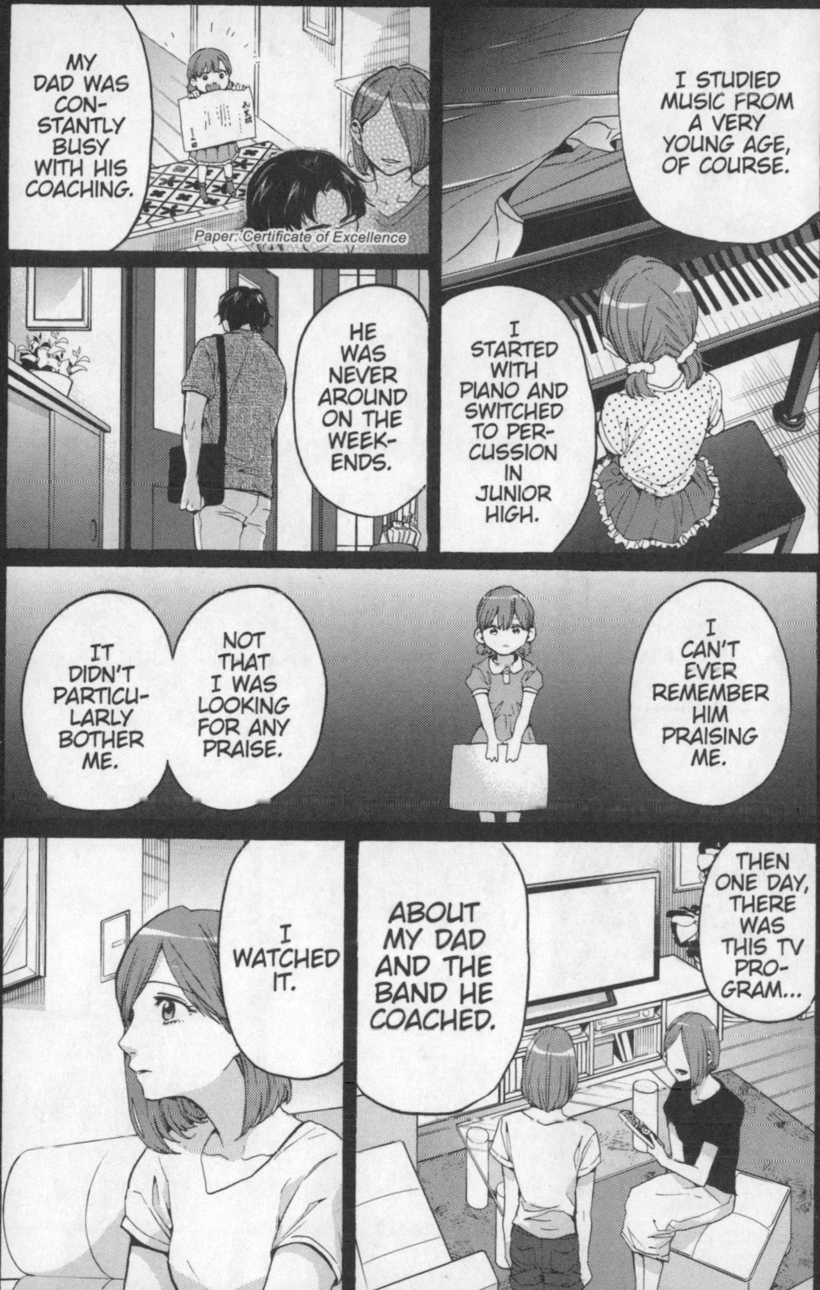
I STUDIED MUSIC FROM A VERY YOUNG AGE, OF COURSE.
I STARTED WITH PIANO AND SWITCHED TO PER-CUSSION IN JUNIOR HIGH.
MY DAD WAS CON-STANTLY BUSY WITH HIS COACHING.
Paper: Certificate of Excellence
HE WAS NEVER AROUND ON THE WEEK-ENDS.
I CAN'T EVER REMEMBER HIM PRAISING ME.
NOT THAT I WAS LOOKING FOR ANY PRAISE.
IT DIDN'T PARTICU-LARLY BOTHER ME.
THEN ONE DAY, THERE WAS THIS TV PRO-GRAM...
ABOUT MY DAD AND THE BAND HE COACHED.
I WATCHED IT.

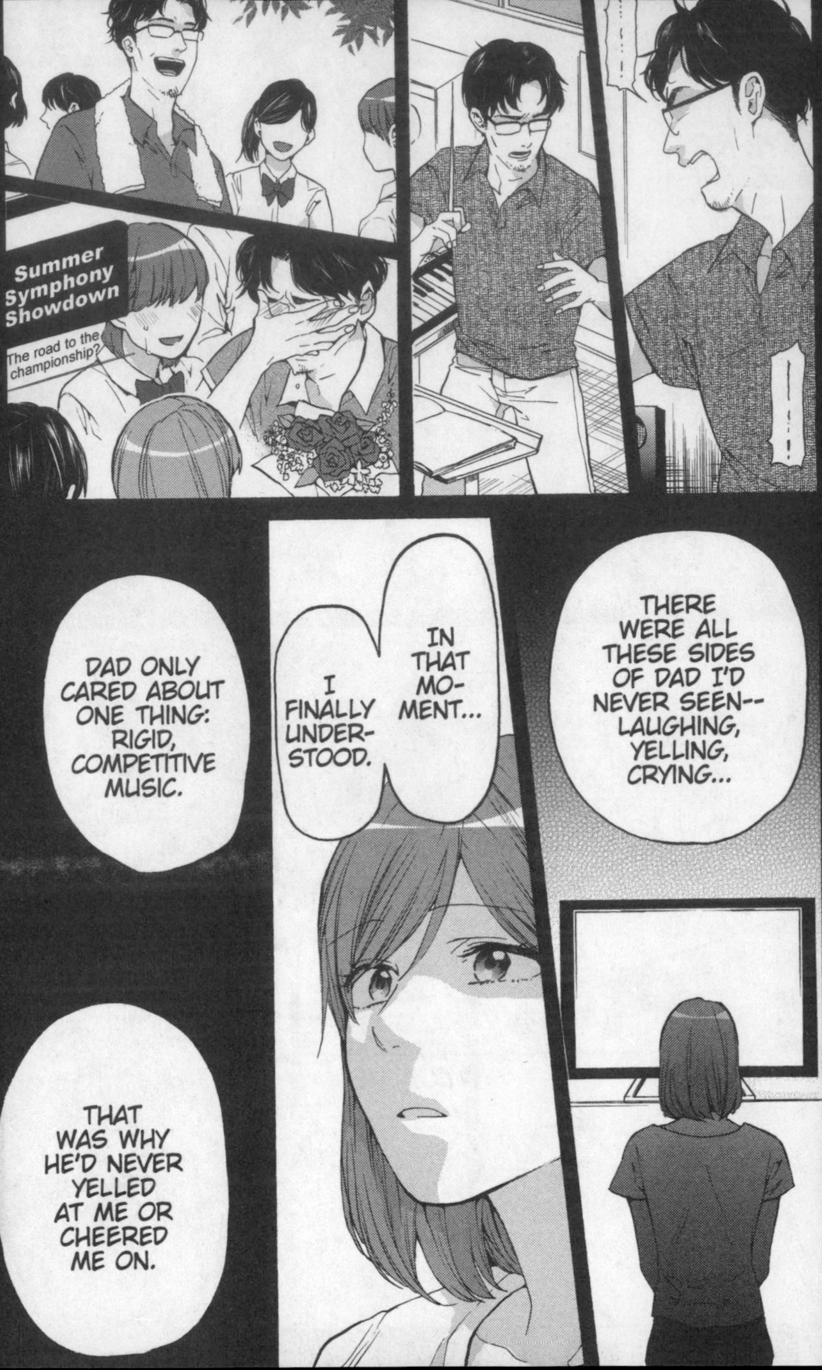

Summer Symphony Showdown
The road to the championship?
THERE WERE ALL THESE SIDES OF DAD I'D NEVER SEEN--LAUGHING, YELLING, CRYING...
IN THAT MOMENT...
I FINALLY UNDERSTOOD.
DAD ONLY CARED ABOUT ONE THING: RIGID, COMPETITIVE MUSIC.
THAT WAS WHY HE'D NEVER YELLED AT ME OR CHEERED ME ON.

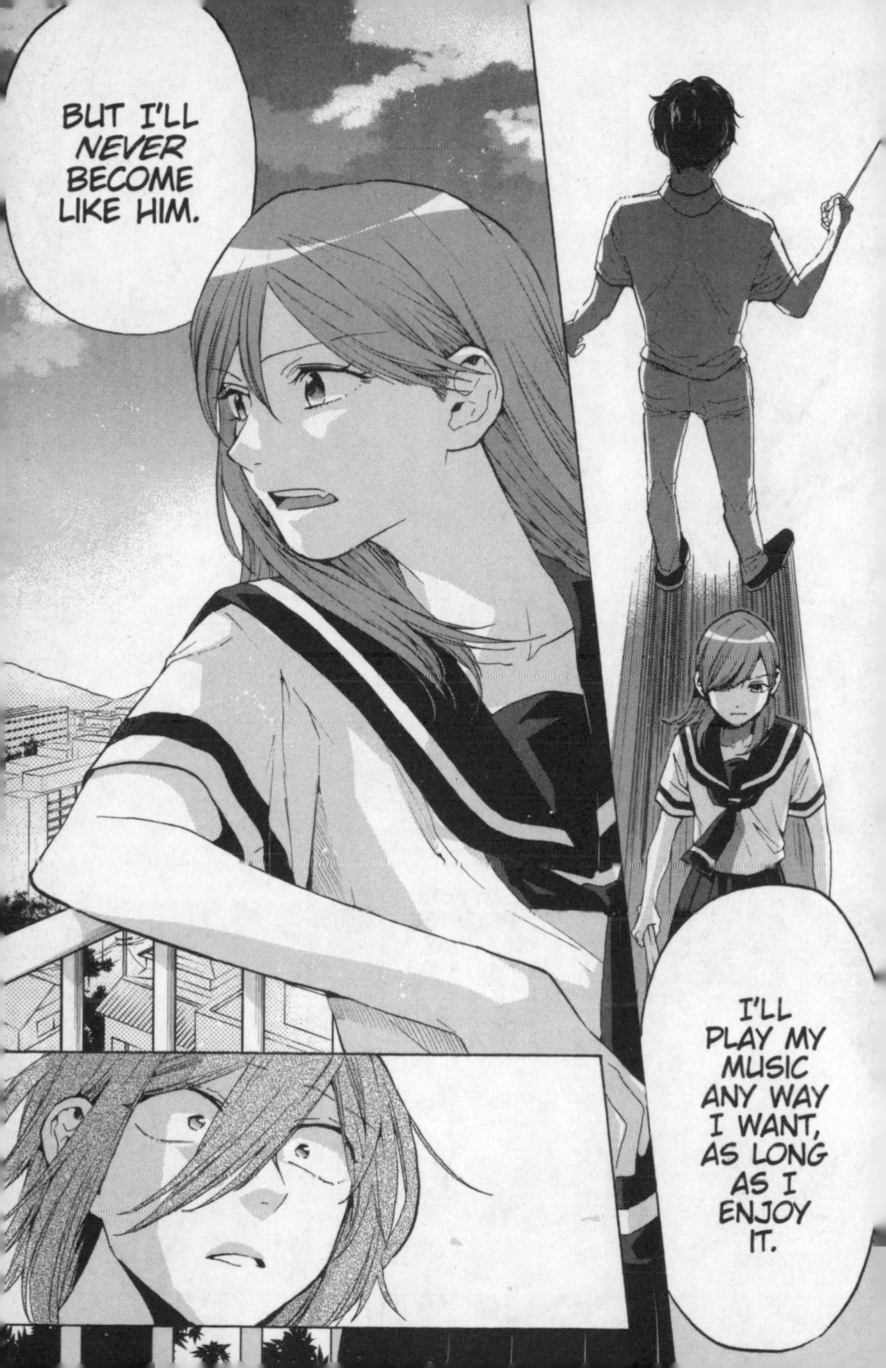
BUT I'LL *NEVER* BECOME LIKE HIM.
I'LL PLAY MY MUSIC ANY WAY I WANT, AS LONG AS I ENJOY IT.

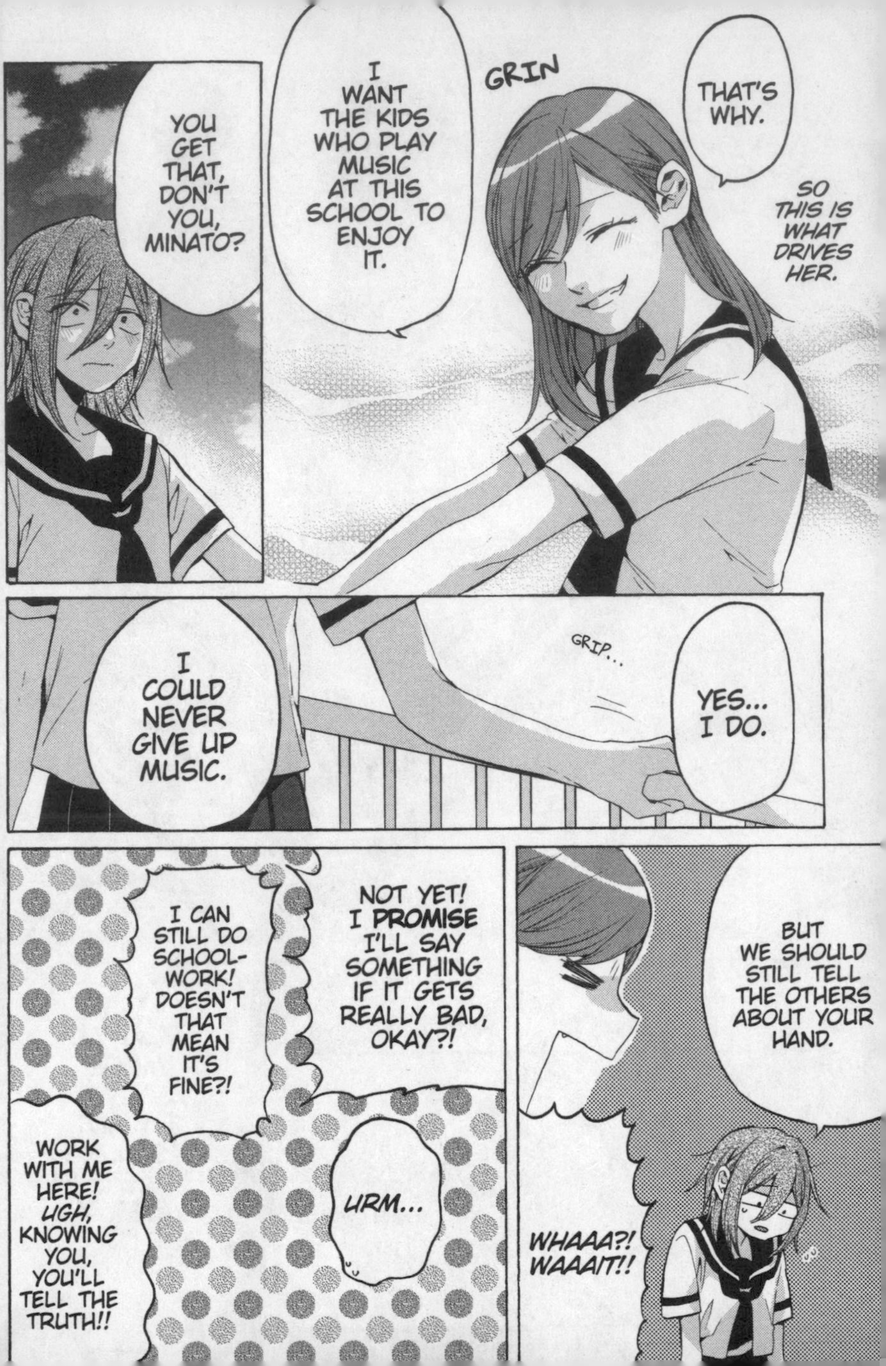
THAT'S WHY.
GRIN
I WANT THE KIDS WHO PLAY MUSIC AT THIS SCHOOL TO ENJOY IT.
SO THIS IS WHAT DRIVES HER.
YOU GET THAT, DON'T YOU, MINATO?
YES... I DO.
GRIP...
I COULD NEVER GIVE UP MUSIC.
BUT WE SHOULD STILL TELL THE OTHERS ABOUT YOUR HAND.
WHAAA?! WAAAIT!!
NOT YET! I **PROMISE** I'LL SAY SOMETHING IF IT GETS REALLY BAD, OKAY?!
I CAN STILL DO SCHOOL-WORK! DOESN'T THAT MEAN IT'S FINE?!
URM...
WORK WITH ME HERE! UGH, KNOWING YOU, YOU'LL TELL THE TRUTH!!

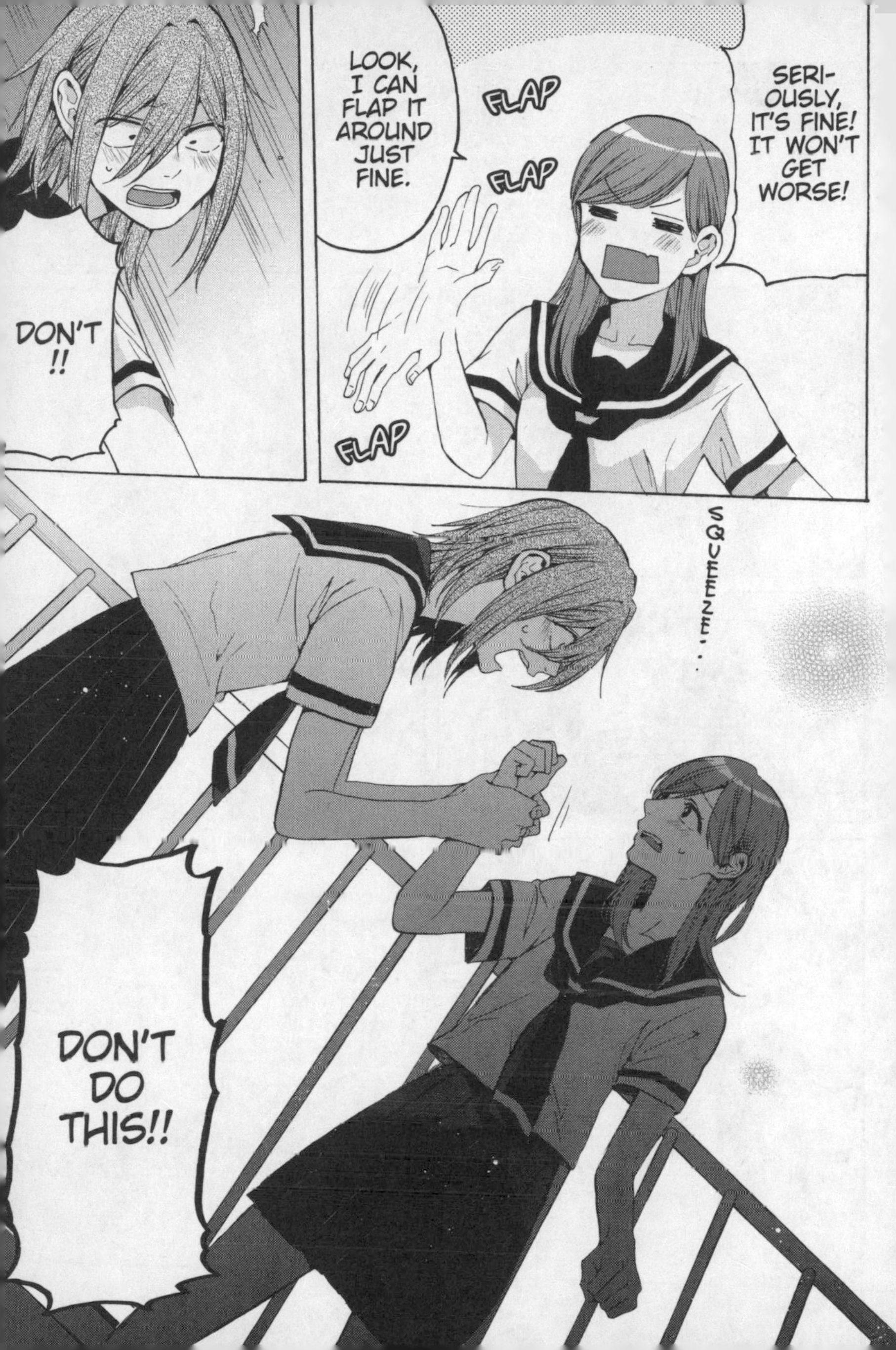
SERI-OUSLY, IT'S FINE! IT WON'T GET WORSE!
LOOK, I CAN FLAP IT AROUND JUST FINE.
FLAP
FLAP
FLAP
DON'T !!
SQUEEZE...
DON'T DO THIS!!

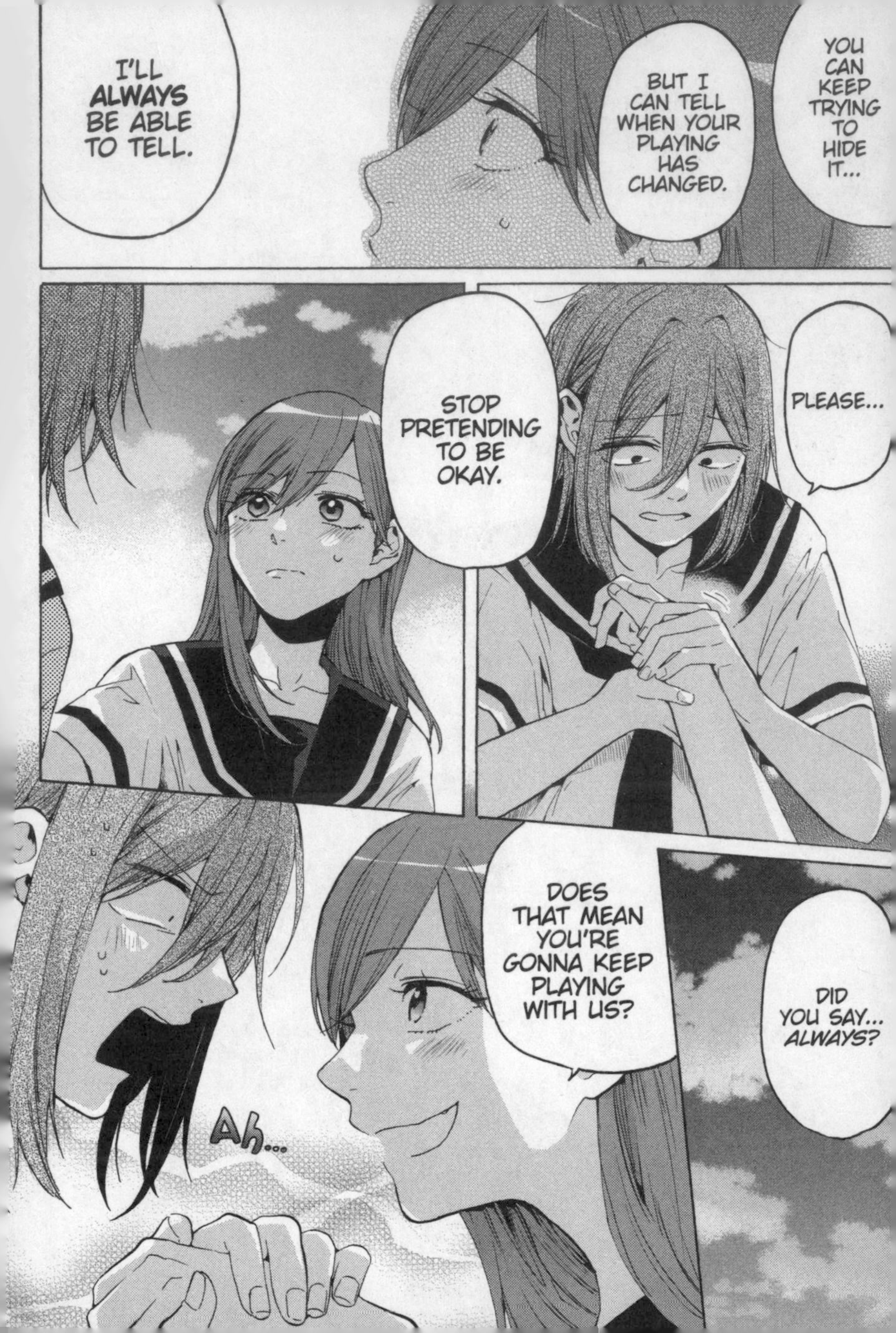
YOU CAN KEEP TRYING TO HIDE IT...
BUT I CAN TELL WHEN YOUR PLAYING HAS CHANGED.
I'LL **ALWAYS** BE ABLE TO TELL.
PLEASE...
STOP PRETENDING TO BE OKAY.
DID YOU SAY... *ALWAYS?*
DOES THAT MEAN YOU'RE GONNA KEEP PLAYING WITH US?
Ah...

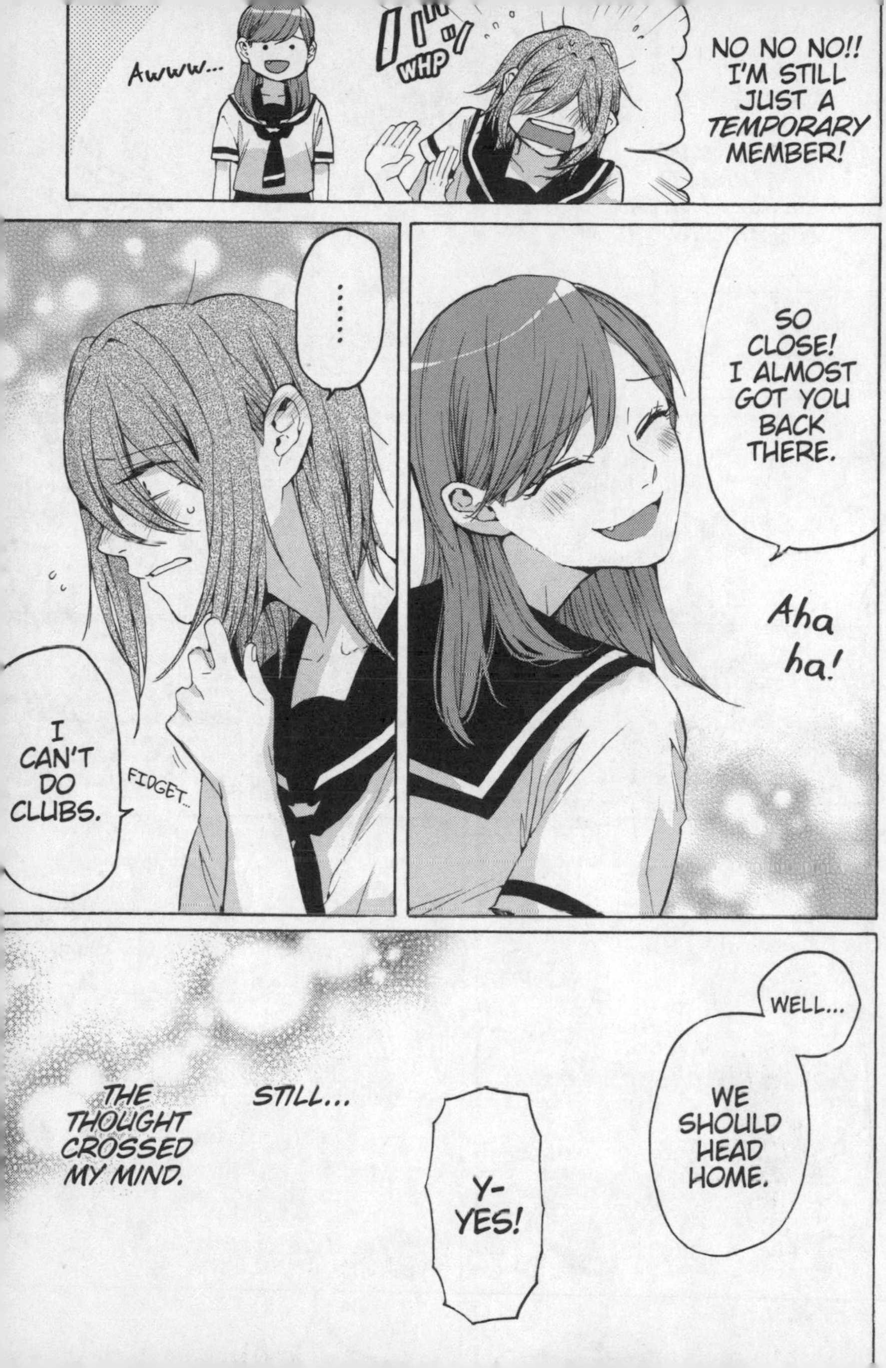
NO NO NO!! I'M STILL JUST A TEMPORARY MEMBER!
WHP
Awww...
SO CLOSE! I ALMOST GOT YOU BACK THERE.
Aha ha!
......
I CAN'T DO CLUBS.
FIDGET...
WELL...
WE SHOULD HEAD HOME.
Y-YES!
STILL...
THE THOUGHT CROSSED MY MIND.

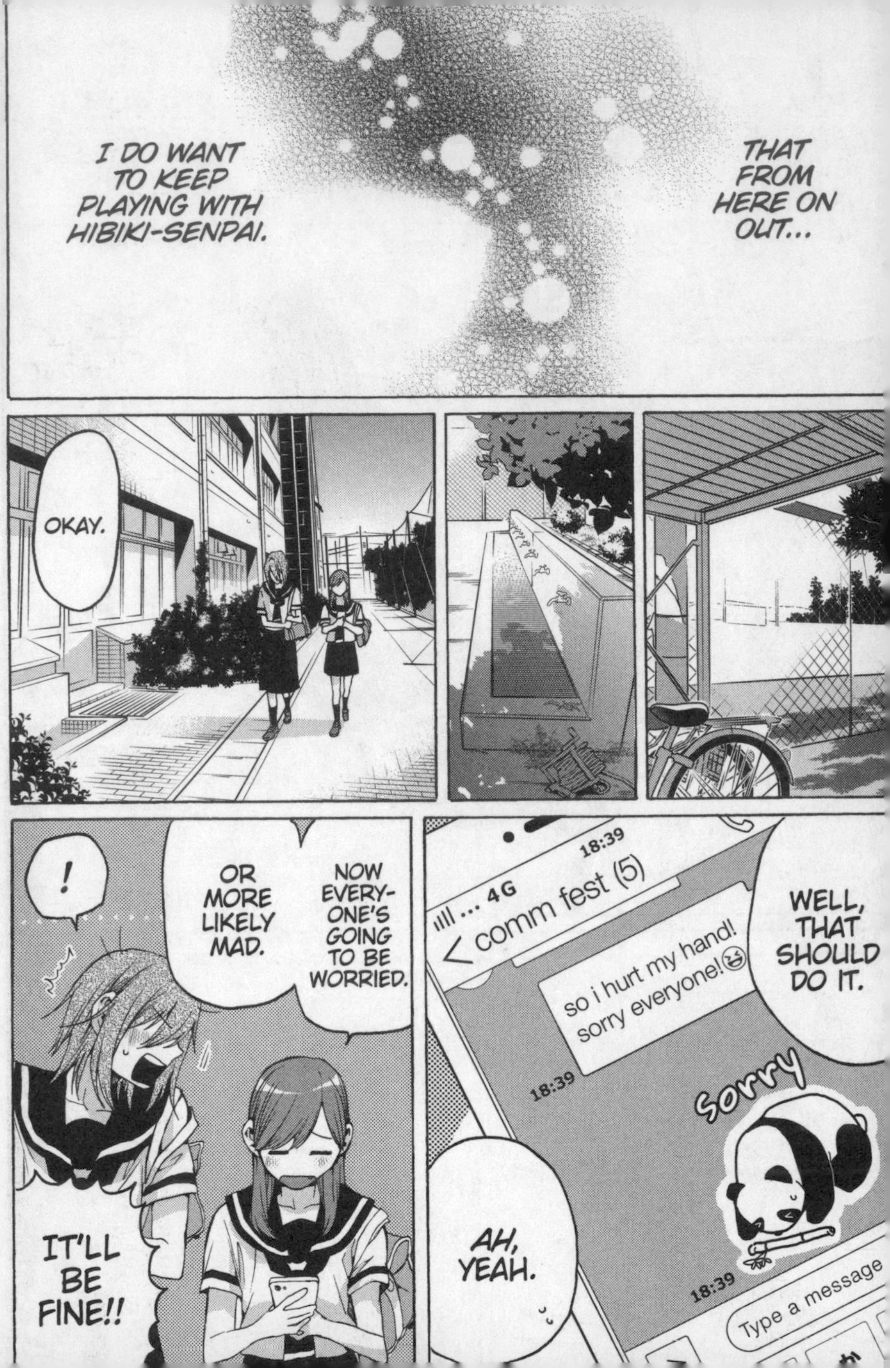
THAT FROM HERE ON OUT...
I DO WANT TO KEEP PLAYING WITH HIBIKI-SENPAI.
OKAY.
WELL, THAT SHOULD DO IT.
18:39
ıııl ... 4G
< comm fest (5)
so i hurt my hand! sorry everyone!
18:39
Sorry
18:39
Type a message
AH, YEAH.
NOW EVERYONE'S GOING TO BE WORRIED.
OR MORE LIKELY MAD.
!
IT'LL BE FINE!!

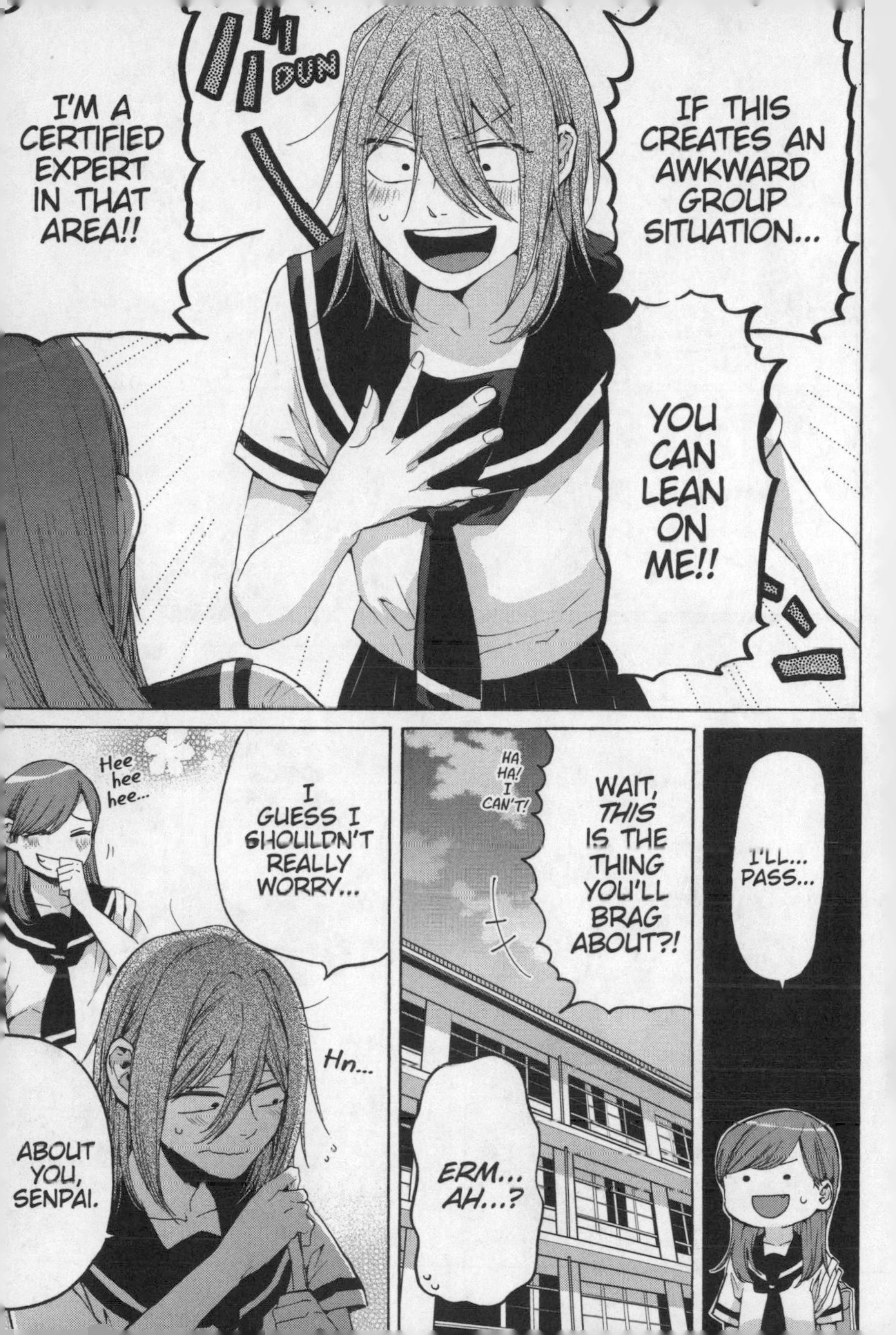
DUN
IF THIS CREATES AN AWKWARD GROUP SITUATION...
I'M A CERTIFIED EXPERT IN THAT AREA!!
YOU CAN LEAN ON ME!!
I'LL... PASS...
WAIT, *THIS* IS THE THING YOU'LL BRAG ABOUT?!
HA HA! I CAN'T!
ERM... AH...?
I GUESS I SHOULDN'T REALLY WORRY...
Hee hee hee...
Hn...
ABOUT YOU, SENPAI.

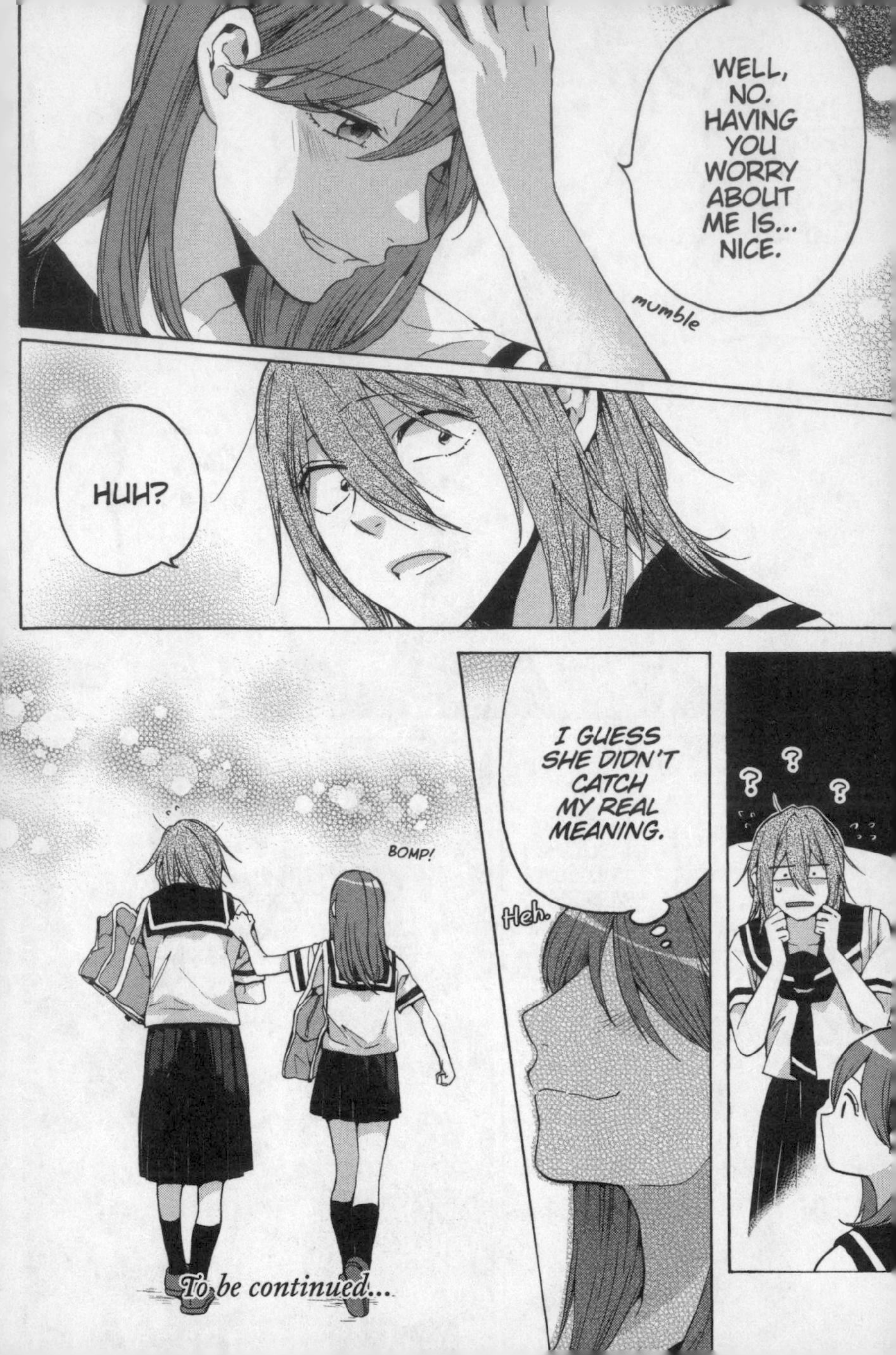
WELL, NO. HAVING YOU WORRY ABOUT ME IS... NICE.
mumble
HUH?
I GUESS SHE DIDN'T CATCH MY REAL MEANING.
Heh.
BOMP!
To be continued...

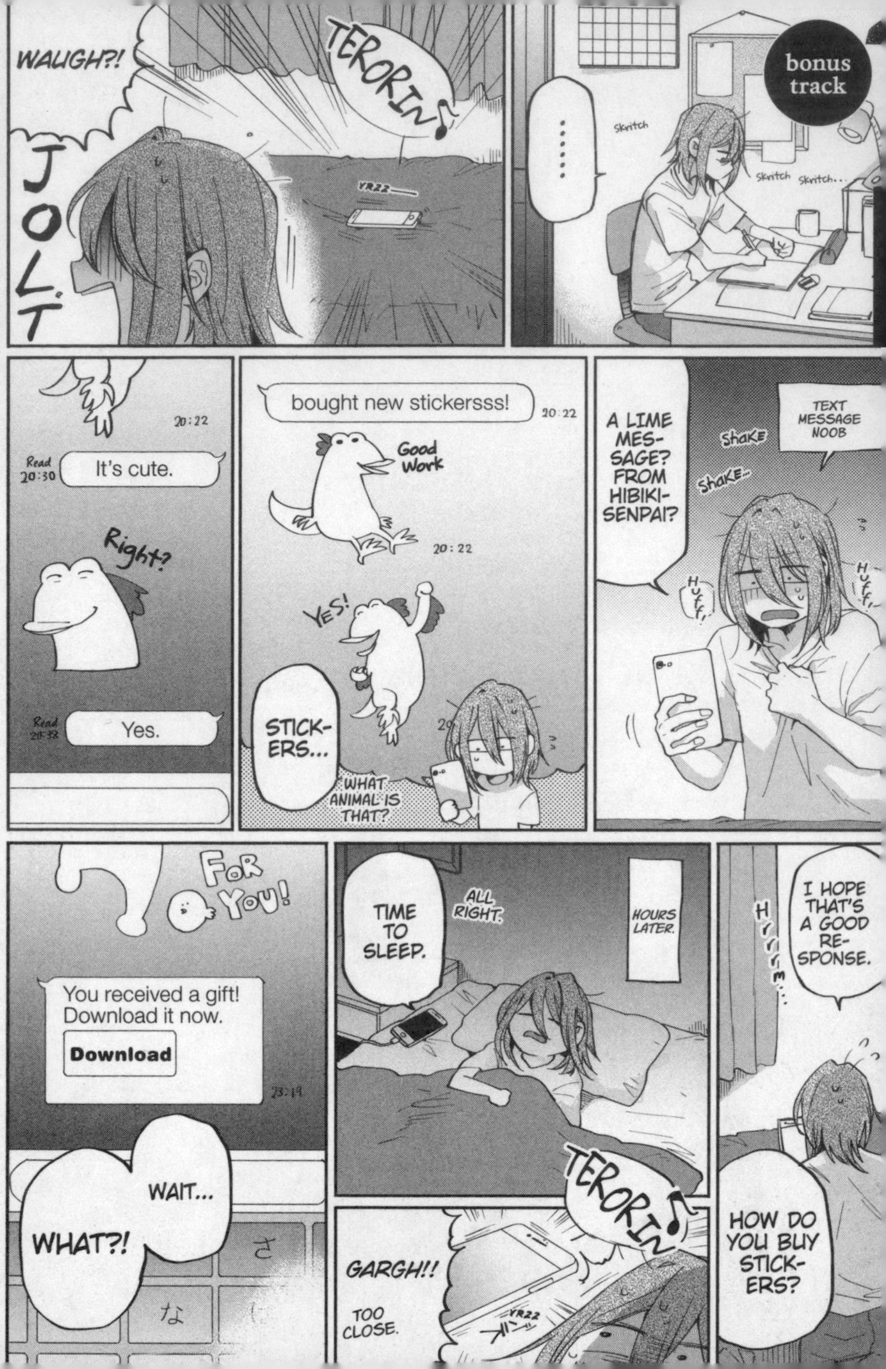
bonus track
......
Skritch
Skritch Skritch...
TERORIN♪
VRZZ
WAUGH?!
JOLT
A LIME MESSAGE? FROM HIBIKI-SENPAI?
TEXT MESSAGE NOOB
Shake
Shake...
Huff!
Huff!
bought new stickersss!
20:22
Good Work
20:22
YES!
STICKERS...
WHAT ANIMAL IS THAT?
20:22
Read 20:30
It's cute.
Right?
Read 20:33
Yes.
I HOPE THAT'S A GOOD RESPONSE.
Hrrrm...
HOW DO YOU BUY STICKERS?
HOURS LATER.
ALL RIGHT.
TIME TO SLEEP.
TERORIN♪
GARGH!!
TOO CLOSE.
VRZZ
FOR YOU!
You received a gift! Download it now.
Download
23:19
WAIT...
WHAT?!
さ
な

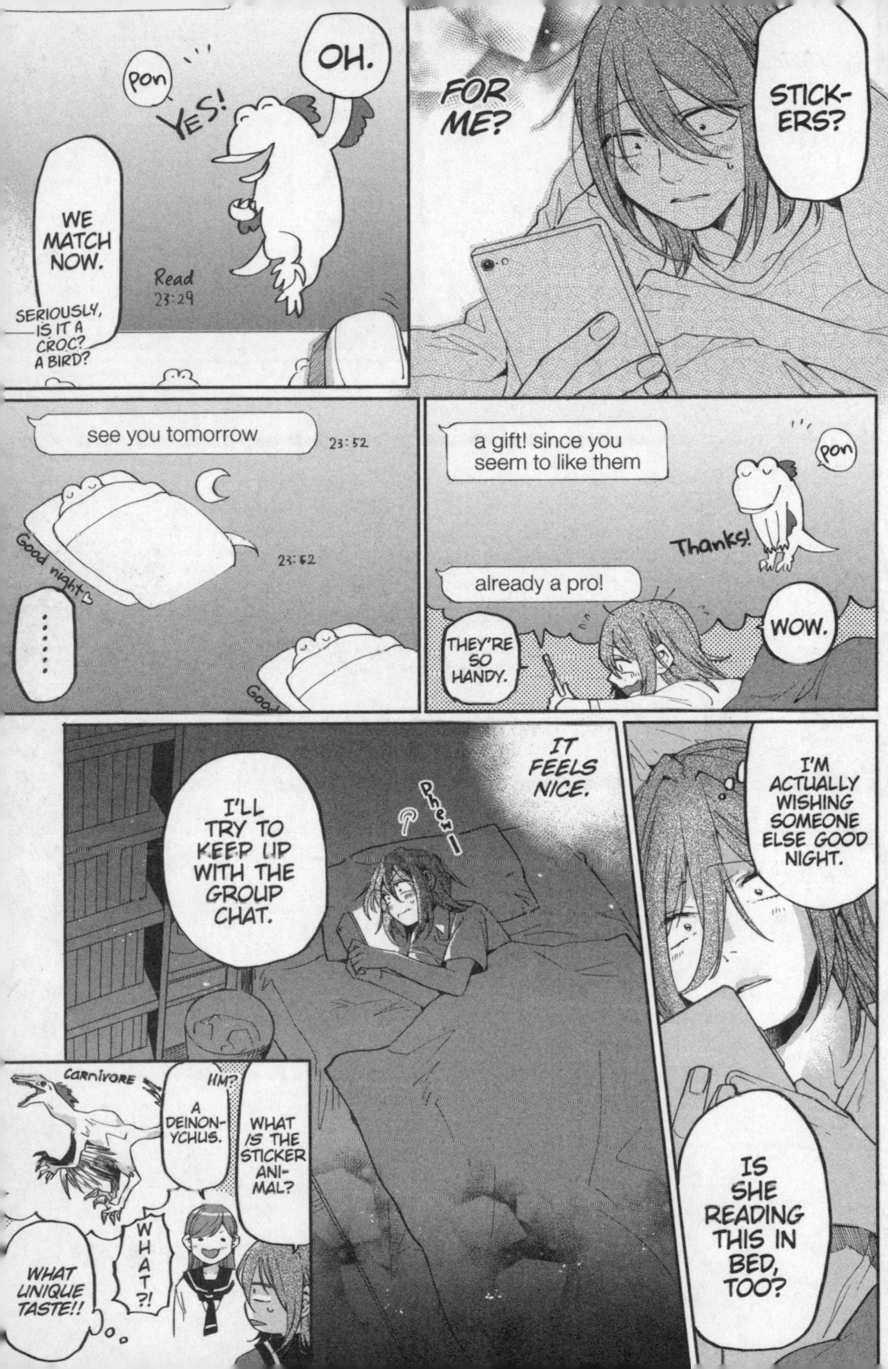
STICK-ERS?
FOR ME?
OH.
pon
YES!
WE MATCH NOW.
Read 23:29
SERIOUSLY, IS IT A CROC? A BIRD?
a gift! since you seem to like them
pon
Thanks!
already a pro!
WOW.
THEY'RE SO HANDY.
see you tomorrow
23:52
Good night♡
23:52
......
Good
I'M ACTUALLY WISHING SOMEONE ELSE GOOD NIGHT.
IS SHE READING THIS IN BED, TOO?
IT FEELS NICE.
Phew
I'LL TRY TO KEEP UP WITH THE GROUP CHAT.
WHAT IS THE STICKER ANIMAL?
HM?
A DEINON-YCHUS.
Carnivore
WHAT?!
WHAT UNIQUE TASTE!!

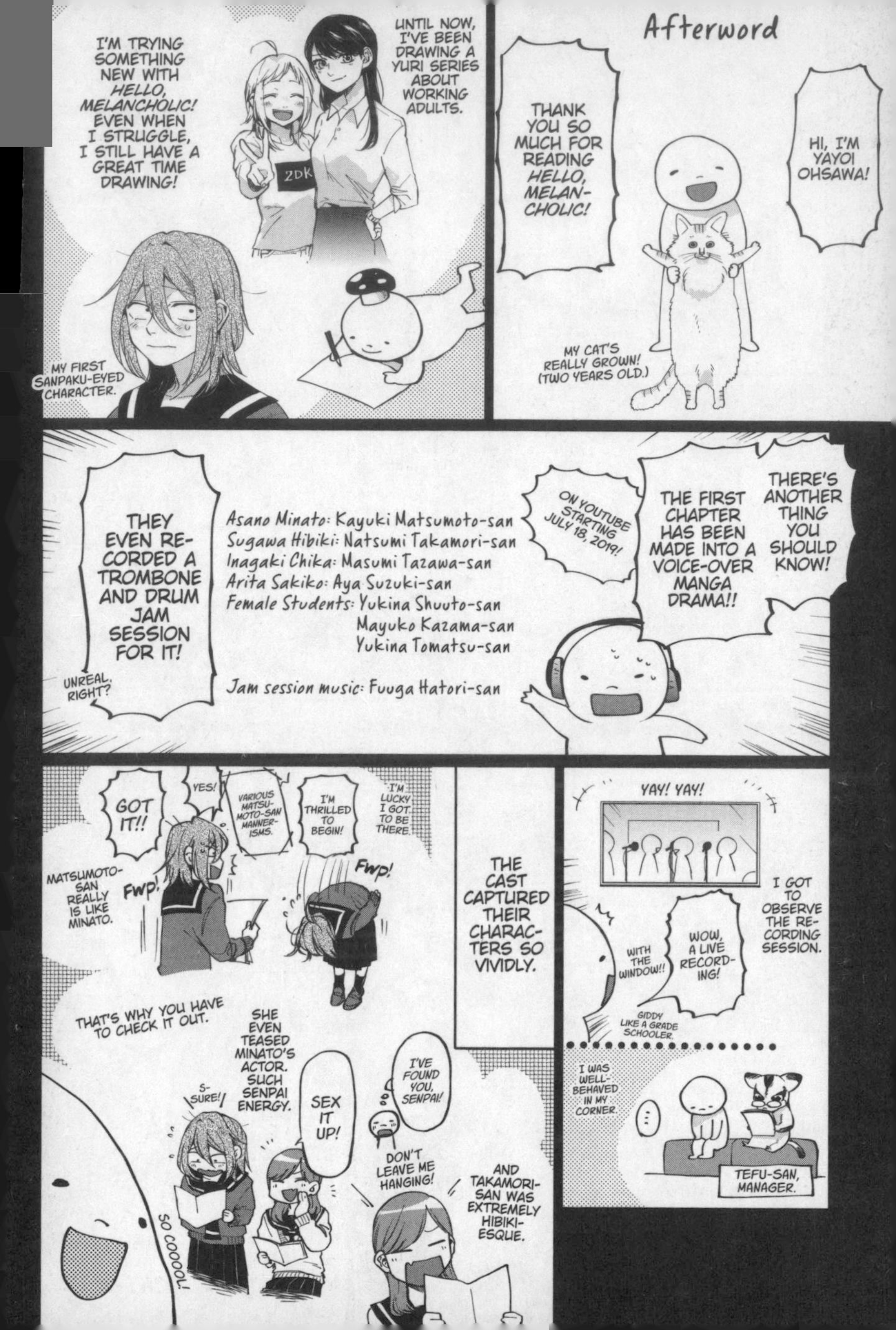
Afterword
HI, I'M YAYOI OHSAWA!
THANK YOU SO MUCH FOR READING *HELLO, MELANCHOLIC!*
MY CAT'S REALLY GROWN! (TWO YEARS OLD.)
UNTIL NOW, I'VE BEEN DRAWING A YURI SERIES ABOUT WORKING ADULTS.
2DK
I'M TRYING SOMETHING NEW WITH *HELLO, MELANCHOLIC!* EVEN WHEN I STRUGGLE, I STILL HAVE A GREAT TIME DRAWING!
MY FIRST SANPAKU-EYED CHARACTER.
THERE'S ANOTHER THING YOU SHOULD KNOW!
THE FIRST CHAPTER HAS BEEN MADE INTO A VOICE-OVER MANGA DRAMA!!
ON YOUTUBE STARTING JULY 18, 2019!
Asano Minato: Kayuki Matsumoto-san
Sugawa Hibiki: Natsumi Takamori-san
Inagaki Chika: Masumi Tazawa-san
Arita Sakiko: Aya Suzuki-san
Female Students: Yukina Shuuto-san
Mayuko Kazama-san
Yukina Tomatsu-san
Jam session music: Fuuga Hatori-san
THEY EVEN RE-CORDED A TROMBONE AND DRUM JAM SESSION FOR IT!
UNREAL, RIGHT?
YAY! YAY!
I GOT TO OBSERVE THE RE-CORDING SESSION.
WOW, A LIVE RECORD-ING!
WITH THE WINDOW!!
GIDDY LIKE A GRADE SCHOOLER.
I WAS WELL-BEHAVED IN MY CORNER.
...
TEFU-SAN, MANAGER.
THE CAST CAPTURED THEIR CHARAC-TERS SO VIVIDLY.
I'M LUCKY I GOT TO BE THERE.
I'M THRILLED TO BEGIN!
VARIOUS MATSU-MOTO-SAN MANNER-ISMS.
YES!
GOT IT!!
MATSUMOTO-SAN REALLY IS LIKE MINATO.
FWP!
FWP!
THAT'S WHY YOU HAVE TO CHECK IT OUT.
SHE EVEN TEASED MINATO'S ACTOR. SUCH SENPAI ENERGY.
I'VE FOUND YOU, SENPAI!
SEX IT UP!
S-SURE!
DON'T LEAVE ME HANGING!
AND TAKAMORI-SAN WAS EXTREMELY HIBIKI-ESQUE.
SO COOOOL!

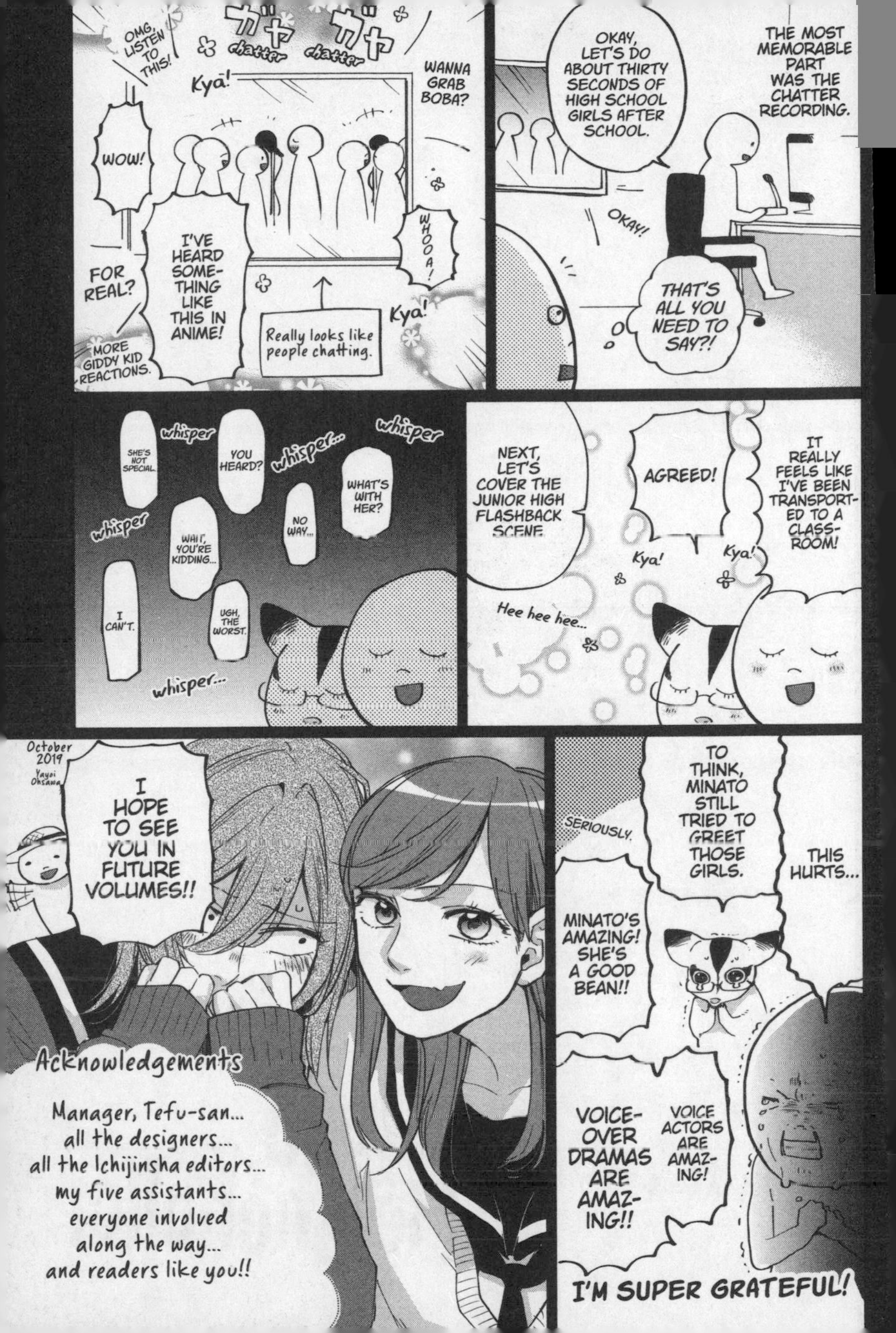
THE MOST MEMORABLE PART WAS THE CHATTER RECORDING.
OKAY, LET'S DO ABOUT THIRTY SECONDS OF HIGH SCHOOL GIRLS AFTER SCHOOL.
OKAY!!
THAT'S ALL YOU NEED TO SAY?!
WANNA GRAB BOBA?
ガヤ chatter ガヤ chatter
OMG, LISTEN TO THIS!
Kya!
WOW!
WHOOOA!
I'VE HEARD SOMETHING LIKE THIS IN ANIME!
FOR REAL?
Kya!
Really looks like people chatting.
MORE GIDDY KID REACTIONS.
IT REALLY FEELS LIKE I'VE BEEN TRANSPORTED TO A CLASSROOM!
AGREED!
NEXT, LET'S COVER THE JUNIOR HIGH FLASHBACK SCENE.
Kya!
Kya!
Hee hee hee...
whisper
WHAT'S WITH HER?
whisper...
YOU HEARD?
whisper
SHE'S NOT SPECIAL.
NO WAY...
WAIT, YOU'RE KIDDING...
whisper
I CAN'T.
UGH, THE WORST.
whisper...
TO THINK, MINATO STILL TRIED TO GREET THOSE GIRLS.
THIS HURTS...
SERIOUSLY.
MINATO'S AMAZING! SHE'S A GOOD BEAN!!
VOICE ACTORS ARE AMAZING!
VOICE-OVER DRAMAS ARE AMAZING!!
I'M SUPER GRATEFUL!
October 2019 Yayoi Ohsawa
I HOPE TO SEE YOU IN FUTURE VOLUMES!!
Acknowledgements
Manager, Tefu-san... all the designers... all the Ichijinsha editors... my five assistants... everyone involved along the way... and readers like you!!

**Hello,
Melancholic!**

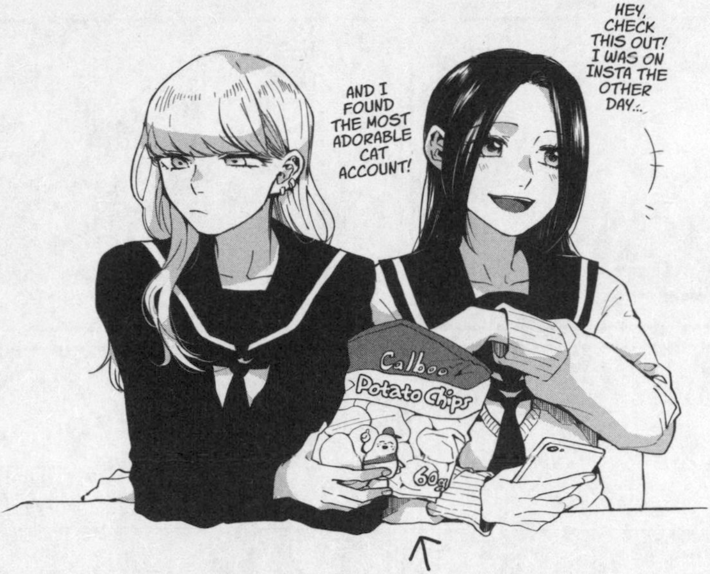
HEY, CHECK THIS OUT! I WAS ON INSTA THE OTHER DAY...
AND I FOUND THE MOST ADORABLE CAT ACCOUNT!
Calboo Potato Chips
60g

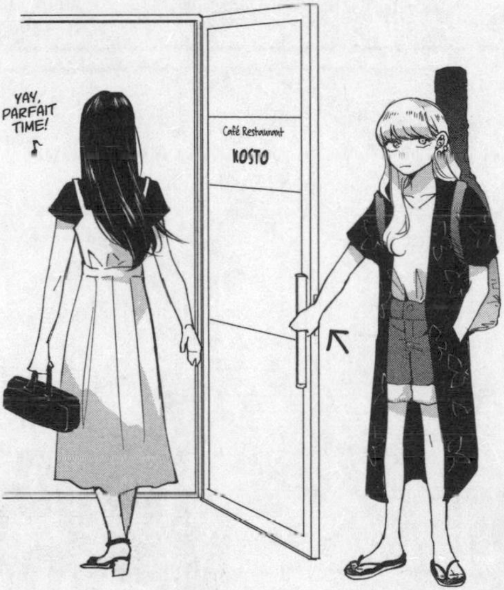
Café Restaurant
KOSTO
YAY, PARFAIT TIME! ♪

Chival-rous Chika-chan

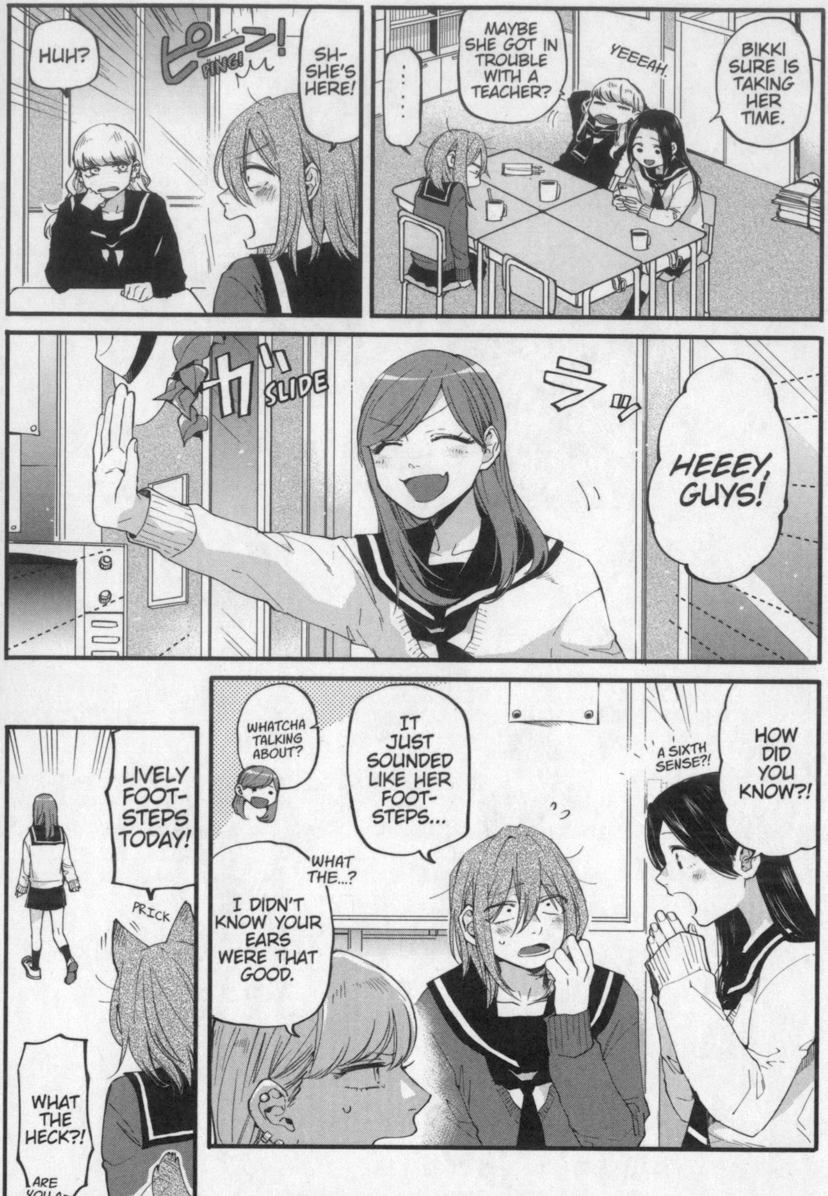

BIKKI SURE IS TAKING HER TIME.
YEEEAH.
MAYBE SHE GOT IN TROUBLE WITH A TEACHER?
......
SH-SHE'S HERE!
PING!
HUH?
HEEEY, GUYS!
SLIDE
HOW DID YOU KNOW?!
A SIXTH SENSE?!
IT JUST SOUNDED LIKE HER FOOT-STEPS...
WHATCHA TALKING ABOUT?
WHAT THE...?
I DIDN'T KNOW YOUR EARS WERE THAT GOOD.
LIVELY FOOT-STEPS TODAY!
PRICK
WHAT THE HECK?!
ARE YOU A DOG?!!!

Hello,
Melancholic!

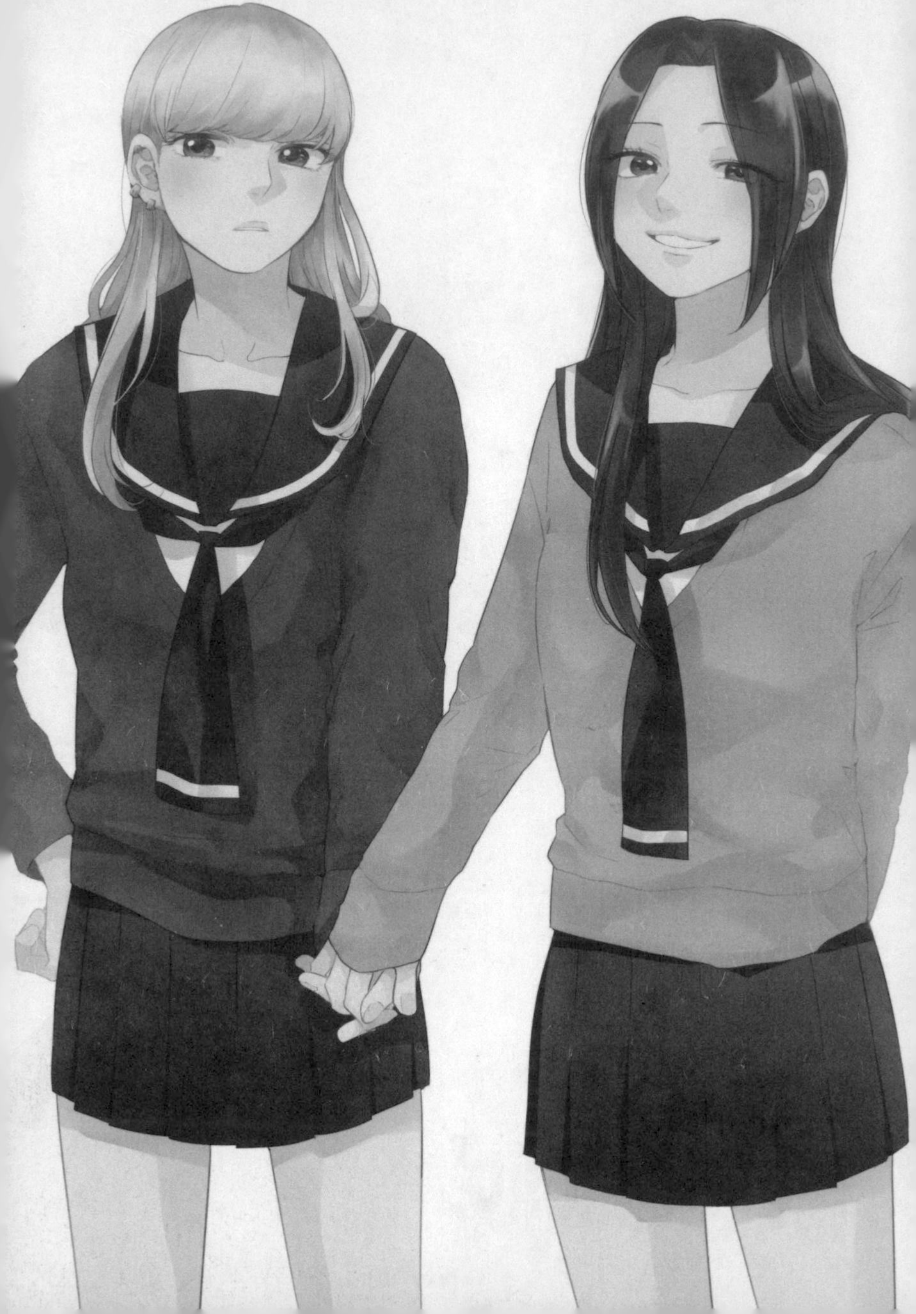

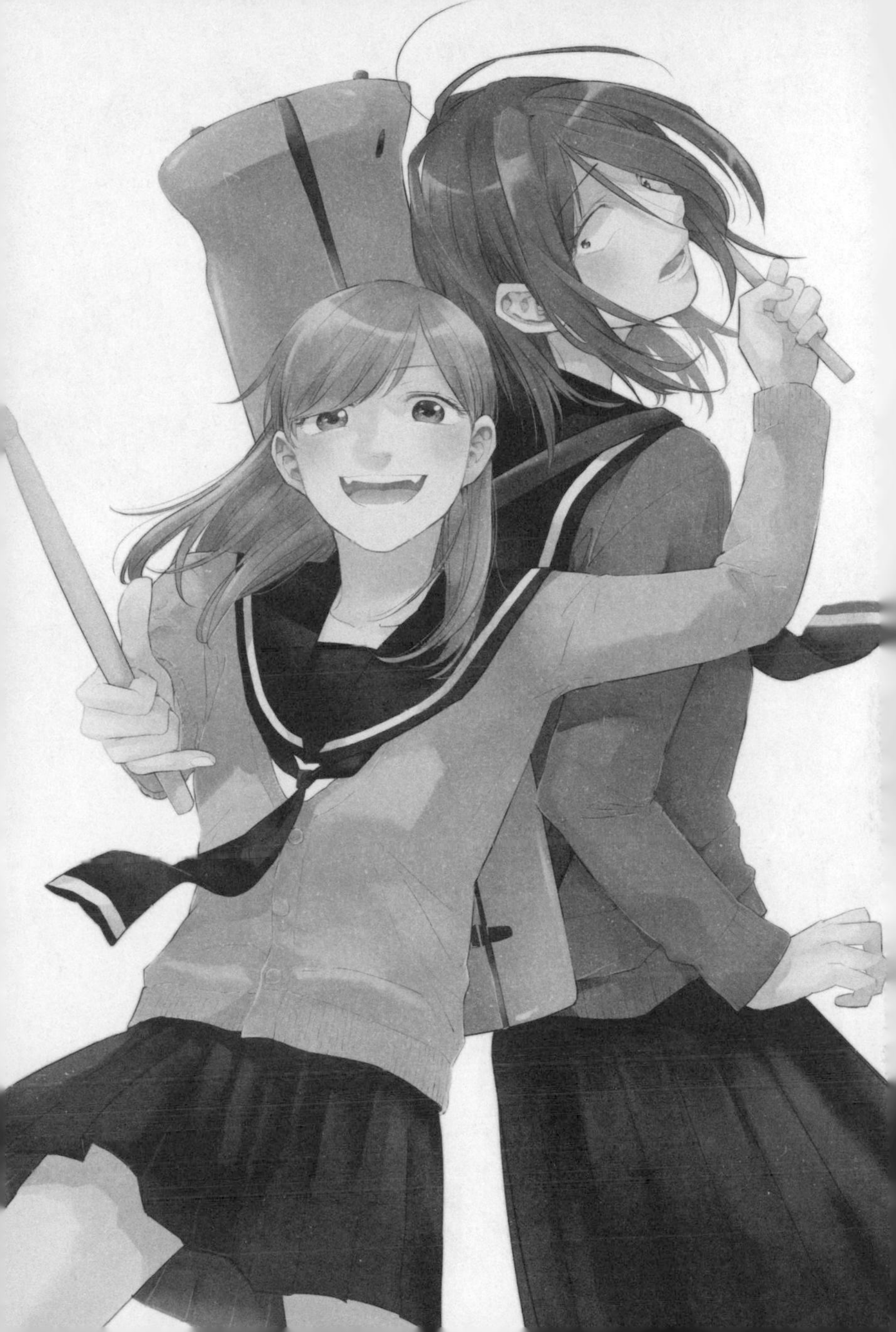

Hello, Melancholic!

SEVEN SEAS ENTERTAINMENT PRESENTS

Hello, Melancholic!

story and art by **YAYOI OHSAWA** **VOLUME 1**

TRANSLATION
Margaret Ngo

ADAPTATION
Marykate Jasper

LETTERING
Mo Harrison

COVER DESIGN
Hanase Qi

PROOFREADER
Leighanna DeRouen

EDITOR
Jenn Grunigen

PREPRESS TECHNICIAN
Melanie Ujimori

PRINT MANAGER
Rhiannon Rasmussen-Silverstein

PRODUCTION ASSOCIATE
Christina McKenzie

PRODUCTION MANAGER
Lissa Pattillo

MANAGING EDITOR
Julie Davis

ASSOCIATE PUBLISHER
Adam Arnold

PUBLISHER
Jason DeAngelis

HELLO, MELANCHOLIC! Vol. 1

First published in Japan in 2019 by Ichijinsha Inc., Tokyo.
Publication rights for this English edition arranged through Kodansha Ltd., Tokyo.

Seven Seas press and purchase enquiries can be sent to Marketing Manager Lianne Sentar at press@gomanga.com. Information regarding the distribution and purchase of digital editions is available from Digital Manager CK Russell at digital@gomanga.com.

ISBN: 978-1-64827-885-3
Printed in Canada
First Printing: February 2022
10 9 8 7 6 5 4 3 2 1

READING DIRECTIONS

This book reads from ***right to left***, Japanese style. If this is your first time reading manga, you start reading from the top right panel on each page and take it from there. If you get lost, just follow the numbered diagram here. It may seem backwards at first, but you'll get the hang of it! Have fun!!

1
2
3
4
5
6
7
8
9

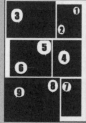

Follow us online: www.SevenSeasEntertainment.com